Walter Ott / Maria Anna Rea-Frauchiger

The Varieties of Legal Positivism

The Hitler Argument and Other Objections to Legal Positivism

Für Frau C. Shannon mit vielem
Dank für die Riesenarbeit mit
dem Proofreading!

25.7.2018

W. Ott

Walter Ott
Prof. Dr. iur., MLaw

Maria Anna Rea-Frauchiger
Dr. iur., MLaw

The Varieties of Legal Positivism

The Hitler Argument and Other Objections
to Legal Positivism

ISBN 978-3-03751-808-3 (Dike Verlag Zürich/St. Gallen)
ISBN 978-3-8487-5146-4 (Nomos Verlag, Baden-Baden)

Walter Ott; Der Rechtspositivismus. Kritische Würdigung auf der Grundlage eines juristischen Pragmatismus. © 2. Auflage 1992, Duncker&Humblot GmbH, Berlin

Bibliographic information published by ‹Die Deutsche Bibliothek›.
Die Deutsche Bibliothek lists this publication in the Deutsche Nationalbibliographie; detailed bibliographic data is available in the Internet at http://dnb.dnb.de

© 2018 Dike Verlag AG, Zürich/St. Gallen

www.dike.ch

Preface

The recent declassificaton of Hitler's "Mein Kampf" by the German federal state of Bavaria caused scientists from around the globe to focus, once again, on issues related to the Hitler phenomenon. This work tries, amongst other things, to shed light on the reasons behind some of the atrocities emerging in the wake of the Nazi regime from a legal historical and jurisprudential perspective (§ 23 D).

Subsequently, new developments were continually incorporated, particularly Dworkin's "general attack on positivism", i.e. the critique of the theses of his teacher H.L.A. Hart, as set forth in his books *Taking Rights Seriously* and *Law's Empire*.

From the Hart-Dworkin debate, two new doctrinal trends have emerged which both build on Hart and attempt to defend him against Dworkin's criticism: "Exclusive Positivism" on the one hand and – depending on the author – "Soft Positivism", "Incorporationism" or "Inclusive Positivism" – on the other hand. For help with the working-up of this discussion, the first undersigned is indebted to Dr. iur. Maria Anna Rea, who was equally responsible for the revision of the pre-existing parts.

This book seeks an approach broader than the one practiced so far to tackle the problem of legal positivism. Thus, the discussion takes in not only the milestones in legal positivism, such as Hans Kelsen's Pure Theory of Law, H.L.A. Hart's Concept of Law and Alf Ross's Realistic Jurisprudence, but also European philosophers probably less well known in the Anglo-American world, such as Karl Bergbohm (German statutory positivism), Ernst Rudolf Bierling, Rudolf Laun, Adolf Merkel, Georg Jellinek, Ernst Beling, Hans Nawiasky, Eugen Ehrlich, Max Weber (with regard to his legal theory), Theodor Geiger and Ota Weinberger. As one can see, the concept of legal positivism is framed more comprehensively than usual: it embraces not only analytical positivism (Austin, Bergbohm, Kelsen, Hart) but also the approach known as legal realism (e.g. Alf Ross or Eugen Ehrlich).

Furthermore, we have tried to precisely disclose the epistemological prerequisites from which this book proceeds. This entailed a fresh approach to legal philosophical thinking which departs from the established conception and accounts for the differences of opinions amongst legal philosophers. We call it *"Axiomatic Theory of Law"*. It follows from this approach that legal theories – unlike scientific theories – are not subject to the truth criterion, but that they must be judged by their consequences.

Particular attention was also paid, however, to the practical aspects of the discussion, viz. to what we call the "Hitler-Argument" which claims that legal positivism was the cause of the perversion of the law in the Third Reich. The discussion gained new and unexpected topicality in the wake of German reunification, since the issues relating to the transition from a state intent on perversion of the rule of law *(ein Unrechtsstaat)* to a constitutional democracy arose afresh (cf. Ott, W., "Did East German Border Guards along The Berlin Wall Act Illegally? Comments on the Decision of the German Federal Constitutional Court of 24 October 1996", Israel Law Review vol. 34, 2000, p. 352 et seqq.).

The first undersigned is indebted to the Council of Education of the Canton of Zurich and to the University of Zurich for providing the opportunity to undertake two research sabbaticals. We also offer our sincerest gratitude to Dr. iur. Franziska Buob, who autonomously elaborated the section on "German Statutory Positivism and National Socialism" (below, § 23 D), revised by Prof. Dr. iur. Clausdieter Schott, to whom we also wish to express our gratitude; to Klaus Füsser we are indebted for pointing out the problems related to the Gumbel murder statistics (below, § 23 D I, N 98); our thanks are due equally to late Prof. H.LA. Hart. We also wish to thank Prof. Dr. Dr. h.c. mult. Stanley Paulson and Bonnie Litschewski Paulson for their very helpful comments and translations.

Finally, we express our thanks to Deborah Shannon, Berlin, who did the proofreading with enthusiasm and very competently, as well as to Prof. Dr. iur. Adrian Künzler for his knowledgeable assistance in revising the manuscript, to Dr. iur. Peter Vollenweider for supplying the infrastructure at the University of Zurich Institute of Law and to Duncker & Humblot, Berlin, publishers, where the first undersigned's book entitled "Der Rechtspositivismus" was published in its first and its second edition, for release of copyright, to BA Ursina Reusser and to BA Anina Knop for drawing up the indeces and to Dike Publishers for the attentive support in printing.

Prof. Dr. iur. Walter Ott, MLaw
Professor for Legal Philosophy,
Legal Theory and Private Law
University of Zurich, Switzerland

Dr. iur. Maria Anna Rea-Frauchiger, MLaw
University of Zurich, Switzerland

Citation System

1. Books listed in the bibliography are, as a matter of principle, cited by giving the author's last name only. Example: Larenz, p. 422, instead of K. Larenz, Methodenlehre der Rechtswissenschaft, 6th edition, Berlin et al.: Springer 1991.

2. Several indepently published works listed in the bibliography by the same author are cited by using an identifier. Example: Hart, Concept of Law; as opposed to Hart, Definition, p. 21.

3. Works which have been published as part of another source are cited by indicating the author's last name and the source only. Example: Kramer, ÖZöR NF 23 (1972), p. 105 et seqq.; instead of E.A. Kramer. Zum Problem der Definition des Rechts. Vier Antworten auf eine Frage des Augustinus. ÖZöR. NF 23 (1972), p. 105 et seqq.

Table of Contents

X

Abbreviations

AcP	Archiv für civilistische Praxis [Tübingen]
ARSP	Archiv für Rechts- und Sozialphilosophie [Wiesbaden]
Art.	Article
BBl	Bundesblatt der Schweizerischen Eidgenossenschaft (Bern)
BGB	Deutsches Bürgerliches Gesetzbuch (German Civil Code)
BGBl	Bundesgesetzblatt (Federal Law Gazette) [Bonn]
BGE	Entscheidungen des Schweizerischen Bundesgerichts. Amtliche Sammlung (Decisions of the Swiss Federal Court) [Lausanne]
BGHSt	Entscheidungen des Bundesgerichtshofs in Strafsachen (Decisions of the Federal Court of Justice of Germany in Criminal Matters) [Cologne/Berlin]
BGHZ	Entscheidungen des Bundesgerichtshofs in Zivilsachen (Decisions of the German Federal Court of Justice in Civil Matters) [Detmold]
BNSDJ	Bund Nationalsozialistischer Deutscher Juristen (National Socialist German Jurists' Association)
BS	Bereinigte Sammlung der Bundesgesetze und Verordnungen von 1848–1947 (Revised Compilation of Federal Acts and Ordinances for the Years 1848-1947)
BV	Bundesverfassung der Schweizerischen Eidgenossenschaft (Federal Constitution of the Swiss Confederation) of 1848 or 1874 or 1999
BVerfGE	Bundesverfassungsgerichtsentscheidungen (Decisions of the Federal Constitutional Court of Germany) [Tübingen]
Cambr. L.J.	Cambridge Law Journal [London]
cf.	confer (compare)
ch.	Chapter
Col. Law Review	Columbia Law Review [New York]
Coll. nouv.	Collection nouvelle
D	Digesta corpus iuris civilis I, ed. by Th. Mommsen/P. Krüger (2nd edn., Berlin 1962)
DRB	Deutscher Richterbund (German Association of Judges)

DRiZ	Deutsche Richterzeitung (Cologne/Berlin/Bonn/Munich)
e.g.	exempli gratia (for example)
edn.	Edition
ed.	Editor
eds.	Editors
EMRK	Konvention zum Schutze der Menschenrechte und Grundfreiheiten (Europäische Menschenrechtskonvention/European Convention of Human Rights) of November 4, 1950
esp.	especially
et seq.	and the following (lat. sequens)
et seqq.	and the following [things] (lat. sequentia)
etc.	et cetera
Gestapo	Geheime Staatspolizei (Secret State Police [in Nazi Germany])
GG	Bonner Grundgesetz (Basic Law for the Federal Republic of Germany)
Harv. L. R.	Harvard Law Review [Cambridge, Massachusetts]
i.e.	that is (id est)
id.	Idem
IRP	Institutionalistischer Rechtspositivismus
ITL	Institutional Theory of Law
IVR	Internationale Vereinigung für Rechts- und Sozialphilosophie
JuS	Juristische Schulung, Zeitschrift für Studium und Ausbildung (Munich/Freiburg)
JW	Juristische Wochenschrift [Leipzig]
JZ	Deutsche Juristenzeitung [Tübingen]
lit.	Litera
loc. cit.	loco citato
Mich. L. R.	Michigan Law Review (Ann Arbor)
n.	Footnote
NF	neue Folge (new series)
NJW	Neue Juristische Wochenschrift [Munich/Frankfurt a. M.]
No.	Number

§ 1 Introduction

A. Objectives

This book was originally born of disappointment about the fact that legal philosophers are seldom in agreement. In this, they are the spitting images of their elder brothers, the general philosophers, who scarcely ever succeed in reaching a consensus, either. In contrast to the various single scientific disciplines, which can boast a stock of assured knowledge to some extent or another – notwithstanding all the uncertainties that current, as yet unresolved problems are prone to raise – it seemed that in the discipline of philosophy in general, and legal philosophy in particular, scholars had been in the habit of turning over the same problems again and again since the year dot, yet failing to come up with results that would gain the recognition of all or even just a majority of their fellow experts.

This duly stirred an interest in looking more deeply into the question of why this is so. However, the analysis could not possibly delve into all the different movements in legal thought and had to be confined to just one, which is nevertheless one of the most important contemporary schools of thought, viz. legal positivism. There are two reasons for this: first, the dismaying inability to reach agreement is just as evident among the legal positivists as in any other circle. And second, they do in principle start from the same epistemological platform, which facilitates the comparison of their theories. These two reasons make the legal positivist theories especially well suited as objects of the kind of investigation envisaged in this book.

The objectives of this work are the following:

- First of all, the most important varieties of legal positivism will be introduced and outlined (below § 2–13).
- In particular, we will address a new doctrinal trend which – depending on the author – is referred to as "soft positivism", "incorporationism" or "inclusive positivism" – as opposed to classical so-called "exclusive positivism" (below, § 12).

1

- On the basis of this presentation, we will then proceed to examine how we intend "legal positivism" to be understood from the point of view of its usefulness (below, § 14/15).

- Next, we disclose the premises on which our investigation is based (below § 16–18).

- Then we attempt to clarify why legal positivists are unable to agree (§ 20 B and C).

- In the following, we shall develop a certain interpretation of legal philosophical thinking (we call it "Axiomatic Theory of Law") which differs from the conventional view and accounts for the differences of opinion amongst the legal positivists (§ 21).

- Finally, with reference to the example of legal positivism, we shall sketch out how legal philosophical theories should be tested on the basis of such an interpretation, which we refer to as "Axiomatic Theory of Law". The question we address is not to what extent the legal positivist theories are true and to what extent they are false, but rather, what are their merits and demerits, i.e. what they are suited for and what are they not (§ 22–24). With the exception of the separation thesis, general assertions will not be made regarding the efficacy of the various legal positivist theories for the understanding of certain issues; rather, this needs to be assessed separately on the basis of each single theory. It is our thesis that it may cause big problems to try to lump all the phenomena of law together in one theory.

- We will attach particular importance to the discussion of what we call the "Hitler argument", which is considered the cardinal proof against legal positivism; at stake is the accusation that legal positivism was the cause of the perversion of the rule of law in the Third Reich.

B. Conceptual Clarifications:
Positivity – Validity – Legitimacy[1]

I. The Criterion for Differentiating between the Variants of Legal Positivism

The first problem we are confronted with is that of determining by which criterion we want to classify the different variants of legal positivist theories. Finding an answer to the question as to the best differentiation criterion does, of course, presuppose knowledge of the subject matter to be discussed in the First Part: only if one exactly knows the individual theories which might be attributed to the different varieties of legal positivism will one be able to find a criterion which may claim to do justice to the matter. Therefore, at the time of writing the authors were forced to tread this path in the opposite direction from the one they now propose to the reader; nevertheless, for the sake of understandability it will undoubtedly be better if we introduce the decisive criterion here and now, and delineate and delimit it against related concepts straight away.

A closer look at the various legal positivist theories will reveal that there is a connection between general philosophical positivism and legal positivism – a connection which has already been noticed by the legal positivists themselves as well as by authors of different provenance. Like the philosophical positivist, the legal positivist aspires to latch on to the "positively given", i.e. to something factual, something *undeniably real*, in order to arrive at sound insights. This being the case, it seems appropriate to base our criterion on what the individual theories recognize as "positivity". Thus, we differentiate between the various legal positivist theories *in terms of the characteristics which each individual theory deems to be constitutive for the positivity of the law.*

---

[1] While reading this section, the reader is advised to refer closely to the chart at § 1 p. 8. below.

II. Positivity

"Positive law" is generally understood as the law *established* by a social authority, in particular by a state authority. The term "positive" in this sense (lat. *ponere* = to put, to place) applies to all treaties, written constitutions, statutes and administrative orders contained in official compilations until they are repealed, irrespective of whether they are approved and actually complied with by the subjects, or whether they are applied by the "law staff".[2] "Paper rules", i.e. rules that exist only on paper, are positive in this sense as well. Furthermore, regardless of the observance of legislative procedures, the commands of a dictator or victor and so-called customary law are also positive in this sense.

Yet this rather narrow concept of "positivity" would not be appropriate for the purpose of this research project. For not everything that appears to be "positively established" in this first sense would be referred to as "positive law" by a sociological legal positivist or a psychological legal positivist. We have mentioned "paper rules" as an example. Paper rules are positive in the sense of "being established by the (state) legislator" but not within the terms of a modern sociological coercion theory, since the law staff is not willing to apply and enforce them. Likewise, an inhumane statute would represent positive law in the first sense; yet within the terms of a variant of psychological positivism based on recognition by the majority of subjects, if the latter disapproved of the statute, then it would not. On the other hand, an illegal practice by the Supreme Court would be positive law according the sociological coercion theory but not in the sense of "being positively established by the legislator." In the sense mentioned last, the term "positivity" could only be used here if it were understood to mean "positively established by the highest judges".

However, we have to choose the differentiation criterion in such a manner that all the theories qualified by us as variants of legal positivism can be based on it. For this reason, it seems advisable to start out from a broader concept of "positivity" which includes *but is not limited to* "being established by a social authority".

---

[2] The term "law staff" is understood as including all authorities involved in the application and enforcement of the law.

For the purpose of this work, positivity in the wider sense shall mean the *actual existence*, the *reality of the law*. By "positive law" we shall approximately mean "actually existing", "real", "factually valid" law. If one analyzes the positivist theories, it becomes evident that they always understand positivity as a physical, *spatiotemporal reality* or as a psychological, i.e. only *temporal reality* or as a combination of the two. The analytical positivist perceives the positivity of the law in its establishment by a state authority, the psychological positivist as a certain psychological condition, such as "ought-experience", "recognition", "*opinio necessitatis*", and the sociological positivist as some external behavior, viz. as actual compliance with the law by the members of the legal community, or as application of the law by a certain staff of officials. When we speak about the "positivity" of the law in the following, as a rule it is this wider sense of the term that we mean.

III. Validity

1. Factual Validity (Effectiveness)

The concept of positivity in the wider sense as just set out above is nothing but the law's "factual validity in the wider sense", so to speak. For the purpose of this book, factually valid law shall mean the same as "positive law" in the wider sense, i.e. actually existing law. "Validity" *in this sense* is therefore nothing normative but something factual, and always refers to the law that has become "real" in some way yet to be defined more closely. If, for example, we say that a legal norm is factually valid, then this neither means that the said norm appears to be justified from some higher standpoint (that it is thus legitimated in the sense to be explained below, sub IV); nor does it mean that it conforms to the validity criteria of the constitution (i.e. that it has what is called "normative validity"), but only that it has come into existence in some way yet to be defined more closely (which does not, of course, rule out the possibility that norms of factual validity may also be normatively valid or legitimated or both).

The actual existence of a factually valid norm may consist in *positivity in the narrower sense* (mentioned above § 1 B.II), or in a *psychological reality*, or in *sociological effectiveness*, or in some combination of these. A norm is psychologically effective for example if it is experienced as "binding" or "obligating", whereas it is sociologically effective if it is actually complied with by the members of the legal society and/or if it is applied by the law staff. Most of the time when there is mention of "effectiveness" in the literature, reference is only made to sociological effectiveness. This would stand in contrast to psychological effectiveness, which we will encompass – together with sociological effectiveness – with the term "factual effectiveness in the narrower sense".

2. Normative Validity

The concepts of factual validity in the narrower sense and in the broader sense are to be kept strictly separate from *normative validity* or *ought-validity* or *legal validity*. The statement that a legal norm is normatively valid shall mean that *it is in compliance with the criteria contained in a higher norm or a set of higher norms concerning the validity of derived norms*. An individual legal norm, e.g. a judicial decision, is normatively valid if it is in compliance with the criteria regarding individual norms contained in the relevant laws; such laws for their part are normatively valid if they are in compliance with the criteria regarding the validity of law contained in the constitution; in Kelsen's system, the constitution is normatively valid if it is in compliance with the validity criteria contained in the so-called "basic norm", i.e. if the constitution can be interpreted as the highest norm of a coercive system that is by and large effective (cf. below § 4 , text n. 10 et seqq.). Thus, normative validity is determined by deductive conclusion from a norm containing one or several validity criteria which functions as major premise and an empirical statement as a minor premise; thus, by logical method.[3] In contrast, factual validity is determined by *observation*, i.e. by empirical method.

---

[3] Example:
   1. What the king commands, one ought to do (major premise containing the validity criterion).
   2. The king commands to do X (empirical statement as minor premise).
   3. One ought to do X (normatively valid conclusion).

IV. Legitimacy

By "validity" of the law one may understand a third thing, viz. what may be referred to as the "legitimacy" of the law. This, too, must be kept strictly separate from the factual validity concepts and from the normative validity concept just set out. "A legal norm is legitimate" shall mean that it appears justified from a higher (philosophical or religious) perspective. Several lines of argumentation may serve to justify the legitimacy of a legal norm, namely value-theoretical (e.g. aligned with value objectivism or utilitarianism, as by John Austin [§ 2]), natural law and religious approaches. As will be seen, usually legal positivists do not address the issue of the legitimacy of the law. However, where this does exceptionally happen, the relevant trains of thought may not be seen as part of positivist theory. In recent times J. Raz and J. Coleman II [§ 15 D] have justified positivism with the moral concept of "legitimate authority", whereas Tom Campbell [§ 14 at the end] defends it on normative grounds.

V. Schematic Overview

For clarification of the aforesaid, please refer to the scheme on p. 8. In the further course of our investigation, we will not always indicate which validity concept is meant when we refer to the "validity of the law", presuming that the attentive reader may easily deduce this from the respective context.

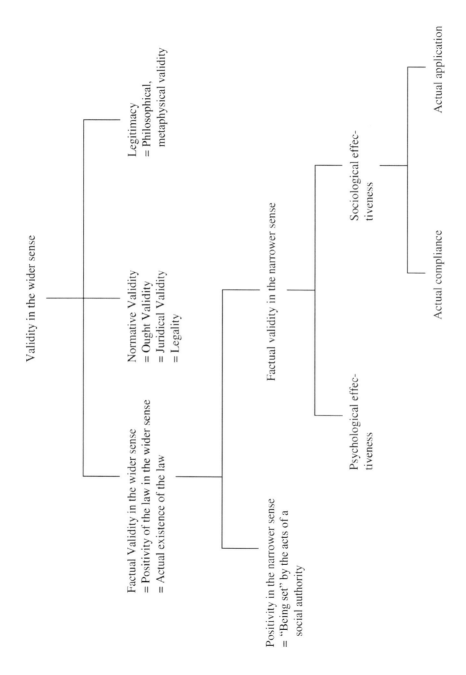

First Part

Varieties and Concept of Legal Positivism

First Chapter

Analytical Positivism

The theories that we will group under the heading of "analytical positivism" all concur in identifying the positivity of the law in the making of rules by a social authority – in fact for the most part by a state authority. With these theories, the term positivity refers to positivity in the narrower sense.[1] The expression positivity acquired the sense of Latin *ponere* "to put, to place" [the law]. These theories are analytical insofar as they analyze the logical relations of the various legal concepts and compile the results in a system. Often, analytical positivism is equated with positivism per se.[2]

§ 2 John Austin's Analytical Jurisprudence[3]

John Austin, significantly influenced by Jeremy Bentham, was the father of what is known as the "analytical" theory (precursors: Jean Bodin and Thomas Hobbes). Austin expounded the greater part of this theory in his

---

[1] Cf. above, § 1 B II and scheme on p. 8.
[2] See for example Brecht, p. 183.
[3] See works of Austin listed in the Bibliography, Lectures on Jurisprudence, I/II, Bristol 1996; same, Province, Cambridge 1995; Löwenhaupt; Eckmann, p. 21 et seqq., p. 28 et seqq., p. 58 et seqq., p. 66; Reich, p. 29 et seqq.; Cattaneo; Eastwood R.A. and Keeton G.W., The Austinian Theories of Law and Sovereignty, London: Methuen, 1929; J.W. Harris, The Concept of Sovereign Will, Acta Juridica 1977, p. 1–15; Hart, The Concept of Law, chs. 2–4; C.A.W. Manning, Austin to-day; or "The Province of Jurisprudence" Re-examined, in: W.I. Jennings (ed.), Modern Theories of Law, London: Oxford University Press, 1933, p. 180–226; W.L. Morison, John Austin, Stanford: University Press, 1982; W. Rumble, The Thought of John Austin, Jurisprudence, Colonial Reform, and the British Constitution, London: Athlone Press, 1985.

"Lectures on Jurisprudence". He distinguishes between "Particular Jurisprudence" and "General Jurisprudence".[4] Particular jurisprudence deals with a particular historical legal system.[5] General jurisprudence, on the other hand, deals with the general legal principles and basic terms common to all, or at least, all advanced legal systems.[6] He does not, however, discuss in detail the principles essential to the law, i.e. legal rules of general content. The main part of his work deals with the necessary concepts and distinctions of the law. Austin's theory is analytical in the sense explained above insofar as it investigates the logical mutual dependence of legal concepts and constructs a system based on the results of his research. Yet it would be wrong to conclude that Austin proceeds in a mere deductive way, i.e. without any reference to experience. On the contrary, more recent studies, by H.L.A. Hart amongst others, have come to the conclusion "…that Austin tried to proceed in a *strictly empirical manner*. He assumes that all terms used by him are strictly empirical, i.e. refer directly or indirectly to impressions on the senses as source of their meaning."[7] To illustrate this, reference may be made to Austin's concept of the legal obligation where he tries to understand the obligation not normatively but as a fact.[8]

A good starting point into Austin's thinking is his famous *conceptual* distinction between the law as it is and the law as it ought to be, which had been emphasized by Bentham, too. Austin puts it like this:

"The existence of law is one thing; its merit or demerit is another. Whether it be or be not is one enquiry; whether it be or be not conformable to an assumed standard, is a different enquiry. A law, which actually exists, is a law, though we happen to dislike it, or though it vary from the text, by which we regulate our approbation and disapprobation."[9] Austin illustrates this by the following example: "Suppose an act innocuous, or positively beneficial, be prohibited by the sovereign under the penalty of

---

[4]   Austin, Lectures I, p. 32.
[5]   Austin, Lectures II, p. 1107.
[6]   Austin, Lectures II, p. 1107.
[7]   Eckmann, p. 23, with reference to Hart, Introduction to Austin, Province p. xi.
[8]   See below, text at n. 25 et seqq.
[9]   Austin, Province, p. 157.

death; if I commit this act, I shall be tried and condemned, and if I object to the sentence, that it is contrary to the law of God ..., the Court of Justice will demonstrate the inconclusiveness of my reasoning by hanging me up, in pursuance of the law of which I have impugned the validity."[10] Critics of the thesis of a conceptual distinction between law and morality often overlook the fact that the positivists affirm an empirical link between law and morality, i.e. they do not deny that moral ideas in a society have a great effect on the content of law, and that this in turn has an effect on social morality.[11]

Corresponding to the *conceptual* distinction between the law as it is and the law as it ought to be, Austin divides legal theory into "jurisprudence" and "science of legislation". While the former is concerned with the positive laws, considered without regard to their goodness or badness,[12] the latter looks into the question of how positive law ought to be.[13] For Austin, the relevant principles are the (revealed) law of God on the one hand and the (not revealed) principle of utility, as stated by Bentham, which is an index to God's commands.[14] *Bentham* formulated the principle of utility as follows:

"Nature has placed mankind under the governance of two sovereign masters, *pleasure* and *pain*. It is for them alone to point out what we ought to do, as well as to determine what we shall do ... They govern us in all we do, in all we say, in all we think: every effort we can make to throw off our subjection, will serve but to demonstrate and confirm it ... The *principle of utility* recognizes this subjection, and assumes it for the foundation of that system, the object of which is to rear the fabric of felicity by the hands of reason and of law."[15, 16] Austin's statement re-

---

[10] Austin, Province, p. 158.
[11] See below, § 11 at n. 8.
[12] Austin, Lectures I, p. 176 et seq.
[13] Austin, Lectures I, p. 33.
[14] Austin, Lectures I, p. 109 et seqq., p. 121.
[15] Bentham, An Introduction to the Principles of Morals and Legislation, coll. works. II/1, ed. by J.H. Burns and H.L.A. Hart, Oxford: Clarendon Press, 1996,, p. 11, chap. 1 n. 1.
[16] Both Austin and Bentham identify the principle of utility with the principle of "the greatest happiness for the largest number of people". Cf. Löwenhaupt, p. 20 n. 5 with further references. It must, however, be emphasized, that Bentham accused

garding the right of resistance may serve as an example of the application of the principle of utility in legal matters. He infers that obedience to established government is generally enjoined by the Lord, for without such obedience there would be little security and enjoyment. If, however, the protection that government yields is too costly because it vexes its subjects with needless restraints and loads them with needless exactions, then at some point the principle of utility may no longer demand obedience but may justify resistance. In such cases "the peculiar good would outweigh the generic evil" of resistance.[17] According to Austin, the statement that a statute is part of the positive law stops short of giving a verdict on whether or not the statute should be obeyed. For in principle, only laws of public utility deserve the obedience of the subjects.

What strikes us as noteworthy about this train of thought is this: Austin's example reveals that legal positivism need not – as is often insinuated – be accompanied by ethical relativism in the supra-positive sphere. A legal positivist may "well be a devout Christian, or an ardent utilitarian, or a radical equalitarian, who would give a definite answer to the question *what rule should or should not be made.*"[18]

---

himself of having put in circulation an unduly shortened formula by speaking of "the greatest happiness for the largest number of people". In reality, the principle of utility is just as much about minimizing pain. Thus Bentham expressly states that he considers slavery inadmissible simply because slaves can suffer from pain as well (Bentham, Chap. I sec. XIII; idem, Principles of the Civil Code, Works I, p. 344 et seq.). Nevertheless, the opponents of utilitarianism often bring forward the argument that utilitarianism would even allow for some having to spend their lives as slaves if social utility were thereby maximized. This argument could be countered with the reasoning of a modern utilitarian like Gesang, who says that any preferential balance yielding victims may be criticized as suboptimal and the utility sum improved by avoiding victims. See Bernward Gesang, Eine Verteidigung des Utilitarismus, Stuttgart: Reclam, 2003, p. 65.

[17] Austin, Lectures I, p. 121.

[18] Brecht 183. Emphasis added by the authors. For an opposing opinion see A.M. Shuman p. 9, p. 15, p. 193, who develops another concept of legal positivism than the one outlined in § 15 and § 14 at n. 19. According to Shuman, the characteristics of legal positivism are the separation thesis, on the one hand, and the tie to the theory of ethical non-cognitivism, on the other. Consequently, for Shuman, Austin's analytical theory – unlike for example Kelsen's pure theory of law – cannot be a positivist theory.

But let us return from Austin's (utilitarian) reflections on the law as it ought to be to his (positivist) analysis of the law as it is: for Austin, the concept of *command* is the key to the understanding of the sciences of jurisprudence and morality.[19] By law, employed in its most general and comprehensive meaning, Austin understood nothing other than the commands given by a human superior to a human inferior which are backed by threats. This definition of the law encompasses both positive law and the divine law.[20] Austin delimits positive law from two sides:

1. First, positive law differs from divine law in the person of the *commander*: divine law is set for men by a transcendental legislator, whereas positive law is set for men by men. Positive law is, therefore, *human* law.[21]

2. Second, positive law as distinguished from positive morality[22] is the aggregate of the rules of behavior set by the sovereign of an independent political society upon its subjects.[23] Thus, positive law is state law.[24]

Now the next question is, what exactly is a legal command? First of all, a legal command, like all commands, expresses a desire of the commander. A command, however, is distinguished from other expressions of desire by the power of the commander to inflict an *evil*[25] if his desire is disregarded by the addressee of the command. A duty, according to Austin, is nothing but the correlative expression of such a command: if somebody is subject to an evil imposed by the commander in case of non-compliance with the commander's wishes, he *lies under a duty* to obey the command.[26] Thus, every command annexed to a threat of coer-

---

[19] Austin, Lectures I, p. 90.
[20] Austin, Lectures I, p. 88.
[21] Austin, Lectures I, p. 88 et seq./173 et seqq.
[22] Austin distinguishes in an exemplary manner between positive (human) morality and morality as such (=divine law), Lectures I 175 et seq.: "If you say that an act or omission violates *morality*, you speak ambiguously. You may mean that it violates which I style *'positive* morality', or that it violates the Divine law which is the measure or test for the former."
[23] Austin, Lectures I, p. 88 et seq.
[24] Austin, Lectures II, p. 550.
[25] Austin, Lectures I, p. 91.
[26] Austin, Lectures I, p. 91.

cion constitutes a legal obligation; the obligation is nothing other than the prospect of an evil in the event of disobedience to the command.[27] The greater the eventual evil tied to the command, the greater the strength of the obligation and the greater the chance that it will be obeyed.[28] Commands which are laws are distinguished from other commands by two further elements:

Only a *general* command may be a rule, a juridical law. Austin does not apply "general" to the number of addressees[29] but to the content of the command. Where a command obliges to a specific act or forbearance, a command is particular, where it obliges to acts or forbearances of a class, a command is general or a rule. A command to the servant to get up at a particular time on a particular morning is a particular command; the command always to get up at such and such time is a rule.[30] A further prerequisite of a legal command is that it emanates from the will of the supreme, legally independent power of an independent political society.[31] Only the commands issued directly by the sovereign or indirectly by its political representatives or private men as political delegates (including all private persons in pursuance of legal rights) are laws or rules.[32]

Sovereignty becomes manifest internally in the fact that the majority of the subjects is in the habit of obeying a determinate and common superior, and externally in the fact that this determinate and common superior is not in the habit of obeying another determinate human superior.[33] Thus, according to Austin, the supremacy of the sovereign need not be absolute, either internally or externally. Neither the occasional disobedience of the subjects nor the occasional obedience of the sovereign jeopardizes the sovereign position.

---

[27] Eckmann, p. 30. *Austin's* understanding of the notion of duty is mere empirical, not normative. Thus, to *Austin*, law is a fact, too, and not an Ought, as it is for example to Kelsen.
[28] Austin, Lectures I, p. 92 et seq.
[29] Löwenhaupt, p. 127.
[30] Austin, Lectures I, p. 95.
[31] Löwenhaupt, p. 143 and references made ibid. in n. 147.
[32] Löwenhaupt, p. 124/125.
[33] Austin, Lectures I, p. 226 et seq.

However, there are several points on which the simple scheme of command, sanction and sovereign as set out in Austin's command theory of law seems not to coincide with legal reality. First of all, Austin himself did not overlook that there are rules which do not lay down a sanction and yet are generally included within the positive law. He refers to laws containing an authentic interpretation or a permission and to so-called *leges imperfectae*. Austin openly admits that such rules form an exception to his proposition that 'laws are species of commands' and are not, therefore, 'laws properly so called'. Even so, Austin emphasizes the imperative function that such rules nevertheless often have: acts of interpretation of the positive law in reality frequently establish new law. Permissive laws create rights; however, since every right correlates with a duty, such rules indirectly create duties. Finally, it is not unusual for the courts to supply imperfect laws with a sanction.[34] Furthermore, the non-existence of an international sovereign made Austin deny the legal nature of international law. He includes the rules of international law with positive (international) morality.[35]

In this context, it is worthwhile to shed some light on Austin's view of the judge's position. It has been claimed that Austin – supposedly influenced by German *Begriffsjurisprudenz* – was a proponent of a purely formalistic theory of interpretation.[36] This is inaccurate, however, as Hart in particular has pointed out.[37] According to Austin, the judge's interpretation of a statute is *usually* a law-making activity. He is not applying previously existing law but is *making new law*.[38] The only exception is constituted by cases where the judge grammatically interprets the terms of a statute to ascertain the underlying will of the legislator.[39] Where the judge interprets extensively or restrictively, he is a subordinate legislator

---

[34] Austin, Lectures I, p. 100 et seqq.
[35] Regarding the problem of international law in Austin's theory, see Löwenhaupt, p. 138 et seqq. with numerous references.
[36] See for example J. Stone, The Province and Function of Law (Sydney 1950), p. 141. For further reference see W.L. Morrison, Some Myths about Positivism, Yale L.J. 68 (1958/59), p. 212 et seqq.
[37] Hart, Positivism and the Separation of Law and Morals, p. 64 et seqq. See also Shuman, p. 192.
[38] Austin, Lectures II, p. 648 et seq.
[39] Austin, Lectures II, p. 649.

(cf. the famous Article 1 para. 2 of the Swiss Civil Code: in the absence of a statutory provision, the court shall decide in accordance with customary law and, in the absence of a custom, *in accordance with the rules that it would enact if it had to legislate*[40]).[41]

In this realistic evaluation of the judicial process, Austin's analytical jurisprudence contrasts favorably with German statutory positivism, to which we will turn in the following.

---

[40] For translation, see Arthur T. von Mehren, Review of: A. Schwarz, "Das Schweizerische Zivilgesetzbuch in der ausländischen Rechtsprechung", The American Journal of Comparative Law 1 (1952), p. 453.
[41] Austin, Lectures II, p. 650.

§ 3 German Statutory Positivism[1]

In terms of its impact on practice, German statutory positivism is the most important variety of the positivist theories. Statutory positivism identifies the law with the (state) norms generated by the constitutionally defined procedure.[2] On the one hand, law exists only in statutes;[3] on the other hand, every statute is *eo ipso* law. Every norm that the sovereign authority has posited in the formally correct procedure, and none that it has not, acquires the quality of law. The reference to a formal, i.e. value-free criterion (in this case the power of the sovereign authority as expressed in the statutes) – as under every positivist theory – leads to abstention from any value-evaluation of the contents of the law. Consequently the sovereign can enact as law *norms of any content whatsoever.*

Thus, statutory positivism proclaims the *juristic omnipotence* of the legislator. The doctrine of *"Quod principi placuit, legis habet vigorem"* goes back to the teachings of Ulpian,[4] and the German *Reichsgericht* in its day delivered the classic coinage of this view by wording it as follows: "The legislator is autocratic and subject to no other limits but those he has drawn himself in the constitution and in other statutes."[5] If one approves of this point of view, then one is, according to Bergbohm, "in the embarrassing situation of having to recognize statutory law of the most despicable content as binding, provided only that it has been enacted in the formally correct manner."[6] Given such an understanding of the juristic theory of validity, it is impossible "to deny validity, on any com-

---

[1] Literature: G. Anschütz/R. Thoma, Handbuch des deutschen Staatsrechts I/II, Tübingen: Mohr Siebeck, 1998, (Reprint of 1930/32 Edition); Bergbohm; Baratta, ARSP 54 (1968), p. 325 et seqq.; Henkel, p. 496 et seqq.; Riebschläger, p. 19 et seqq.; Rüthers, Unbegrenzte Auslegung, p. 91 et seqq.; Wieacker, p. 458 et seqq.; F. Somló, Juristische Grundlehre, Second Edition, Leipzig 1927 (Reprint Aalen, 1973), p. 298 et seqq., in particular p. 308 and p. 431.

[2] By law, we mean, in this context, written constitutions, statutes and regulations.

[3] From a statutory positivist perspective, customary law is consequently only valid in as much as it is explicitly or implicitly recognized by statutory law.

[4] D 1, 4, 1 pr.

[5] RGZ 118 (1928) 327 (our translation). For reference with regard to the historical context of this decision, see below, § 23 at n. 128.

[6] Bergbohm, p. 144 (our translation), referring only to legal but not moral validity.

pelling grounds, to the imperatives of a paranoiac who believes himself to be king."[7] However, precisely when confronted with "law displeasing for its disgracefulness or its inhumanity", Bergbohm says, "the pure jurist's noblest virtue can prove itself: the capability to abjure from the deepest personal prejudices and most burning passions, expecting their fulfillment only by way of legal change."[8]

It is to be emphasized that the statutory positivists usually do not try to give reasons for the legitimacy (in the sense of a philosophical validity) of the positive law.[9] This would result not only in a legal, but also in a moral obligation to obey the law. When Bergbohm says in the quotation above that despicable statutory law has to be recognized as binding as long as it has been enacted in the formally correct manner, other parts of his exposition corroborate that he is only referring to "a formal validity of the rules duly promulgated as law" (i.e., in our terminology, the normative validity) which must be sharply distinguished from its "material integrity" (in our terminology: its legitimacy).[10] Likewise, Somló observes that there may be "absolutely immoral law" and therefore declares "the impositions of the law to be burdens independent of moral obligations."[11] From the fact that somebody is – legally – obliged to comply with the positive law, it does not necessarily follow that they are morally obliged to do so. Similarly, Anschütz and Thoma turn their attention to the case where the legislator does not intend a certain legal rule to be a just and charitable one.[12] In such a case, moral conscience could drive the individual to publicly incite disobedience or, indeed, to the point of rebellion.[13]

---

[7] Radbruch, p. 79 (our translation).
[8] Bergbohm, p. 398.
[9] See above, and scheme p. 8.
[10] Bergbohm, 397/398.
[11] Somló, (quoted in § 3 n. 1), p. 431.
[12] Anschütz/Thoma II (quoted in § 3 n. 1), p. 141.
[13] Anschütz/Thoma II (quoted in § 3 n. 1), p. 142. Note, however, that Anschütz modifies this statement in another one of his works for the judge (Die Verfassung des deutschen Reiches vom 11. August 1919, 12th Edition, Berlin 1931, p. 417): "If one cannot admit that the judge is authorized to rule on the constitutionality of the law then much less can one admit that the judge would be allowed to refuse obedience to a law which materialized as a result of the constitutionally defined procedure because such law – in the opinion of the judge – violates rules (e.g. custom, morality,

Thus, if a statutory positivist declares that positive law imposes the obligation of unconditional obedience, it is important to recognize that this is meant only in the legal and not in the moral sense, i.e. there is no legal justification for refusing to obey. Even from a statutory positivist standpoint, this allows for the adoption of a critical distance towards the positive law.

A foundation of the positivist theory of power based on value philosophy was attempted by Radbruch in 1932. Being a value relativist, Radbruch proceeds from the impossibility of scientific cognition of ultimate values.[14] It is by that very impossibility that we can justify the binding character (in the philosophical sense) of the positive law. The order of co-existence cannot be left to the legal precepts of the co-existing individuals but must be clearly regulated by a supra-individual authority: "Since, however, reason and science are unable to perform this task, *will and power have to assume it. If nobody is able to determine what is just, then somebody has to stipulate what ought to be just*, and if the law that is enacted is supposed to fulfill the task of ending by authoritative fiat the conflict between antagonistic views of the law, *then the enactment of the law must be backed by a will that is able to prevail against every opposing view of the law.*"[15]

---

good faith, "natural law") which stand above the legislator or because it does not bear up under certain value judgments (justice, equity, reason)."

[14] Reference is made to Radbruch's position before World War II (i.e. before his conversion to natural law). Cf. below, § 11 and § 23 A and Stanley Paulson, Radbruch on Unjust Laws: Competing Earlier and Later Views? Oxford Journal of Legal Studies 15 (1995), p. 490. Apart from the attempt to justify the binding character of the law based on value philosophy, Gustav Radbruch's theory differs from German statutory positivism in that it does not confine the application of the law to logical operations. See Radbruch (1946), p. 106 et seqq. With regard to Radbruch, cf. A. Kaufmann, Gustav Radbruch. Rechtsdenker, Philosoph, Sozialdemokrat, Munich: Piper, 1987, and H. Dreier, Die Radbruch'sche Formel – Erkenntnis oder Bekenntnis? in: H. Mayer (ed.), Essays in Honour of Robert Walter zum 60. Geburtstag, Vienna: Manz 1991, p. 117 et seqq.

[15] Radbruch, p. 82 (our emphasis) [Radbruch, Rechtsphilosophie, Third Edition, Leipzig: Quelle und Meyer, 1932, p. 81]. Regarding the second half of the translation, see Stanley Paulson, Radbruch on Unjust Laws: Competing Earlier and Later Views? Oxford Journal of Legal Studies 15 (1995), p. 490. Note that Radbruch uses a wording here of which he accused positivism after the war (see below, § 23 A). "Wer

Understood like this, the positive law is thus not only legally valid but also legitimated since, by its sheer existence, it at least ensures the value of legal certainty: the resulting consequence is that the judge has not only a legal but also a moral obligation to obey the law:

"The judge, *by utilizing the law irrespective of its justice*, will nevertheless not become a servant of accidental goals of arbitrariness. *Even if he, since that is the way law wants it, ceases to be a servant of justice, he still remains a servant of legal certainty.* We hold in contempt the clergyman who preaches contrary to his own convictions, *but we revere the judge whose fidelity to the statutes is not compromised by his own conflicting sense of what is right.*"[16]

We contend that a justification of the positive law's claim to legitimacy such as the one put forward by Radbruch is not possible within the frame of a positivist theory but only by recourse to a position of value philosophy. The statutory positivist theories – like all the other legal positivist theories – do not justify the law and can therefore only correctly assume a legal but not a moral obligation to obey.

The statutory positivist thesis of the identity of law and statute – more precisely: the identity of the law as expressed in statute and the law per se – necessarily leads to the conclusion that the application of law must be understood exclusively as the application of statutes. To apply the law means to subsume to the norms of a statute. From this, the idea proceeds that the judge is only stating the law, is nothing but "*la bouche, qui prononce les paroles de la loi.*"[17] The judge discovers the law in the statutes, he does not invent it. The function of the court is the determination of law, not the making of law. A statutory positivist therefore entirely distrusts arguments by analogy and by the "nature of things", and there have even been cases where the judge was forbidden to interpret the law alto-

---

Recht durchzusetzen vermag, beweist damit, dass er Recht zu setzen berufen ist." "Who can enforce the law proves that he is competent to make law."

[16] Radbruch, p. 84 (our emphasis) [Radbruch, Rechtsphilosophie, Third Edition, Leipzig: Quelle und Meyer, 1932, p. 83 et seq.] (on the translation of second sentence, refer to Stanley Paulson, quoted in § 3 n. 15, p. 496). However, Radbruch rates the position of the ordinary person subject to the law – whose unconditional obedience he obviously does not assume – as different from that of the judge (ibidem).

[17] Montesquieu, De l'Esprit des Lois, Livre XI, chapitre 6.

gether.[18] On the other hand, it must be emphasized that the principle of *"nulla poena sine lege"*,[19] regarded today as the epitome of criminal law in accordance with the rule of law and as "the criminal's Magna Carta", is an offshoot of liberal, Enlightenment-influenced statutory positivism. The statutory positivist method of processing enacted law therefore precludes broadening or even changing the law with reference to political, moral or sociological – i.e. extra-legal – principles.[20]

This entails the following significant consequences: the judge must prove his decision to be legally justified (rather than just morally justified); and, on the principle that forbids the denial of justice, this must be proven even in cases where the law does not directly yield an answer. However, since the statutory positivist's view only allows for such a deduction to be derived from the positive law and not from extra-legal principles, the statutory positivist must postulate the *gaplessness of statutory law*, or the more frequent assumption by far, the gaplessness of law per se.

Plathner, for example, pleads for the gaplessness of *statutory law* by demanding that legislation be "sufficient and precise" and that "every decision be made in accordance with no other norm than the provisions of statutory law."[21] Any other norm is merely arbitrary to the party concerned, and would remain so even when ascertained by a judge.

The theory of the *law* as a gapless order goes back mainly to Bergbohm. If the legal system does not yield an answer to a particular question, Bergbohm wants us to distinguish between two cases: if, after summon-

---

[18] Rules that forbid such techniques of interpretation can be found e.g. in: Justinian, Constitutio Tanta (C 1, 17, 2, 21 in fine) und especially in decrees in times of absolutism.

[19] Written by the jurist Paul Johann Anselm Ritter von Feuerbach (1775–1833) as part of the Bavarian Code in 1813.

[20] Baratta, ARSP 54 (1968), p. 332. Representative for this e.g. P. Laband, Das Staatsrecht des Deutschen Reiches I, 4th Edition, Tübingen/Leipzig: Mohr, 1901, p. IX. It must be emphasized that Anschütz/Thoma are expressly rejecting this view and may therefore not be qualified as absolute and pure statutory positivists.

[21] Plathner, Geist des preussischen Privatrechts, p. XXXIII; quoted from Kohler, Über die Interpretation von Gesetzen, Zeitschrift für das Privat- und öffentliche Recht, Vienna 1874–1916, established by Grünhut, 13 (1886), p. 49 (our translation).

ing all aid, positive law still fails to deliver an answer, then the supposed question must be "retrospectively" declared a "non-legal" one;[22] it is deemed to fall within the unlegislated area surrounding the legal system. If one is unable to admit this, however, a decision – a "quantum of positive law" – must be found, which fits exactly in this gap and automatically fills the apparent vacuum.[23] In such a case, the gap is not in the law itself but in the person searching for the law.[24] The existence and the evidence of the law must not be confused. The evidence of the law is tied to the formal sources of the law, which have never been exhaustive.[25] By means of "difficult deductions", the judge can nevertheless arrive at the necessary norms. The argument that such a norm, because it was discovered with such difficulty, is less positive than one that can be deduced directly from the wording of the law, is unpersuasive.[26] This argumentation, which has in the main been endorsed by most proponents of the dogma of the law as a gapless order,[27] illuminates that Bergbohm's explanations, strictly speaking, are aimed at demonstrating the *incompleteness* of the *wording* of the statute and the *gaplessness* of the *law expressed in the wording* of the statute.[28] The law obtained only by (allegedly) logically conclusive deductions must, in order to be meaningful, be regarded as part of the system of statutory law; it cannot be interpreted as a system of norms independent of the statutory law, since this would be inconsistent with the theory of the identity of statute and law.

From a statutory positivist view, it makes sense to speak of gaps in a system of positive law only in cases where a second and equally positive system of legal norms is available to supplement and correct the first system; for example, the supplementing of state law by federal law.

---

[22] Bergbohm, p. 381.
[23] Bergbohm, p. 381.
[24] Bergbohm, p. 382.
[25] Bergbohm, p. 382.
[26] Bergbohm, p. 381.
[27] Riebschläger, p. 24.
[28] Bergbohm, p. 382, distinguishes between the law and its meaning: "The statutes are not the law, they only stand for legal thoughts that everyone must reproduce himself from the thought-givers: the words of the statutes." (our translation).

§ 4 Hans Kelsen's Pure Theory of Law[1]

The 'pure' theory of law aspires to be a theory of the positive law, in fact of *positive law as such* as opposed to a specific legal system.[2] For Kelsen, the "positivity" of the law is twofold: the law must be the product of specifically qualified *human* acts on the one hand, and it must be *effective* up to a certain degree on the other.[3] As a theory, the 'pure' theory of law seeks *cognition* of its object, i.e. an answer to the question of what law *is* as opposed to what law *ought to be*.[4] The postulate of "purity" means the elimination from legal science of all "non-legal" methods and ways of looking at things (particularly psychology, ethics and political theory). Cognition of the law should not be dulled by a "methodological syncretism".

[1] Literature: Kelsen, Pure Theory of Law, Translated from the Second (Revised and Enlarged) German Edition by Max Knight, Clark, N.J.: The Lawbook Exchange, Ltd., 2005; idem, Introduction to the Problems of Legal Theory, A Translation of the First Edition of the Reine Rechtslehre or Pure Theory of Law, translated by Bonnie Litschewski Paulson and Stanley L. Paulson, Oxford: Clarendon Press, 1992; idem, Reine Rechtslehre, Reprint of Second Edition (1960), Vienna: Österreichische Staatsdruckerei, 1992; idem, General Theory of Law and State, translated by Anders Wedberg, Reprint of the 1945 Harvard University Press Edition, Clark, N.J.: The Lawbook Exchange, Ltd., 1999; idem, What is Justice? Justice, Law and Politics in the Mirror of Science. Reprint of the 1957 University of California Press Edition, Clark, N.J.: The Lawbook Exchange, Ltd., 2000; Walter, Rechtstheorie 1 (1970), p. 69 et seqq., A. Verdross (ed.), Gesellschaft, Staat und Recht. Untersuchungen zur Reinen Rechtslehre, Festschrift für Hans Kelsen zum 50. Geburtstag, Reprint of 1931 Edition, Topos Ruggell 1983; A.J. Merkl/A. Verdross/R. Marcic/R. Walter (Editors), Festschrift für Hans Kelsen zum 90. Geburtstag, Vienna: Franz Deuticke, 1971. The life and work of Hans Kelsen are portrayed in the book by Métall. See also Kelsen, Autobiographie (1947), in: M. Jestaedt (ed.), Hans Kelsen im Selbstzeugnis, Sonderpublikation anlässlich des 125. Geburtstages von Hans Kelsen am 11. Oktober 2006, Tübingen: Mohr Siebeck, 2006; P. Koller, in: O. Weinberger/W. Krawietz (Editors), Reine Rechtslehre im Spiegel ihrer Fortsetzer und Kritiker, Forschungen aus Staat und Recht No. 81, Vienna/New York: Springer, 1988, p. 129 et seqq.; H. Klecatsky/R. Marcic/H. Schambeck (Editors), Die Wiener rechtstheoretische Schule, Schriften von Hans Kelsen, Adolf Merkl, Alfred Verdross I-III, Vienna et al., 1968; J. Behrend, Untersuchungen zur Stufenbaulehre Adolf Merkls und Hans Kelsens, Schriften zur Rechtstheorie No. 65, Berlin: Duncker & Humblot, 1977; E. Weinreb, Legal Formalism: On the Immanent Rationality of Law, Yale Law Journal 97 (1988), p. 949 et seqq.; idem, Law as a Kantian Idea of Reason, Columbia Law Review 87 (1987), p. 472 et seqq.; V. Kubeš/O. Weinberger, Die Brünner rechtstheoretische Schule, Vienna: Manz'sche 1980; E. Kaufmann, Kritik der neukantischen

The cognition of the law is aimed at the cognition of *norms*. A norm does not exist in time and space; it is not a perceptible fact in the external world, but rather the *meaning* of an act of will given in time and space. In the case of facts related to the law in any way (e.g. parliamentary enactment, administrative act, judicial decision, private law transaction or tort), one can always discern two elements: one is an *external event* of human behavior taking place in time and space; the other is the *legal*

Rechtsphilosophie, Tübingen: Mohr Siebeck, 1921; Brookfield, F.M., The Courts, Kelsen and the Rhodesian Revolution, University of Toronto Law Journal 19 (1969), p. 326; J.M. Finnis, Revolutions and Continuity of Law, in: A.W.B. Simpson (ed.), Oxford Essays in Jurisprudence, Second Series, Oxford: Clarendon Press, 1973; L. Gianformaggio (ed.), Hans Kelsen's Legal Theory. A Diachronic Point of View, Turin: G. Giappichelli Editore, 1990; M.P. Golding, Kelsen and the Concept of "Legal System", in: R.S. Summers (ed.), More Essays in Legal Philosophy: General Assessment of Legal Philosophies, Berkeley: University of California Press, 1971; J.W. Harris, Kelsen's Concept of Authority, Cambridge Law Journal 36 (1977), p. 353; idem, Law and Legal Science, Oxford: Clarendon Press, 1979; idem, Kelsen, Revolutions and Normativity, in: E. Attwooll, Shaping Revolution, Aberdeen: Aberdeen University Press, 1991; idem, The Basic Norm and the Basic Law, Hong Kong Law Journal 24 (1994), p. 207; idem, Kelsen's Pallid Normativity, Ratio Juris 9 (1996), p. 94; H.L.A. Hart, Essays in Jurisprudence and Philosophy, chapters 14 and 15, Oxford: Clarendon Press, 1983; D.N. MacCormick, Legal Obligation and the Imperative Fallacy, in: A.W.B. Simpson (ed.), Oxford Essays in Jurisprudence, Second Series, Oxford: Clarendon Press, 1973; Stanley L. Paulson, Material and Formal Authorisation in Kelsen's Pure Theory, Cambridge Law Journal 39 (1980), p. 172; idem, The Neo-Kantian Dimension of Kelsen's Pure Theory of Law, Oxford Journal of Legal Studies 12 (1992), p. 311; Stanley L. Paulson/R. Walter (Editors), Untersuchungen zur Reinen Rechtslehre (Vienna: Manz 1986), Stanley L. Paulson/Michael Stolleis (Editors), Hans Kelsen, Tübingen: Mohr Siebeck, 2005; J. Raz, The Concept of a Legal System, 2nd Edition, Oxford: Clarendon Press, 1980; idem, The Authority of Law; J. Stone, Legal Systems and Lawyers' Reasonings, London: Stevens & Sons, 1964; R. Tur/W. Twining (Editors), Essays on Kelsen, New York: Oxford University Press 1986.

2   Kelsen, Pure Theory, p. 1.
3   Kelsen, JZ 20 (1965) 465; idem, Reine Rechtslehre, p. 207, footnote **. It should be taken into consideration that according to the pure theory of law – contrary to most of the other positivist theories – the positivity of the law is not identical with its "validity", since Kelsen understands validity only as normative validity. The usage of the word positivity is not entirely uniform amongst the representatives of the 'pure' theory of law. On p. 9 and 198 et seq. of the Pure Theory of Law, Kelsen uses the term "positivity" in the narrower sense "posited by men" whilst in the aforementioned places, he also embraces the aspect of sociological effectiveness with the term "positivity".
4   Kelsen, Pure Theory of Law, p. 1.

meaning of that event. Let us suppose, for instance, that a businessman writes a letter with a specific content to another businessman and the latter writes back in reply; it is perceptible to the senses as a sequence of events but, as such, will not be the object of specifically legal cognition. What turns something into a legal (or illegal) act *is not an Is* defined by the laws of causality but the *objective meaning* linked with the said act.[5] This objective meaning – in the example: that a contract has been concluded – is conferred on the act only by a *norm* referring to the act in such a way that the act can be interpreted accordingly. The norm functions as *scheme of interpretation*. It states that something ought to be or ought to happen, and, especially, that a human being *ought to* act in a certain way. Kelsen attributes to the term "ought" a wider meaning than common linguistic usage: a norm can not only *command* a certain behavior, it can also *allow* or *authorize* it; his "ought" also encompasses the senses of "may" (on the basis of a permission) and "can" (on the basis of an authorization).[6] The norm is therefore an Ought (German: *Sollen*); the act of will which brings the norm into being and the sense of which the norm is representing is an Is (German: *Sein*).

Consequently, Kelsen is sharply emphasizing the *dichotomy between Is and Ought*. The statement that something *is* is substantially different from the statement that something ought to be! *From the fact that something is, it cannot be inferred that something ought to be, and from the fact that something ought to be, it cannot be inferred that something is.* For example, from the fact that certain people commit suicide, it does not follow that human beings ought to commit suicide. From the fact that human beings have always waged wars, it does not follow that human beings ought to wage wars. Nevertheless, Is and Ought do not exist as

---

[5] The meaning attributed to the act by the objective legal system must be distinguished from the subjective meaning developing from self-interpretation by the acting individual. These meanings may but need not coincide: a person who states in writing what is to happen to his belongings when he dies (a bequeather) may have considered that document, subjectively, to be a last will and testament, whereas the document may lack that quality – because of the breach of certain forms – from the standpoint of the law. See Kelsen, Introduction to the Problems of Legal Theory, p. 9–10; Pure Theory of Law, p. 3.

[6] Kelsen, Pure Theory of Law, p. 5. Apart from this "normative" Ought, Kelsen also uses the concept of a "descriptive" Ought. See below, § 6 n. 20.

completely unrelated propositions, since they can refer to the same content, especially the same human behavior: a human behavior can be something that is or something that ought to be.

The specific existence of a norm is its "validity". What Kelsen understands by validity – in contrast to certain realist theories – is not a factual validity, in the sense of the "effectiveness" of a norm, for example, but a "normative validity". The effectiveness of a norm is the fact that it is actually applied and complied with; this must not be identified with its "validity". It is true that a minimal effectiveness is a *condition* for the validity of a norm, since a norm that is never applied or complied with is usually considered not to be valid.[7] However, effectiveness is never the *reason* for the validity of a norm: such a reason can have its roots only in a higher norm which regulates the generation of the lower norm and possibly even predetermines its contents.[8] An order issuing from a tax officer to pay a certain amount of money can only be interpreted as a valid (individual) norm – unlike the same order coming from a gangster – because it was issued in accordance with the tax law.[9] The norm of the tax law is valid solely because it has been decided upon by the legislative body authorized by a constitutional norm to enact such norms. If one inquires into the basis of the validity of the constitution, one may come across an earlier constitution and infer the validity of the current constitution from the fact that it was issued in accordance with the provisions of this earlier constitution; however, the validity of the historically first constitution can no longer be inferred from a norm enacted by the legally competent authority.[10] If one also wants to *interpret* the norms of the historically first constitution as objectively valid norms, one must, according to Kelsen, *presuppose* a norm, one which can no longer claim any real existence but which is, instead, imagined. This *hypothetically presupposed norm* that is not part of the positive law appoints the historically first constitution as a norm-setting fact and reads as follows: *"Coercive acts ought to be performed under the conditions and in the manner*

---

[7] Kelsen, Pure Theory of Law, p. 10. The classic example is a legal order annulled by revolution or coup d'état.
[8] Kelsen, JZ 20 (1965) 467.
[9] Kelsen, Pure Theory of Law, p. 8.
[10] Kelsen, Pure Theory of Law, p. 200.

which the historically first constitution, and the norms created according to it, prescribe."[11] The statement that the law has objective validity is, as emphatically stressed by Kelsen, *by no means a necessary interpretation* of legislative acts but just one *possible* interpretation, viz. the one possible under the condition of the *basic norm.*[12] *Nobody can be prevented with cogent arguments from interpreting the respective interhuman relationships not normatively but sociologically, i.e. as mere power relations,*[13] and thus from seeing anything but naked power where jurists speak of the law.[14]

Kelsen's basic norm provides the hypothetical foundation of the positive legal system – indeed, of *every* positive legal system. For the content of a positive legal system is completely independent from the basic norm[15] in that it cannot be deduced from it; whereas the content of a legal system can certainly be deduced from the historically first constitution and the norms created in accordance with it. As a consequence, no positive legal system can be deemed not to correspond with its basic norm and hence not to be valid. However, since effectiveness is, as we have seen, a condition of the validity of norms, and therefore of the whole legal system, only a coercive system that is by and large effective can be interpreted as a legal system in accordance with the 'pure' theory of law. Thus the basic norm only ever refers to a legal system with continuous effectiveness;[16] and conversely, every coercive system living up to the said con-

---

[11] Kelsen, Pure Theory of Law, p. 201 (emphasis by the authors). This paraphrasing of the basic norm shows that, contrary to the opinion of critics, it does not always have the same content. Every legal order has its own historically first constitution and hence its own hypothetical basic norm. There are as many basic norms as there are legal systems. Cf. critique by Raz and Hart § 6.

[12] Kelsen, Reine Rechtslehre, p. 218 (footnote). Regarding the further development of the Pure Theory of Law by R. Walter, see below, § 20 B.III.

[13] Kelsen, Pure Theory of Law, p. 218.

[14] Kelsen, Introduction to the Problems of Legal Theory, Translation of the First Edition of the Reine Rechtslehre or Pure Theory of Law, p. 34.

[15] Kelsen, Pure Theory of Law, p. 217.

[16] To corroborate his opinion, Kelsen, Pure Theory of Law, p. 50, makes reference to fact that the courts of the United States of that time refused to recognize the acts of the revolutionary Russian government as legal acts; this on the grounds that such acts were acts of a robber band and not of a state. As soon as the coercive systems established by revolution had proven to be lasting, they had been recognized as legal systems.

dition can be understood as an objectively valid normative system. Kelsen exemplifies this by raising the problem (first brought up long ago in St. Augustine's De Civitate Dei) of the difference between a state (as a legal community) and a gang of robbers.[17] According to the 'pure' theory of law, the acts of a gang of robbers can only be denied legal quality if the legal system of the state proves to be more efficient, by virtue of the fact that sanctions against members of the robber gang can be enforced. However, as soon as the robbers' own coercive system becomes efficient enough within a certain territory to exclude the validity of any other coercive system, it can be considered a legal system and the community that it constitutes may well be viewed as a legal state. Kelsen quotes the example of the pirate states which existed along the north-east coast of Africa (Algeria, Tunisia, Tripoli) between the 16th and the early 19th centuries, whose ships preyed upon navigation in the Mediterranean.[18]

It follows from the above that according to the 'pure' theory of law, any content can become a legal content. "There is no human behavior which, as such, is excluded from being the content of a legal norm."[19] This statement demonstrates the *separation of law and morals* that is characteristic of all positivist theories. According to Kelsen, there are very different and contradicting moral systems and the opposing postulate of a moral law amounts to an uncritical justification of one's *own* [national] coercive system. For it is taken for granted that *this* system be law, and thus it follows from the theory that it must also be moral. In Kelsen's view, it is not acceptable for a discipline of legal *science* to put forward that kind of legitimization of positive law.[20]

Kelsen does not see the difference between law and other social normative systems, summarized by Kelsen under the term of "morals"[21], as

---

[17] St. Augustine, Civitas Dei, IV, 4. St. Augustine is asking: "Set justice aside then, and what are kingdoms but robber bands? Because what are robber bands but little kingdoms?" According to St. Augustine, the difference between law and other coercive systems is the *justice* of its contents.
[18] Kelsen, Pure Theory of Law, p. 48.
[19] Kelsen, Pure Theory of Law, p. 198.
[20] Kelsen, Pure Theory of Law, p. 68 et seq.
[21] Kelsen, Pure Theory of Law, p. 59.

residing in what the two systems – as regards their content – forbid or command, nor in how they are created or applied.[22] The difference lies rather in *the manner in which they forbid or command* a certain behavior. The law is a normative system which seeks to bring about a certain human behavior by linking the *opposite behavior* to a *socially organized coercive act* (deprivation of certain goods such as life, freedom or economic values).[23] The sanctions of morality, on the other hand, consist only in *approval of the norm-conforming and disapproval of the norm-opposing behavior.*[24] Morality exerts only psychological, not physical coercion.

The characterization of the law as a coercive system as explained above leads to a fundamental reinterpretation of the unlawful act: a human behavior is not linked to a coercive act as a legal consequence of its unlawfulness; on the contrary, it is unlawful because it is linked to a coercive act.[25] The decisive criterion is not that a material fact is socially harmful, but that the fact in question is the condition for a coercive act of the state. Thus, according to the 'pure' theory of law, there are no "*mala in se*" but only "*mala prohibita*". Take homosexuality as an example: in the past, numerous countries including many Western countries made sexual intercourse between men a punishable offense, so at that time it was a "*malum prohibitum*". Nowadays, homosexuality is no longer punishable in most Western countries; it is no longer "unlawful".

Furthermore, conceptualizing law in the manner described gives rise to the following important consequence: because it is common practice to characterize the state as a political organization and because, according to Kelsen, the "political" element consists in the coercion regulated by such an organization and exerted by human being upon human being, the state is, in a legal sense, nothing but the legal system itself.[26] For the coercive acts of the state are precisely those coercive acts which the legal

---

[22] Kelsen, Pure Theory of Law, p. 62.
[23] Kelsen, Pure Theory of Law, p. 33/62. Kelsen's conception is, however, presupposing that there is a *factual consensus* on the values of life, freedom and economic goods. The observer of such society may, in contrast, keep at value relativism.
[24] Kelsen, Pure Theory of Law, p. 62.
[25] Kelsen, Pure Theory of Law, p. 111.
[26] Kelsen, Pure Theory of Law, p. 286.

system imposes under certain conditions. The state qua subject of the state's acts is no more or less than the "personification" of the legal system;[27] it is a "point of imputation" which expresses the unity of the legal system, and which the human mind in pursuit of intuitive understanding is all too inclined to hypostatize, to posit as real, and to imagine as some entity behind the legal system.[28] Every state, then, is a legal system; but not every legal system is a state. To be characterized as a state, a legal system must have achieved a certain degree of centralization. This is true neither for the legal system of a tribal community nor for the present-day international legal system. The state, then, is a relatively centralized legal system.[29] Kelsen also systematically relates the three elements of the state, i.e. the people of the state, the territory of the state and the so-called power of the state, to the legal system: the people of the state may be comprehended as the personal sphere of validity, the territory of the state as the spatial sphere of validity and the power of the state as the validity of the legal system.[30] Furthermore, the identity of law and state has the consequence that every state is – from a formal point of view – a state governed by rule of law (= *Rechtsstaat*, if one understands '*Rechtsstaat*' to mean a state that 'has' a legal system).[31]

With regard to the *problem of interpretation and the problem of gaps,* insights significant for the 'pure' theory of law ensue from the hierarchical structure of the law as depicted above: interpretation is an intellectual activity that accompanies the law-creating process as it moves from a higher level to a lower level governed by this higher level.[32] Legislation is interpretation of the constitution, judicial decisions are interpretation of statutes, and law enforcement is interpretation of the individual norms of a court decision or an administrative act. The higher-level norm determines the process whereby the lower-level norm is to be created and

---

[27] Kelsen, Pure Theory of Law, p. 293.
[28] Kelsen, Pure Theory of Law, p. 291.
[29] Kelsen, Pure Theory of Law, p. 286.
[30] Kelsen, Pure Theory of Law, p. 287.
[31] Kelsen, Pure Theory of Law, p. 313. The term "state governed by the rule of law" is, however, generally used in a content-based sense for a state which conforms with the postulates of democracy and legality and with certain rights and freedoms. Cf. Kelsen, ibidem.
[32] Kelsen, Pure Theory of Law, p. 348.

possibly the content of the lower-level norm. It is crucial, however, that this *determination is never complete* so that interpretation, on any level, is of *constitutive character*. This is true in two regards for judicial decisions, to which we will confine the following discussion:

On the one hand, the very "finding" that there is a concrete set of facts which must be linked to a legal consequence represents a constitutive function of the court.[33] Strictly speaking, it is not the set of facts that is the condition for the legal consequence but the *opinion of the court* as to whether such a set of facts exists. In order for somebody to be sentenced for murder, the decisive factor is not whether the accused really committed the murder, but whether the court believes that the accused committed the murder! This is documented by several recent cases in the United States where university law professors supported by their students have succeeded in proving the innocence of many prisoners awaiting execution on 'Death Row'.

On the other hand, every norm only ever represents a frame within which various options for application are given.[34] There is always a variable degree of freedom to exercise discretion. Every act that remains within that frame conforms to the applicable general norm. Thus, Kelsen clearly disapproves of the German statutory positivist thesis that the judge is simply discovering done-and-dusted, fully formed law.[35] For this reason, the 'pure' theory of law cannot simply be pigeonholed as a type of German statutory positivism. According to Kelsen's theory, the judicial process is essentially a creative activity; for he regards the interpretation of norms – as long as the relevant matter falls within the frame set by the norm – as an act of will, not as an act of cognition.[36]

Regarding the problem of gaps in the law, Kelsen subscribes to the view that a positive legal order may *always* be applied to a concrete case.[37] Yet this so-called "dogma of gaplessness" is substantially different from that of the German statutory positivists. For Kelsen does not ignore the fact

---

[33] Cf. Kelsen, Pure Theory of Law, p. 239 et seqq.
[34] Kelsen, Pure Theory of Law, p. 350.
[35] Kelsen, Pure Theory of Law, p. 237; above, text at n. 17 et seqq.
[36] Kelsen, Pure Theory of Law, p. 354.
[37] Kelsen, Pure Theory of Law, p. 245.

that there may be cases where it is impossible to apply a *particular* legal norm; nevertheless, he argues, it is still possible to apply the *legal system*. For then the 'negative norm' applies, which states that if the legal system does not impose upon an individual any obligation regarding a certain behavior, it *permits* that behavior.[38] If, for example, a statute stipulates that an organ must be established by election but does not regulate the electoral procedure, then it means that any kind of procedure (e.g. proportional representation, majority, public or secret) is in accordance with the law. The body entitled to carry out the election may determine the procedure at its own discretion.[39]

Kelsen's methodology as just depicted here had considerable influence on the Constitutional Court of Austria at which Kelsen served from 1919 to 1930. Kelsen's judicial votes, which were supported by the court most of the time, appear surprisingly modern and are far from a stubborn clinging to the wording of the constitution.[40]

---

[38] Kelsen, Introduction to the Problems of Legal Theory, Translation of the First Edition of the Reine Rechtslehre or Pure Theory of Law, p. 84 et seq.; idem, Pure Theory of Law, p. 245 et seq.

[39] Kelsen, Pure Theory of Law, p. 249.

[40] R. Walter, Hans Kelsen als Verfassungsrichter, Vienna: Manz, 2005.

Second Chapter

Psychological Positivism

The different variants of psychological positivism concur in locating the positivity of the law in certain contents of feeling and consciousness. Since these contents of feeling and consciousness are, however, usually expressed in some external behavior of both the subjects of the law and the 'law staff' (viz. in actual compliance with or application of the law), it is not possible to draw a sharp distinction between psychological positivism and sociological positivism. A particular approach can only be ascribed to one or the other school of thought based on its preponderant tendency.[1]

As a consequence, the meaning of 'validity' for psychological as well as sociological legal theory is "in general, a factual validity in the sense of the actual existence of law, although for the former it consists less in any external behavior than in ideas and feelings."[2]

The following theories may be considered as varieties of psychological positivism:

---

[1] Eckmann, p. 20 (our translation).
[2] Eckmann, p. 21.

§ 5 Theories of Recognition[3, 4]

A. Theories of Individual Recognition

When referring to the positions in legal theory labeled "theories of recognition", one has to differentiate between theories of individual recognition and theories of general recognition. Whereas under theories of individual recognition, the law is constituted by the recognition of *every single norm-addressee*, under theories of general recognition this is the case as soon as the *majority of norm-addressees consent*.[5]

Initial stages of a theory of individual recognition are to be found in an essay published back in 1813 by the young Carl Theodor Welcker,[6] rediscovered for legal philosophy by H.-L. Schreiber. Welcker does not pursue the psychological approach in a consistent way, however, since – in contradiction to his own individual-empirical premises – he constantly presupposes supra-individual, material values in order to arrive at an objective law related to morality.[7]

I. Ernst Rudolf Bierling's Psychological Legal Theory

Ernst Rudolf Bierling was the first to develop an elaborate psychological legal theory. Bierling's positivist attitude is expressed, first of all, in that he dismisses all theories which base the binding power of the law on God's majesty, on a pre-legal ethical principle, on a superordinate moral

---

[3] Literature: Kramer, Festschrift Merkl, p. 187 et seqq.; Bierling, Prinzipienlehre I/IV; idem, Kritik I; Beling, Festgabe für Philipp Heck, Max Rümelin und Arthur Benno Schmidt, Tübingen: J.C.B. Mohr, 1931, p. 1 et seqq.; Laun; Jellinek; Merkel, Elemente; idem, Enzyklopädie; Kelsen, Hauptprobleme, p. 346 et seqq.; Larenz, p. 39 et seqq.; Nawiasky; Schreiber, p. 85 et seqq.; Welzel, p. 7 et seqq.; Yoon, Rechtsgeltung und Anerkennung. Probleme der Anerkennungstheorie am Beispiel von Ernst Rudolf Bierling: Nomos, Baden-Baden, 2009.

[4] "Recognition" is used in this context as meaning "acknowledgement".

[5] Kramer, Festschrift Merkl, p. 188.

[6] Die letzten Gründe von Recht, Staat und Strafe, Giessen 1813. In this regard Schreiber, p. 85 et seqq.

[7] Schreiber, p. 90.

law or on any other supra-positive principles.[8] In his terms, it is a tacit but never to be overlooked prerequisite of any legal theory of principles 'that only the positive law has a right to the title "law"...'[9] Aside from that, he equally opposes those positivist conceptions which trace the law back to the sovereign's actual position of power or to a common will. In Bierling's view, sheer power, coercion by the state are not sufficient to constitute the binding force of the law.[10] Rather, Bierling argues, the law in a juristic sense is "generally everything that men who live together in some sort of a community mutually recognize as norm and rule of such living together."[11] In fact the law must be recognized by *everybody* belonging to a certain legal community, and not – as per theories of general recognition – just by a majority. For in the latter case, the duty of any minority to obey a majority would be derived from a purely numerical ratio, a concept which, according to Bierling, is patently absurd.[12] The binding power of legal norms upon an individual is thus explained by the fact that *the individual himself* has consented to them.

That gives rise to the question of what happens if a norm is to be applied to a law-breaker. Since non-compliance must be interpreted as lack of recognition by the law-breaker, the norm would lose its legal quality at the very moment it had to be enforced against a recalcitrant individual. At this point, Bierling resorts to the theory of *indirect* recognition. Recognition need not always be direct, "i.e. immediately directed at each single norm. Rather, a *merely indirect* recognition is also sufficient, viz. the kind of recognition that is nothing but the plain and logically necessary consequence of another kind of recognition of legal norms, which is of course ultimately and necessarily direct. For this fact alone, all norms found in laws which have materialized as a result of the constitutionally determined procedure appear to be indirectly recognized legal

---

[8] Bierling, Kritik I, p. 19 et seqq.; Schreiber, p. 91/92.
[9] Bierling, Prinzipienlehre, I 5 n. 1 at the end.
[10] Schreiber, p. 92. Moreover, Bierling is a representative of the so-called command theory according to which all law consists of commands so that his theory can at the same time, as Eckmann, p. 21, emphasizes, be qualified as an analytical legal theory.
[11] Bierling, Prinzipienlehre I, p. 19. For the differentiation from religion, morality, customs and fashion see Prinzipienlehre, I, p. 54 et seqq.
[12] Bierling, Kritik I, p. 79.

norms in as much as and provided that a genuine recognition of law, with reference to the respective constitution or even just to the norms concerning the enactment and the validity of laws, prevails."[13] To be sure, Bierling does not mistake the fact that this indirect law-recognition is only a peculiar sort of *ideal* recognition. As Larenz has rightly pointed out, here Bierling strays beyond the territory of a purely psychological legal theory.[14]

However, if Bierling's conclusion from recognition (psychological fact) were to be acceptable for the validity (in the normative sense) of the constitution, he would have to presuppose a basic norm, stated approximately as follows:

> If everybody directly recognizes Constitution X, it is valid.
>
> (= basic norm, containing the validity criterion; first premise)
>
> Everybody directly recognizes Constitution X.
>
> (= factual judgement; second premise)
>
> Constitution X is valid.
>
> (= normative conclusion; the constitution is interpreted as a valid one with the help of the basic norm)

Strictly psychologically, on the other hand, Bierling frames the concepts of legal duty and legal rights. He defines a right as "that – imperatively expressible – *claim, the content of which represents a legal rule* ...that is not only recognized by the one or the ones addressing a claim to one or more other persons but also by these addressed persons as a duty to be fulfilled; in other words, as their legal duty."[15] Thus, a legal duty and a legal right are correlates: "just as the latter is the expression of the norm-making will vis à vis another person within a specific relationship, so legal duty is the expression of the corresponding – i.e. within that same specific relationship – norm-taking will vis à vis the other person."[16] This conception, however, leads to problems in cases where real

---

[13] Bierling, Prinzipienlehre I, p. 46 (our translation).
[14] Larenz, p. 40.
[15] Bierling, Prinzipienlehre I, p. 161 (our translation).
[16] Bierling, Prinzipienlehre I, p. 171 (our translation).

norm recognition is beyond debate – e.g. in the case of children, people with mental illnesses, or legal entities.[17]

With regard to the problem of the interpretation of statutes, Bierling's view is based in principle on a subjective-historical method of interpretation. Since he views laws as the expression of the legislator's will,[18] interpretation is about exploring the real (i.e. the real psychological) will of the legislator[19] by examining the history of the law's origins.[20] In order to be logically consistent, he must therefore dismiss objective theories of interpretation.[21]

II. Rudolf Laun's Theory of the Autonomy of the Law

Elements of a theory of individual recognition are also to be found in Rudolf Laun's "theory of the autonomy of the law",[22] which he has set out in his inaugural address as a university rector in 1924.[23] In later addenda, however, he has further developed his approach, veering towards the theories of general recognition[24] and finally even abandoning his positivist-psychological starting point by tending to adopt a "transcendental validity of a moral world order."[25]

Fundamental to Laun's theory is his differentiation between the positive law and the "autonomous" law.

By positive law, he originally denoted the law whose sources of origin can be seen in customs, statutes and treaties as well as in the "commands of a ruler or a victor to whose will weaker or conquered individuals effectively submit without any presumption of an enduring custom or

---

[17] See objections in this point by Larenz, p. 41, Schreiber, p. 96, and Kelsen, Hauptprobleme, p. 355 et seqq.
[18] Bierling, Prinzipienlehre IV, p. 256.
[19] Bierling, Prinzipienlehre IV, p. 280.
[20] Bierling, Prinzipienlehre IV, p. 275.
[21] Bierling, Prinzipienlehre IV, p. 257 et seqq.
[22] Laun, p. 59.
[23] Laun, p. 1 et seqq. (section I).
[24] Laun, p. 52 et seqq.
[25] Laun, p. 77.

compliance with a certain statute or a certain form of contract …".[26] We encounter these provisions of the positive law as heteronomous commands.[27] Thus, according to Laun, they do not contain any obligation. For he holds, and in this his individualistic approach shows: *"A clause ordering me to do something is either the expression of somebody else's will, then it cannot oblige me; or it obliges me and then cannot be the expression of somebody else's will."*[28] As an expression of somebody else's will, the positive law therefore contains no Ought at all,[29] it does not oblige, it only forces. *"The so-called positive law is sheer force."*[30] It would therefore be more accurate to speak of "positive force" than of "positive law".[31]

The contents of the Ought cannot be derived from the causal world, of which, according to Laun, the positive law is also part. Rather, the decisive source of cognition is the elemental experience of the Ought in each individual.[32] *"Of what we ought, of the contents of our duty, we can only become aware by our own direct experience."*[33] It is true that this experience of the Ought is at first something purely subjective;[34] but it acquires relative empirical objectivity if several people are in agreement on it. The true, "autonomous" law, according to Laun, is "never given in any different way than in a sum of individual, subjective, autonomous

---

[26] Laun, p. 7 (our translation).

[27] Laun, p. 7.

[28] Laun, p. 6/7 (our translation).

[29] The positive law belongs thus exclusively to the sphere of facts. Since Laun as a Neo-Kantian acts on the assumption of disparity between Is and Ought, it is clear that an obligation can never be derived from the fact of force, "not even if one calls the force 'law'." (Laun, p. 9, our translation).

[30] Laun, p. 8.

[31] Laun, p. 9.

[32] That this experience is also nothing else but a psychological *fact* from which, from a Neo-Kantian point of view, no ought can be derived, seems to be the reason for Schreiber, p. 104, that Laun is ultimately attempting to infer inductively an act-transcendent, universally valid ought from the experience of the ought. See explanations following hereinbelow for further details.

[33] Laun, p. 10/11 (our translation). See also E.-J. Lampe (Editor), Das sog. Rechtsgefühl, Jahrbuch für Rechtssoziologie und Rechtstheorie 10, Opladen: Westdeutscher Verlag, 1985.

[34] Laun, p. 12.

experiences of the Ought, of duty."[35] The heteronomous, positive "law of power" thus stands counter to the autonomous, real "emotional law".[36]

These two laws, however, do not stand in unrelated juxtaposition. What has been decreed by force and obliges nobody, per se, becomes law when applied in an *individual* case if the individual approves of it by virtue of his conscience or his sense of justice.[37] The significant feature of Laun's conception is that – contrary to all the other varieties of theories of recognition – he does not content himself with recognition of the legal order as a whole, in other words with *carte-blanche* acceptance, but asks for real recognition of every single norm: "Thus, in every single case of application, the individual's response to so-called positive law, the statutes and the treaties etc. is dualistic: either he approves of them and experiences them in the individual application as an Ought, as an inner constraint of his conscience or sense of law, in which case they are *law* to him, even if he does not comply with them; or else no such approval is forthcoming, in which case they are *nothing but brute force* to him, even if he submits to them."[38]

Due to this, Laun arrives at a modified concept of "positivity": The "positivity" of the law consists of two real facts: viz. that the masses actually obey the law and that they experience their obedience in the large part not only as a Must but as an Ought.[39] In order to be able to speak of a positive law in this sense, actual obedience *and* approval out of an autonomous sense of duty must exist amongst a *sufficient majority*.[40] In this

---

[35] Laun, p. 13, *mutatis mutandis* the same p. 49.

[36] Laun, p. 14.

[37] Laun, p. 14. Laun is obviously trying to derive a "binding power" of the law (i.e. something normative) from the approval of the individual (i.e. from something factual) in the sense explained above, a point about which legal positivists usually remain mute. This conclusion would only be admissible if Laun presupposed a "hypothetical basic norm" which would have to read for his system approximately as follows: "What the individual experiences as an Ought is binding." Cf. the corresponding basic norm for Bierling's system in the passage following n. 14, above.

[38] Laun, p. 15.

[39] Laun, p. 52.

[40] Laun, p. 52/54. Therefore, Laun argues, there are different "degrees of positivity" (p. 53), depending on how many actually obey autonomously.

point, which concerns the problem of the validity of the law (in a factual sense), Laun's theory shades off into a theory of *general* recognition.[41]

There remains the question of whether it would be possible to assert something universally valid about the contents of the Ought, despite the elements of variation between subjective Ought-experiences. For an obligation upon the minority that disapproves of the law cannot be derived from a law supported by the approving feelings of the majority either, unless one is willing to abandon the idea of autonomy. The quintessence of Laun's explanations in this point can briefly be summarized as follows:[42] we must, he says, infer by means of induction – only hypothetically, but with a high probability – the existence of a real, general, transcendental world order, i.e. a general Ought, from the fact of the Ought-experiences. Otherwise, absolute skepticism and anarchy are inevitable. In pursuing this course, Laun departs from the territory of a purely empirical-psychological legal theory. As regards the content of an absolute Ought, he gives no more than hints of what this might be.[43]

B. Theories of General Recognition[44]

I. Adolf Merkel

The first to develop a theory of general recognition in the more recent past has apparently been Adolf Merkel.[45] Merkel emphasizes the following dual nature of the law:[46]

Generally, the coercion emanating from the law is in one respect a Must, i.e. "a sensory necessity to behave in accordance with it."[47] On the one hand, then, law is material power.[48] This becomes manifest in that the

---

[41] Schreiber, p. 103.
[42] Laun, p. 60 et seqq.
[43] Laun, p. 80/81.
[44] See literature quoted by Welzel, p. 12/13 n. 28.
[45] Like this Schreiber, p. 105. As precursors, Welzel, p. 10/11, mentions J. Brehmer and O. Bülow.
[46] Merkel, Enzyklopädie § 46 p. 39.
[47] Merkel, Enzyklopädie § 46 p. 39.
[48] Merkel, Elemente, p. 588.

law holds ready physical instruments of power which are intended to enforce compliance with its commands, as far as possible.[49]

On the other hand, however, it would be wrong to characterize the law as the entirety of the social coercion norms.[50] For not every legal rule is backed by a sanction; and the law of a people would not cease to be law if the application of mechanical instruments of power had become superfluous.[51] A characteristic of the law is rather, and above all, a moral dimension in that those to whom the commands are addressed are made to feel morally obliged to obey them.[52] This explains why law can rely on voluntary compliance in the majority of cases.[53]

But what is the binding force of the law rooted in? According to Merkel, it is rooted in the fact that the law partakes of support from the norm-addressees' sense of duty; it is nothing but "the alliance with the moral powers which reside in the people and from which some coercion emanates to comply with the commands of the law."[54] From that, it is evident that law can emanate from injustice and brute force; to wit, if – under the influence of habit and other mediating factors – the "energies of the conscience of the people" enter into an "abetting relation" to the facts created (by injustice and brute force, e.g. by revolution and coup d'état). Conversely, law can turn into injustice if "the law in its development does not keep up with the ethical views of a people...".[55]

Merkel expressly opposes theories which attribute the binding force of the law to an act of recognition by *an individual*.[56] Rather, the law is dependent on the "*ethical value judgments* which prove to be *those that prevail among a given people at a given time*."[57] Essential to the law is that it is in accord with the "prevailing conviction". Approval by the

---

[49] Merkel, Enzyklopädie § 50 p. 42.
[50] Merkel, Elemente, p. 588.
[51] Merkel, Elemente, p. 588.
[52] Merkel, Enzyklopädie § 46 p. 39.
[53] Merkel, Enzyklopädie § 47 p. 39; Elemente, p. 589.
[54] Merkel, Elemente, p. 590. With regard to this, see also the omnibus volume by Lampe quoted above, § 5 n. 33.
[55] Merkel, Elemente, p. 590.
[56] Merkel. Elemente, p. 607; Enzyklopädie § 49 p. 42.
[57] Merkel, Enzyklopädie § 32 p. 29 (our translation; emphasis ours).

individuals is not necessary with regard to each single norm, but only with regard to the supreme imperative ("obey my directions"); in other words, with regard to the legal system as a whole.[58] The binding force of the law (emanating from conformity with the prevailing value ideas) already includes the element of recognition.[59] Merkel apparently does not consider necessary an independent act of recognition.

II. Georg Jellinek

Georg Jellinek represents a methodically clear psychological positivism. To get an idea of the "the hard-to-grasp nature of the law", one can pursue a dual strategy:

Either one can seek to explore the nature of the law "as a power independent of the human being based on the objective nature of what exists."[60] This is the strategy of metaphysical speculation. Jellinek does not consider it to be his task to identify the "transcendental value of human institutions."[61]

Or, one can understand the law as "subjective, i.e. intrapersonal human phenomenon". According to this psychological method, which Jellinek favors, the law is "part of human ideas, it exists in our heads and any further determination of the law must be aimed at identifying which part of the content of our consciousness is to be called law."[62]

In application of this method, Jellinek characterizes the legal rules (as opposed to the rules of religion, morality and customs) as follows: these are rules which regulate the *external behavior* of people towards one another; which emanate from a *recognized* external authority; and the validity of which is guaranteed by *external* powers.[63] Therefore, the positivity of the law is ultimately based upon a purely subjective ele-

---

[58] Merkel, Enzyklopädie § 80 p. 55; § 48 p. 39/40.
[59] Merkel, Enzyklopädie § 49 p. 42 (our translation).
[60] Jellinek, p. 332.
[61] Jellinek, p. 332
[62] Jellinek, p. 332.
[63] Jellinek, p. 333.

ment, upon a psychological fact, viz. the *belief in its validity*.[64] This belief is not inferable any further, it is simply empirically given. The transformation of the state's initially only factual power into legal power is thus effected by a purely internal process taking place in people's heads; by precisely this idea "that this factual reality is normative in nature, that it should be the way it is."[65]

In this regard, the decisive belief is that of the "average of a people".[66] With all mass-psychological assessments, the opposing acts of a minority are, according to Jellinek, necessarily neglected.[67] The victims of the Spanish inquisition would scarcely have felt the norms by which they were found guilty to be lawful. From this it follows that a *social* consideration of state and law is subject to the highly significant possibility of conflicting views about the legal quality of certain parts of the state order, which is capable of exerting a deep influence on the evolution of the legal order. The lawyer, however, need not expect to encounter this conflict as long as he confines himself to a limited community of individuals and to isolated cases.[68]

Thus, Jellinek discards theories of individual recognition. In his view, the validity of a norm is by no means left to "subjective arbitrariness".[69]

C. Theories of Recognition by the Leading Class (Ernst Beling, Hans Nawiasky)

The theories of Beling and Nawiasky, which are not based on the recognition by the individual or by a majority of the members of a legal order but on the beliefs of a leading class which sets the tone within a society, occupy an intermediate position between the theories of general and of

---

[64] Jellinek, p. 333/334.
[65] Jellinek, p. 342.
[66] Jellinek, p. 334 n. 1.
[67] Jellinek, p. 334 n. 1.
[68] Jellinek, p. 334 n. 1. The conflict only amounts to *legal* relevance if it escalates to the point of a dispute over whether the controversial norm should be replaced by derogative customary law.
[69] Jellinek, p. 333 n. 1.

individual recognition.[70] In their view, within the spatially delimited community which we call a state, only a very small number of people are truly authoritative;[71] in the value judgments of this class alone the law is rooted;[72] they constitute the "real prime cause of the law".[73]

Therefore, the positivity of law rests on the will or the recognition of this authoritative group.[74] For the law to have positive validity, however, it is not necessary for every single norm to be accepted by the authoritative group. Rather, the recognition of the system as a whole is sufficient: "If one recognizes the system, one also recognizes the individual norms that belong to it, unless the express opposite is proven for particular norms."[75] Actually, according to Beling, the members of the authoritative class do not even need to know the contents of the norms; it is sufficient "that they delegate a free rein to certain persons as representatives, giving *carte-blanche* 'recognition' to what they decree as having been enacted on behalf of the collective."[76]

---

[70] Nawiasky, p. 18; Beling, Festgabe für Heck, Rümelin und Schmidt, p. 10 et seqq. A similar theory is also represented by E. Riezler, Der totgesagte Positivismus, in: W. Maihofer (Eds.): Naturrecht oder Rechtspositivismus?, Bad Homburg v.d.H.: Wissenschaftliche Buchges., 1962, Reprint 1966, p. 242; according to this author, what is decisive is recognition by "the power which has attained a not entirely ephemeral, real supremacy and to which the general public ... is subordinated".

[71] Nawiasky, p. 18.

[72] Beling, Festgabe für Heck, Rümelin und Schmidt, p. 11.

[73] Beling, Festgabe für Heck, Rümelin und Schmidt, p. 15.

[74] Nawiasky, p. 19, Beling, Festgabe für Heck, Rümelin und Schmidt, p. 10.

[75] Nawiasky, p. 21.

[76] Beling, Festgabe für Heck, Rümelin und Schmidt, p. 11.

§ 6 Scandinavian Legal Realism[1]

A. General Characterization

Scandinavian legal realism, centered in Sweden, is a line of thought in legal theory that has had a profound influence on basic research in jurisprudence in Scandinavia over the last eighty years.[2] Its general philosophical foundation is rooted in the Uppsala school of philosophy, the father of which is Axel Hägerström. This school is characterized by a pronounced hostility to metaphysics, as expressed programmatically in Hägerström's motto, with which he prefaced his self-portrayal: "*Praeterea censeo metaphysicam esse delendam.*"[3] Scandinavian legal realism is a psychological and sociological legal theory with an emphasis on the psychological element, which justifies its inclusion in this chapter.[4]

The Uppsala school teaches[5] that value judgments are not statements of anything real. A value is determined by the *feeling* affiliated to it.[6] It loses any significance whatsoever if it is not sustained by a feeling of pleasure or reluctance in the person making the judgment.[7] Now, such a feeling does not state any characteristic of the observed object. As a consequence, value judgments cannot express any scientific knowledge

---

[1] Ross, On Law and Justice; idem, Realistic Jurisprudence; idem, Kritik der sogenannten praktischen Erkenntnis, zugleich Prolegomena zu einer Kritik der Rechtswissenschaft, Kopenhagen/Leipzig 1933; Bulygin, ARSP Beiheft 41 (1965), p. 39 et seqq.; Kelsen, ÖZöR NF 10 (1959/60), p. 1 et seqq.; Vogel; Hart, Scandinavian Realism, Cambr. L.J. 1959, p. 233 et seqq., reprinted in: Hart, Essays in Jurisprudence and Philosophy, Oxford: Clarendon Press, 1983, p. 161 et seqq.; for further references see Coing, p. 63 n. 9. Bjarup; E. Kamenka/R.S. Summers/W.L. Twining, Soziologische Jurisprudenz und realistische Theorien des Rechts, Rechtstheorie Beiheft 9, Berlin: Duncker & Humblot, 1986, Teil III.

[2] Michael Martin, Legal Realism, American University Studies, Series 5, Philosophie, New York, Bern et al.: Lang 1997, p. 123.

[3] R. Schmidt (ed.), Die Philosophie der Gegenwart in Selbstdarstellungen VII, Leipzig: Felix Meiner, 1929, p. 111.

[4] See Kramer, Festschrift Merkl, p. 198 n. 37, Eckmann, p. 19/20.

[5] For the value-theoretical position of the Uppsala School, see Vogel, p. 26 et seqq.

[6] Vogel, p. 27; Martin p. 132.

[7] Vogel, p. 28.

or cognition; they can be neither true nor false, and they are not scientifically meaningful statements.[8]

Like value judgments, legal rules do not convey any cognitive substance. Rules are not descriptive, they contain imperative elements. Their function is not a theoretical one, in the sense of describing reality, but a practical one: they make use of psychological mechanisms as a means of governing people's behavior.[9] Olivecrona phrased the realist critique of the concept of "valid law" from traditional jurisprudence as follows: "Any attempt to claim on a scientific basis that the legal system has binding power by any means other than by exerting factual pressure on people is doomed to fail. Such an attempt can only give rise to contradictions and other errors. Thus, this demarcates the borderline between realism and metaphysics, between scientific method and mysticism in the explanation of legal systems. If we stick to the facts, we are only dealing with the *idea* of a binding power. It is a psychological reality which is meaningful enough. But that is all."[10]

What are the tasks of legal science according to the Scandinavian realists? According to the principles of the Uppsala school, an occupation is scientific only on condition that it is dealing with something perceptible *in time and space*.[11] Since, according to the legal realists, the law can only be determined in real ideas which have an imperative effect – in legislative and adjudicative material, to begin with – an activity is jurisprudential if it is devoted to the *ideas of behavior* as expressed in the *legislative* and *adjudicative material.*[12] The methodological means to this end is the analysis of legal concepts.[13] Legal concepts such as "property", "claim", "validity" stand for human ideas. Since the latter cannot be directly accessed, the analysis must address their expressed form. "The result of the linguistic analysis is the establishment of a linkage with a

---

[8] Vogel, p. 30.
[9] Vogel, p. 49.
[10] K. Olivecrona, Om lagen och staten, København/Lund:Ejnar Munksgaard, 1940, p. 19 et seq., quoted from Vogel, p. 43 and 43 n. 162.
[11] Vogel, p. 61.
[12] Vogel, p. 61. Therefore, independent value deliberations by a judge when reaching a verdict would not qualify as scientific for the purpose of the Uppsala school.
[13] See Martin, p. 139 et seqq.; Vogel, p. 60/66 et seqq.

particular content of consciousness."[14] The word "duty", for example, has no objective content. "It is simply a rationalized expression of an irrational experience, a sense of duty on a mystical or metaphysical basis which is only given an air of objectivity by language."[15]

B. Alf Ross's Realist Theory in Particular

To further clarify the concerns of the Scandinavian Legal Realists, we will examine more closely the theory of the internationally best-known proponent of this school, Alf Ross. Ross's theory aspires to be a realistic, i.e. an empirical theory.[16] According to Ross's approach, jurisprudence is to be understood as part of the science of human behavior; thus, its object must be within the realm of psychological phenomena.[17] Jurisprudence is thus a branch of psychology and sociology.[18] The propositions of the doctrinal study of law (legal doctrine) about the legal norms must therefore be Is-statements which are subject to the criterion of verification,[19] and not Ought-statements which can be neither true nor false, despite the fact that, grammatically, they often appear in the guise of normative sentences. If, for example, a legal scientist says: "Under this rule, the legal consequences ought to be y", then this is not a normative statement, despite the grammatical form, but an assertion which can be true or false.[20] The sentence is not prescribing anything, but it is describing something. Grammatically, it is an imperative but semantically, it is an indicative. How such sentences can be verified, in Ross's view, we

---

[14] Vogel, p. 68.
[15] Eckmann, p. 20.
[16] Ross, On Law and Justice, Preface p. ix.
[17] Ross, Towards a Realistic Jurisprudence, p. 77.
[18] Like that the correct characterization by Kelsen, ÖZöR NF 10 (1959/60), p. 14.
[19] Ross, On Law and Justice, p. 6 et seqq.
[20] Kelsen, Pure Theory of Law, p. 71 et seqq., also draws a clear distinction between propositions of legal doctrine and legal rules. Contrary to Ross, he refers to the propositions of legal doctrine as *Ought*-statements but emphasizes at the same time that these have a *descriptive*, not a *prescriptive* function. Materially, there is no difference from Ross in this point, but the terminology of a "descriptive Ought" is extremely ambiguous. See Pure Theory of Law, p. 79.

will pursue after looking into his concept of "validity" and his concept of law.

From his perspective whereby attention is directed towards the social reality of human behavior, Ross vehemently rejects any definition of "validity" based on an objective Ought-validity. Understood like this, validity is, Ross argues, nothing objectively comprehensible, but only a senseless word: "... validity in the sense of a category or sphere of existence co-ordinated with reality is nonsense in the literal meaning of the word!"[21] His endeavors are aimed at reinterpreting the concept of validity in terms of empirically provable facts.[22] Approaching the problem from a purely behaviorist angle would not work, according to Ross, as he attempts to illustrate with the *example of chess*. For a person watching a game of chess without knowing anything about chess could only observe a meaningless sequence of individual moves and, at best, some regularities in the course of the game. The individual moves become meaningful only if the onlooker knows the *rules of chess* which serve him as a scheme for interpretation of the individual moves that the players are making. The rules of chess could not be established by observation of the external behavior of the players alone, for one would be unable to distinguish between rule-motivated behavior and mere habitual behavior (for example, conditioned by chess theory). For this reason, the behaviorist method needs to be supplemented by a method that Ross – somewhat unfortunately – labels as 'introspective'.[23] It is imperative to find out (for example by asking the players) which rules the players feel to be binding. Only rules which are effectively adhered to by the players (external aspect) and which are felt by them to be binding (internal aspect) are valid rules of chess.[24]

Ross makes an analogous distinction between these two aspects when he goes on to deal with the concept of the validity of legal norms:[25]

---

[21] Ross, Towards a Realistic Jurisprudence, p. 77.
[22] Ross, On Law and Justice, Preface, ix.
[23] We consider the choice of the word "introspective" unfortunate because "introspective" usually refers to contemplation of one's *own* inner life and not the observation of aspects of somebody else's.
[24] Ross, On Law and Justice, p. 16.
[25] Ross, On Law and Justice, p. 34 et seqq.

That a legal norm is valid *means only that it is felt by the judge to be socially binding and is therefore applied by him.*[26] For Ross, the concept of validity includes two aspects, an external, physical one, and an internal, psychological one:[27] the former consists in an external behavior, viz. in the actual application of the norm, the latter in a particular emotional condition of the judge, viz. the feeling of being bound by the norm. Thus, validity, according to Ross, is nothing normative but something real, viz. a psycho-physical reality.

In keeping with this view, Ross's interpretation of the concept of law is equally realistic: by "valid law", Ross means a normative ideology[28] "… the abstract set of normative ideas which serve as a scheme of interpretation for the phenomena of law in action, which again means, that these norms are effectively followed, and followed because they are experienced and felt to be socially binding."[29] According to this definition, one might presume that not all norms which are actually applied are valid norms. A legal norm is valid only if it is based on certain psychological experiences of the judge (viz. the feeling of the binding nature of the norm). This brings up the question of how things stand if for example the judges of an occupied country feel the laws of the occupying power to be arbitrary and "illegal" but – perhaps out of fear or self-interest – apply them nevertheless.[30] On the basis of the criterion of validity advocated by Ross, such norms would not qualify as valid norms since the ideolog-

---

[26] The terms "judge" and "court" are understood by Ross as comprehensive terms including all authorities involved in the administration of justice and law enforcement. See Ross, On Law and Justice, p. 18 n. 2, and Bulygin, ARSP Beiheft 41 (1965), p. 42 n. 12.

[27] Ross, On Law and Justice, p. 37: "In the concept of validity two points are involved: partially the outward, observable and regular compliance with a pattern of action, and partly the experience of this pattern of action as being a socially binding norm." In his book, *Towards a Realistic Jurisprudence*, p. 78 et seqq., Ross had still framed his concept of validity in a purely psychological manner.

[28] The expression "normative ideology" need not be misunderstood: ideology as such is, according to Ross, a psychological factor motivating the judge (Ross, On Law and Justice, p. 37). The content of the ideology is, however, normative insofar as it consists of directives, viz. legal rules.

[29] Ross, On Law and Justice, p. 18

[30] Bulygin, ARSP Beiheft 41 (1965), p. 44.

ical element of the feeling of being bound is lacking.[31] Ross expressly rejects this consequence, however, by explaining that from a purely cognitive-descriptive standpoint, it is not possible to distinguish between a legal system and a system of tyranny. He admits that it would be possible, in principle, to delimit the concept of law such that only a system that gained the approval of a majority could be called a "legal system". Except that Ross sees no advantage in such a definition of the law, only the disadvantage of linking the concept with a criterion that is impracticable. Moreover, Ross argues, no tyranny can be maintained in the long run unless it wins a certain measure of goodwill, at least from the group handling the system of sanctions. Ross expressly rejects the opinion that Hitler's dictatorship was not a legal order.[32] This tension in Ross's concept of validity, which has been pointed out in particular by R. Schreiber[33] and E. Bulygin,[34] is a result of Ross's endeavor to synthesize psychological and sociological legal theory.[35]

We will return now to the problem of how doctrinal propositions about valid law can be verified. As we have seen, Ross argues that the doctrinal study of law must be recognized as empirical social science:[36] consequently, its propositions must ultimately be open to confirmation or falsification by experience. As the verification criterion, Ross chooses observation of the *behavior of the courts*. From observation of the behavior of the courts, one shall be able to infer whether a certain norm is valid or not.

Furthermore, Ross says that the following must be taken into consideration: if somebody claims, "This rule is valid law", he undoubtedly wants to say something about *how a future court action on which the particular legal rule has a bearing will be decided*. The assertion, therefore, refers to a future behavior of the courts and not how the courts have ruled hitherto (although consistent practice in the past does of course provide a

---

[31] Bulygin, ARSP Beiheft 41 (1965), p. 44.
[32] Ross, On Law and Justice, p. 31/32.
[33] Schreiber, Die Geltung von Rechtsnormen, Berlin/Heidelberg/New York: Springer 1966, p. 99 et seqq.
[34] Bulygin, ARSP Beiheft 41 (1965), p. 43 et seqq.
[35] Ross, On Law and Justice, p. 73.
[36] Ross, On Law and Justice, p. 40.

good basis for forecasting future decisions). From this, Ross also draws the conclusion that a rule which has recently been promulgated may be considered valid law, too, although it has never been applied by the courts.

Thus, Ross arrives at the following conclusion: doctrinal propositions refer to a future judicial behavior; or more precisely: if somebody claims, "this rule is valid law", it is a prediction to the effect that if an action is brought before the courts in which the conditioning facts given in this particular rule are considered to exist, the directive to the judge contained in this rule will be one of the decisive factors determining the conclusion reached by the judge.[37] Whether a doctrinal proposition is true or false can in the present merely be assumed with a greater or lesser degree of probability.[38] Only when the courts actually rule in accordance with what was asserted by prediction does one know that it was right; and only when judicial behavior does not conform to the doctrinal assertion is it proven wrong.

Ross's realistic conception further leads him to radically reject the scientific nature of the thoughts of natural law and value theory; consequently, he regards rational legal policy as something impossible.

Ross carries his thought to a logical conclusion by emphasizing the creative character of the interpretation by the judge.[39] The various maxims of interpretation are, in his opinion, so imprecise in meaning that the judge can – within certain limits – arrive at any result he deems desirable. The judge can, for example, justify a restrictive interpretation by appealing to the alleged intention of the legislator. If, on the other hand, he desires an extensive interpretation, he will simply claim that the conditions for the use of analogy are satisfied. "If the judge cannot think of any other possibility, he may resort to mere postulates as to what would have been the legislator's intention, simply presuming that the legislator must have desired what is desirable to the judge himself."[40]

---

[37] Ross, On Law and Justice, p. 42.
[38] Ross, On Law and Justice, p. 44/45.
[39] Ross, On Law and Justice, p. 152.
[40] Ross, On Law and Justice, p. 152/153.

Third Chapter

Sociological Positivism

Sociological positivism identifies the positivity of the law with a sociological reality, viz. with a certain observable human behavior (of the group members or the so-called "law staff"). This limitation of scope to the reality that is susceptible to sensory perception is explained by the endeavor to thereby arrive at claims about the law which are intersubjectively verifiable. For the purpose of sociology of law, the propositions of jurisprudence should be verifiable or falsifiable by experience. Therefore the sociological way of looking at things necessarily results in an elimination of the ideal and metaphysical dimensions of the law insofar as they have not become socially effective.[1] The sociological positivist, too, understands by validity of the law its factual validity in the sense of its actual existence; he is, however, referring to different criteria than the psychological positivist.[2]

§ 7 Eugen Ehrlich[3]

Eugen Ehrlich is considered to be the father of modern sociology of law. Within the context of our work, Ehrlich's significance consists in his

---

[1] Of course, the sociologist can look into for example the convictions of faith effective in a society, too, he does not do this, however, by asking – as the theologian – for their transcendental truth but by understanding them as factors guiding the social events.

[2] See E. Kamenka/R.S. Summers/W.L. Twining (Editors), Soziologische Jurisprudenz und realistische Theorien des Rechts, Rechtstheorie Beiheft 9, Berlin: Duncker & Humblot, 1986.

[3] Literature: Ehrlich, Fundamental Principles of the Sociology of Law, translation of Grundlegung der Soziologie des Rechts by Walter L. Moll, Reprint Edition, New York: Arno Press, Inc., 1975; idem, Recht und Leben. Gesammelte Schriften zur Rechtstatsachenforschung und zur Freirechtslehre, Schriftenreihe des Instituts für Rechtssoziologie und Rechtstatsachenforschung der Freien Universität Berlin No. 7, Berlin: Duncker & Humblot, 1967; M. Rehbinder, Einführung in die Rechtssoziologie, Frankfurt am Main: Athenäum Verlag, 1971, p. 21 et seqq.; idem, Die Begründung der Rechtssoziologie durch Eugen Ehrlich, Second Edition, Berlin: Duncker & Humblot, 1986.

confronting 19th century German statutory positivism with a new – and, in his eyes, more scientific – positivism which identifies the positivity of law not with the legislative power of the state but with social reality. In the famous foreword to "Fundamental Principles of the Sociology of Law", Ehrlich writes that the centre of gravity of legal development at any time lies not in legislation, nor in juristic science, nor in judicial decisions, but in *society itself.*

Precisely Ehrlich's example demonstrates the close interweavement of the psychological and the sociological view which has already been pointed out. According to Ehrlich, law "is a matter of intellectual concept which does not exist in the sphere of tangible reality, but in the minds of men. There would be no law if there were not men who bear the concept of law in their consciousness."[4] However, Ehrlich abandons this psychological starting point almost immediately by remarking: "But here, as everywhere else, our concepts are fashioned from the material which we take from tangible reality. They are always based on *facts* which we have *observed*. These facts must have been in existence before the concept of law and legal relation began to dawn in the human brain ... It is here that we must look for the workshop of the law."[5] The first question of juristic science is the question as to the origin of law and thus leads up to the question as to which facts the human mind associates with certain rules. Ehrlich's answer is: The basic facts of law are *usages, domination, possession*, and *declaration of will*[6] (particularly articles of association, contract and testamentary dispositions[7]). Ehrlich argues that it is from concrete usages, from relations of domination or possession, contracts, articles of association and testamentary dispositions – and only these can be directly observed by the scientist – that the rules of conduct which determine the behavior of people in a society proceed. "These facts alone, therefore, and not the legal propositions, according to which the courts render decisions, and according to which the administrative tribu-

---

4   Ehrlich, Fundamental Principles, p. 84.
5   Ehrlich, Fundamental Principles, p. 84 et seq. (emphasis by authors).
6   Ehrlich, Fundamental Principles, p. 85.
7   Ehrlich, Fundamental Principles, p. 192.

nals of the state proceed, are of authoritative significance for the legal order in human society."[8]

According to Ehrlich, the law may be divided into three different classes of norms:[9] the first consists of "the rules of organization of human communities, which have spontaneously developed in society [= social law; authors' note]."[10] These rules are the ones emanating *directly* from the aforementioned facts of law. The law, therefore, does not primarily consist of the norms for decision, but of the norms with which humans actually align their conduct:[11] indicative of this is that sanctions by the state to enforce compliance with norms are only necessary in a very limited number of cases.[12] It is at this point that Ehrlich is confronted with the problem of how to distinguish legal norms from other kinds of social norms (especially from norms belonging to the realm of custom, morality, religion or fashion). The answer is: by the difference in feeling triggered by a breach of norm: "Compare the feeling of revolt that follows a violation of law with the indignation at a violation of a law of morality, with the feeling of disgust occasioned by an indecency, with the disapproval of tactlessness, the ridiculousness of an offense against etiquette, and lastly with the critical feeling of superiority with which a votary of fashion looks down upon those who have not attained the heights which he has scaled."[13] Peculiar to the legal norm is the feeling of the *opinio necessitatis*, a point which, interestingly, brings Ehrlich back towards psychological positivism (in the sense of the theories of recognition).[14]

The second class of norms that make up the material of law is juristic law. By origin, juristic law is a creation of the lawyers (although they are,

---

[8] Ehrlich, Fundamental Principles, p. 192.
[9] Rehbinder, Einführung, p. 29.
[10] Rehbinder, Einführung, p. 29 (our translation).
[11] According to Ehrlich, it is therefore always necessary to ask how much of what has been promulgated by the lawgiver, proclaimed by the founder of a religion or taught by a philosopher is not only applied by the courts, preached from the pulpit or taught in books or schools but is also actually practised and lived. Only what is actually brought to life will become a living norm, the rest is only doctrine, decisional norm, dogma or theory. See Ehrlich, Fundamental Principles, p. 41.
[12] Ehrlich, Fundamental Principles, p. 67.
[13] Ehrlich, Fundamental Principles, p. 165.
[14] Explicitly qualified as theory of recognition by Rehbinder, Einführung, p. 59.

of course, always acting under the influence of society), and it consists for the most part of decisional norms which are primarily addressed to the courts and aimed at the settlement of disputes within the community.[15]

The third class of norms comprises the law which, by *content*, emanates from the *state*. "State law consists of commands directed by the state to its tribunals."[16] The borderline with juristic law, especially with regard to decisional norms, is not clear. Thus, according to Ehrlich, the rules governing the passage of risk in sales contracts are juristic law, whilst the norms found in the German Civil Code on the prerequisites to the acquisition of legal capacity by legal organizations are to be regarded as state law.[17]

These three classes of norms – the associations' norms of organization [= social law], juristic law and state law – which are in many ways interrelated, constitute the "living law".[18] Thus, Ehrlich avoids identifying the so-called "living law" with social law. Nor does he cut the normative element out of his considerations. His theory is sociological only in the sense of his seeking the origin of all legal norms in social reality by starting out from what is actually practiced.[19] On top of that, Ehrlich complements his theory – as shown – with psychological and normative considerations.

---

[15] Rehbinder, Einführung, p. 28 f.
[16] Ehrlich, Fundamental Principles, p. 188.
[17] Ehrlich, Fundamental Principles, p. 188.
[18] Ehrlich, Fundamental Principles, p. 486 et seqq.
[19] For Ehrlich, however, not only is the law a phenomenon determined by social reality [= the normative power of the factual], but it also has a reciprocal effect on reality [= the factual power of the normative]: "The legal proposition is not only the result, it is also a lever, of social development ..."(Fundamental Principles, p. 202).

§ 8 Max Weber[1]

Max Weber's thinking is characterized primarily by its exemplary methodological stringency. This is seen, for instance, in the way that Weber begins the discussion about "Legal Order and Economic Order" with a strict separation of the juridical point of view and the sociological point of view: "Taking the former, we ask: What is intrinsically valid as Law? That is to say: What significance or, in other words, what *normative* meaning ought to be attributed in correct logic to a verbal pattern having the form of a legal proposition. But if we take the latter point of view, we ask: What *actually* happens in a community owing to the *probability* that persons participating in the communal activity *(Gemeinschaftshandeln)* … subjectively consider certain norms as valid and practically act according to them, in other words, orient their own conduct towards these norms? This distinction also determines, in principle, the relationship between *law* and *economy*."[2] According to Weber, the two points of view raise entirely heterogeneous problems; their objectives can never come directly into contact with one another on the same plane: "The ideal 'legal order' of legal theory has nothing directly to do with the world of real economic conduct, since the two things exist on different levels. One exists in the ideal realm of the 'ought', while the other deals with the real world of the 'is'."[3] Nevertheless, legal and economic systems can be interrelated to a very intimate degree, in which case, however – and this is the crucial point – the meaning of the word "legal system" changes completely: it is no longer to be understood as a world of "norms of logically demonstrable correctness" in the juristic sense but as "a com-

---

[1] Weber, On Law in Economy and Society, translated from Max Weber, Wirtschaft und Gesellschaft, Second Edition (1925) by Edward Shils and Max Rheinstein, Cambridge, 1954; Rehbinder, Max Webers Rechtssoziologie: Eine Bestandesaufnahme, in: R. König/J. Winckelmann: Max Weber zum Gedächtnis, Opladen: Westdeutscher Verlag, 1963, p. 470 et seqq.; idem, Einführung, p. 35 et seqq.; Raiser, Grundlagen, p. 86 et seqq.; M. Baurmann, Grundzüge der Rechtssoziologie Max Webers, JuS 31 (1991), p. 97 et seqq. The following comments are based on the main work published only posthumously.

[2] Weber, On Law in Economy and Society, p. 11.

[3] Weber, On Law in Economy and Society, p. 12.

plex of actual determinants *(Bestimmungsgründe)* of actual human conduct" in the sociological sense.[4]

Weber goes on to elucidate this sociological concept of the law, as opposed to other social systems such as usage and convention, as follows:

By usage, Weber means a typically uniform activity which is simply kept on the beaten track by custom and unreflected imitation.[5] However, the individual is in no way "required" by anyone to perpetuate this collective way of acting.[6] Thus, for Weber, usage is only an actual regularity in behavior.[7]

On the other hand, an order shall be called convention where "its validity is externally guaranteed by the probability that a violation will be met with the (relatively) general and practically significant *disapproval* of a determinable group of people."[8] The difference from "usage", which is merely an actual regularity in behavior, consists in the incorporation of the normative element; convention is, according to Weber, something normative, usage, on the other hand, something factual. The non-conventional behavior of the actor – unlike usage – leads to a reaction from the environment, albeit limited to disapproval.

Regarding the legal order, the characteristic added on is the *staff* which engages in enforcement. According to Weber, an order shall "be called law if it is externally guaranteed by the probability that coercion (physical or psychological), to bring about conformity or avenge violation, will be applied by a *staff* of people holding themselves specially ready for that purpose."[9] The existence of the enforcement staff need not be at all similar to what we are used to today. In particular, it is not necessary for there to be any specifically judicial organ. According to Weber, a clan

---

4 Weber, On Law in Economy and Society, p. 12.
5 Weber, On Law in Economy and Society, p. 20.
6 Weber, On Law in Economy and Society, p. 20.
7 Weber, On Law in Economy and Society, p. 5, takes the manner of cooking as an example of usage. See also Hart, p. 55, who quotes the habit of going to the cinema on Saturday night as an example.
8 Weber, On Law in Economy and Society, p. 5. Weber quotes as an example for a conventional order the common way of dressing decently.
9 Weber, On Law in Economy and Society, p. 5, e.g. the excommunication of the Roman Catholic Church.

(in the cases of blood vengeance or feud) represents such a staff, too, if some sort of regulatory order exists which determines their reactions. Furthermore, ecclesiastical rules enforced by psychological coercion as the specific disciplinary means of the church, or the rules of a college fraternity[10] are included in this concept of law whereas in the case of international law, this very point is at least debatable.[11] Thus for Weber, the validity of law in the sociological sense is constituted by the chance (probability) of the actual occurrence of physical or psychological coercion by a staff specialized in serving this purpose in cases of deviance.[12] Unlike Ehrlich who sees the *"opinio necessitatis"* as the decisive distinguishing feature of law in comparison with other social orders, Weber champions a theory of coercion.[13] His concept of law has proved largely practical in contemporary legal sociology, certainly more practical than Ehrlich's.[14] His thoughts, however, have been rendered more precise – especially with regard to the so-called "efficiency rate" – by the scholar to be addressed next.

---

[10] The rules of German students' fraternities regulating such matters as convivial drinking or singing are set out in a *"Komment"*. See Weber, On Law in Economy and Society, p. 7.

[11] Weber, On Law in Economy and Society, p. 6 et seq.

[12] Weber, On Law in Economy and Society, p. 12 et seq.

[13] Apart from Weber, other representatives of the coercion theory include Geiger, Pound, Olivecrona, Durkheim and Kelsen.

[14] Raiser, Grundlagen, p. 102.

§ 9 Theodor Geiger[1]

A consistent sociological positivism can be found in Theodor Geiger's works. Geiger seeks to study the law in particular and the social order in general "as facticities, as *relations in reality*".[2] The aim of his endeavors is to analyze metaphysically and ideologically laden complexes of ideas, such as norm, validity, duty, right etc., in order to determine the relations of fact that are distorted by them, and to express these relations in terms of *perceptible reality*.[3] A general jurisprudence which is not inclined to wallow in the "thought swamps of metaphysics and ideology" has to be developed, Geiger argues, from sociological starting points; in fact it coincides with the theoretical sociology of law.[4] Geiger himself characterizes his position as "sociological legal realism".[5] In doing so, he clearly comes out against classical legal philosophy, which believed itself equal to drawing normative conclusions from the "alleged nature" of the law, and also against conventional legal dogmatics which, due to its rule fetishism, is always inclined to attribute some kind of objective validity to the positive law.[6]

---

[1] Literature: Geiger, On Social Order and Mass Society, Selected Papers, Chicago: The University of Chicago Press, 1969; idem, Vorstudien zu einer Soziologie des Rechts, Fourth Edition, Schriftenreihe zur Rechtssoziologie und Rechtstatsachenforschung, vol. 65, 4th Edition, Berlin: Duncker & Humblot, 1987; Raiser, Grundlagen, p. 107 et seqq.; H. Oetjens, Kritischer Rationalismus und Rechtssoziologie, in: W. Naucke/P. Trappe (Editors), Rechtssoziologie und Rechtspraxis, Neuwied/Berlin: Luchterhand, 1970, p. 11 et seqq.; W. Naucke, Wissenschaftsbegriff – Rechtssoziologie – Rechtspraxis. Bemerkungen zu einem konkret-humanen juristischen Pragmatismus, in: W. Naucke/P. Trappe, p. 79 et seqq; P. Trappe, Die Rechssoziologie Theodor Geigers, Diss. Mainz 1959. W. Zitscher, Normen und Feldtheorie, Schriften zur Rechtstheorie Nr. 110, Berlin: Duncker & Humblot, 1983, offers a further development of Theodor Geiger's theory.

[2] Geiger, Vorstudien, p. 6.

[3] Geiger, Vorstudien, p. 2.

[4] Geiger, Vorstudien, p. 1/2.

[5] Geiger, Vorstudien, p. 329. Geiger is clearly rejecting a psychological theory of law (p. 340 et seqq., p. 6). He factors out legal consciousness for methodological reasons, not because he denies its existence but because it is not a suitable object for the purpose of scientific research (p. 343). From the standpoint of empirical science, one must, Geiger argues, keep to *actions as such*.

[6] Geiger, Vorstudien, p. 6.

Finally, regarding the question of values, Geiger expressly endorses the "theoretical value nihilism" of the Scandinavian Uppsala School.[7] Good and bad are "completely imaginary concepts …, impervious to any empirical framing of their alleged contents and therefore non-existent at least as far as a rational conception of the world is concerned."[8] Empirical science can deal with such ideas only in a way which marks and analyzes them as "psychological curiosities".[9] Consequently, nothing can be said scientifically concerning the contents that a concrete decision ought to have.

At first, Geiger's analyses look into all kinds of social orders without differing between norms of the law, of morality and of custom. His starting point is the fact given by "direct observation" that men are attuned to and dependent on each other in their existence.[10] They live "in mutual dependence on one another", a fact that Geiger describes by "social interdependence".[11] "In order to live together, people must be able to predict with reasonable certainty how others will behave in recurrent typical situations."[12] A social order is thus based upon the fact that there is a specific stable relationship between certain typical situations s and the corresponding typical modes of behavior g.[13] Geiger describes this unity of a given situation and a given behavior in terms of the formula $s \rightarrow g$ ("s is followed by g"). He explains the genesis of such a reaction-model with reference to (the zoologist) Richard Semon's mnemic[14] theory as follows:[15] every psychological experience leaves a lasting trace on the memory, a so-called "engram". When the impression

---

[7] Geiger, Vorstudien, p. 271 et seqq. Geiger is close to the Uppsala school but reprimands the "sociological shortcomings" of the Scandinavian legal theories whose adherents – with the exception of Alf Ross – reveal "an astonishing lack of sociological understanding of their object" (Geiger, Vorstudien, p. 7).

[8] Geiger, Vorstudien, p. 257.

[9] Geiger, Vorstudien, p. 257.

[10] Geiger, Vorstudien, p. 8 et seq.

[11] Geiger, Vorstudien, p. 8.

[12] Geiger, On Social Order and Mass Society, p. 39.

[13] Geiger, On Social Order and Mass Society, p. 39.

[14] Mneme means memory.

[15] R. Semon, Die Mneme als erhaltendes Prinzip im Wechsel des organischen Geschehens (Leipzig: Wilhelm Engelmann, 1904). For the following see Geiger, On Social Order and Mass Society, p. 61 n. 4 as well as idem, Vorstudien, p. 54 et seq. *The*

consists of two or more elements, the result is an "engram-complex". Now if an agent H has ever been in situation *s* and has responded with behavior *g*, the complex of impressions s and g leave behind a memory trace, an engram-complex. This engram-complex is characterized by the following idiosyncrasy: if H is later faced with a new impression, one element of which resembles an element of the engram-complex, this current impression tends to elicit recall of the *entire* engram-complex. Semon calls this process "ecphory" (triggering). The mneme (memory) thus ecphorically supplements the image associated with the situation *s* with the image of behavior *g* so that H will supposedly respond in the new situation s with reaction g. Every repetition will deepen the memory trace. An individual action has turned into an individual habit (s → g). The same mechanism operates in a group, too, in that the group members – after repeated observation of the H's behavior – on the one hand expect behavior g, and on the other hand adopt it themselves in similar s situations. Through response-expectation and social imitation, the confirmed habit of an individual becomes a social custom s → g. At first, this means nothing more than a "factual regularity", i.e. a normative element is not yet included.[16] Once a social custom is established in that way and, contrary to expectations, an individual fails to act in accordance with the scheme s → g, but in accordance with $s \rightarrow \overline{g}$ (s is followed by non-g), the group members will respond with astonishment, possibly with indignation. For social interdependency demands predictability of behavior in typical cases.[17] The group members will demand response g from person H acting in situation s. The model s → g is supplemented with the factor of the binding obligation v and is thus turned into a social norm (*s* → *g*) *v*.

But what does the binding nature of a norm consist of? It is clear that Geiger, if he wants to abide by his own methodological precepts, must attribute the binding nature of norms to facts identifiable in the external

---

results of modern brain research have in large parts corroborated Semon's hypotheses.
[16] Geiger, On Social Order and Mass Society, p. 54.
[17] See above.

world.[18] The binding nature of a norm cannot therefore be anything but its own reality, and *the reality of a norm is its effectuality potential*.[19] What does that mean?

In a situation s, every individual of the group in question is faced with the following alternative: either he acts in accordance with the requested response g and is thereby complying with the norm. Or he acts in a deviant manner by opting for response c (crime) and is thereby exposing himself to a reaction on part of the group (r). Geiger describes these facts in the following formula:[20]

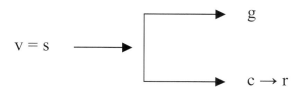

It is not absolutely certain, however, that c is followed in all events by an r. The crime might remain undiscovered, the group may act negligently or the delinquent may be able to escape the sanction. It would thus be wrong to identify the binding nature of the norm exclusively with the described alternative effectuality, because this would mean that the norm is not binding in case of lack of norm-compliance and of a reaction. A norm can therefore not be seen as absolutely binding or absolutely non-binding, Geiger argues, but only as *more or less* binding.[21] The binding force of a norm can be of *higher or lower degree* and is a measurable parameter. It can be expressed by the fraction $\frac{e}{s}$, where e is the number of cases in which the norm proved effective by either being complied with or by a reaction to non-compliance, and s is the total number of cases in which the norm-addressees are faced with the

---

[18] "Binding nature" is thus, according to Geiger, not the same than what we have characterized as the "legitimacy of the law", above, § 1 B.IV. For Geiger, binding nature is something real, i.e. the validity in the sense of the sociological effectiveness of the law.
[19] Geiger, On Social Order and Mass Society, p. 49.
[20] Geiger, On Social Order and Mass Society, p. 51.
[21] Geiger, Vorstudien, p. 34.

norm-typical situation.[22] For example, an efficiency of 70% would mean that in 70% of cases, the norm is complied with or followed by a sanction in case of breach, whilst in 30% of cases the delinquent goes scot-free. The binding nature and reality of a norm is therefore nothing but the described "probability of this alternative" (i.e. its effectuality potential).[23] As for why this and not some other reaction has had the v-stigma attached, i.e. has been elevated to the level of a norm, Geiger states that (for the time being) this question is unanswerable.[24]

According to Geiger, the law differs from other normative systems by virtue of the following characteristics:

1. First, one can only speak of law in a meaningful way if such law refers to a "differentiated and structured large social aggregate".[25] The regulatory structure of the law thus only belongs to relatively advanced human societies.[26] In tribal societies, law and customs cannot be distinguished.

2. Second, one speaks of law only under condition that a *superordinate central authority* has been constituted within a social milieu consisting of separate coexistent or interlocking groups.[27]

3. Third, in case of a legal order, the reaction activity, i.e. the imposition and execution of sanctions, has been *monopolized* by the central authority.[28]

4. Fourth, the legal order differs from the pre-legal order by the fact that there is a *special apparatus* for the administration of the order, that *specific administrative organs* are established.[29] The reaction activity is assigned to the central power's administrative organs.[30]

5. Fifth, the reaction activity is regulated by a *formal procedure*.[31]

---

[22] Geiger, On Social Order and Mass Society, p. 52.
[23] Geiger, On Social Order and Mass Society, p. 52.
[24] Geiger, On Social Order and Mass Society, p. 67.
[25] Geiger, Vorstudien, p. 128.
[25] Geiger, Vorstudien, p. 85.
[27] Geiger, On Social Order and Mass Society, p. 69.
[28] Geiger, Vorstudien, p. 128.
[29] Geiger, On Social Order and Mass Society ,p. 70.
[30] Geiger, On Social Order and Mass Society, p. 71.
[31] Geiger, On Social Order and Mass Society, p. 74.

6. And sixth, the legal order indicates a special way of *reaction allot-ment*.[32] Norm violations of all kinds are each assigned a specific re-action deemed adequate.[33] These assignments replace the spontane-ous reactions of extra-legal regulatory systems taking place without applying any standards.

Summing up, Geiger defines the law as "the social regulatory system of a centrally organized large social aggregate, provided that such a system is based on an apparatus of sanctions operated monopolistically by spe-cial administrative bodies."[34] Nevertheless, Geiger does not claim that his characterization of the law is absolutely irrefutable but emphasizes in a methodically exemplary way that one is dealing here with a *question of definition*. Definitions are "crutches of cognition".[35] Above all, how-ever, crutches should be "serviceable". What he means by this is that a stipulative definition should be judged for its fruitfulness, not for its truth.[36]

---

[32] Geiger, On Social Order and Mass Society, p. 76.
[33] Geiger, On Social Order and Mass Society, p. 77.
[34] Geiger, Vorstudien, p. 297 (our translation).
[35] Geiger, On Social Order and Mass Society, p. 68.
[36] See below, § 20 B.I.

§ 10 American Legal Realism[1]

Further elements of a sociological positivism are found in American legal realism.[2] It is difficult to reduce the American realist movement to a common denominator, however, since it neither formed an actual school whose representatives agreed with one another on substantial issues[3] nor did it produce a uniform and coherent theory of law. The realists support postulates as different as

- the disapproval of excessive conceptualism[4]
- the inclusion of empirical data in the process of judging[5]

---

[1] Literature: M. Martin, Legal Realism, American University Studies, Series V: Philosophy, New York: Peter Lang Publishing 1997; M.A. Rea-Frauchiger, Der Amerikanische Rechtsrealismus: Karl N. Llewellyn, Jerome Frank, Underhill Moore, Berlin: Duncker & Humblot, 2005; W. Twining, Karl Llewellyn and the Realist Movement, London: Weidenfeld and Nicolson, 1973; H. Coing, Neue Strömungen in der nordamerikanischen Rechtsphilosophie, ARSP 38 (1949/50), p. 536 et seqq.; Casper, Gerhard: Juristischer Realismus und politische Theorie im amerikanischen Rechtsdenken, Schriften zur Rechtstheorie, Heft 10, Berlin: Duncker & Humblot, 1967; Reich; Kantorowicz, Hermann: Rechtswissenschaft und Soziologie, Freiburger Rechts- und Staatswissenschaftliche Abhandlungen, Band 19, Karlsruhe: C.F. Müller, 1962, p. 101 et seqq.; idem, Some Rationalism About Realism, in: Yale Law Journal 43 (1934), p. 1240–1253; W. Fikentscher, Gedanken zu einer rechtsvergleichenden Methodenlehre, in: Recht im Wandel, Festschrift 150 Jahre Carl Heymanns Verlag KG, Cologne/Berlin/Bonn/Munich: Carl Heymanns, 1965, p. 141 et seqq.; idem, Methoden des Rechts in vergleichender Darstellung, Vol. 2: Anglo-amerikanischer Rechtskreis, Tübingen: Mohr Siebeck, 1975; F.K. Beutel, Die Experimentelle Rechtswissenschaft. Möglichkeiten eines neuen Zweiges der Sozialwissenschaft, Schriftenreihe zur Rechtssoziologie und Rechtstatsachenforschung No. 21, Berlin: Duncker & Humblot, 1971; R.S. Summers, Pragmatic Instrumentalism and American Legal Theory, Rechtstheorie 13 (1982), p. 257; idem, Pragmatischer Instrumentalismus und amerikanische Rechtstheorie, Freiburg/Munich 1983.

[2] The main representatives of legal realism are: K.N. Llewellyn, J. Frank, U. Moore, F.K. Beutel and F.S. Cohen. Legal realism continued after 1930 where sociological jurisprudence – developed by O.W. Holmes, R. Pound, L.D. Brandeis and B.N. Cardozo – had left off, and can no longer be clearly separated from the latter. Regarding legal realism in general, see Reich, p. 82 et seqq.

[3] Fikentscher, Gedanken zur einer rechtsvergleichenden Methodenlehre (quoted in § 10 Fn. 1), p. 153; Kantorowicz, in: Rechtswissenschaft und Soziologie, p. 101.

[4] Casper (quoted in § 10 n. 1), p. 59.

[5] Seminal in this regard was a legal brief written by Judge Brandeis in Muller v. Oregon, US Supreme Court Reports 208 (1907) 412 (the so-called "Brandeis Brief") in which Judge Brandeis – by means of medical opinions and sociological case-studies

- the approval of a so-called "functional teleological method" (i.e. the judge is held to look into the ends and the consequences of a legal rule)[6]
- the concept of interest identification and interest evaluation[7]
- the adjustment of the law to changing circumstances
- the identification of the law with certain behavior or propositions of behavior (see below)
- psychological evaluation of judicial decisions with the objective of uncovering of the real reasons motivating them,[8] etc.

Only the concepts that attempt to define the so-called 'nature' of law sociologically – which are by no means uncontested, even amongst the realists themselves – fall within the scope of this book:

Bingham, for example, uses "the phrase 'the law' in the sense of sequences of external facts and their concrete legal consequences through the concrete operation of governmental machinery."[9] Frank writes that the law "consists of decisions, not of rules. If so, *whenever a judge decides a case he is making law.*"[10] Llewellyn declared that "[w]hat these officials do about disputes is, to my mind, the law itself."[11] Kantorowicz has summarized these statements of the realists as follows: "[T]he Law is not a body of rules, not an Ought, but a factual reality. It is the real

---

    – submitted empirical proof of the negative impact of long working hours on the psychological and physical health of women. Subsequently, the Supreme Court upheld an Oregon State Statute, according to which the working hours of women are to be limited to a maximum of 10 hours, as constitutional. See Reich, p. 70 et seqq.

6   Reich, p. 103.

7   Reich, p. 101.

8   Regarding the psychological phase of legal realism, see Reich, p. 86 et seqq., in particular p. 90 et seqq.

9   Bingham, What is law, Mich. L.R. 11 (1912) 109 n. 29 (quoted from Kantorowicz, Yale L.J. 43 [1934], p. 1243 who notes that Bingham "obviously defines 'the law' by the concept of 'legal'", ibidem, n. 9).

10   J. Frank, Law and the Modern Mind, 6th Edition, New York: Coward-McCann, Inc., 1949, p. 128.

11   Llewellyn, The Bramble Bush, p. 8: Llewellyn refers to his realist "behaviorist definition" of the law as "unhappy words" which are at best "a very partial statement of the whole truth". (Llewellyn, The Bramble Bush – On Our Law and Its Study, Revised Edition, New York: Oceana Publications 1960).

behavior of certain people, especially of the officials of the Law, more especially of the judges who make the Law through their decisions, which, therefore, constitutes the Law."[12]

Every now and then the law is not identified with an actual behavior but with *propositions describing* an actual behavior. Amongst these is Holmes' famous "prediction theory of law". "If you want to know the law and nothing else, you must look at it as a bad man ... we shall find that he does not care two straws for the axioms or deductions, but that he does want to know what the Massachusetts or English Courts are likely to do in fact ... *The prophecies of what the courts are likely to do in fact, and nothing more pretentious, are what I mean by the law.* "[13] In this conception, legal rules are "rules of description and prediction";[14] their real value can be assessed by testing them against future court decisions and evaluating the degree of conformity or non-conformity.[15] A high degree of conformity indicates "real rules", i.e. rules embodying the real law, since they are applied by the courts; the opposite result indicates "paper rules", i.e. rules that are not followed by the courts and are thus nothing more than what the books say the law is (i.e. on paper).[16] According to the realists, the most important task of jurisprudence is the analysis of the real rules; the traditional dogmatic problems, on the other hand, tend to receive less attention.[17]

A further advantage of the positivist theories consists in their having directed our attention to the so-called "real factors of law-making".[18] Only the realist movements have started to investigate factors actually

---

[12] Kantorowicz, Some Rationalism about Realism, Yale Law Journal 43 (1934), p. 1243.

[13] O.W. Holmes, The Path of the Law, in: Collected Legal Papers, New York: Harcourt, Brace and Company, 1921, pp. 171/173.

[14] Llewellyn, A Realistic Jurisprudence – The Next Step, Columbia Law Review 30 (1930), p. 439. As emphasized by Rehbinder, Einführung, p. 55, Llewellyn has well seen that the word "rule" may be used in a normative sense; Llewellyn addresses rules in this sense as "prescriptive rules" or "ought-rules".

[15] Llewellyn, Columbia Law Review 30 (1930), p. 444.

[16] Regarding the differentiation of "real rules" and "paper rules" see Llewellyn, Columbia Law Review 30 (1930), p. 448.

[17] Llewellyn, Columbia Law Review 30 (1930), p. 457 et seqq. as well as literature quoted by Reich, p. 104 n. 6.

[18] So the accurate denomination by Henkel, p. 525 et seqq.

influencing judicial decisional behavior. Thus Underhill Moore and Gilbert Sussmann investigated, in a detailed study,[19] whether the banks in certain regions displayed institutional (i.e. frequent and regular) patterns of behavior when debiting direct discounts and if so, what influence such behavior patterns had on court decisions regarding matters of debiting direct discounts. The three cases, brought before court in South Carolina, New York and Pennsylvania respectively, were each based on similar facts: the plaintiff, having a checking account with the defendant bank, presented a promissory note to the bank which the bank discounted. On or after the day of maturity of the note or notes, the bank debited the amount discounted to the plaintiff's account which regularly resulted in a debit balance. In each of the three cases, a check issued by the plaintiff was presented and dishonored following the debiting of his account. In South Carolina it turned out that it was highly unusual for a bank to debit the amount due before the customer had issued a check on the bank or given instructions to debit[20] whilst the equivalent behavior in New York and Pennsylvania was judged to be common or common enough to classify as foreseeable. These results not only account for why the South Carolina court gave judgment for the customer whilst the New York and Pennsylvania courts decided in favor of the bank, but they also confirmed the working hypothesis underlying the studies that each of the judges had rendered judgment in accordance with the cultural conventions or, more specifically, institutional behavior patterns of the locality.[21] If such surveys were conducted on a larger scale, this would certainly contribute to convey a more realistic picture of the administration of justice.

---

[19] Published in a series of 6 articles entitled "Legal and Institutional Method Applied to the Debiting of Direct Disounts, Yale Law Journal 40 (1931), p. 381–400, 555–575, 752–778, 928–953, 1055–1073, 1219–1250; see also Rea-Frauchiger, Der amerikanische Rechtsrealismus: Karl N. Llewellyn, Jerome Frank, Underhill Moore, p. 134 et seqq.

[20] Moore and Sussman, Legal and Institutional Methods Applied to the Debiting of Direct Discounts – VI. The Decisions, the Institutions, and the Degrees of Deviation, p. 1226.

[21] Cf. Moore and Sussman, Legal and Institutional Methods Applied to the Debiting of Direct Discounts – VI. The Decisions, the Institutions, and the Degree of Deviation, Yale Law Journal 40 (1931), p. 1219 et seq., 1226, 1238 et seq. and 1244 et seq.

Fourth Chapter

Mixed Forms of Positivism

§ 11 H.L.A. Hart's Legal Theory[1]

H.L.A. (Herbert) Hart, who is one of the most important legal philosophers in the English-speaking world, expounds in his work a legal posi-

---

[1] Biography: Lacey, N.: A Life of H.L.A. Hart, Oxford: Oxford University Press 2004;
Bibliographical references: R. Alexy, On Necessary Relations between Law and Mo-
rality, Ratio Juris 2 (1989), p. 168 et seqq.; L.J. Cohen, H.L.A. Hart: The Concept of
Law, Mind 71 (1962), p. 395 et seqq.; J.L. Coleman, Negative and Positive Positiv-
ism, Journal of Legal Studies 11 (1982), p. 140 et seqq.; M.J. Detmold, The Unity of
Law and Morality: A Refutation of Legal Positivism, London: Routledge & Kegan
Paul, 1984, chapter 2; R.M. Dworkin, Taking Rights Seriously, chs. 2–3; Eckmann;
B. Edgeworth, Legal Positivism and the Philosophy of Language, Legal Studies 6
(1986), p. 115 et seqq.; R. Gavison (Editor), Issues in Contemporary Legal Philoso-
phy, Oxford: Clarendon Press 1987, chs. 1–3; R.P. George, The Autonomy of Law,
Oxford: Clarendon Press, 1996; K. Greenawalt, Hart's Rule of Recognition and the
United States, Ratio Juris 1 (1988), p. 40 et seqq.; P.M.S. Hacker, Hart's Philosophy
of Law, in: Hacker and Raz (Editors), Law, Morality and Society, Oxford: Clarendon
Press 1977; J.W. Harris, Law and Legal Science, Oxford: Oxford University Press,
1979; Hart, The Concept of Law; idem; Positivism and the Separation of Law and
Morals, in: Essays in Jurisprudence and Philosophy, p. 49 et seqq.; idem, Definition
and Theory in Jurisprudence, in: Essays in Jurisprudence and Philosophy, p. 21 et
seqq.; idem, Essays on Bentham, Oxford: Oxford University Press, 1982, p. 141 et
seqq.; R.E. Hill, Legal Validity and Legal Obligations, Yale Law Journal 80 (1970),
p. 47 et seqq.; N. Hoerster, Grundthesen analytischer Rechtstheorie, Jahrbuch für
Rechtssoziologie und Rechtstheorie 2 (1971), p. 115 et seqq.; idem, Was ist Recht?
Grundfragen der Rechtsphilosophie, Munich: C.H. Beck, 2006, chs. 1–8; S. Hotz/K.
Mathis, Recht, Moral und Faktizität, Essays in Honour of Walter Ott, p. 53 et seqq.
and p. 79 et seqq.; L. Kanowicz, The Palace of Sanctions in Professor Hart's Concept
of Law, Ducane University Law Review (1966–67), p. 1 et seqq.; M. Krygier, The
Concept of Law and Legal Theory, Oxford Journal of Legal Studies 2 (1982), p. 155
et seqq.; D.N. MacCormick, Legal Reasoning and Legal Theory, Oxford: Clarendon
Press, 1994, appendix; idem, H.L.A. Hart, 2nd Edition, Stanford: Stanford University
Press, 2008; M. Martin, The Legal Philosophy of H.L.A. Hart, Philadelphia: Temple
University Press, 1987; J. Raz, The Authority of Law, Oxford: Oxford University
Press 1979, chapters 2–3; idem, The Concept of a Legal System, 2nd Edition, Oxford:
Oxford University Press, 1980, postscript; idem, The Morality of Freedom, Oxford:
Clarendon Press, 1986; idem, Practical Reason and Norms, 2nd Edition, New Jersey:

tivist theory that combines elements of all the main lines of thought so far introduced in this book. It is characterized by the attempt at a synthesis of the psychological, the sociological and the analytical view.[2] Moreover, particularly characteristic is Hart's endeavor (in the analytical parts of his work) to use for the benefit of law the methods and starting points of the modern philosophy of language under the formative influence of Wittgenstein, which was the prevailing trend in the Anglo-Saxon countries and had its centre in Oxford.[3] The larger and more important part of Hart's work is dedicated to the logical-empirical research of the structure of law,[4] on which we will exclusively focus in the following. Apart from that, Hart published contributions to material legal issues in which he subjects problems of the criminal law reform to critical analysis from a liberal point of view.[5]

Hart's legal positivist approach shows first of all in the *conceptual* separation of law and morals. He takes up from Bentham and Austin, who had constantly and firmly insisted on the need to distinguish, uncompromisingly and with a maximum of clarity, law *as it is* from law *as it ought to be*.[6] What mattered to Bentham and Austin were the following two simple things:

Princeton University Press, 1990, chs. 2 and 5; idem, Ethics in the Public Domain, Oxford: Oxford University Press, 1994, chs. 8 and 9; R.A. Samek, The Legal Point of View, New York: Philosophical Library, 1974; R.E. Sartorious, Hart's Concept of Law, in: Summers (Editor), More Essays in Legal Philosophy, Berkeley: University of California Press, 1971; J.C. Smith; Legal Obligation, London: The Athlone Press, 1976, ch. 2; P. Soper, A Theory of Law, Cambridge, Mass.: Harvard University Press, 1984, ch. 2; R.S. Summers, Professor Hart's Concept of Law, Duke Law Journal 1963, No. 4, pp. 629–670; Watkins-Bienz.

[2] Eckmann, p. 128.

[3] Hoerster, Einleitung, p. 5; Hart held the chair of jurisprudence in Oxford until he became emeritus in 1968.

[4] Eckmann, p. 12.

[5] Hart, Punishment and Responsibility, Essays in Philosophy of Law, New York and Toronto: Oxford University Press, 1968; idem, The Morality of the Criminal Law, Two Lectures, Jerusalem: Magnes Press/London: Oxford University Press, 1965; idem, Law, Liberty and Morality, London 1963, idem, Prolegomenon to the Principles of Punishment, in: Proceedings of the Aristotelian Society 60 (1959/60) p. 1 et seqq.; idem, Essays on Bentham, Studies in Jurisprudence and Political Theory, New York: Clarendon Press: Oxford University Press, 1982.

[6] Hart, Positivism and the Separation of Law and Morals, p. 50.

First: *from the mere fact that a rule violates standards of morality, it cannot follow that it is not a rule of law* (unless there is an express constitutional or legal provision to this exact end).

Second: *from the mere fact that a rule is morally desirable, it cannot follow that it is a rule of law.*[7]

This conceptual separation of law and morals which Hart heartily endorses does not lead him into denying *empirical influences of morality on the law* (and vice versa), in which point he refers once again to Austin and Bentham: both "never denied that, as a matter of historical fact, the development of legal systems *had been powerfully influenced by moral opinion, and, conversely, that moral standards had been profoundly influenced by law,* so that the content of many legal rules mirrored moral rules or principles."[8] This momentous differentiation has been overlooked by many critics of the positivist separation thesis: law and morals are *conceptually distinct but empirically related.* Instead they often write only about the positivist separation of law and morals, e.g. they insinuate that according to positivism, law and morals are *completely separate* systems of norms.

Hart defends the positivist separation thesis by dealing with the arguments raised by its critics:[9]

A first criticism is that the so-called "command theory of law", as represented most notably by Austin, demonstrates the untenability of the separation of law and morals.[10] For the difference between the command of a gunman saying to his victim "Give me money or your life" and a legal command can only consist – or so, at least, it seems – in a moral qualification. Since the simple trilogy of command, sanction, and sovereign as taught by the command theory of law applies to the gunman's situation, too,[11] this conception yields no distinction between a gunman's command and a legal command, with the sole exception that, in the case

---

[7]   Hart, Positivism and the Separation of Law and Morals, p. 55.
[8]   Hart, Positivism and the Separation of Law and Morals, p. 54.
[9]   Coleman's II critique follows below, § 15 D.
[10] Hart, Positivism and the Separation of Law and Morals, p. 57 et seqq.
[11] Hart, Positivism and the Separation of Law and Morals, p. 59.

of a legal system, a gunman on a grand scale is at work. Hart's replies on this point amount to arguments which attribute the fallibility of the command theory to different reasons, which we will set out in another context.[12] Above all, however, Hart points out that disapproval of one of Austin's theses, viz. to conceive of the law as essentially identical in character with commands, does not necessary entail disapproval of the separation thesis, because the two are logically independent of one another.[13]

A second objection against the separation of law and morals is that an essential connection of law and morality becomes apparent when one investigates how laws of disputed meaning are interpreted and applied to a concrete case. It seems obvious that the judge must turn to principles of morality to bridge the uncertainty and incompleteness of the law. Hart shows with a plausible example how the wording of rules in fact often allows for several interpretations.[14] However, Hart rejects the statutory positivist thesis according to which the judge can find the one correct decision by way of logical deduction alone.[15] But what is the real issue when an opinion is denounced as being too formalistic? Hart's reply is: the social aims on which the rule is based have been left out of consideration. The "formalistic" opinion is not distinguished – as has often, erroneously, been said – by excessive use of logic but rather by a fair amount of stupidity (for so-called formalistic reasoning in jurisprudence is in fact seldom logically conclusive).[16] Thus, the fact that the judge must appeal to social aims when applying rules or filling in gaps in the legal system does not mean by any measure that such social aims are *eo ipso* moral! The social aims on which a particular legal system is based

---

[12] See below, § 24 B.

[13] Hart, Positivism and the Separation of Law and Morals, p. 57; Hoerster, Einleitung, p. 6.

[14] Hart, Positivism and the Separation of Law and Morals, p. 63 et seqq.

[15] Hart, Positivism and the Separation of Law and Morals, p. 64. Hart emphasizes the creative character of interpretation (Positivism and the Separation of Law and Morals, p. 87). As soon as the penumbral area of uncertainty outside the hard core of settled meaning surrounding a rule is arrived at, the judge has a leeway in decision-making covering several alternatives. For a comprehensive account of Hart's theory of interpretation, see Eckmann, 53 et seqq.

[16] Hart, Positivism and the Separation of Law and Morals, p. 66/67.

can be evil, too,[17] a fact which in turn, according to Hart, provides evidence for the fruitfulness of the distinction between the law as it is and the law as it ought to be. We may refer to the National Socialist legal system: its principles were the *Führer*-principle, the Aryan racial theory, the belief in a sound popular feeling *("gesundes Volksempfinden")* and the party program of the NSDAP, principles which must, from the standpoint of critical morality, be judged as highly immoral. It is just at this point that the positivist separation thesis proves of value: the law as it was, i.e. National Socialist law inclusive of its ideological principles, cannot be justified from the standpoint of critical morality. By this example, the thesis of a separation of positive law and positive morality may equally be upheld: for the entire duration of the Nazi regime, the individualist, liberal contract law of the German Civil Code (BGB) remained in force although it was at odds with the ideological principle of the racially defined "people's community" *(Volksgemeinschaft)*.

Yet another objection against the separation of law and morals originated from Gustav Radbruch.[18] In an essay that garnered considerable attention, Radbruch had held the opinion that positivism (in the sense of insistence on the separation of the law as it is from the law as it ought to be) had powerfully contributed to the horrors of the Nazi regime. This objection is, as will be shown below, historically wrong.[19] The fundamental principles of humanitarian morality must, Radbruch argues, be included in the very concept of law: no positive enactment or statute, however clearly it conforms to the formal criteria of validity of a given legal system, could be valid if it contravened basic principles of morality.[20] Hart points out that recognition of a norm as a valid norm of a given legal system does not conclusively answer the question of whether that norm must be obeyed.[21] It is precisely the separation of law and morals

---

[17] Hart, Positivism and the Separation of Law and Morals, p. 69/70.
[18] See below, § 23 A.
[19] See below, § 23 D.
[20] Hart, Positivism and the Separation of Law and Morals, p. 74. As legal history research has shown (see below, § 23 D), Radbruch's argument is wrong. Furthermore, Radbruch is attacking a position he had himself held until 1932 (cf. Radbruch, p. 82 and 84 [Radbruch, Rechtsphilosophie, Third Edition, Leipzig: Quelle und Meyer, 1932, p. 83 et seq.]). See above, § 3, text at n. 14 et seqq. and below § 23.
[21] Hart, Positivism and the Separation of Law and Morals, p. 75.

that enables us to take a moral-critical attitude towards the law: since such an attitude will not be advanced, as Hoerster explains in his interpretation of Hart's reflections, by mixing up the question of what the law says in a particular situation with the question of how one ought to act, as a citizen or as judge, in such a situation, but rather by "making it a self-evident habit of thought that often an act only becomes *morally* dubious at the very point it is deemed to be *legally* imperative."[22] Consequently, Hart is against the inclusion of principles of natural law within the concept of law.[23]

Interestingly, he nevertheless sees a necessary correspondence between law and morality, which he sets out in his theory of the "minimum content of Natural Law".[24] Hart's starting point is the – possibly only coincidental – fact that men generally desire to live.[25] From this actual desire to survive he concludes that a legal system cannot be viable unless it protects the lives of at least some individuals.[26] Human vulnerability results in the ban on inflicting bodily harm and on killing;[27] from the fact that food, clothes and shelter do not exist in limitless abundance, there follows a minimum form of the institution and protection of property (though not necessarily individual property);[28] and the limited understanding and strength of will of men make sanctions necessary to guarantee the efficacy of the law.[29] As Eckmann points out, one should take note of the fact that Hart is not drawing an inadmissible conclusion from Is to Ought.[30] Hart does not derive the aim "Man ought to survive" from the fact of the desire to survive.[31] What follows from the nature of man is not an Ought but an Is, viz. the actual existence of the rules mentioned.

---

[22] Hoerster, Einleitung, p. 9.
[23] Hart would want to adhere to the separation of law and morals even if there were "cognitive" theories of morality. See below, § 15 B.II.
[24] Hart, The Concept of Law, p. 193.
[25] Hart, The Concept of Law, p. 192.
[26] Eckmann, p. 49.
[27] Hart, The Concept of Law, p. 194 et seq.
[28] Hart, The Concept of Law, p. 196 et seq.
[29] Hart, The Concept of Law, p. 197 et seq.
[30] Eckmann, p. 49.
[31] The assumption that men wish to survive because this is their predestined goal, Hart is expressly discarding as too metaphysical: Hart, The Concept of Law, p. 192; Eckmann, p. 49.

Hart thus *explains* the existence of the relevant rules, he *does not justify* them. Moreover, Hart's explanations do not contain any assessment of the rightness and binding nature of the law in the sense of the traditional doctrine of Natural Law.[32] According to Hart's criteria, it is not at all necessary that a legal system, to be law, must protect the lives of all men or even of most of them.[33] Only if the rules failed to provide the benefit of protection to anybody – even to a small group of slave-owners – would we no longer be dealing with law but with a number of meaningless taboos.[34] Moreover, the minimum content of law postulated by Hart is by no means conclusive and immutable forever. If, for example, men became invulnerable from attack by each other or could extract the food they needed from the air by some internal chemical process, rules forbidding the free use of violence or constituting the minimum form of property would obviously become superfluous.[35] It follows from the above that to refer to Hart's "minimum content" theory as natural law theory could be misleading, to say the least.[36]

What, then, is Hart's vision of the structure of the positive law? According to Hart, the law consists of general rules: in fact he discriminates between two fundamentally different types of rules, which he calls the primary rules and the secondary rules.[37] Primary rules *create duties*, and do so independently of the will of the person thereby obligated.[38] The social function they perform is that of motivating a certain conduct on the part of those to whom they apply by attaching a sanction to violations of the legal obligation. Prototypes for primary rules are the rules of the criminal law.[39] By secondary rules, on the other hand, Hart means rules that *confer power*.[40] Secondary rules which confer *private* powers provide facilities for individuals to mould their legal relations at their own discretion by concluding legal transactions; some of them state the min-

---

[32] Eckmann, p. 48.
[33] Eckmann, p. 46.
[34] Hart, Positivism and the Separation of Law and Morals, p.81/82.
[35] Hart, Positivism and the Separation of Law and Morals, p. 80.
[36] Eckmann, p. 48/49/50.
[37] Hart, The Concept of Law, p. 79 et seqq.
[38] Hart, The Concept of Law, p. 81 and 283.
[39] Hart, The Concept of Law, p. 27.
[40] Hart, The Concept of Law, p. 81.

imum personal qualification for exercising such powers (such as being adult or sane); others lay down the manners and forms in which the power is to be exercised.[41] The rules conferring *public* power define the contents and scope of the three functions of the state (legislation, adjudication and administration); for example, by determining the necessary qualifications of the organs of the state and the procedure for these state functions. Such secondary rules are remedies for three defects which a legal system consisting only of primary rules would prove to have: the first defect of a regime of primary rules would consist in the *static* character of its rules. Special secondary rules which Hart calls *"rules of change"* remedy this matter.[42] The simplest form of such a rule is that which empowers an individual or body of persons to introduce new primary rules for the conduct of the life of persons, and to eliminate old rules. The second defect of a regime of primary rules would be the *inefficiency* of the diffuse social pressure with which the rules would be equipped.[43] To eliminate this defect, so-called *rules of adjudication* must be introduced which, on the one hand, will empower individuals to authoritatively determine whether a primary rule has been broken, and which, on the other hand, will define the procedure that has to be followed in doing so.[44] Therefore, as stressed by Eckmann, the rules of change and of adjudication are, for the most part, obviously identical with those secondary rules that confer public power and that refer to the state functions of legislation and adjudication.[45]

A regime of primary rules would, however, suffer from a third defect, viz. that of *uncertainty*.[46] It is uncertain according to which criteria a certain rule could be allocated to a given system. The remedy for this defect is the *rule of recognition*.[47] The rule of recognition will specify the features a rule must possess to be classified as forming part of the system and, as a consequence, to be supported by the social pressure that is

---

[41] Hart, The Concept of Law, p. 28.
[42] Hart, The Concept of Law, p. 95.
[43] Hart, The Concept of Law, p. 93.
[44] Hart, The Concept of Law, p. 96 et seq.
[45] Eckmann, p. 87.
[46] Hart, The Concept of Law, p. 92.
[47] Hart, The Concept of Law, p. 94.

characteristic of such system. The rule of recognition, therefore, contains *the identification and validity criteria* of the legal system and is the most important secondary rule. There is, according to Hart, a very intimate connection between the rule of recognition and the fundamental rules of change and of adjudication; a connection in this sense that the rule of recognition is already included in the rules of change and of adjudication. If, for example, the fundamental rule of change in Switzerland states that the people and the states are appointed to exercise constitutional power,[48] then it implicitly contains the rule of recognition that what the people and the states decide must be recognized as law.[49] The criterion for the legal validity of the constitutional legislation as contained in the rule of recognition is basically just the other side of the rule of change which confers the basic power of constitutional legislation upon the people and the states.[50] The same applies to the rules of adjudication: if a rule of adjudication empowers a court to decide authoritatively on the breach of a primary rule, it is implicitly empowered to decide on the validity of such a primary rule, too. Therefore, according to Hart, a rule of recognition exists which says that the rules expressed in a judicial decision are to be recognized as valid law.[51] As a consequence, judicial decisions are recognized as sources of law. In a modern legal system, the rule of recognition commonly includes several criteria for identifying the law: in particular, it may provide for a written constitution, legislative enactments, judicial precedents and custom.[52]

---

[48]   Art. 140 para. 1 lit. a and Art. 142 para. 2 of the Federal Constitution of the Swiss Confederation in force since 1 January 2000.

[49]   For a general outline of this relationship, see Hart, The Concept of Law, p. 96 et seq.

[50]   Eckmann, p. 91/92.

[51]   Hart, The Concept of Law, p. 97: "… if courts are empowered to make authoritative determinations of the fact that a rule has been broken, these cannot avoid being taken as authoritative determinations of what the rules are. So the rule which confers jurisdiction will also be a rule of recognition, identifying the primary rules through the judgments of the courts and these judgments will become a 'source' of law."

[52]   Hart, The Concept of Law, p. 101: "In a modern legal system where there are a variety of 'sources' of law, the rule of recognition is correspondingly more complex: the criteria for identifying the law are multiple and commonly include a written constitution, enactment by legislature, and judicial precedents." Hart mentions customary rules as a source of law on p. 95; for Hart's theory of the hierarchy of the different criteria see The Concept of Law, p. 106.

In the original version of his theory, Hart furthermore acknowledges that a legal system *may impose substantial limitations on the legislative body by incorporating moral principles in the constitution.* As an example, he cites the Fifth Amendment of the Constitution of the United States. "This provides, among other things, that no person shall be deprived 'of life, liberty, or property, without due process of law'; and statutes of Congress have been declared invalid by the courts when found to conflict with these or with other restrictions *placed by the constitution on their legislative powers.*"[53]

Hart characterizes himself as a *soft positivist*[54] since, as just explained, "… the ultimate criteria of law might explicitly incorporate … *principles of justice* or *substantive moral values,* and these may form the content of legal constitutional restraints.*"[55] In the postscript, he does, however, revoke the thesis that moral principles "may be among the criteria of legal validity, since if it is an open question whether moral principles and values have objective standing, *it must also be an open question whether 'soft positivism' provisions purporting to include conformity with them among the tests for existing law can have that effect …*"[56] This revocation is explained by Hart's intention to create a theory independent of philosophical controversies. And the question of whether moral judgments have objective standing belongs to the realm of philosophical dispute.[57]

But this problem only arises when the criterion is *content based.* One such example would be if a constitution included, alongside the usual criteria for legal validity, the stipulation: a rule is also invalid if it offends "against common decency". Here there would be philosophical controversies about when this is the case. – But as soon as the moral criterion is *source based,* as for example in the amendments to the US Constitution, and Hart expressly invokes such examples, this philosophical problem is no longer raised. The fundamental basic rights are already listed

---

[53] Hart, The Concept of Law, p. 72 (our emphasis).
[54] Hart, The Concept of Law, p. 250.
[55] Hart, The Concept of Law, p. 247.
[56] Hart, The Concept of Law, p. 254.
[57] Hart, The Concept of Law, p. 253 et seq.

in the amendments, after all. What remains is the problem of the *inter-pretation* of these basic rights, but no theory can avoid this problem. Hart, then, could have stayed with his original thesis of *soft positivism.*

The rule of recognition sets out the ultimate validity criteria for all the rules of a system. Since Hart, when speaking of the "validity" of a rule, always refers exclusively to an internal validity,[58] i.e. the validity of a rule within a given system, the question as to the validity of the very rule of recognition can no longer be raised. The rule of recognition is neither valid nor invalid,[59] because the validity of the rule of recognition as the ultimate rule of the system can no longer be assessed with reference to a superior rule.

But what exactly, then, makes for the specific existence of the rule of recognition in Hart's system? The rule of recognition exists – so Hart explains – *"only as a complex, but normally concordant, practice of the courts, officials, and private persons in identifying the law by reference to certain criteria. Its existence is a matter of fact."*[60] The existence of the rule of recognition has, according to this proposition, its roots *in an external behavior of certain members of the society, viz. in the actual application of the rule of recognition by them.*[61] Thus Hart's theory seems to boil down to a variant of *sociological* positivism. However, such a characterization would be too one-sided. For apart from this external aspect, i.e. the sociological fact of the application of the rule by certain members of the society, Hart emphasizes the *"internal aspect"*:[62] this consists in the *psychological fact* that the secondary rule in question is *accepted by the officials.* Thus, it is not necessary that the majority of the citizens acknowledge the rule of recognition (even though this will in-

---

[58] Hart, The Concept of Law, p. 107/108.
[59] Hart, The Concept of Law, p. 109.
[60] Hart, The Concept of Law, p. 110.
[61] In this sense Eckmann, p. 95.
[62] Hart, The Concept of Law, p. 56. Hart expressly speaks of "internal aspect" and "external aspect only when discussing the so-called system-independent primary rules (e.g. "rules of etiquette"). The internal aspect of a social rule consists of its acceptance as a public standard; the external aspect is constituted by a concordant external behavior of a social group. However, Hart's theory of the rule of recognition is, as has been shown by Eckmann, p. 93 et seqq., also based on this scheme.

deed be the case most of the time, viz. when the citizens acquiesce in the official legislation and judicial and administrative decisions[63]); but a legal system exists as soon as the officials accept the fundamental rule of recognition and the criteria included therein.[64] Hart does not distinguish sharply between acceptance and application of the fundamental rule of recognition.[65] Rather, the two are linked in that its acceptance is betokened by its application. The legislators acknowledge the fundamental rules of change (and with them implicitly the corresponding criterion provided for by the rule of recognition) when they make law in accordance with these rules; the courts acknowledge them when they identify rules thus made as law to be applied by them; and experts do the same when they guide the ordinary citizens by making reference to the said law.[66] An acceptance of the legal system on the part of the *ordinary* citizens is not necessary. For the existence of a legal system, it is *sufficient if they by and large obey the rules.*

For the legal system of Switzerland, the rule of recognition may be framed as follows:

- What the People and Cantons of Switzerland decide, is constitutional law (Art. 140 para. 1 lit.a and Art. 142 para 2 and 3 of the Constitution of the Swiss Confederation of 18 April 1999).

- What the legislative power (Parliament or the majority of those who vote in case of a *referendum)* decide, is law (concerning the competences of the Parliament:Art. 148, 163, 164, 165, 166 para 2, 172 para 2, 173 para 1 lit. c : concerning the competences of the People: Art. 140 para 2 lit. a–c, 141 para 1 lit. a–d, 142 para 1).

- Decisions of the Swiss courts which have obtained legal force are law (Art.197b para 1). The doctrine that judicial holdings of the Federal Supreme Court of Switzerland (Art 189 and Art. 190 of the Federal Constitution of the Swiss Confederation) have binding precedential value, known to Common Law systems as *stare decisis*, is not valid in Switzerland.

---

[63] Hart, The Concept of Law, p. 61.
[64] Hart, The Concept of Law, p. 117.
[65] Eckmann, p. 96.
[66] Hart, The Concept of Law, p. 61.

- What is in accordance with a settled, sustained practice based on the opinion on matters of right and justice (*opinio necessitatis*), is law (Art. 1 para. 2 of the Swiss Civil Code).

Although Hart refuses to give a definition *per genus proximum* and *differentiam specificam*,[67] he writes in *The Concept of Law*: "There are therefore two minimum conditions necessary and sufficient for the existence of a legal system. On the one hand, those rules of behavior which are valid according to the system's ultimate criteria of validity must be generally obeyed, and, on the other hand, its rules of recognition specifying the criteria of legal validity and its rules of change and adjudication must be effectively accepted as common public standards of official behaviour by its officials."[68]

With minor change and rearrangement of the words, as we shall see forthwith, this may be read as a definition of the positive law: the positive law in terms of Hart is *a system of primary and secondary rules*[69] whose most important secondary rule, *the rule of recognition* containing the identification and validity criteria of the system (commonly including a written constitution, enactment by legislature, judicial precedents[70] and long customary practice[71]), must be accepted and applied by the officials, whilst for the ordinary citizens, it is sufficient to by and large obey the primary rules.[72]

---

[67] Hart, The Concept of Law, pp. 15–17, particularly p. 15 and 17. The main reason why Hart does not want to give such a definition is that according to Hart, no wider family of things or genus of law may be found. (Concept of Law, p. 15). It is, however, obvious, that Hart, after clarifying the concept of rule, (p. 55–57 and ch. V: Law as a Union of Primary and Secondary Rules) has found of which genus law is a member: viz. "rules". The rules of morals, religious rules, table manners, social etiquette may be quoted as examples for other rules.

[68] Hart, The Concept of Law, p. 116.

[69] Hart does not intend in his use of the word "rule" to restrict the content of a legal system to "all-or-nothing" rules. Cf. Hart, The Concept of Law, p. 263.

[70] Hart, The Concept of Law, p. 101.

[71] Hart, The Concept of Law, p. 95.

[72] Cf. Hart, The Concept of Law, p. 60. Although Hart acknowledges that there are secondary rules conferring power to private persons (The Concept of Law, p. 28), it is probably sufficient for a legal system to exist that the citizens comply with the primary rules.

Therefore, Hart's theory is to be qualified as psychological-sociological positivism. Eckmann rightly calls it a "legal theory of acceptance and obedience".[73] Furthermore, Hart agrees with German statutory positivism and Kelsen's pure theory of law in that he uses, as shown above, a normative concept of legal validity and that his theory is analytical. Modifications of Hart's theory can be found in work of his disciple Joseph Raz.[74]

---

[73] Eckmann, p. 97.
[74] Raz, Concept, ch. VI-IX ; *idem*, AL; below, § 12 A and § 24 H at n. 168.

§ 12 Exclusive – Inclusive Positivism[1]

The basis for the positivisms to be delineated in this paragraph – Sebok calls them *New Positivism*[2] – was provided by H.L.A. Hart in 1958 with his famous essay "Positivism and the Separation of Law and Morals"[3] and in 1961 with his book *The Concept of Law*. As we have seen in paragraph § 11 , Hart supported the thesis that the rule of recognition of a modern legal system may, apart from the traditional criteria (legislative acts, case law, customs), incorporate *moral* requirements – such as, for example, those contained in the Amendments to the American Constitution – in terms of which legal validity is to be tested. In the postscript to the second edition of The Concept of Law, Hart called this – his own view – *soft positivism*.[4]

The next step was taken by Ronald Dworkin who launched a "general attack on positivism",[5] which centered on theses of his teacher H.L.A. Hart, by publishing his essay *The Model of Rules I*[6] (1967) and, in particular, his book *Taking Rights Seriously* (1978).[7] Although Dworkin is an anti-positivist, his contributions exerted a significant influence on the development of New Legal Positivism. Dworkin argued that in hard cases judges are obligated to turn to *principles* (as opposed to rules).[8] Such principles cannot be identified by applying a positivist pedigree test

---

[1] For general overview, see Himma, K. E., Inclusive Legal Positivism, in: Jules Coleman and Scott Shapiro (eds.), Kenneth Himma (assoc. ed.), Oxford Handbook of Jurisprudence and Legal Philosophy, Oxford: Oxford University Press, 2002; hereinafter referred to as "Inclusive Legal Positivism"; Marmor A., Exclusive Legal Positivism, ididem, p. 104; Székessy, L.: Gerechtigkeit und inklusiver Rechtspositivismus, Münsterische Beiträge zur Rechtswissenschaft, Band 150, Berlin: Duncker & Humblot 2003.

[2] Sebok, p. 268.

[3] Harvard Law Review 71 (1958), p. 593 et seqq., reprinted in: Essays in Jurisprudence and Philosophy, p. 49 et seqq., particularly p. 54 et seq.

[4] Hart, Concept of Law, p. 250.

[5] Dworkin, Taking Rights Seriously, p. 22. See below, § 22 D.

[6] The Model of Rules I, University of Chicago Law Review 14 (1967), p. 35 et seqq.

[7] For a detailed analysis of the Hart-Dworkin debate see Renée Watkins-Bienz, Die Hart-Dworkin Debatte, Schriften zur Rechtstheorie 220, Berlin: Duncker & Humblot, 2004.

[8] See below, § 22 D.

but the judge must engage in *moral* evaluations in order to find them. Furthermore, he advocated a kind of a *dogma of gaplessness*. According to him, there is a uniquely correct answer even in hard cases *(the right answer thesis)* though not based on rules but on principles. The judge does not have discretion. Consequently, the judge does not make the law in *hard cases* but he *discovers,* by means of principles, rights which the parties *already have*.

The third stage was characterized by the emergence of two doctrinal tendencies which both build on Hart and try to defend him against Dworkin's criticisms. One group abides by Hart's *conceptual* separation of law and morality but refers to Hart's confirmation that in some systems of law, the ultimate criteria of legal validity may explicitly incorporate moral criteria. This position became generally known as *inclusive legal positivism* (Lyons,[9] Soper,[10] Coleman I,[11] Waluchow,[12] and Sebok[13]). The other group defends Hart's *conceptual* separation of law and morality but denies that the rule of recognition can include moral principles in the standards that set out the conditions of legality.[14] These theories are generally summarized under the term *"exclusive positivism"*.

---

[9] David Lyons, Principles, Positivism and Legal Theory, Yale Law Journal 87 (1977), p. 415, 428.

[10] E. Philip Soper, Legal Theory and the Obligation of a Judge: The Hart/Dworkin Dispute, Michigan Law Review 75 (1977), p. 473 et seqq.

[11] J.L. Coleman I, p. 139 et seqq. Reprinted in Coleman, Markets, Morals and the Law, Cambridge: Cambridge University Press, 1988. Coleman has recently switched to exclusive positivism (quoted as Coleman II, cf. below § 15 D).

[12] W.J. Waluchow, Inclusive Legal Positivism, Oxford: Clarendon Press, 1994.

[13] A.J. Sebok, Legal Positivism in American Jurisprudence, Cambridge University Press, Cambridge 1998.

[14] Like this e.g. J. Raz, The Authority of Law, Reprint of 1979 edition, Oxford: Oxford University Press, 2002 (hereinafter AL); idem, Authority, Law, and Morality, in: Ethics in the Public Domain: Essays in the Morality of Law and Politics, Oxford: Clarendon Press, 1994 [hereinafter ALM]; Coleman II, p. 2 et seqq.; F. Schauer, Rules and the Rule of Law, Harvard Journal of Law and Public Policy 14 (1991), p. 645, 670 n. 49, S.J. Shapiro, On Hart's Way Out, in: Jules Coleman (Editor), Hart's Postscript: Essays on the Postscript to the Concept of Law, Oxford: Oxford University Press, 2005. A critical exploration of Raz's theory can be found in: M. Martin, Judging Positivism, Oxford: Hart Publishing, 2014.

A. Exclusive Positivism

Central to Raz's position is the *sources thesis*: "A jurisprudential theory is acceptable only if its tests for identifying the content of the law and determining its existence depend exclusively on facts of human behaviour capable of being described in value-neutral terms, and applied without resort to moral argument."[15] In other words, the norms to be tested must emanate from *legislation*, *judicial decisions* or *custom*.

There are three arguments which, combined, militate, according to Raz, in favor of the sources thesis. On the one hand, Raz believes, the thesis explains our conception of the law. The other arguments show that there are sound reasons for adhering to this conception:

I. Our Conception of the Law

Raz argues that there are two kinds of characteristics which we consider desirable in a judge: on the one hand, we highly esteem his knowledge of the law and his skills to interpret the law. However, we equally appreciate his wisdom and his comprehension of human nature, his moral sensibility etc. Whilst it is generally recognized that all these characteristics are important for a judge, usually only the first group is looked upon as establishing the *legal* skills of a judge. Likewise, we differentiate, when we assess a court decision as good or as bad, between *legally* acceptable and unacceptable arguments, and only then verify their *moral* tenability. Thus, the use of a *moral* judgment is seen not as a special case of applying the *law* or *legal* argumentation but as separate and complementary to them.

Furthermore, it corresponds to the common view that judges *apply* as well as *develop* the law. In doing the first, they apply their *legal* skills whereas in doing the second they use *moral* arguments. The sources thesis explains and systematizes this distinction. If a legal question is not answered by norms emanating from legal sources, the *law* is not settled in this point. A judge deciding such a case is necessarily breaking fresh

---

[15] Raz, AL, p. 39 et seq.

legal ground and his decision *creates new law*. Such decisions are, by nature, at least partially based upon *moral and other non-legal* considerations.[16]

II. The Argument from Function

However, the sources thesis equally brings out a basic insight regarding the function of the law. It is commonplace that social life requires cooperation, coordination and forbearance. Different members may be of different opinions as to which schemes of cooperation, coordination and forbearance are appropriate: "It is an *essential* part of the function of law in society to mark the point at which a *private* view of members of the society [...] *ceases to be* their private view and becomes [...] a view binding on all members *notwithstanding their disagreement* with it. It does so and can only do so by providing publicly ascertainable ways of guiding behaviour and regulating aspects of social life."[17]

III. The Authority Argument

Raz tries to develop his own *conception of authority*.[18] This conception can best be explained if we start with an example:

Until 1967, traffic in Sweden drove on the left side of the road. In order to decide whether to change to driving on the right, the legislator first had to weigh up the "first order reasons" (balancing of reasons). An argument in favor of the changeover was that traffic drove on the right in the neighboring countries of Norway, Finland and Denmark. A counter argument was the increased number of accidents until such time as Swedish drivers had become accustomed to driving on the right. Also taken into the balance were the considerable infrastructure costs of adjustment and the information material for the population. The authority of the Swedish legislator was legitimate:

---

[16] Raz, AL, p. 48 et seqq. (our emphasis).
[17] Raz, AL, p. 51.
[18] Raz, ALM, p. 198 et seqq.

(1) because it had a better overview of the international environment, the psychological preconditions of Swedish motorists, and the expected costs; and

(2) because the individual driver drives better if he follows the decision of the legislator than if he had relied upon his own assessment. Or expressed abstractly:

First, the decision of the legislator is a reason for action for the drivers. This reason for action should in principle be the result of the consideration of the reasons already applicable to the problem. Raz calls these reasons "first order" or "dependent" reasons (from our assessment).[19] Second, the decision of the legislator is meant to *replace* the reasons already applicable to the problem (= preemptive reason).[20]

That is to say, the reasons which one might have been able to call upon in order to justify an action before the decision was passed can no longer be relied on after it has been given.

This leads to the following conclusion: *the only decisive reason for a person to have authority over another is that one sees the decision as a reason for action which replaces those reasons for action on the basis of which the decision has been made.*

As a consequence, Raz builds the *normal justification thesis*: "The normal and primary way to establish that a person should be acknowledged to have authority over another person involves showing that the alleged subject is *likely better to comply with reasons which apply to him* (other than the alleged authoritative directives) *if he accepts the directives of the alleged authority as authoritatively binding*, and tries to follow them, than if he tries to follow the reasons which apply to him directly."[21]

With this, the core of Raz's *concept of legitimacy* has been ascertained: only if the authority is likely to better conform to the dependent reasons is the authority's claim to legitimacy justified.[22]

---

[19] Raz, ALM, p. 196.
[20] Raz, ALM, p. 196.
[21] Raz, ALM, p. 198.
[22] Raz, ALM, p. 198 et seq.

In order that something can be authoritatively binding, it must be endowed with the following characteristics:

First, a directive which *does not* mirror the judgment *of an alleged authority* or *is at least presented as such* fails *not* because it is *wrong* but because it is *not a directive of the right kind*, e.g. because it was issued for a different occasion or was the threat of a gangster who is only concerned with himself.[23]

Second, it must be possible to identify the order as emanating from the authority *without having to resort to the reasons which the order purports to decide*. This would, for example, not be the case if *the drivers* were merely told that the *legislator* had passed the uniquely correct law. The *drivers* could only make out its content by means of recourse to the reasons which led to the decision (dependent reasons). However, if they were able to do so, they would not have needed *a law of the legislator* to begin with.

Decisive for the derivation of the *sources thesis from the authority* argument is that *legal sources meet both conditions*: laws (legislator), decisions (judge) and customary law (the bulk of the population) all represent somebody's opinion as to how the subjects have to behave. Likewise, *legal sources can be identified without recourse to the reasons they are meant to decide*.[24]

B. Inclusive Positivism

Inclusive positivists start out from what they see as the obvious fact that there are legal systems which include moral principles as ultimate validity criteria (e.g. the Amendments to the US Constitution or the Canadian Charter of Rights and Freedoms).[25]

Likewise, they believe that the inclusive approach allows for acknowledging the potential role of moral deliberations in defining what the law

---

[23] Raz, ALM, p. 203.
[24] Raz, ALM, p. 205.
[25] Waluchow, p. 4.

is without denying that the criteria of the law must feature adequate institutional relations: "Unlike traditional natural-law theory which denies the necessity of such connections, inclusive positivism places them front and centre by insisting that moral reasons are sometimes relevant *but only to the extent that the legal system recognizes them as such.*"[26]

Thus, inclusive positivism is based on the following theses:

I. Social Fact Thesis

All variants of positivism subscribe to the social fact thesis but in doing so take different social facts as a basis. This corresponds to the result set out below that all variants of positivism define the law by way of empirical criteria, albeit by drawing on different facts.[27] According to Austin, such a social fact consists in the presence of a sovereign who is willing and capable to impose sanctions in case of failure to comply with his rules.[28]

Hart rejected Austin's version of the social fact thesis mainly for one reason: it overlooks the existence of meta-rules which are concerned with the existence of primary rules.[29] According to Hart, it is the presence of a binding rule of recognition, not of a sovereign, that is accountable for the existence of a binding legal system. In order for a binding rule of recognition to exist, two conditions must be met:

First: the validity criteria provided for by the rule of recognition must be recognized and applied by the officials of the state S as a standard for their official conduct.

---

[26] Waluchow, p. 141 (our emphasis).
[27] See below, § 15 B and § 15 C. We would like to point out that *isolated social facts* can only be so-called *"brute" facts.* Only once one asks for *the meaning* of these facts do they become *"institutional" facts* (§ 13 at n. 15). With respect to the rule of recognition, one has to consult the constitution of the country in question. Only *this reveals the meaning* of the social facts.
[28] See above, § 2.
[29] Himma, Inclusive Legal Positivism, p. 126.

Second: the ordinary citizens of S usually comply with the primary rules validated by the rule of recognition.[30] However, in our opinion, the citizens must by and large *also comply with the rules conferring private power* (which are part of the secondary rules), *for if people never made their last wills or contracts in compliance with the formal regulations,* for example, then such formal regulations would be mere paper rules.[31]

As has been shown above,[32] the rule of recognition of a modern legal system commonly contains several validity criteria: in particular, it may provide for legislative, judicial and customary law-making.[33]

The proponents of exclusive positivism content themselves with these formal criteria (sources thesis). The proponents of inclusive positivism, however, consider such a rule of recognition too narrow, since they want the rule of recognition to include moral principles, which may not always be attributed to a formal source, too.[34] However, it must not be forgotten that the proponents of inclusive positivism are bound to include formal criteria in the rule of recognition as well, for a rule of recognition according to which "all and only moral rules are legally valid" would not provide a mechanism to change the law on the basis of rules of change in Hart's terms.[35]

II. The Conventionality Thesis

This thesis supplements the social fact thesis by a more in-depth explanation of the authority of the validity criteria: according to the conventionality thesis, the validity criteria constitute the content of a *social convention amongst the persons which hold an official function,*[36] the

---

[30] Himma, Inclusive Legal Positivism, p. 127.
[31] See below, § 24 G, text at n. 120 et seqq.
[32] See above, § 11 towards the end.
[33] Hart, The Concept of Law, p. 95; cf. above, § 11.
[34] Most of the time moral principles may be identified by means of pedigree as well, e.g. the Amendments to the US Constitution or a reference of the positive law to morality such as Art. 20 para. 1 of the Swiss Code of Obligations which provides for the nullity of contracts that violate common decency.
[35] Himma, Inclusive Legal Positivism, p. 129, with reference to Hart, The Concept of Law, p. 92 et seq.
[36] Himma, Inclusive Legal Positivism, p. 129.

existence of a *convention thereby being dependent on conformity of conduct as well as attitude* (belief that non-conforming behavior is a legitimate ground for criticism).[37] All positivists who base their theories on Hart's theory as well as the proponents of the *theories of recognition*[38] agree that the validity criteria are authoritative in virtue of a convention.

III. The Separability Thesis

As we have seen,[39] all positivists draw a *conceptual distinction* between the law as it is and *the law as it ought to be*, or, in short, they separate between law and morality. An example of this would be if a lawyer said "This tax law is unjust and should therefore be changed". By this simple sentence, the jurist has completed the conceptual separation of law and morality since he has distinguished between the tax law (the positive law) and justice (which forms part of morality). In contrast, Hart has equally emphasized the *empirical relation* between law and morality. As we have seen, he refers to Bentham and Austin: both would never have denied that *moral convictions have exerted a strong influence on the development of legal systems* and, conversely, *that the law has significantly shaped morality*.[40]

Thus, the question arises of whether the proponents of inclusive positivism, who call for the inclusion of moral principles in the rule of recognition, limit the separability thesis or even reject it. The answer is no: for the rule of recognition is dependent on a particular legal system. For each system, it is different. If a legal system contains moral principles, so will its rule of recognition. If this is not the case, the rule of recognition will not incorporate moral validity criteria, either. Even regarding legal systems which contain moral criteria in the manner described above, inclusive positivism remains a descriptive theory. For: "A description may still be a description, even when what is described is an evaluation."[41]

---

[37] Himma, Inclusive Legal Positivism, p. 130.
[38] Above, § 5.
[39] Cf. beginning of § 2 above, § 3 text at notes 9–13, § 4 text at notes 19–20, § 11 text at notes 6–35 and below, § 15 B.II.
[40] Below, § 11 at n. 6; Hart, Positivism and the Separation of Law and Morals, p. 54.
[41] Hart, The Concept of Law, p. 244.

Let us look at a legal system like that of the National Socialist state. In addition to formal sources, it also contained ideological principles, such as the *Führer* principle, the racial theory, the sound popular feeling ("*gesundes Volksempfinden*") and the party program of the NSDAP, as principles of the positive law. These principles of the Nazi system were surely condemnable, which is why one should contrast them with the principles of a "critical morality". If one does so, one will accept once again the conceptual separation of Nazi law, including its principles and critical morality, i.e. again, one separates law from morality.

IV. The Incorporation Thesis

One can only infer from the separability thesis that the rule of recognition *does not necessarily* contain moral criteria, but not that it cannot contain moral criteria.[42] This latter claim – viz. that the rule of recognition *can* contain moral criteria – is made by the incorporation thesis, which may be regarded as the core of inclusive or soft positivism.

The validity of a norm can depend on the moral merit of its content in two ways corresponding to the two components of the incorporation thesis.

a) According to the *sufficiency component* which was first developed in response to Dworkin's analysis of Riggs v. Palmer[43] there are conceptually possible legal systems in which it is a sufficient condition for a rule to be valid that it reproduces a moral principle. This version was represented by Coleman I.[44] Thus, an *unpromulgated* norm can be legally valid in virtue of its moral content only.

b) According to the *necessity component* which was first articulated by Hart in his debate with Lon Fuller,[45] a rule must, in order to be valid, not only have an appropriate social source, but necessarily also comply with the requirements of some *set of* moral principles,[46] for Hart

---

[42] Coleman I, Negative and Positive Positivism, p. 141 et seq.
[43] The foremost issue addressed was whether a murderer could be his victim's heir.
[44] Coleman, Negative and Positive Positivism, p. 163.
[45] Cf. Hart, Lon L. Fuller: *The Morality of Law,* reprinted in: Essays in Jurisprudence and Philosophy, p. 361; cf. also Hart, The Concept of Law, p. 250.
[46] Himma, Inclusive Legal Positivism, p. 136 et seq.

has said that the constitution may impose legal constraints of moral content on the legislator (e.g. the amendments of the US-Constitution). It follows from this that no rule of American law may be contradictory to these amendments.

Even though the opponents of inclusive positivism reject the incorporation thesis, they do not deny that legal systems often contain validity criteria which are described using "moral language". They argue, however, that this does not amount to validity being dependent on moral criteria, but that such provisions only direct judges to engage in moral evaluations under certain circumstances.[47]

---

[47] Himma, Inclusive Legal Positivism, p. 140.

§ 13 Neil MacCormick's and Ota Weinberger's Institutional Theory of Law[1]

The institutional theory of law is a legal theory which has been developed by Neil MacCormick (Edinburgh) and Ota Weinberger (Graz) in mutual independence approximately at the same time. Neil MacCormick presented the first program of institutional positivism in his inaugural lecture "Law as Institutional Fact"[2] in 1973, and Weinberger had published essentially the same thoughts in his essay *"Die Norm als Gedanke und Realität"*[3] in 1970.

The 'institutional theory of law' (or ITL for short) is based on the following general premises:

1. For the purpose of practical philosophy, one should start out from an 'epistemologically differentiated semantics', i.e. purely descriptive sentences (theoretical sentences) are fundamentally different from practical sentences (e.g. normative sentences).[4]

2. From this categorical dichotomy between descriptive and practical sentences follow the two *postulates of non-derivability*:

   a) No normative sentence can be deduced from a class of purely declarative sentences.[5]

---

[1] Literature: MacCormick N./Weinberger O., An Institutional Theory of Law – New Approaches to Legal Positivism, Dordrecht/Boston/Lancaster/Tokyo: Reidel, 1986 [ITL]. This collection of essays is, dependent on the author, quoted as MacCormick, ITL, or Weinberger, ITL. German Version: MacCormick N./Weinberger O., Grundlagen des Institutionalistischen Rechtspositivismus, Berlin: Duncker & Humblot, 1985 [IRP]; Weinberger O., Recht, Institution und Rechtspolitik. Grundprobleme der Rechtstheorie und Sozialphilosophie, Stuttgart: Franz Steiner, 1987; idem, Revue Internationale de Philosophie 35 (1981), p. 487 et seqq.; idem, in: W. Krawietz/R. Alexy (Editors), Metatheorie juristischer Argumentation, Berlin: Duncker & Humblot, 1983, p. 159 et seqq., particularly p. 214 et seqq.; idem, Norm und Institution. Eine Einführung in die Theorie des Rechts, Vienna: Manz, 1988.

[2] Inaugural Lectures No. 52, University of Edinburgh 1973, reprinted in: ITL, p. 49 et seqq.

[3] ÖzöR 20 (1970) 203 et seqq., published in English in 1986, "The Norm as Thought and as Reality", in: ITL, p. 31 et seqq.

[4] Weinberger, ITL, p. 35 and 154/155.

[5] Weinberger, ITL, p. 155.

b) No declarative conclusion can be deduced from premises containing only normative sentences.[6]

These two postulates of non-derivability do not constitute logical
principles the rightness of which can be proved, but they are *me-
ta-logical* postulates with which every norm-logic system must comply.[7]

3. In addition to the two postulates of non-deducibility, the thesis of
non-cognitivism applies: it is impossible "to justify informative practical sentences in any purely cognitive way, that is, without recourse
to arguments of the sort which include some adoption of a particular
attitude."[8] There is no such thing as practical cognition, i.e. there is
no possibility to identify fair law, particularly natural law, in a purely
objective way.[9] Nevertheless, rational arguments about values based
on non-cognitivism are possible: viz. (a) by goal-means analysis and
analysis of the consequences of our actions and (b) by evaluation of
the inner consequences of our value-judgments.[10] Thus, the possibility of rational *de lege ferenda* reasoning is recognized in this restricted sense.

4. The law is always a sociological fact, i.e. it is rooted in human will
and not in speculative principles of reason or in a sphere of absolute
values.[11]

5. The law is a normative system which must be distinguished from
positive morality and which only brings into play norms of social
morality where explicit reference to them is made.[12] In colloquial
language, the term "law" is, for good reasons, not used in a value-free
manner because ordinary legal systems are claiming that their commands and interdictions are socially justified. The legal theorist,
however, should "work with a neutral concept of law (of the legal
order) and not regard 'unjust law', 'immoral law and the like as *con-*

---

6   Weinberger, ITL, p. 155.
7   Weinberger, IRP, p. 21.
8   Weinberger, ITL, p. 155.
9   Weinberger, ITL, p. 116 et seq.
10 Weinberger, IRP, p. 46; *idem,* ITL p. 156.
11 Weinberger, IRP, p. 41.
12 Weinberger, IRP, p. 50.

tradictio in adjecto …, for this is a necessary prerequisite for being able to portray the institutionally existing reality in every case."[13]

The ITL aims to be an ontology of law which will answer adequately the following questions:

How can a legal "Ought" be ascribed to have a real existence even though the "Ought" is fundamentally (i.e. in the sense of the aforementioned postulates 1 and 2) different from the "Is"?[14]

The answer, which takes up Searle's distinction between *brute* facts and *institutional* facts,[15] is this:

In the human world, there are some facts like states, religions, games, cultures and legal systems for which the means we have at our disposal to adequately represent brute facts (e.g. stones, lakes, planets) are insufficient. To portray such institutional facts it is necessary to have recourse to *practical* concepts,[16] in particular the concepts of *action* and *of practical sentences*. The basic ontological thesis is, therefore:

There is an intrinsic relationship between "institutional facts on the one hand and practical sentences (norm systems, systems of ends and value systems) on the other hand. Institutions are functionally connected with systems of practical sentences that really exist (especially normative regulations); institutional facts and their observable sequences of action can only be understood under the condition that they are interpreted in the context of normative rules which means in the end that they are understood in the context of actions."[17] The moves of chess players, for example, cannot be understood if they are interpreted as mere regularities in behavior, but only if the rules of chess are known. The same holds true for socially relevant acts of persons: they cannot be understood unless the applicable normative rules of the law and morality are known.

---

[13] Weinberger, IRP, p. 48.
[14] Weinberger, Revue Internationale de Philosophie 35 (1981), p. 501.
[15] Speech Acts – An Essay in the Philosophy of Language, Cambridge: Cambridge University Press 1969, p. 50 et seqq.
[16] Weinberger, ITL, p. 82.
[17] Weinberger, Rechtspolitik, p. 149 et seq.

In summary, Weinberger emphasizes:

Institutions are frameworks for human behavior. They have a core of practical information. They consist of a classified system of practical information which is interrelated with psychological and sociological facts. In this sense, they are always of a complex nature.[18]

Taking this as a basis, one can draw two distinctions:

On the one hand, one can distinguish between normative and social institutions.[19] Amongst the normative institutions are legal institutions such as property, marriage, the last will, legal succession, corporate bodies, legal personality etc. Institutions such as hospitals, universities, games, the banking industry or the market belong to the class of social institutions. The distinction between these two classes is, sure enough, not absolutely clear-cut. "Marriage is a legal institution; it is, however, also a social entity – a social institution – including persons, role relationships and artefacts."[20] Reciprocally, games such as football or chess are not only social institutions but also normative institutions, viz. systems of rules. The distinction only indicates whether more emphasis is placed on the normative part or on the social part.

On the other hand, one must, according to MacCormick, distinguish between institutions (e.g. marriage or contract) and *individual instances* of them (concrete marriages or contracts).[21] With regard to legal institutions, we will find three kinds of rules:[22]

1. *Institutive* rules which lay down on the occurrence of which acts or events a specific instance of the institution comes into existence (e.g. the rules about getting married).

2. *Consequential* rules determining the consequences of the existence of an instance of an institution (e.g. the rules concerning effects of marriage).

---

[18] Weinberger, Rechtspolitik, p. 33.
[19] Weinberger, Rechtspolitik, p. 34/154.
[20] Weinberger, Rechtspolitik, p. 33.
[21] MacCormick, ITL, p. 53 et seq.
[22] MacCormick, ITL, p. 52 et seq.

3. *Terminative* rules providing for the circumstances under which an instance of an institution is terminated (e.g. the divorce law).

The law itself also numbers among the institutional facts.[23] A norm is, on the one hand, an ideal entity (a thought in the objective sense) which is normally given linguistic expression.[24] It is not a platonic idea but simply the meaning of a string of linguistic characters.[25] As an ideal entity, it is subject to linguistic analysis and stands in logical relations.[26] The norm in this sense must not be confused with psychological facts. If, for example, passengers get on a bus and pay the fare, it is fairly certain that many of them do not know that they have made a contract with the bus corporation. But this lack of knowledge is completely immaterial to the proposition that there exist as many contracts as passengers.[27] Understood like this, the concept of 'rules of law' is an *institutional* concept in the *philosophical* sense.[28]

On the other hand, however, the norm has a real existence, too. This existence is conveyed by two factors:

First, a norm exists in the realm of human consciousness: "There is something like an experience of obligatoriness, the consciousness that something ought to be the case."[29] Apart from that, there is knowledge of obligatoriness, the knowledge that a group is bound by something, although the holder of such knowledge need not necessarily accept that norm.[30] Thus, norms function as behavior determinants in humans.

Secondly, the real existence of a norm is closely related to the existence of social institutions like government offices, courts, legislative bodies etc.[31] "The law is, *in a sociological sense, institutional* in that it is in various ways made, sustained, enforced and elaborated by an interacting

---

[23] MacCormick, ITL, p. 49 et seqq.
[24] The norms of customary law need not be expressed linguistically, but one always *can* express them linguistically.
[25] Weinberger, IRP, p. 16.
[26] Weinberger, Revue Internationale de Philosophie 35 (1981), p. 502.
[27] MacCormick, ITL, p. 50.
[28] MacCormick, ITL, p. 57.
[29] Weinberger, ITL, p. 40.
[30] Weinberger, ITL, p. 40.
[31] Weinberger, ITL, p. 41.

set of social institutions."[32] The work of the apparatus of state consists partially of processes which are perceptible by senses, which are observable.

From this dual nature of the norm, it follows that, according to the ITL, cognition of the law means understanding of the normative meaning-content as well as cognition of the corresponding social effects. Legal norms as such cannot be observed, but can only be conceived comprehensively as meaningful thought-objects.[33] This results in the necessity of developing an *analytical hermeneutics* in terms of ITL;[34] however, so far hardly any contributions have been made towards resolving this problem.[35] The only thing that is clear so far is that interpretation must be recognized as a necessary element of *communication in pragmatic languages* and that hermeneutics has to be regarded as a systematic development of "natural interpretation".[36]

From the twofold nature of the law, it further ensues that ITL is taking a position *beyond normativism and realism*.[37] It corresponds with normativism (particularly Kelsen) in regarding the law primarily as meaning-contents which are statable in normative sentences, i.e. as a system of norms, and in Is and Ought and descriptive and practical sentences respectively, being fundamentally different semantic categories. However, ITL differs from normativism mainly in three points:

1. Kelsen's postulate of purity[38] is rejected.[39] Non-normative methods, as for example those of psychology and sociology, are admitted for the cognition of the law, too.

---

[32] MacCormick, ITL, p. 56.
[33] See Weinberger, in: Metatheorie juristischer Argumentation, p. 215.
[34] See Weinberger, in: Metatheorie juristischer Argumentation, p. 225 et seqq.
[35] Cf. H. Alwart, Recht und Handlung. Die Rechtsphilosophie in ihrer Entwicklung vom Naturrechtsdenken und vom Positivismus zu einer analytischen Hermeneutik des Rechts, Tübingen 1987, p. 86 et seqq. and 110 et seqq.
[36] Weinberger, Rechtspolitik, p. 105.
[37] Weinberger, IRP, p. 15.
[38] See above, § 4 at n. 4.
[39] MacCormick, ITL, p. 19 et seq.

2. The reason of validity of a particular norm of a legal system is not only a higher (conditioning) norm,[40] but the combination of higher norms and observable facts:

a) What the king commands, one ought to do.

b) The king commands one to do X.

c) One ought to do X.

The example demonstrates that the validity of the derived norm sentence c) is dependent on the combination of the presupposed norm sentence a) and the declarative sentence b), not on the norm sentence a) alone.

3. The validity of the legal system as a whole cannot be constituted by a *hypothetical* basic norm alone, for such a basic norm is not suitable to account for the validity of *real* norms. The validity of a legal system in social reality is always dependent on facts which can only be recognized through sociological observation.[41]

From legal realism, ITL differs as follows: legal realism either completely eliminates the normative element (like Hägerström[42] and certain forms of American legal realism[43]) or keeps the normative element but defines legal validity in terms of facts so that legal validity and positivity coincide.[44] The psychological positivist explains legal validity as a psychological condition such as an "ought-experience", "approval", "*opinio necessitatis*",[45] the sociological realist as certain external forms of behavior,[46] in particular as the application of the law by the state apparatus, and Alf Ross tries to combine the two, in saying that legal validity means that the judge feels bound by the norm and consequently applies it.[47] In contrast, ITL, like German statutory positivism and the pure theory of law, works with a *normative* concept of legal validity as set out above. To

---

[40] See above § 4 at n. 8 et seqq. and Kelsen, Pure Theory of Law, p. 194 et seq.

[41] Weinberger, ITL, p. 114.

[42] A. Hägerström, in: R. Schmidt (ed.), Die Philosophie der Gegenwart in Selbstdarstellungen VII, Leipzig: Felix Meiner, 1929, p. 132, p. 155.

[43] See above, § 10.

[44] Above § 1 B.III.

[45] Above § 5 and § 6.

[46] Above, § 7–10.

[47] Above § 6 at n. 26.

sociological positivism in particular, ITL raises the objection that the legal system is real in the entirety of the social institutions created by it and that to exclusively focus on the behavior of the legal officials amounts to an inadmissibly curtailed view.

The approach of ITL results in a considerable extension of the realm of positive law:[48]

The law does not only comprise *explicitly enacted primary and secondary rules in Hart's sense* (norms of conduct and power-conferring norms respectively) but also the so-called *legal principles,* indeed *the entire teleological underpinning* of the legal system (e.g. principles of justice) as well as the *legal doctrine* as far as these elements have *a positive-social existence,* i.e. affect the *argumentation* in *legal practice*. According to ITL, these elements are not part of natural law at all, but constituents of *positive* law. This is – as we will see – the most significant consequence of the institutional theory of law.

---

[48] Weinberger, IRP, p. 33 and Rechtspolitik, p.119 et seq.

Fifth Chapter

The Concept of Legal Positivism

§ 14 The Ambiguity of the Term "Legal Positivism"

In order to round off the preceding depiction of the different varieties of legal positivism, an attempt is made in the following to define, as concisely as possible, legal positivism. As always when it comes to specifying the exact meaning of a word, it is advisable to start out from *linguistic usage*. In principle, use in *habitual language* and use in *scientific-philosophical language* come into consideration. Regarding the term "legal positivism", it is obvious that only the scientific-philosophical use is a suitable starting point since this word is not used in habitual language. Therefore, we will first of all inquire what meaning different authors attribute to the term "legal positivism". The result will be that the term is ambiguous.

According to Hart, at least five different meanings of positivism (logically independent of one another) circulate in contemporary legal theory, meanings which are expressed in the following five theses:[1]

1. Laws are human commands.
2. There is no conceptual connection between law and morality (i.e. between the law as it is and the law as it ought to be).
3. The analysis of concepts must be distinguished from empirical investigations of the law as well as from criticism of the law on the basis of morals or other social objectives.
4. The law is "a closed logical system", from which the right decision can be extracted by way of logical deduction – regardless of extra-legal principles.
5. Moral (especially political) judgments cannot be justified rationally (ethical non-cognitivism).

---

[1] Hart, Positivism and the Separation of Law and Morals, p. 57.

Similarly, Alessandro Baratta distinguishes between the following three meanings of legal positivism:

In the *first* instance, legal positivism proves to be a legal theory "which infers the validity of legal norms exclusively from the fact that they have been enacted by legal officials whose legislative power results from norms which are regulating the organization of the legal system."[2] This meaning links legal positivism to a mentality according to which the law as it is and the law as it ought to be are two issues which can be and are to be kept separate.[3]

In its *second* meaning, legal positivism proves to be a value theory according to which the Ought cannot be derived from the Is. Therefore, value judgments (especially value judgments with regard to the law as it ought to be) are not rationally justifiable, i.e. provable.[4]

In its *third* meaning, legal positivism proves to be a method for the framing and the interpretation of laws based on the idea of legal certainty. This legal certainty is achieved by the legislator by framing laws of unambiguous conditioning facts as well as by the subordination of the interpreter to the legislator's intention.[5] However, Baratta emphasizes that the linking of the term "legal positivism" to these three theses does not cover all meanings.[6]

Other authors put the main emphasis on the affinity of legal positivism to general philosophical positivism.[7] Like the first, the latter rejects met-

---

[2] Baratta, ARSP 54 (1968), p. 330 (our translation).
[3] Baratta, ARSP 54 (1968), p. 330.
[4] Baratta, ARSP 54 (1968), p. 330.
[5] Baratta, ARSP 54 (1968), p. 332.
[6] Baratta, ARSP 54 (1968), p. 329. Coing, p. 77/78, too, reduces legal positivism to three theses, viz.: a) Only positive law constitutes law. b) Positive law calls for absolute obedience; this because moral judgments are subjective convictions only. c) The interpretation of laws must, as a matter of principle, be restricted to grammatical-logical interpretation. Yet another classification can be found with Bobbio, p. 103 et seqq.
[7] Likewise, for example, Coing's comments, p. 59 et seqq.; Henkel, p. 487 et seqq; Kelsen, JZ 20 (1965), p. 465; Larenz, p. 36 et seqq.; Eckmann, p. 16 et seqq./25/33/35; Wieacker, p. 431 et seq.; W. Krawietz, Neues Naturrecht oder Rechtspositivismus?, Rechtstheorie 18 (1987), p. 216 n. 21. See also L. Kolakowski, Positivist Philosophy, London: Penguin Books, 1972.

aphysical speculations and in contrast wants to adhere to the "positively given", to incontestable facts (e.g. legislating acts by a state authority; the content of consciousness, especially the feelings of certain individuals; observable behavior patterns of the "law staff" or the members of a certain society and more besides), whereas – depending on the facts in which one sees the positivity – different varieties are to be distinguished.

What is understood by legal positivism is often limited to analytical positivism, especially German statutory positivism.[8] According to Brecht, legal positivism designates "the theory that only those norms are juridically valid which have been established or recognized by the government of a sovereign state in the forms prescribed by its written or unwritten constitution."[9] According to Fechner, legal positivism in the conventional meaning of the word accepts the act of legislation as a fact which does not require further clarification. The only theory that is positivistic in the narrower sense of the word, this author argues, is the theory of power, according to which the law is a human imposition out of the arbitrariness of the powerful one who is, within the area of his power, enacting and enforcing whatever he deems desirable or necessary.[10] Kaufmann, on the other hand, equates legal positivism with German statutory positivism in various essays.[11]

We have seen above[12] that Hart acknowledges in the original version of his theory that a legal system may impose substantial limitations on the legislative body by incorporating moral principles in the constitution, as for example in the Fifth Amendment to the Constitution of the United

---

[8] J. Hoffmeister, for example, Wörterbuch der philosophischen Begriffe (Second Edition, Hamburg: Meiner, 1955), defines legal positivism as "the equation of the law with the so-called positive law given in statutes, other legislative acts/regulations etc." Quoted from Kelsen, JZ 20 (1965), p. 466 and ibidem, n. 10.

[9] Brecht, p. 183.

[10] Fechner, p. 36.

[11] Kaufmann, p. 102, 132 et seq. and p. 208/275 (Rechtsphilosophie im Wandel. Stationen eines Weges Frankfurt a.M.: C. Heymanns, 1972). Statutory positivism is distinguished from other varieties of analytical positivism particularly by the fact that it is linked with a certain method of application of the law which ties the judge tightly to the wording of the laws. See above, text § 3 at n. 17 et seqq.

[12] Above, § 11 text at n. 53 et seqq.

States (the view known as soft positivism). As set out above,[13] a new form of positivism has developed from this statement, viz. the view known as inclusive positivism.[14] According to this theory, there are legal systems which include moral principles as ultimate validity criteria in their rule of recognition, e.g. the amendments of the Constitution of the United States and the Canadian Charter of Rights and Freedoms.

The host of such opinions documents clearly that the term "legal positivism" is ambiguous. There is no uniform use of language; consequently, a purely analytic definition as set out below cannot be contemplated.[15] We are therefore assigned the task of proposing a concept of legal positivism which is as useful as possible; in other words *it is not a matter of declaring what legal positivism is but a matter of deciding what should usefully be understood by legal positivism.* For this purpose, it seems necessary to us to maintain a clear separation between three complexes of issues which have been touched on in the characterizations above:[16]

The first complex of issues concerns the *definition of law.* Aspects of this issue are questions on the characteristics of positivity, on the validity of the law, on the separation or combination of law and morals, on the relativity and arbitrariness of the content of law, on legal duty and the right to resist in *terms of law* as well as on the affinity of legal positivism to general philosophical positivism. The problem of how soft positivism and inclusive positivism are to be classified equally pertains here.

The second complex of issues concerns the problem of interpretation and gaps: it includes questions as to what extent the judge is bound by the law, on the justifiability or non-justifiability of a purely formalistic method of application of law.

---

[13] § 12 above.

[14] Represented by David Lyons, E. Philip Soper, Jules Coleman I, Wil J. Waluchow, Anthony James Sebok and L. Székessy.

[15] See below, § 19 A. Of course this does not mean that we can completely abstract our definition from the hitherto habitual, though not uniform, language use. On the contrary, our definition should as far as possible be compatible with the language use habitual up to now.

[16] See the distinction of these three issues by Cattaneo, Chapter 1.

The third complex of issues concerns the problem of values. Part of this issue are questions on the possibility or impossibility of a rational justification of value judgments (and therefore also on the possibility or impossibility of rational legal politics), on the relation of Is and Ought and on the right to resist *in terms of morals*.

The question now is which complex of issues we should advantageously take up first to arrive at a concept of legal positivism. If we decide in favor of the second issue, we will have to define as "positivist" a legal theory which proposes a formal method of application of law, that is to say which takes the stand of the judge being a subsumption machine.[17] From this it would follow that the theories of Austin, Kelsen, Bierling, Ehrlich, Ross, Geiger and Hart would not qualify as "positivist" since these authors have stressed the creative nature of the application of law. Such a definition, therefore, would be far off the habitual language use because these authors are portrayed for the most part as typical proponents of positivism, sometimes even as exponents (Kelsen and Hart) of legal positivism;[18] it would therefore be quite an unhappy choice. If we decide in favor of the third issue, then we choose as a starting point for the characterization of legal positivism an area that belongs also, and primarily, to general philosophy, viz. to value philosophy. Whether value judgments are rationally justifiable and whether ought-sentences can be derived from is-sentences is of as much interest for the general philosopher, particularly the moral philosopher, as for the jurist. Therefore, we do not deem it expedient to start a characterization of legal theories at this point. Aside from that, value relativism forms part of the fundament of continental positivist theories only. Value relativism and legal positivism are not necessarily logically interconnected.[19] The British legal positivists (Hobbes, Bentham, Austin, Hart) always deemed value judgments to be rationally justifiable. For these reasons, we opt for the first issue: decisive for our definition shall be which *concept of law* the relevant theories imply.

---

[17] Whether other characteristics would have to be included in this concept need not be examined at this point.

[18] See for example A. Kaufmann/W. Hassemer, Grundprobleme der zeitgenössischen Rechtsphilosophie und Rechtstheorie, Frankfurt a.M.: Athenäum, 1971, p. 11.

[19] See above, § 2 at n. 18 and below, § 15 B.II at n. 28 et seqq.

At this point, the issue of Campbell's "Legal Theory of Ethical Positivism" (LEP) is to be addressed briefly. Contrary to most other positivist theories discussed in the course of this book, Campbell's theory is *not* a *descriptive* but a *prescriptive* theory of law.[20] Campbell does not intend to change the concept of law in H.L.A. Hart's sense but he is committed to portraying positivism as a *normative political philosophy*. LEP is the theory which focuses on the ethical functions and premises of the positivist concepts of the law. LEP provides the insight that the reasons justifying legal positivism can be seen as being primarily ethical instead of analytical, explanatory or empirical.

The central tenet of LEP is that a legal system should be a system of *rules*.[21] Rules have many assets. Usually, the courts will be able to identify them without recourse to moral reasoning. Mere rules of thumb, i.e. general principles for decision-making, are not sufficient; they are not "trumps" in the sense of the metaphor introduced by Dworkin in relation to rights. The main limitation imposed by the law on political decision-making is that political authority is to be restricted by means of such rules. It must not simply be a question of ad-hoc discretion.[22] Rules often stand in contrast with principles but they are the best expression of decision-making guided by principles.[23]

Some political implications result from the LEP approach; for example:

1. Statute law is to be preferred to common law. For statute rules have to be clearly formulated even if they must in some points delegate legislative authority to the judge. Moreover, the common law is undemocratic and confusing owing to the indeterminacy of the judicial reasoning.[24]

2. LEP opposes excessive use of blanket clauses and strong judicial discretion.[25]

---

[20] Campbell, LEP, p. 3.
[21] Campbell, LEP, p. 5.
[22] Campbell, LEP, p. 6.
[23] Campbell, LEP, p. 6.
[24] Campbell, LEP, p. 9.
[25] Campbell, LEP, p. 9.

3. LEP disapproves of the judge determining the content of fundamental rights and freedoms since it is against delegating authority to unaccountable persons for what are, in reality, major legislative decisions.[26]

---

[26] Campbell, LEP, p. 9 and p. 161 et seqq.; see also idem, Prescriptive Legal Positivism: Law, Rights and Democracy, London: UCL Press, 2004.

§ 15 Definitions and Characterization of Legal Positivism[1]

We define legal positivism as follows:

For the purpose of this book, any theory which – under avoidance of metaphysical assumptions[2] – defines the law by means of *empirical criteria which are subject to change at any time* shall qualify as legal positivism (= legal positivism in the *broader* sense).

In a *narrower* sense than the one determined above, one might also understand by legal positivism *analytical positivism* only. Legal positivism in this sense may be contrasted with *legal realism* (psychological and sociological theories).[3]

Only *German statutory positivism* which is characterized by a specific theory of application of law, on the other hand, qualifies as positivist in the narrowest sense.[4]

The characteristics indicated in the above definition are now to be explained in more detail:

A. Rejection of "Metaphysical" Assumptions

Metaphysics is understood as "the philosophical theory of the most general principles of being and the last recognizable interrelations between what is and what has been".[5] Metaphysics is therefore dealing with the "ultimate" things, the transcendental, the inexperiencable, the supernat-

---

[1] See also A. Aarnio, Form and Content in the Law: Dimensions and Definitions of Legal Positivism, in: idem, Philosophical Perspectives in Jurisprudence, Helsinki: Societas Philosophica Fennica, 1983, p. 76 et seqq.; F. Müller, Artikel: Positivismus, in: N. Achterberg (Editor), Ergänzbares Lexikon des Rechts, Neuwied: Luchterhand, 1986, p. 1 et seqq.
[2] I.e. especially of the existence of God, of a world of ideas, of an invariable nature of mankind or of a teleologically determined nature.
[3] See scheme below.
[4] Above, § 3 at n. 17 et seqq.
[5] R. Eisler, Wörterbuch der philosophischen Begriffe II, Fourth Edition, Berlin: Mittler, 1929, p. 126 (our translation).

ural, the absolute. Statements are of a metaphysical nature if they cannot be traced back to internal or external experience and its intellectual working up by way of logic and mathematics.

It is characteristic for all positivist theories that they try to do without such metaphysical assumptions.[6] They refrain in particular from presupposing the existence of God, a world of absolute ideas or values, a teleologically determined nature or an invariable nature of mankind and/or from searching for the "nature", the "idea" or the "essence" of the law.

For some legal positivists, this concern is paired with a downright adverseness towards metaphysics. This is particularly true of proponents of the Uppsala school like Geiger or Ross, for example. Others, however, reject metaphysical assumptions only *within the framework of their positivist theory* but otherwise do not regard attempted metaphysical cognition as an undertaking that is impossible from the outset; sometimes the existence of God[7] or a transcendental moral world order[8] is even openly assumed.

This second attitude is the more appropriate one, because from the positivist concept of cognition it only follows that metaphysical cognition must necessarily be cognition of a different kind, but not that it is impossible as a matter of principle.[9]

---

[6] Within this context, Kelsen's basic norm which has been assessed as metaphysical already by representatives of other lines of positivism has an exceptional position. However, we would in any case deal with an example of critical, not of dogmatic metaphysics.

[7] See for example Austin, § 2 at n. 10 et seqq. above.

[8] See Laun, above.

[9] See below, § 18 A and § 18 D.

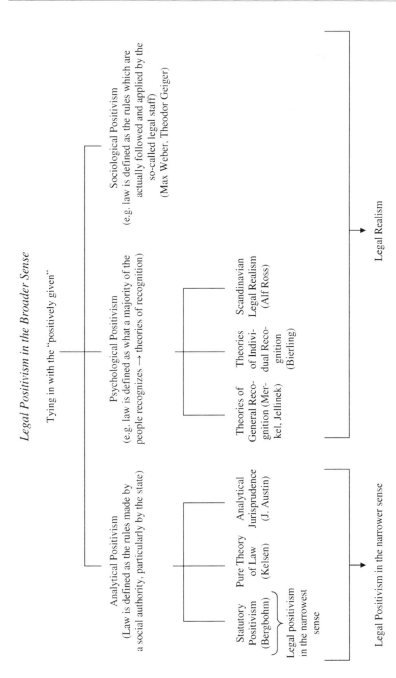

Legal Positivism in the Broader Sense

Tying in with the "positively given"

Analytical Positivism
(Law is defined as the rules made by
a social authority, particularly by the state)

Psychological Positivism
(e.g. law is defined as what a majority of the
people recognizes → theories of recognition)

Sociological Positivism
(e.g. law is defined as the rules which are
actually followed and applied by the
so-called legal staff)
(Max Weber, Theodor Geiger)

Statutory
Positivism
(Bergbohm)

Pure Theory
of Law
(Kelsen)

Analytical
Jurisprudence
(J. Austin)

Theories of
General Reco-
gnition (Mer-
kel, Jellinek)

Theories
of Indivi-
dual Reco-
gnition
(Bierling)

Scandinavian
Legal Realism
(Alf Ross)

Legal positivism
in the narrowest
sense

Legal Positivism in the narrower sense

Legal Realism

Note: The legal theories of H.L.A. Hart and Donald Neil MacCormick/Ota Weinberger as well Inclusive and Exclusive Positivism contain elements of all three main forms.

111

B. Definition of Law by Way of Empirical Criteria (Social Fact Thesis)

Refraining from taking recourse to metaphysical assumptions leads the legal positivists to define the law by way of *social facts alone* which, as such, do not allude *to any values*. The exclusion of content-based criteria from the concept of law becomes plain with all legal positivists: if, for example, one traces the law back to the will of a ruler, or to what is recognized by the majority of the members of a society, or to actual real-life behavior, the *content* of what the ruler commands or what the majority of the society recognizes or *how* people *actually* behave obviously does not matter. Legal positivism uses as a criterion for its concept of the law solely the factor of "positivity": the law is always defined by reference to a physical or a psychological reality; the constitutive characteristics of the law are facts of the spatiotemporal outside world (acts of a ruler or legislator, or actual application of or compliance with rules) or of the mental inner life (psychological facts such as "recognition", "ought-experience", "sense of duty").

The question that now arises is whether "soft positivism" or "inclusive legal positivism" fit into this picture as well, and this must be answered in the affirmative. For all variants of legal positivism, including inclusive positivism, endorse the social facts thesis,[10] albeit on the basis of different social facts. According to Austin, the relevant social fact is to be seen in the presence of a sovereign who is willing and able to impose sanctions in case of non-compliance with his orders. According to Hart, it is the existence of a binding rule of recognition that is responsible for the existence of a legal system. For a binding rule of recognition to exist, two conditions must be met:[11]

First: the validity criteria provided for by the rule of recognition must be accepted and applied by the officials as a standard of their official behavior.

---

[10]   The terminology was coined by Coleman I, passim.
[11]   Above, text at § 11 n. 60 et seqq.

Second: the ordinary citizens of a legal system must by and large obey the primary rules that are valid according to the rule of recognition.[12]

The proponents of inclusive legal positivism furthermore embrace the incorporation thesis and the separation thesis. From the conceptual separation of law and morality, however, it only follows that the rule of recognition does *not necessarily* have to include moral validity criteria. Therefore, according to the proponents of inclusive positivism, legal systems *are conceivable which do not contain moral criteria* for the identification and validation of the law. If one seeks to frame a concept of law applicable *to all developed legal systems* from the standpoint of inclusive positivism it is thus not advisable to take as a basis moral criteria which can be observed with only some but not all legal systems. The *continental European legal systems*, for example, do not contain moral validity criteria since in continental Europe, constitutional rights (e.g. freedom of religion, freedom of speech etc.) are considered to be *legal* rights and *not moral* rights. Furthermore, it remains to be pointed out that even if moral criteria are incorporated in a particular instance of a rule of recognition, such moral criteria must find their expression in the concordant practice of the officials to which the rule of recognition owes its very existence. To that extent, we are still concerned with observable, i.e. social facts.

The law only exists if and in as much as it has become positive, i.e. *real* in one of the aforementioned ways. The positivists' way of defining the law by means of empirical criteria entails two important consequences:

I. The Law as Positive Law

In principle, Bergbohm's proposition is applicable to the positivist theories: "All law is positive … and only positive law is law."[13] This proposition must, however, be delimited for a positivist like Austin, who recognizes aside from the positive law the existence of natural "law". But

---

[12] Himma, Inclusive Legal Positivism, p. 127.
[13] Bergbohm, p. 52, footnote; it must be noted, however, that Bergbohm as a statutory positivist understands "positivity" in a narrower sense as "an enactment" of a legislator.

for Austin, too, only the positive law qualifies as law in the all-inclusive sense of the word, which is expressed, for instance, in the following statements: "... every law properly so called is set by a superior to an inferior or inferiors ..."[14] and: "Every positive law, or every law simply and strictly so called, is set by a sovereign person, or a sovereign body of persons ..."[15]

The prerequisite that law can only ever be something for which certain occurrences belonging to the factual sphere can be proven clearly shows the affinity of legal positivism with trends of general philosophical positivism[16] even though several forms of legal positivism (in particular the theory of Hobbes (1588–1679) precede at least some of the modern philosophical positivists.[17] This affinity is first of all evident for the realist theories (psychological and sociological positivism) and is sometimes openly emphasized by their proponents.[18] As we will see later, cognition is – roughly speaking – scientific in accordance with a positivist concept of cognition only on condition that it is based either upon experience and its processing by way of logic and mathematics or upon a logically necessary deduction within a axiomatic system without reference to experience. The attempt of the realist theories to put the law down to physical or psychological realities conforms to the prerequisite of empirical cognition in terms of philosophical positivism. The affinity of legal positivism and philosophical positivism, however, applies equally to analyt-

---

[14] Austin, Lectures I, p. 340.

[15] Austin, Lectures I, p. 225 et seq.

[16] See authors quoted above § 14 n. 7. Likewise Noll, p. 20 et seqq.; of a different opinion, Weinberger, ITL, p. 116, and Alwart, p. 12.

[17] The fathers of modern philosophical positivism, impressed with the groundbreaking accomplishments of natural science, were: David Hume (1711–1776), John Stuart Mill (1806–1873), Auguste Comte (1798–1857), Herbert Spencer (1820–1903), Ernst Laas (1837–1885), and furthermore the Vienna Circle of Neopositivism around Moritz Schlick (1882–1936) with Otto Neurath (1882–1936), Rudolph Carnap (1891–1970), Philipp Frank (1884–1966) and Victor Kraft (1880–1975). For an introduction to the general philosophy of positivism see L. Kolakowski, Positivist Philosophy, London: Penguin Books, 1972.

[18] See for example Ehrlich, Fundamental Principles, p. 9, who explains that the prevailing method of true science is an inductive one which seeks to increase the depth of our insight into the nature of things through observation and experience. In a similar way Ross, On Law and Justice, p. ix.

114

ical positivism. With regard to the pure theory of law, this was clearly emphasized by Kelsen himself.[19] The postulates of philosophical positivism are not directly applicable to *legal norms* because legal norms are not facts but the *meaning* of facts. Yet facts are a condition for the validity of legal norms since norms have to be *stated* and must be *effective* up to a certain degree.[20] This connection has been proved for German statutory positivism by Coing on the basis of a Bergbohm passage. According to Bergbohm, a norm or rule only qualifies as positive in terms of jurisprudence and legal science if it has been awarded such quality by the competent legislative power following the applicable, externally recognizable procedure.[21] The clear parallel to the prerequisite of philosophical positivism, as Coing rightly observes, consists in the fact that an external historical act must be established for every norm to be recognized as a legal norm.[22]

II. The Conceptual Distinction Between the Law as it Is, and the Law as it Ought to Be (Positivist Separation Thesis)

The second consequence of the positivist concept of law is the conceptual distinction between the law as it is and the law as it ought to be, or, to paraphrase it as it is often stated: the conceptual (logical or analytical) separation of law and morality. Since law is defined by means of empirical characteristics, for a norm to qualify as law, it is not really decisive whether its content is just to a higher or lesser degree. The dualism of the concept and idea of law is therefore – at least from the standpoint of a juristic handling of the problem – not known to the positivist theories. In fact they arrive at a monism: any fact oriented to the empirical characteristics mentioned above – and only such a fact – matches up to the concept and therefore qualifies eo ipso as law. Its legal quality cannot be

---

[19] Kelsen, JZ 20 (1965), p. 465: "Legal positivism must be distinguished from philosophical positivism; but there is a close connection between the two of them."
[20] Kelsen, JZ 20 (1965), p. 465.
[21] Bergbohm, p. 549.
[22] Coing, p. 77.

lost by force of any discrepancy with an idea of law, however serious (in relative or absolute terms) such a discrepancy may be.

When the British proponents of legal positivism speak of the separation thesis, they mean not only the conceptual differentiation of positive law from positive morality, i.e. the morality actually in force, but also from so-called *"critical morality"*, i.e. from enlightened morality.[23] By critical morality, they mean the general moral principles which are needed for the purpose of criticizing actually existing social institutions including positive morality.[24]

The positivist demand for a conceptual separation of law and morality *on no account means that the law does not have to be moral in any way*, i.e. need not live up to a certain (absolute or relative) standard of justice. *Nor does it mean that actual influences of moral ideas of the law as it ought to be on the shaping of the content of positive law are denied.* Quite the contrary, the interconnection between law and morality is emphasized.[25] Disapproval is reserved for the proposition to include content-based criteria within the concept of law; the subject of the positivist approach is the law as it effectively is, as it actually exists, and not some ideal law. The positivist standpoint allows for criticizing the positive law, too, the only consequence of this being, however, that positive law is, where applicable, *disqualified as bad, morally condemnable law; never* can the consequence of criticizing positive law be that such law *loses its quality as law*, i.e. becomes non-law because of its being contradictory to justice. For the positivist, *unjust law is never tantamount to "non-*

---

[23] With regard to this differentiation see Hart, Concept of Law, p. 185 and 205 et seq. and even more articulate Hart, Law, Liberty and Morality, London 1963, p. 20. That Hart understands the separation thesis in this dual sense became apparent on the occasion of a conversation I was able to have with him in Oxford in Summer 1985. See my report of this conversation in: Rechtstheorie 18 (1987), p. 538 et seqq.

[24] J.-C. Wolf, Studia Philosophica 44 (1985), p. 35, is describing critical morality as follows: "Critical morality is not the sum of what people regard as morally correct but it is rather a way of thinking which is allowing us to rationally revise moral decisions. Validity claims of moral convictions are the topic of critical morality. It is different from a descriptive or genetic morality which rubricates different opinions on moral questions and searches for the causes." See also below, § 22 A.

[25] See above, § 11 n. 8 and text ibid.

law"[26] *but only to "morally condemnable" law.*[27] *Even the system in Nazi Germany* was therefore – from the standpoint of the pure theory of law, for example – a legal system. For when a positivist refers to a "legal" system (*"eine Rechtsordnung"*), it does not necessarily encompass any judgment on his part that the given system is just and equitable, qualities to which the German word for law (*"Recht"*) always alludes. (The English language, in contrast, clearly differentiates between justice and law.) Even to the German ear, however, the phrase can be stripped of much of its offensive character if one replaces "legal system" with Kelsen's positivist concept of law. It then reads: *even the system in Nazi Germany was "a by and large effective coercive system"* – a proposition which we dare say none of those who know the historical reality will contest.

The fact that the positivist defines the law without reference to any values has led to the widespread opinion that legal positivism is always accompanied by an ethical relativism in the supra-positive sphere. As Hart's subtle comments show, however, this does not necessarily have to be the case. Let us assume, Hart suggests, that moral judgments are rationally defensible just as easily as any other kind of judgment. This alone would not yield any argument against the positivist separation thesis. For the only difference it would make would be that the moral iniquity of such legal norms would be susceptible to proof; one could prove that a norm is morally wrong and should not be law or, conversely, that it is morally desirable and therefore should be law. Such proof, however, would not attest whether something is or is not law. Provability of moral principles would not alter the fact "that there are laws which may have any degree of iniquity or stupidity and still be laws. And conversely there are rules that have every moral qualification to be laws and yet are not laws."[28] A positivist concept of law is therefore – contrary to popular opinion – compatible with the recognition of absolute values. A legal historian can

---

[26] Geiger, Vorstudien, p. 167.

[27] The positivist's attitude towards the right to resist is a necessary result of this. He can only approve of such a right if it falls within his concept of law, i.e. for example when such a right is provided for by the legislator or is recognized by society. Where this is not the case, a "right" to resist exists, according to the positivist, at the utmost in a moral sense, but never in a juristic sense.

[28] Hart, Positivism, Law, and Morals, p. 84.

base his research, for example, on a positivist concept of law and never-theless – in the supra-positive sphere – believe in the existence of a natural law. "Political and legal positivism simply fails to deal with transpositive questions, either in a relativist or in an absolute manner."[29]

For this reason, we suggest distinguishing between strong and weak versions of positivism. A strong version of legal positivism shall mean a version which is combined with an ethical relativism in the supra-positive sphere (as in the Continental positivisms, for example, in particular Scandinavian legal realism and Kelsen's pure theory of law). A weak version of positivism shall mean a version which considers a rational moral justification in the supra-positive sphere possible (as in British positivism, as represented by Hobbes, Bentham, Austin and Hart).

For the realist theories, the *characteristics of the positivity* simultaneous-ly represent the characteristics of the *validity*. For the psychological positivist, for example, the positivity of the law consists of the "recogni-tion", the "experience of ought", the "sense of duty" of certain persons; and the law is valid because it is recognized, felt as imposing a duty or experienced as something which ought to be by these persons. For the sociological positivist, the positivity of the law is a social reality, viz. the behavior pattern "actually requested, practiced and – in case of non-com-pliance – enforced" by the members of a society.[30] And the law is *valid in a sociological sense* insofar as it *conforms to such a social reality* which can be expressed for example in an efficiency rate.

Things are different in the case of German statutory positivism, the pure theory of law and in Hart's theory where a *normative* concept of validity is used, with the necessary consequence that the positivity is something different. Thus, validity and positivity of the law diverge in these theo-ries.

---

[29] Brecht, p. 184. Nevertheless, this logical independence of value relativism and legal positivism does not necessarily rule out the possibility that value relativists may in fact often be legal positivists and vice versa. For the changeability of the character-istics of a positivist concept of law (see below, C) inclines the adherents of legal pos-itivism to think in relative categories in the supra-positive sphere, too. Conversely, a value relativist is inclined to be a legal positivist because he is denying the verifiabil-ity of a higher law. This is, however, not a logical necessity.

[30] Raiser, Einführung, p. 104.

C. Definition of the Law by way of Variable Characteristics

A further distinguishing mark of the legal positivist theories is their tendency to be relativist. The social facts identified by the different theories do not tie in with constant factors, as the reference to certain human drives (such as the self-preservation instinct) would be, for example, but with variable parameters. Analytical positivism takes as a basis the power of the respective sovereign, psychological positivism the content of consciousness of the respective persons and sociological positivism the respective factual behavior patterns. The contents of the law are therefore different from place to place and time to time. There is simply no law that is universally valid irrespective of time and sphere.[31]

For this reason, the German conceptual jurisprudence of the 19th century cannot be classified as a positivist theory in terms of the definition suggested by us. For it was – as more recent research studies have shown – not relativist, nor did it lack a basis of legal ethics: "In fact even if in a very sublimate, diluted form, the fundamental ethical ideas of German Idealism, and especially Kant's ideas, live on e.g. in Windscheid's or A. v. Tuhr's conceptual systems …, even though this connection is almost forgotten at the end of the century and a substantiation on the grounds of legal philosophy is completely evaded."[32] According to the opinion of the proponents of this school of thought, in legal concepts such as right, accessoriness of pledge, elasticity of property, "*agelessly valid* statements on the right law have become independent in such a manner that their logical application (like the one of a mechanical law or a physical formula) must necessarily lead to the right (i.e. just) decision, too."[33] We

---

[31] At any rate, Lampe has called our attention to the limits of legal positivism. The legislator cannot, for example, shorten the duration of a pregnancy; he cannot deviate much from linguistic laws or else the legal text becomes incomprehensible; and he cannot breach the laws of logic without the contents becoming absurd, i.e when he proclaims for example that something is retained in sole proprietorship by several persons. See E.-J. Lampe, Grenzen des Rechtspositivismus, Schriften zur Rechtstheorie No. 128, Berlin: Duncker & Humblot, 1988.

[32] Larenz, p. 22/23.

[33] Wieacker, p. 433/434 (our emphasis).

therefore agree with Wieacker who proposes that it is better at this point to speak of a "jurisprudential formalism" than of "positivism".[34]

D. Excursus: Coleman's II Rejection of the Separability Thesis

Since the 1980s, Coleman I had been one of the most notable proponents of so-called inclusive legal positivism (ILP).[35] In a recently published article (The Architecture of Jurisprudence, The Yale Law Journal, 10/4/2011, pp. 2 et seqq., cited as Coleman II), Coleman then switched entirely to the opposing position of so-called exclusive legal positivism (ELP). His argumentation begins with the objection levelled by Raz against ILP, which is based on the simple insight that judges are people too.[36] Because they are human beings, all moral reasons are also applicable to them. Moral reasons are always applicable to people, irrespective of whether they are legal actors or not. If moral reasons are now always applicable to legal actors, according to Coleman II it is utterly confusing to think that the law – assisted by the actions of the enforcing officials – has the power to determine that moral reasons are applicable to certain actors (Coleman II, p.48).

Here it must be kept in mind that morality is a more extensive normative system than the law and demands *more* from people than the law; for the latter only ensures the "ethical minimum" (Georg Jellinek). For this reason the law can, and often does, refer to morality by means of blanket clauses and indeterminate legal concepts. Let us consider a famous case from Roman law, namely the case of the so-called "Jealous Wall", and

---

[34] Wieacker, p. 432. Conceptual jurisprudence is often referred to as "jurisprudential positivism", e.g. by Wieacker, p. 433 et seq., and by D. Tripp, Der Einfluss des naturwissenschaftlichen, philosophischen und historischen Positivismus auf die deutsche Rechtslehre im 19. Jahrhundert, Schriften zur Rechtsgeschichte No. 31, Berlin: Duncker & Humblot, 1983, ch. 7. Regarding conceptual jurisprudence, see W. Krawietz (ed.), Theorie und Technik der Begriffsjurisprudenz, Darmstadt: Wissenschaftliche Buchgesellschaft, 1976.

[35] Cf. afore § 12 B and below § 24 H, cited as Coleman I.

[36] J. Raz, Incorporation by Law, 10 LEGAL THEORY 1,2 (2004), cited after Coleman II, p.48 n. 56.

let us assume that it had to be ruled upon according to modern-day Swiss private law (example 1): there are two neighbors, each of whom owns his plot of land. From a legal perspective both are allowed to build whatever they like on their own plots. Now one neighbor erects a wall on his plot for the sole purpose of blocking the other's view. Article 2 of the Swiss Civil Code reads: "Every person must act in good faith in the exercise of his or her rights and in the performance of his or her obligations. The manifest abuse of a right is not protected by law"

With this blanket clause, the law makes reference to morality. But the law does not say what is morally right in the individual case. This answer is supplied by morality: in our case, morality says that it is obviously abusive if one builds a wall for the sole purpose of blocking a neighbor's view. The builder of such a wall must break it down again, on the basis of a court judgment if necessary.

A second example: Article 20 para. 1 of the Swiss Code of Obligations reads: "A contract is void if its terms are impossible, unlawful or against common decency." In making use of the indeterminate concept "against common decency", here too the law refers to morality. One example is the prostitute's contract. The contract between a prostitute and her client has no impossible content, nor does it breach the law. But it violates what is, in Switzerland today, the prevailing view of common decency. Therefore it is null and void. In both cases, the law determines when morality is to be applied. It can do so because law and morality are not identical. Morality demands more than law.

But the converse question also arises: under which conditions should one act on the basis of *legal* reasons? Because morality is always applicable to actors, then it must be because morality advises or demands this. Hence the question is: when does morality demand or advise this? Here Coleman II relies on Raz's authority argument[37] which we encountered earlier.[38] Morality demands action for legal reasons when *one probably satisfies morality better by acting out of legal reasons* than by acting on the basis of one's own assessment of the moral reasons that are applica-

---

[37] Coleman II, p. 50 et seqq.
[38] Afore § 2 A III.

ble to one.[39] This is the case when those who pass the directives *are in a better position to judge* what the *balancing of moral and other reasons* demands.

Let us take the example used above once again:[40] until 1967 Swedish drivers used to drive on the left. In order to decide whether to convert to driving on the right, the legislator had to weigh up the so-called first order reasons (international context, increased danger of accidents, substantial costs of the infrastructure adjustments). The authority of the Swedish legislator was a legitimate one for the following reasons:

1. because it had a better overview of the international context, the existing mindsets of Swedish drivers and the expected costs; and

2. because the individual driver drove better if he complied with the legislator's ruling than if everybody were to rely on their own assessment.

According to Coleman II, morality delineates areas out of the moral landscape where acting directly on the basis of one's own assessment is probably less successful than if one acts on the basis of reasons (moral, etc.) specified by others. Nevertheless, the concept of law, according to Raz, is positivistic through and through. The drivers now had to look solely at the law in order to know what was valid. It would not have been opportune if every driver were to decide for himself whether to drive on the right or the left. According to Raz, resorting to first-order reasons is not permissible. The law is source-based, to wit, in the sense of the *strong* sources thesis, i.e. the law is based on its social sources *alone*. That means that the validity of any law is only based on facts of compliant behavior, which can be presented value-neutrally.[41] Hence it is quite clear that according to Raz, moral principles cannot be part of positive law.[42]

The social fact thesis is the kernel of Raz's positivism. Because of the fact that the concept and the content of the law are determined through

---

[39] Coleman II, loc. cit.
[40] Afore § 12 A III.
[41] Székessy, p. 68.
[42] Székessy, p. 71 et seqq.

value-neutral social facts *alone*, the reverse inference (argumentum e contrario) is *compelling* that following Raz, everything with value-content, including morality, stands *outside of* the law, i.e. that law and morality are conceptually (analytically, logically) separate. The separation thesis is *not a premise* but a *compelling implication* of the social fact thesis. The attempt by Coleman II to refute the separation thesis therefore failed.

Now it is very important that Coleman II himself concedes that moral considerations play no part: "[they] cannot bear on determining the identity or content of law: as regards these issues, morality and law must be separated"![43] – The discussion hitherto about the separation thesis revolved *exclusively around these questions*, however: what turns a rule into a legal rule? How does one ascertain the content of law? What is the basis of the validity of a legal rule? It is most remarkable that, in relation to these questions which are still debated to this day, Coleman II *expressly holds fast to the separation thesis*![44] He elaborates further: "The Razian version of exclusive legal positivism is not a way of giving expression to the separability thesis for it derives from rejecting the separability thesis. It is only because at the most fundamental levels law and morality are necessarily connected that, *at the level of determining the identity and content of law, they necessarily must be kept apart*"[45]. He therefore *re*locates the thesis of a necessary link between law and morality on the most fundamental level of the legitimacy of law in the sense intended by Raz.

Let us take a fourth example: in the year 1935 the German Reichstag, completely dominated by the NSDAP and Hitler, unanimously passed the Nuremberg racial laws. They were published on 16 September 1935 in the Imperial Law Gazette (Reichsgesetzblatt, RGBl., Part I pp. 1146). These laws subjected Jews to substantial discrimination. For example, marriage and extramarital sexual intercourse between Jews and non-Jews were prohibited and the offence of "racial defilement" was punishable with prison or penal labor.

---

[43] Coleman II, p. 52.
[44] Coleman II, pp. 52/53.
[45] Coleman II, pp. 52/53, authors' emphasis.

The initial question here is whether Hitler even exerted the claim to be a legitimate authority. It is conceivable that certain dictators and mass murderers make no such claim. But so as not to destroy the argument at this premature point, we assume that Hitler exerted this claim. Everybody will agree that Hitler or his executive organs like the NSDAP or the German Reichstag were illegitimate authorities. This does not change the fact that – as we will assume – the claim to be a legitimate authority pertained although it was wrong; it suffices that it was not necessarily wrong.

The necessary connection to positive law must now only pertain between this claim of (illegitimate, in this case) authority and the positive (illegitimate, in this case) law. One can say, then, that a necessary connection existed between Nazi morality (i.e. Hitler's claim to be a legitimate authority) and the Nuremberg racial laws. Hence in this example a necessary relationship pertains on the level of legitimacy between Nazi morality and positive law. But what is gained by assuming a *necessary* relationship between the *moral* claim to be a legitimate authority and the law on the level of *legitimacy?* If, in other words, a necessary connection pertains between morality and law on the level of *legitimacy*? Does it not make more sense to contrast positive Nazi law, as it once pertained, with a morally good law? And would it not make more sense to contrast Hitler's illegitimate authority with a morally good authority, which can rightly claim legitimacy for itself? That is to say, *even on the most fundamental level of legitimacy it is absolutely possible to hold fast to the separability thesis.* Coleman II thus pursues a curious dual strategy: on the level of identification and determination of the content of law, he holds fast to the separability thesis. On the level of legitimacy, in contrast, he advocates the thesis of a necessary connection of law and morality.

Hence, Coleman II's attempt to refute the separability thesis on the most fundamental level of legitimate authority likewise failed.

The following conclusions can be drawn:

1. That law can make reference to morality, which insofar as morality is then *incorporated* into positive law through judicial decisions, transforms it into positive law (examples 1 and 2).

2. That conversely, a moral conception like that of Raz can delineate the domain in which positive law is applicable (example 3).

3. In questions concerning the identification and determination of the content of law, law and morality must be kept separate.

4. The assumption of any necessary connection between the claim to be a legitimate authority (= morality) and positive law yields no progress.

The separation thesis is *not* a premise but a *compelling implication* from the social fact thesis. *Both* form the *kernel* of each variant of legal positivism.

Second Part

The Axiomatic Character of Legal Positivism

First Chapter

The Problem of Scientific Cognition

As shown in the last section, all varieties of legal positivism are implicitly or expressly based upon the postulates of philosophical positivism. The Second Part focuses on assessment of the theories of legal positivism on the basis of their own premises. For this purpose, the First Chapter will set out in more detail the understanding of science as it has been developed by the more recent positivistically oriented philosophy of science.[1] We will adhere to this variety of modern philosophy of science in an endeavor not to apply the critical probe to legal positivism based on "alien" premises, i.e. premises that start out from a different understanding of science. Rather, we try to home in on the understanding of science on which the theories of legal positivism are based. Thus, if at the end of this chapter a positivist concept of cognition is postulated, this does not mean that we are of the opinion that jurisprudence should generally start out from such a concept. The question as to the adequacy or inadequacy of the positivist concept of cognition is not the subject of this book. We are only interested in creating a platform for a fair criticism of legal positivism, namely by placing ourselves on the same epistemological ground as legal positivism.

---

[1] I.e. the neopositivism of the Vienna Circle (e.g. Mortiz Schlick, Victor Kraft, Rudolf Carnap and Otto Neurath) as well as Karl Popper, The Logic of Scientific Discovery, London and New York: Routledge Classics, 2002 (Popper calls his philosophy "critical rationalism"), and W. Stegmüller, Probleme und Resultate der Wissenschaftstheorie und Analytischen Philosophie, Band I, Erklärung, Begründung, Kausalität, 2nd, extended and improved Edition, Berlin/Heidelberg/New York: Springer, 1983.

Modern epistemological positivism accepts only two basic methods which serve to secure scientific cognition, viz. the axiomatic and the empirical method. Both methods shall be explained in the following paragraphs. In doing so, it will be indispensable to go somewhat further afield and to point out correlations which are not strictly required knowledge for the advancement of our analysis.[2] They are nevertheless essential for a deeper understanding of the positivist concept of cognition and shall therefore be mentioned as the opportunity arises.

§ 16 The Axiomatic Method[3]

A. Characterization of the Axiomatic Method in General

I. The Axioms

The axiomatic method is the most rigorous amongst the scientific methods so far known. All theorems (= derived propositions) of an axiomatic system are to be proven in a strictly logical-deductive procedure in accordance with certain rules:[4] namely, they must be reducible to certain

---

[2] E.g. the methods for the verification or falsification of hypotheses on laws of nature.

[3] Literature: Hilbert, Grundlagen; idem, Axiomatisches Denken, in: D. Hilbert, Gesammelte Abhandlungen III, Berlin: Springer 1935, p. 164 et seqq.; Klug, Juristische Logik, p. 15/16 and ibidem, literature quoted in n. 49; Gonseth; Bochénski, p. 65 et seqq; Seiffert I, p. 127 et seqq.; Weinberger, Rechtslogik, p. 361 et seqq.; E. v. Savigny, Zur Rolle der deduktiv-axiomatischen Methode in der Rechtswissenschaft, in: G. Jahr/W. Maihofer (Editors), Rechtstheorie, Beiträge zur Grundlagendiskussion, Frankfurt am Main: Klostermann, 1971, p. 315 et seqq.; Austeda, p. 28 et seqq., 64 et seqq.; H. Scholz, Die Axiomatik der Alten, in: H. Scholz, Mathesis universalis, Abhandlungen zur Philosophie als strenger Wissenschaft, Basel/Stuttgart: Wissenschaftliche Buchgesellschaft, 1961, p. 27 et seqq.; idem, David Hilbert, der Altmeister der mathematischen Grundlagenforschung, in: Mathesis universalis, p. 279 et seqq.; Fuchs, p. 28 et seqq., 35 et seqq., 203 et seqq.; A. Szabó, article "Axiom", in: J. Ritter (Editor), Historisches Wörterbuch der Philosophie I, Basel/Stuttgart: Schwabe, 1971, p. 737 et seqq.; H. Freudenthal, article "Axiomatik", in: J. Ritter (Editor), p. 748 et seqq.; L. Kolakowski, Positivist Philosophy, London: Penguin Books, 1972.

[4] Regarding the problems entailed by Kurt Gödel's incompleteness theorems (1931), reference is made to Eckehart Köhler, Wie Gödel den Rechtspositivismus widerlegen würde, in: Clemens Jabloner/Friedrich Stadler (Hrsg.), Logischer Empirismus

basic precepts, the axioms. "For the term axiom, one can equally use the synonymous expressions postulate, maxim, basic precept or basic premise."[5] The crucial point is that the basic precepts are introduced without proof. The following list of examples of axioms shall serve as an illustration:

> The so-called "axioms of connection", which represent one of the groups of axioms on which Euclidean Geometry is based, read in Gonseth's wording as follows:
>
> 1. "For any point A and any straight line a it is certain whether A is on a or not"
> 2. "There are at least two points on any straight line."
> 3. "Any two points can be joined by one and only one straight line."

We will deal with the fundamental significance of these axioms separately at a later stage (below B I and II).

II. Chain Definitions

Furthermore, some basic terms are introduced into the system without definition. With regard to the aforementioned geometrical axioms, the terms "point" and "straight line" would be such undefined basic terms (one could define "point" as "circle of radius 0", but only to the result that "circle" would be an undefined basic term). However, all the other terms must then be defined as terms derived step by step from the basic terms in accordance with certain rules (rules of definition). The meaning of every term within the system is therefore exactly set.

III. Rules of Inference

In addition, in order to advance to new statements in a system of axioms, certain rules must be established which describe in detail the operations

---

und Reine Rechtslehre: Beziehungen zwischen dem Wiener Kreis und der Hans Kelsen-Schule, Vienna/ New York: Springer, 2001 (Veröffentlichungen des Instituts Wiener Kreis, 10), p. 245–274.

[5] Klug, Juristische Logik, p. 16.

necessary thereto. By means of such rules, new statements are inferred from the axioms and, in turn, further statements are inferred step by step from the new statements.

Attention is drawn, for example, to the rule of inference known as "modus ponens" which can be represented as follows:

> If A, then B.
>
> A.
>
> Therefore, B.[6]
>
> If it rains, the street gets wet.
>
> It rains.
>
> Therefore, the street gets wet.

IV. Axiomatic System Requirements

Nowadays the following three demands are made on an axiomatic system:

1. The axioms must be independent from one another. That means: one must not be able to infer the individual axioms from the system itself. For such an axiom deduced from the others would be superfluous. We will take the following sentence as an example:

    "Two straight lines have one or no point of intersection."[7]

    At first view, in its plausible manner it seems to belong to the geometrical axioms of connection mentioned above (see § 16 A I). This is, however, not true, as the following consideration proves: if one supposes that a straight line s is intersected by another straight line f in two points A and B, it follows that the straight line f also contains these two points A and B. With this, one is immediately faced with a contradiction to the third axiom of connection (above, § 16 A I). The sentence that two straight lines have one or no point of intersection is therefore not an axiom but a conclusion from the other axioms. To set

---

6   Bochénski, p. 67.
7   Gonseth, p. 17.

this sentence up as an autonomous axiom would therefore violate the requirement of independence of axioms.

2. The most important property of an axiomatic system is its consistency. An axiomatic system is consistent if it does not allow for the possibility to derive both a statement and its negation simultaneously from the system's axioms.[8] Thus it loses its consistency if and only if a combination of statements in the form of "A and non-A" can be proved.[9] As can be demonstrated, any statement from the respective field is derivable from an inconsistent system.[10] The consequence of this is that it is no longer possible to differentiate between true and false statements, which of course makes any scientific activity impossible. The proof of the consistency of an axiomatic system turns out to be different according to the circumstances. David Hilbert, for example, demonstrates the consistency of his *Foundations of Geometry* by introducing an interpretation whereby the axioms are translated into sentences of an approved mathematical theory, viz. into the theory of real numbers.[11] The consistency of the Hilbert's system was consequently proven under the condition that the theory of real numbers is consistent.[12]

3. A further requirement on an axiomatic system is its completeness. "A system is called 'complete' if all true statements in its field are derivable from its axioms ..."[13] That the first three axioms of connection (see above, § 16 A I) do not, of course, amount to a complete basis for Euclidian geometry can be shown as follows:

Assume a straight line a and on it two points A_1 and A_2.[14] This formation is in compliance with the first three axioms of connection, as anyone can easily verify. That there is more than one straight line and

---

[8] Like this Weinberger, Rechtslogik, p. 367.
[9] Fuchs, p. 58.
[10] Bocheński, p. 72.
[11] See Hilbert, Grundlagen (also published in English as: Foundations of Geometry), p. 34 et seqq.
[12] Scholz, David Hilbert (quoted in § 16 n. 3), p. 284.
[13] Bocheński, p. 72. Regarding the problems entailed by Kurt Gödel's incompleteness theorems (1931), see above § 16 A I n. 4.
[14] Gonseth, p. 17.

more than two points, though, cannot be derived from these three axioms. Therefore, one must assume more axioms and groups of axioms in order to be able to construct Euclidean geometry consistently.

After this short characterization of the axiomatic method in general, we will now turn to a closer examination of the epistemological significance of axioms.

B. The Axioms in Particular

I. The Old-Fashioned Perception: Axioms as Evident Truths

The traditional perception of the epistemological significance of axioms which prevailed into the 19th century was that axioms had to be judged according to their *evidence*. The first to give a clear statement of the evidence postulate was Aristotle. It reads as follows:[15] "A basic truth is a statement which owes its evidence … to itself and not to some other statements; for the principles of a science must not require *any further* justification but must be … evident … directly." Indeed: An unbiased observer with "common sense" who is visualizing the aforementioned geometrical principles by means of a graph would probably accept these sentences as evident truths offhand. Admittedly, a closer examination would unearth that they are *unprovable* unless one makes use of other premises. For example, one could replace Euclid's parallel axiom (see below) with the following statement: "From any point within an angle, one can draw a straight line which intersects both sides of the angle."[16] This would, however, just come down to the unprovability of this premise which would then be an axiom; which makes it clear that there is no way around presupposing certain *ultimate* premises which cannot be inferred any further, an issue which is very accurately expressed by Aristotle's statement just quoted above.

---

[15] Quoted from Scholz, Die Axiomatik der Alten (quoted in § 16 n. 3), p. 32, with references (translation by authors).

[16] Gonseth, p. 39.

The view that axioms state evident truths does, however, cause difficulties. Above all, the question arises as to "how the relation between the obviously psychological category of evidence and the logical category of truth must be imagined."[17] The subjectivity of the feeling of evidence became apparent in the dispute on Euclid's parallel axiom, which came into the focus of interest since it was not believed to be evident enough.

In Gonseth's wording, it reads as follows: "*Through a point, there is only one non-intersecting straight line (parallel) to a straight line.*" The efforts of mathematicians to prove the parallel axiom from the other axioms, which lasted for no less than two millennia, failed (and were doomed to fail, as is known today). A proof of the parallel axiom only succeeded whenever another postulate was presupposed without proof; whether this possessed greater self-evidence than Euclid's postulate always remained questionable.

II. The Modern Perception: Axioms as Postulates

The decisive change in the meaning of the term "axiom" only took place in the 19th century through the beginning of the 20th century following the development in non-Euclidean geometries.[18] The analyses of Gauss, Lobatschewskij, Bolyai, Riemann and Hilbert led to the proof that it is possible to construe logically consistent systems of geometrical sentences to which Euclid's parallel axiom or other axioms of Euclidean geometry *do not apply*! Though these new axioms are in contradiction to our (Euclidean) view, they are by no means unthinkable.

Thus, evidence was produced that the parallel axiom (or any premise equivalent to it) was in fact independent of the other axioms of Euclidean geometry, i.e. could not be inferred and proved from them. Above all, however, *the perception of the axioms as evident truths was shattered.* If Euclidean geometry is not the only possible system, and – depending on the choice of the axiomatic basis – other, logically equal geometries can be established, then one will obviously no longer be able to interpret the axioms of a geometry as self-evident truths. The relativity of axioms has

---

[17] Scholz, Die Axiomatik der Alten (quoted in § 16 n. 3), p. 33.
[18] Freudenthal (quoted in § 16 n. 3), p. 750.

meanwhile also become apparent in logic: the early phase of logic – before 1921 – may not have offered different systems. "But in 1921 (simultaneously and independently from one another) J. Lukasiewicz and E. Post set up so-called many-valued systems of logic differing radically from 'classical' logic. Lukasiewicz's systems have since been strictly axiomatized, their consistency and completeness proved, etc. There followed the so-called intuitionist logic of L. Brouwer; in 1930 this too was formulated in strictly axiomatic terms by Heyting. Today there are dozens of alternative systems, and the difference between them is considerable. Thus, for example, the *tertium non datur* (the law of the excluded middle) holds neither in the three-valued logic of Lukasiewicz, nor in Heyting's intuitionist logic, although it is a law of 'classical' mathematical logic (such as that of the *Principia Mathematica* for example)."[19]

The conclusion that must be drawn from this – which will strike the layperson as highly surprising – is this: axioms may only be interpreted – if the interpretation is to make sense – as *postulates or conventions*. Thus, axioms do not make assertions about reality, they do not discover truths, they are not statements which convey cognition but they invite us to think in a certain way; they postulate certain relations between concepts. Consequently, axioms can neither be true nor false; in the opinion of the conventionalists, they are stipulations based on conventions which have to be judged in accordance with their usefulness.[20] In contrast, Austeda differs between arbitrarily chosen and necessarily valid axioms.[21] Whilst the conventionalist standpoint is true for the former (e.g. the axioms of non-Euclidean geometry),[22] the latter are "*postulates* rooted in the human constitution, imperative demands of our intellect according to which we are forced to think, recognize, understand ...". Thus, they exert coercion on our thinking, cognition, understanding and to that extent are not arbitrary-conventional. Among them is for example the identity theorem of logic "A = A". The axioms of common geometry are

---

[19] Bocheński, p. 78.
[20] H. Poincaré, Science and Hypothesis, New Dover Edition, Mineola: Dover Publications Inc, 1952, p. 50: "*The geometrical axioms are therefore neither synthetic à priori intuitions nor experimental facts. They are conventions.*"
[21] Austeda, p. 65.
[22] Austeda, p. 192/193 n. 184.

not conventions insofar as they are rooted – from a psychological stand-point – in our Euclidean view.[23]

The common denominator of the opinions outlined above is that axioms do not represent invariable truths and therefore have nothing to do with "evident certainty" (Evidenz) or "essential intuition" (Wesensschau) and the like. Axioms are, according to the currently predominant perception, not assertions about reality, but postulates. Ultimate justifications of mathematical or logical systems are consequently not possible.

This does not rule out the possibility of assigning an external meaning to the axiomatic system and making reference to it for the purpose of de-scribing empirical interrelations (e.g. in classical mechanics).[24] In this sense, the axioms are to be qualified as empirical scientific hypotheses which can be proved true or false by experience.[25] The internal structure and the external meaning of an axiomatic system must thus be kept strictly separate. Whilst the former is independent of experience, the latter is in principle open to experience. With these questions, we touch on a significant issue which we will deal with in a concluding paragraph. To illustrate it, we will once again turn our attention to geometry.

C. Genetic and Logical Approach Illustrated by the Example of Euclidean Geometry[26]

If one asks why a geometrical proposition is considered to be true, then the answer can only be: since it can be inferred from the axioms, some basic terms and chain definitions, based on the rules of inference of the relevant system. This means: *external phenomena must never be ad-duced to prove a geometrical proposition.* Proof can only be produced *by logical deductive method based on a well founded axiomatic system.* It would be erroneous to deduce the Pythagorean Theorem from mea-surements of real triangles, even if those were extracted from the most

---

[23] Austeda, p. 38/39.
[24] Savigny (quoted in § 16 n. 3) p. 340/341.
[25] Regarding the interpretation of axioms as empiric scientific hypotheses see Popper, p. 51 et seqq.
[26] For what follows, cf. detailed comments by Austeda, p. 9 et seqq.

accurate and highest possible number of graphs. Equally, it would be mistaken to seek the validity of a geometrical axiom in the external reality of the physical space surrounding us. This already follows from the possibility of geometries which contradict real observations, but it can also be inferred from the following consideration: geometrical thinking starts "with the transfer of the physically real into the geometrically ideal."[27] The notion of the straight line, for example, is suggested to us by certain spatial factors: by the edge of a ruler or of a table, by a straight line on a drawing or by a stretched string. However, this is only possible due to the fact that the human eye only produces rough images of reality. Physically speaking, the matter consists of adjoining (but separate) atoms with the result that the perfect, continuing straight line *does not exist at all* in the exterior world! Reality is inspiring us to certain geometrical concepts, we abstract them from exterior phenomena; once thought, however, they adopt a perfectly autonomous character; they transform into a *scheme of thoughts* which is possibly in rough compliance with certain phenomena of the physical space. From a *logical* standpoint one must thus admit that geometry is *completely independent* of experience. From a *genetic* standpoint, however, things look different: if one asks about the genesis of geometry, in other words about how geometry developed, one will be able to attribute considerable significance to experience; in this particular case, to observation. For in the case of the Euclidean geometry, it was obviously reality that inspired man to the construction of an axiomatic basis (and the non-Euclidean geometries have emanated from the Euclidean geometry). *"If, then, there were no solid bodies in nature there would be no geometry"*[28] Poincaré rightly observes. Nevertheless, in reality, pure geometry is – in logical terms – not concerned "with natural solids: its object is certain ideal solids, absolutely invariable, which are but a greatly simplified and very remote image of them. The concept of these ideal bodies is entirely mental, and experiment is but the opportunity which enables us to reach the idea."[29] That is how we arrive at the seemingly paradoxical conclusion that *geometry*

---

[27] Gonseth, p. 13.

[28] Poincaré, Science and Hypothesis, New Dover Edition, Mineola: Dover Publications Inc, 1952, p. 61.

[29] Poincaré, p. 70.

– in genetic terms – emanates from experience and is at the same time – in logical terms – independent of experience! Or, as Poincaré has put it: "It is seen that experiment plays a considerable rôle in the genesis of geometry; but it would be a mistake to conclude from that that geometry is, even in part, an experimental science."[30] The paradox is, however, only an imaginary one if one bears in mind that we are dealing with two different approaches, the genetic and the logical. This differentiation between the genetic and the logical view is epistemologically significant far beyond geometry. We will encounter it once more in § 19 B IV below when dealing with the problem of whether it is possible to prove a certain concept of law by empirical means. It has been introduced at this earlier point because Euclidean geometry provides for a particularly clear illustration.

---

[30] Poincaré, p. 70.

§ 17 The Empirical Method

A. Schematic Overview

Empirical statements can be classified as follows:[1, 2]

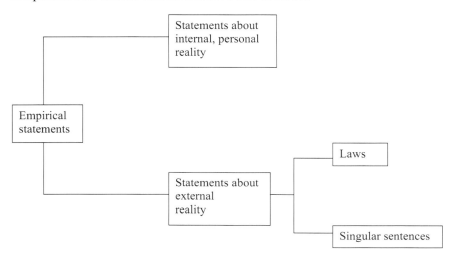

This classification is based on the differentiation between "inner" and "outer" experience. Whilst reflection on subjective experience (introspection) serves the former as a source of cognition, it is sense perception that serves the latter.

---

[1] Literature: Bocheński, p. 91 et seqq.; Kraft; B. Juhos/H. Schleichert, Die erkenntnis-theoretischen Grundlagen der klassischen Physik, Erfahrung und Denken No. 12, Berlin: Duncker & Humblot, 1963, p. 23 et seqq.; B. Juhos, Die Erkenntnis und ihre Leistung, Vienna: Springer, 1950; Popper; Austeda, p. 75 et seqq.; Seiffert I, p. 153 et seqq., p. 201 et seqq.; Brecht, p. 27 et seqq.; Stegmüller I; Bonifacio, p. 28–35.
[2] The classification is based on Juhos' table (quoted in § 17 n. 1), p. 83, and on Austeda's comments, p. 75 et seqq.

B. Observation Statements (Basic Statements, "Konstatierungen")

By "observation statements" one means statements about the existence of a direct personal experience,[3] such as for example "I feel pain", "I see an auburn roof" or "I smell the scent of roses". Thus, observation statements say something about the *personal* experiential reality of the individual who is making the statement. In this connection, it is irrelevant whether the personal experiences stem from objects of the inner or of the outer world. For the outer world initially becomes known to the individual by subjective experience, too, as for example in the statement: "I see an auburn roof." It follows from this that a statement about one's own experiential reality is not false for the mere fact that it is objectively untrue – if, for example, the object identified by the individual as an "auburn roof" is in reality an auburn horse. Rather, the observation statement is already true if it correctly describes the respective experience. For somebody can without a doubt have the subjective experience of seeing an auburn roof when in reality the object is something entirely different, or even – in the case of a hallucination – nothing whatsoever.

It is a matter of controversy whether, to this limited extent (i.e. only with regard to personal experiences), observation statements vouch for absolute certainty. This opinion is represented by several authors such as for example Schlick, Russell, Ayer[4] and also Juhos.[5] They view these sentences as the final, not further challengeable fundamentals of empirical cognition. Statements on experiential reality may therefore be lies, at most, but never errors. In fact, one will not normally be able to doubt observation statements; all the same, experiences with regard to introspection in psychological experiments teach us that errors happen.[6] This is confirmed by the doubts regarding the accuracy of a patient's description of pains, which are familiar to every doctor.

---

[3] Juhos/Schleichert (quoted in § 17 n. 1), p. 24.
[4] Kraft, p. 206 with further references.
[5] Juhos (quoted in § 17 n. 1), p. 10; Juhos/Schleichert (quoted in § 17 n. 1), p. 24. Take note of the restriction, p. 25.
[6] Kraft, p. 210 and literature quoted there in n. 414.

In order to make the subjective observations contained in basic statements viable for science, statements on experiences are usually transformed into a different logical form, viz. into so-called *protocol sentences*.[7] For this purpose, the indicative variables (I, here, now) contained in the observation statements are replaced by constants,[8] viz. by the exact statement of the name of the observer, of the date and place of observation, i.e. for example "On 12/25/2017, at 7 p.m., Mr. M. observed such and such at the observatory in Z." The observation statement as a statement of the individual about his personal experiential reality *is transformed thereby into a statement about the external reality of which Mr. M's observation experience now has become a part.*

C. Laws

A further question is how one arrives at formulating empirical laws from the unorganized class of protocol sentences framing the individual observational data. Science is confronted here with one of its most challenging problems, viz. the so-called "problem of induction". According to Bocheński, it seems that some aspects of nature were successfully covered by means of the inductive method; how this is possible defies our knowledge to this day. "The great work achieved by induction appears to the logician like the successful deciphering of a cipher text, to which we still lack the key. That some things have been deciphered seems certain; it is just that we do not know how this has happened."[9]

Nevertheless, the following steps can be distinguished:

---

[7] For an empirical positivist such as Kraft, the observational statement in a protocol sentence is constituted by the perceptive experience (Kraft, p. 294). Popper accused this view of "psychologism". Therefore, Popper does not speak of "protocol sentences" but of "basic statements" (Popper, p. 11 et seq. and p. 12 n. 2). Unlike the protocol sentences, these are recognized by *convention*. The perceptive experiences which underlie *also* basic statements are only the *motives* for the determination *but not its justification* (Popper, p. 85). These differentiations do not play an important part in research practice or in the further course of our analysis. We subscribe, however, to Kraft's conception since it results in a clearer differentiation between empirical science and philosophy.

[8] Kraft, 212.

[9] Bocheński, p. 114.

I. Hypothesization

First of all, it must be mentioned that there is no logically imperative procedure on the basis of which one could infer an unobserved fact from an observed single fact (without reference to *a higher premise*). A logically admissible, specific inductive inference from the particular to the general does not exist.[10] For one can only logically deduce from a statement that which is already contained in the statement; the inductive method, however, is aimed at an extrapolation exceeding the known particular case. The new cases are in no way already contained in the original set of facts.

Therefore, universal statements expressing relations between an indefinite multiplicity of facts can initially only be introduced as *hypotheses*. By hypothesis, one means a tentative claim, an assumption, the truth of which is yet uncertain since one cannot be sure whether the alleged facts apply to reality. The assumption must be chosen in such a way that the protocol sentences known hitherto may be deduced from it. In this way, it "explains" the observations made hitherto for the time being.

Epistemologically, the following seems important: the formation of hypotheses is based on the *premise of nature's constant regularity*, i.e. "that under similar circumstances, a pattern of events will recur in the same way as it has done on every previous regular occurrence."[11] Only this condition permits one to hope that the as-yet unobserved facts will confirm the hypothesis in the future. Without regularity, the world would remain "a chaos inaccessible to our reason!"[12]

As is well known, quantum physics brought about a fundamental change of view on this point.[13] The insight into the indeterministic character of modern physics was gained as soon as the Heisenberg uncertainty prin-

---

[10] Kraft, Einführung in die Philosophie, Second Edition, Vienna/New York 1967: Springer, p. 145.
[11] Juhos/Schleichert (quoted in § 17 n. 1), p. 26. This does not hold true for quantum physics (cf. below).
[12] Austeda, p. 48.
[13] Stegmüller I, p. 565.

ciple had been accepted.[14] It states that *on principle* it is impossible[15] to determine simultaneously and with unlimited accuracy, for example, the position and the momentum[16] or the energy of a particle[17,18]

"With the acceptance of the Heisenberg principle, the belief in the exact predictability of physical properties and thus the belief that the physical universe is a deterministic system had to be dropped. For the first time, physical laws were formulated as *statistical laws*."[19] This meant a radical break with traditional physical and philosophical views.

For us it is, however, important to emphasize the following: the indeterminism addressed in the above paragraph applies practically only to micro-physical systems, viz. to the microparticle level. "For the macroparticle level, on the other hand, it is of purely theoretical nature and neither of practical nor experimental relevance."[20] For the further course of our investigations, it is therefore unimportant. We can thus leave the classical causality principle unchallenged.

II. Verification and Falsification

The validation of a hypothesis is usually performed as follows: from the statement covering observations so far made, one infers new statements about single facts so far not observed. Thus, one is formulating predictions of future events on the basis of the assumed law. The final goal of this procedure consists, however, not in the making of forecasts but in the confirmation or refutation of the hypothesis.[21] This happens by means

---

[14] Stegmüller I, p. 565.

[15] I.e. absolutely impossible, not only temporarily practically-technically impossible.

[16] The momentum is the product of mass and velocity, Bonifazio, p. 29 n. 12.

[17] E.g. electron, neutron, proton.

[18] Bonifacio, p. 29.; Stegmüller I, p. 565 et seq. If, for example, the standard deviation of the momentum measurement is Δp and Δq stands for the standard deviation of the position measurement, then the product of $\Delta p \times \Delta q$ cannot be smaller than a fix constant (viz. $\frac{h}{4\pi}$), i.e.: $\Delta p \times \Delta q \geq \frac{h}{4\pi}$.
h is Planck's constant whose value is 6.625×10^{-27} erg. sec. (erg. = energy; sec. = time); $\pi = 3.14159. \ldots$

[19] Stegmüller I, p. 566.

[20] Stegmüller I, p. 573.

[21] Seiffert I, p. 181.

of a "deduction within the induction". The single facts are deduced from the assumed law "as if the law formed part of a deductive system".[22] The statements arrived at in this way are formally protocol sentences; their truth value must be "technically ascertainable"[23] but does not have to be ascertained yet. Since they focus on directly observable events, they may be evaluated by means of experiments and other observation techniques. If the actual observations correspond with the conclusions drawn from the hypothesis, then the hypothesis is considered indirectly confirmed; otherwise it is falsified.

The installation of a lightning arrester may serve as an example: lightning and thunder are explained physically as non-visible particles in an air stream rising because of temperature rise. The particles rub against each other and consequently pick up energy charges. Lightning is the discharge of this energy. The sound waves created in this process we hear as thunder. If this explanation is true it must be possible, according to the laws of electricity, to capture the lightning by means of a lightning arrester and to redirect it innocuously to the ground. That this is in fact possible confirms the correctness of the explanation of the lightening as an electrical discharge. All technical applications rest, if they are to be successful, on such correct prophecies on the basis of laws of nature.

If a hypothesis has been confirmed in several instances but has never been disproved, it is assigned law status. An empirical law is understood to be a *verified* statement of *universal* content.[24] Thus, the law does not describe a singular occurrence (that would be described by a so-called "singular statement", see below, § 17 D) but refers to an unlimited multitude of occurrences by expressing an empirical entailment (implication): if conditions A are given, then the consequences will always be B. This apodictic wording re-leads to the immediate revelation of the problem of induction: an empirical law is *obviously never verifiable once and for all*. For this purpose, one would have to be able to observe all occurrences taking place in the past, the present or the future which fall with-

---

[22] Seiffert I, p. 181.
[23] Bocheński, p. 98.
[24] We will have to get back to the important distinction between the "hypotheses of law" and the "individual hypotheses" at a later point of this work, § 17 D.

in the scope of the law. This is obviously not possible. On the other hand, the observance of a single occurrence inconsistent with the law is sufficient to disprove it for good, as long as the inconsistency cannot be unmasked as only apparent and due to the influence of additional factors. This *"asymmetry"* between (logically valid) falsifiability and (never final) verifiability has led Karl Popper to propose the *falsifiability* of the system as a criterion for an empirical system.[25] That means, in order to be recognized as empirical or scientific, a system need not be conclusively (positively) verifiable; it is sufficient for it to be refutable by experience.[26] Thus, according to Popper, too, a system must be open to validation by experience. This may be expressed as follows: *the "verification" of an empirical law consists in the failure of its falsification.* In research practice, however, the principle of the ultimate falsification of a law by contradicting observations is not handled as strictly. According to Bocheński, "[i]t would be naive to suppose that a scientist abandons a well-verified law when he finds one or two protocol statements which contradict it ..."[27] It is more likely that the accuracy of the protocol statements will be doubted or – in case such accuracy is established – that one will look for interfering factors influencing the result in order to uphold the law in case such factors can actually be proved.

Unfortunately, falsifications as understood by Popper have turned out not to be definite, either. There are many examples in the history of science. A simple one is the following:

Nowadays we know that the speed of sound is approximately 340 m/s. Since the measuring instruments available in his days were so inexact that they yielded results either much higher or much lower than the actual value, Isaac Newton preferred to calculate the speed of sound "by means of theory taking the already known oscillation laws as a basis."[28] In doing so, he obtained a first theoretical value of about 295 m/s. However, after other scientists had come up with completely different measurement results, Newton decided to carry out measurements himself. He

---

[25] Popper, p. 18.
[26] Popper, p. 18.
[27] Bocheński, p. 99.
[28] Di Trocchio, p. 25.

obtained results which were partly higher, partly lower than the value calculated by means of theory. Had Newton proceeded in accordance with Popper, he would have had to regard his calculation as falsified. Luckily, he did not do so. It was not until 1802 that Pierre-Simon Marquis de Laplace (1749–1827) was able to account for the difference between the theoretical value of 295 m/s and the actual one of approximately 340 m/s: under compression, sound waves liberate heat as they expand which reduces the air resistance and thus generates a higher velocity.[29] After all, the "falsified" Newtonian calculation had been correct.

Nevertheless, it remains to be summarized: any empirical law is, strictly speaking, only valid for the time being! That means *it may be overturned at any time by future, as yet unknown experiences.* Therefore, in principle, empirical research never results in apodictic certainty. One is always faced with the possibility of future changes. The more often a law is corroborated by occurrences observed at a later stage, the greater the likelihood of its correctness. Thus, *there is only a gradual and not a categorical difference between a hypothesis in the technical sense of the term* (statement at the stage of an assumption) *and a law: empirical laws, too, are only valid hypothetically.*

III. Formation of Theories

Normally, one does not content oneself with the setting up of laws; one proceeds to formulate a third level of statements which, for their part, explain the law. "If these statements are sufficiently general and explain many laws, they are usually called theories (the methodological terminology is still somewhat variable). The process which leads to the formation of theories is, from a logical point of view, basically the same as that which led to the enunciation of laws…"[30] Therefore, a theory is a "combination of several laws in a 'major law'."[31] It is based directly on the laws which it explains, and indirectly on the protocol statements on which the laws are based.

---

[29] Di Trocchio, p. 27.
[30] Bocheński, p. 97.
[31] Seiffert I, p. 165.

D. Singular Statements

Singular statements refer, unlike empirical laws, to a *concrete* fact. They "claim empirical relations of validity between basic statements. Thus for the individual case at hand, the singular statement 'This is a table' claims simultaneous validity, that is to say 'empirical equivalence', for certain basic statements of optical, haptic etc. sensory impressions; relations of validity which have always been observed hitherto between basic statements of this kind."[32] The claim "This is a table" based on the optical impression, for example, can be verified by touching the object referred to as a table. Just like empirical laws, singular statements are, strictly speaking, of a hypothetical nature. In the aforementioned example, a closer examination could bring to light that the object referred to as a table is in reality a big mirror which is showing the reflection of a table. The hypothesis "This is a table" would then be falsified. In this case, the term "hypothesis" takes on a slightly different meaning from the one we have so far assigned to it (see above, § 17 C.I). Whereas general hypotheses which articulate an assumption on an unlimited multitude of cases were at stake there, here we are concerned with "singular scientific hypotheses" which claim an individual set of facts. Confirmed general hypotheses result – as we have seen – in empirical laws, confirmed singular hypotheses in singular statements.

This differentiation between general scientific hypotheses and singular scientific hypotheses as well as between empirical laws and singular sentences is very important; it makes it clear that one may *legitimately speak of empirical research already when singular occurrences have been exactly secured* and not only – as for the most part in natural science – when universal statements have been established. The equation "empirical science = natural science" is very unfortunate since in the other sciences, too, one can find a great many statements which can be verified directly or indirectly in an "intersubjective" manner and may therefore quite rightly be called "empirical", although only the securing of single facts (for example in history or sociology) as opposed to universal laws is at stake. Therefore, we treat as empirically testable not only claims like

---

[32] Juhos/Schleichert (quoted in § 17 n. 1), p. 26.

the one that a temperature rise of 1° C causes nitrogen to expand its volume by 1/273, but also, for example, the following: "The majority of students at the University of G law school are against capital punishment", or "Composition X was written by composer A", or "The decisions of the highest Court of the country of Z regarding legal issue Y can be summarized as such and such." The first of these claims would be testable by means of a survey, the second by analysis of the historical sources (the dependability of the historian's findings being dependent upon the concrete availability of sources), and the third by review of the decisions of the respective court.

E. Empirical Statements as Determinations

In summary, we can characterize empirical statements as follows: empirical statements make claims about reality. They are not stipulations but reports and therefore convey cognition. Their validity can be tested by the methods indicated; they can be verified or falsified respectively by anybody of sound mind who possesses normal perception and (where necessary) is equipped with the requisite scientific education. "In terms of traditional logic, they are 'synthetic' or 'judgments of extension' insofar as they extend the meaning of the subject term by a predicate and state a characteristic not yet included therein. Thus, on the one hand they are not 'empty' like logical sentences, but on the other hand, neither do they constitute apodictic knowledge as those do ..."[33] Strictly speaking, all empirical sentences are only valid hypothetically.

Their first and most important validity basis is *experience*. This experience can be "internal" or "external" experience, i.e. it can refer to one's own experiential reality conceived by introspection, or to external reality ultimately conceived by sense perception. Other components of this external experience are, however, facts which cannot be directly observed but which are inferable from observation data (and in psychology also from introspection) on the basis of (possibly quite complicated) conclusions, such as, for example, processes forming part of somebody

---

[33] Austeda, p. 77.

else's inner life. By means of logical conclusions from observation, *mental* realities can – under certain conditions – also be established as inter-subjectively testable: for example a custom, by observation of actual human behavior, or the law in force in a country, by the relevant codes and court decisions. In this context, the following example of Bocheński is instructive, too: "Take an unknown word, for example, 'tar'. What it means will gradually come to be understood as the following axioms are set forth: (1) the tar has two feet, (2) the tar speaks English, (3) the tar smokes a pipe. On the basis of 1 alone 'tar' could mean a piece of furniture; 1 and 2 indicate that it is certainly alive, but it could still be a parrot; with all three axioms, however, it is clear that 'tar' can mean only a human being."[34] The meaning of the word "tar" – thus something mental – can here be established in an inter-subjectively testable manner.

The rules of *logic* constitute the second validity basis of empirical sentences. Since experience alone could only convey a chaos of impressions to us, we must acknowledge the rules of logic in order to be able to organize the world of experience in an orderly manner. These rules of logic which are the basis of all thinking, concluding and proving, cannot themselves be proved right by experience but are valid independent of all experience and before all experience.

Thirdly, empirical research is based upon certain additional theoretical conditions which can neither be verified by experience nor are part of the rules of logic. One of them is the assumption – immediately clear to common sense – that there is a physical reality beyond our experiential reality. This corresponds to the basic thesis of epistemological realism which advocates a dualism of consciousness and a reality that is independent therefrom.[35] This is not the place to unpick the extraordinary complicated problem of the basic principles of science and to demonstrate in detail which premises science must presuppose as "axiomatic"

---

[34] Bocheński, p. 84.

[35] This does not apply to quantum physics. Whether, for example, light displays its wave quality or its particle quality *is dependent on the test arrangement of the observer*. The measurements are then, however, *strictly objective in terms of classical physics*. Regarding quantum physics see above, § 17 C.I.

since they cannot be proved on the basis of and by means of scientific method. We confine ourselves to pointing out the fact that in any case, even empirical scientific research cannot do without any premises (not to mention philosophical thinking!). From this it is clear that in the empirical sciences, too, ultimate justifications are not possible.[36]

---

[36] Cf. § 16 B II above with reference to the mathematical-logical axioms.

§ 18 Scientific Truth and Scientific Cognition

A. The Definition of Cognition as Stipulation

We have so far repeatedly used the terms "truth" and "cognition" without explicitly stating their meaning. Our approach was legitimate insofar as that the use of these words and their position in the context in which they were used already illuminated their meaning up to a certain degree. This meaning shall now be developed in more detail. It shall not be the purpose to investigate what truth or cognition is, as such, since both these terms rank amongst the most controversial ones in philosophy. Many things may be understood by them. It is rather a matter of clarifying what we mean to be understood by them in the following; which meaning these words shall be assigned based on the conception developed in the course of this work.

If we begin by asking the question: "What is cognition?", a closer look will reveal that the question has been worded in an unfortunate way. For the attempt to identify what cognition is will inevitably lead to an infinite regress or a circular argument.[1] In order to understand what cognition is one needs a criterion which, itself, represents cognition. In order to prove that this criterion represents cognition, one is in need of a further criterion which verifies the first one as cognition, and so on ad infinitum. If this infinite regress is avoided by simply *declaring* a certain concept of cognition as the result of true cognition, the argument becomes obviously circular.

Therefore, the concept of cognition cannot itself be based on cognition but can only be introduced as a definition. Thus, the question does not read "What is cognition" but "What shall cognition be?"[2] or "What shall we accept as cognition?" or "What do we *want* to accept as cognition?" This said, it should be clear that it is not our intention to propagate a weltanschauung with the concept of cognition to be developed in the following, but to create a methodological instrument for the further

---

[1] For the following, see Kraft, p. 21 et seqq.
[2] Kraft, p. 27.

150

course of our investigation. Even the metaphysician may – and justifiably so – pass off as cognition what he has viewed in the state of enlightenment. Only then, his statements are based on a different concept of cognition than the one to be developed here; his assertions may at best be tested by another enlightened person, but not universally.

It goes without saying that we will not determine the concept of cognition arbitrarily but will turn to certain motifs for guidance. These motifs are the following:

First of all, we must *stipulate* the concept of cognition in such a way that statements about psychological processes are, in principle, equally regarded as testable. If we considered only sentences about facts of the external physical world, i.e. about facts of time and space, as empirically testable, the psychological varieties of positivism would be discredited from the beginning: they would be considered as unprovable on the basis of our stipulation of the concept of cognition alone.

Furthermore, sentences about meanings shall be considered cognitions if they can be substantiated by logical empirical investigations. If we did not allow for this, then for example sentences about legal *norms,* i.e. about the *meaning* of certain empirically given facts, would not be testable from the outset. It is, however – as has been demonstrated in the two preceding paragraphs – overhasty to conclude that something which is not directly observable is beyond the scope of empirical cognition. Only a small proportion of the content of a physical theory, for example, is directly observable; nevertheless the whole theory may be regarded as an empirical system because it can be refuted as a whole by experience. Likewise, a *meaning is not perceptible to senses.* Nevertheless, it may be open to logical empirical analysis.[3] Kelsen has clearly formulated this for legal theory as follows: "A science is 'empirical', as opposed to 'metaphysical', not only if it describes facts taking place in space and time but also if it describes the meaning of certain human acts. A theory of law remains empirical if it is limited to the description of norms which

---

[3] See above, § 17 E. Whether it will in fact be open to such analysis is of course dependent on the concrete circumstances and especially on whether the expressions used are assigned a particular, constant meaning in everyday or technical language usage.

are the meaning of empirical, human-set acts in time and space without reference to superhuman entities such as God or a God-created nature, as long as the 'ought' of such norms described by such theory is not the ought of a metaphysical justice."[4]

Only statements which can be tested for their truth by *everybody of sound mind* who possesses *normal perception* and is equipped with the necessary *education* shall therefore be referred to as statements conveying cognition (determinations). *As cognition, we shall regard what can be proved to be true.* We are thus referencing the concept of truth. This shall be defined as follows:

B. Logical Truth

A sentence shall be considered logically true if, within a deductive system, it can be inferred from the presupposed axioms, basic terms, chain definitions and rules of operation of the system.[5]

Therefore, a logically true sentence is nothing more than an "if-then-statement": If one accepts the axioms, basic terms, chain definitions and rules of operation, then such and such is true. We are always concerned just with an "internal" truth, i.e. with a truth within the respective system: thus, logical truth is relative insofar as it depends on the premises of the respective system. On the other hand, logical truth is an absolute truth insofar as it is determined within the system once and for all, i.e. it cannot be refuted, like empirical truth, by later investigations.

---

[4] Kelsen, ÖZöR NF 10 (1959/60), p. 5 (our translation).
[5] Regarding the problems entailed by Kurt Gödel's incompleteness theorems (1931), reference is made to Eckehart Köhler, Wie Gödel den Rechtspositivismus widerlegen würde, in: Clemens Jabloner, Friedrich Stadler (Eds.), Logischer Empirismus und Reine Rechtslehre: Beziehungen zwischen dem Wiener Kreis und der Hans Kelsen-Schule, Vienna, New York: Springer, 2001 (Veröffentlichungen des Instituts Wiener Kreis, 10), p. 245–274.

C. Empirical Truth

A sentence shall be considered empirically true if it can be integrated without contradiction into an ordered context of a multitude of perception statements – which may be based on internal or external perception – and certain theoretical premises.[6]

Included in this definition are, first of all, the previously discussed validity bases of empirical sentences (viz. logic, experience and certain theoretical premises).[7] Furthermore, the following issues are to be emphasized:

In this context, "empirical" is not to be understood in the narrow sense of natural science, and this is meant in two respects. First, we have also characterized as empirical statements about one's own experiential reality (basic statements or *Konstatierungen*). Hence, inner experience is admissible! Second, even a statement of single facts confirmed by observation or inferred logically therefrom (i.e. not only statements of laws) shall be considered "empirical". An historian investigating sources or a psychologist checking a patient proceeds "empirically" in this sense.

An authoritative standard for the truth of an empirical sentence (a basic statement as well as a statement about external reality) cannot be just a single subjective experience such as a sense-perception. *Sense perception alone is not a sufficient criterion for truth.* Rather, the sentence describing the relevant experience must be capable of integration within the logical context of a multitude of experiences and theoretical premises. Only the fact that it can be integrated without contradiction into an already known system vouches for the truth of an empirical sentence. The following example may serve as an illustration: if one dips a straight stick into the water, it is well known that it appears to be refracted. An observer who is not familiar with the laws of optics would therefore have to hypothesize, on the basis of this *one* perception, that a stick breaks in the said circumstances. If the observer pulls the stick out of the water, it

---

[6] The concept of truth defined herein consists thus in a combination of the so-called "theory of correspondence" and the so-called "theory of coherence".

[7] See above, § 17 E.

will prove to have remained unbroken. The observer thus obtains two conflicting optical impressions. Furthermore, by touching the seemingly broken stick under water, his sense of touch will confirm the second optical impression. A further point that militates in favor of the stick actually not breaking is the fact that it is possible to propel a boat forward by rowing, which would otherwise be impossible. By this and other impressions obtained under any number of different circumstances, the counter-hypothesis of the non-breaking stick is confirmed, whilst the original hypothesis is proven wrong. Doubt cannot be smoothed out completely, however, as long as the deceptive impression is unaccounted for. Only if one is familiar with the law according to which the light deviates from its original straight path when it passes from one medium (e.g. air) to another one of different density (e.g. water) may one consider the issue clarified.

D. Epistemological Positivism and Value Relativism

A widely-held belief following from the approach of an epistemological positivism is that any kind of value judgment is of irrational nature and therefore beyond scientific cognition.[8] This belief is true only insofar as the cognition of values is not possible by the means of scientific cognition described herein, and that most positivists are *de facto* value-relativists. In our opinion, however, a positivist approach does not rule out that there can be a different kind of cognition of values, e.g. on the basis of a utilitarian conception, and that a rational discussion of value issues is therefore possible. *From a positivist approach it only follows that value cognition must be cognition of a different kind, but not that it is impossible.* Therefore, epistemological positivism and value relativism are logically independent theses even though they tend de facto to appear connected to each other in the works of many philosophers.

---

[8] Like this e.g. Coing, p. 62.

Second Chapter

Proving the Unprovability of Legal Positivism

In order to answer the main question that we set out to address in the following, viz. the question of whether one of the legal theories described above is "right", and if so, which one, we must first recall that the decisive divergences between the different legal positivisms consist in a *definition*: positivist theories differ principally in the *concept of law* which they presuppose. We are then confronted with the question of verification, i.e. the question of whether one of the definitions of law given by the positivists can be proven true, which implies that all the other theories would have to be considered false. In accordance with the concept of cognition laid out in the preceding paragraphs, only logical-empirical methods are suitable.

Since, as just said, we focus on definitions, it seems appropriate to resort to the theory of definition from the discipline of logic at this point.[1] In fact we will draw upon the *modern theory of definition* since the classical theory of definition has proven to be insufficient in various respects.[2] To us, the most important distinction consists of the qualification of a definition as a determination (below, A) which can be true or false, or as stipulation (below B) which can only be useful or non-useful.[3]

§ 19 Statements

Two subgroups are to be kept apart: claims about habitual language use and real definitions.

---

[1] Literature: R. Robinson, Definition, Oxford: Oxford University Press, 1950; Austeda, p. 73 et seqq.; Bocheński, p. 81 et seqq.; Klug, p. 80 et seqq.; idem, Festschrift Emge, p. 33 et seqq.; Kantorowicz, p. 1 et seqq.; Dubislav; E. v. Savigny, Grundkurs im wissenschaftlichen Definieren, Munich: Deutscher Taschenbuchverlag, 1970; L. Kuhlen, Typuskonzeptionen in der Rechtstheorie, Schriften zur Rechtstheorie No. 66, Berlin: Duncker & Humblot, 1977, p. 30 et seqq.
[2] Klug, Juristische Logik, p. 89.
[3] Klug, Festschrift Emge, p. 40.

A. Claims about Habitual Language Use
(Analytic Definitions)

I. Basics

An analytic definition is claiming something about the *existence of a habitual language use*.[4] It is a "determination, and not a stipulation, of the meaning which a word or a sign in general possesses, in other words the determination of the usage it has."[5] According to Bochénski, by an analytic definition "a meaning is explicitly attributed to a sign which is already appropriate to it in some way or another".[6] It is thus presupposed that a certain meaning of the sign is already recognized by a certain person (e.g. in the works of a scholar) or a certain group of people. The respective determination thereof can obviously be correct or incorrect; i.e. it makes sense to ask whether it is true or false.

As explained above, we only consider logical empirical methods suitable for the verification of definitions.

II. Examples

Let us take a look at the following examples: "A bumblebee is any of the various large, hairy, social bees that nest underground and belong to the genus *Bombus*." Or: "A wife is a woman joined to a man in marriage; a female spouse." Or: "A stallion is an adult male horse that has not been castrated." The definitions at hand represent analytical definitions, i.e. the precise meaning on which the terms "bumblebee", "wife" or "stallion" are based is worked out in detail. Said words are thus *expressly assigned* the meaning they actually have in *habitual language use*. These definitions assert some claim. They are therefore subject to the truth criterion and can be verified by analysis of habitual language use. Hence they are based on scientific cognition, not on a stipulation. If, for example, wife was defined as follows: "A wife is a woman joined to a man in

---

[4] Robinson (quoted in § 19 n. 1), p. 35 et seqq., refers to it as "lexical definition".
[5] Dubislav, p. 131.
[6] Bocheński, p. 82.

a shared household" (= concubinage), then this definition would not be inexpedient, but simply wrong. For it is not our custom to refer to a partner in a quasi-marital relationship as "wife". Analytical definitions have the purpose of *reflecting* a certain linguistic usage, not of *stipulating* a certain linguistic usage.

III. The Positivist Definitions of Law as Analytic Definitions?

We will now concern ourselves with the question of whether the positivist definitions of law may be qualified as analytic definitions in the sense laid out above.

Even on cursory consideration, this seems unlikely since, as Kantorowicz notes, scholars have filled whole libraries with writings devoted to the question of what is meant by "law", but, as the sheer volume of their output testifies, without having arrived at definitive answers.[7] This would scarcely be the case if there was a clear-cut language usage and if it had been the intention of the legal theorists to simply outline such usage. Since in this case criteria would be available which allowed for the verification of the various definitions, sooner or later one of the definitions would have proven to be the uniquely correct one, and would have been bound to gain general recognition.

Today's international legal theory also distinguishes between three different dimensions of law[8] which are attributed to different juristic disciplines and which correspond with different approaches to concept formation.[9] The first approach is directed at the *facts* of the law. In this sense, the law is the subject-matter of the legal empirical sciences, viz. sociology of law,[10] ethnology of law and psychology of law. All these sciences inquire into the *reality* of the law.

---

[7] Kantorowicz, p. 1.
[8] Rehbinder, Einführung, p. 2; idem, Eugen Ehrlich, p. 130 et seqq. and literature quoted in n. 19/20/21, ibidem.
[9] Raiser, Einführung, p. 103 et seq.
[10] Modern sociologists of law, such as Rehbinder, do no longer lapse into the extreme of identifying the law in a sociological sense, the so-called "law in action", by certain *facts* only. The law in action consists of "those *norms* which the law staff is prepared to apply or to comply with" (Rehbinder, Eugen Ehrlich, p. 130; accentuation by the

Secondly, the law may be viewed as a system of *norms* in force (in the sense of ought-validity) which are contained primarily in legislative acts, but aside from these, also in judicial decisions and in formations of customary law. The law in *this* sense is the object of legal dogmatics; however, many modern legal logics studies are also concerned with the law as norm.[11]

Thirdly, the law may be understood in the sense of an *ideal;* the task of inquiring into the contents of the idea of law is assigned to philosophy of law. The legal philosopher seeks to establish the 'just content' of the law.

Provided that the positivist definitions of the law are, according to their logical structure, to be qualified as analytic definitions, they have to identify the meanings attributed to the word "law" and the corresponding expressions "*ius*", "*Recht*", "*droit*", "*diritto*", "*derecho*" by actual language usage. One glance at the aforementioned three dimensions of the law immediately reveals that all positivist concepts of the law ignore the third dimension. This fact is so obvious that we have qualified it as a typical characteristic of our concept of legal positivism. It is, however, indisputable that, when employed in the compounds "natural law", "*ius naturale*", "*Natur-Recht*", "*droit naturel*", "*diritto naturale*" and "*derecho natural*", the terms "law", "*ius*", "*Recht*", "*droit*", "*diritto*", "*derecho*" are evidently used in their third meaning. Consequently, in certain contexts, the word "law" and its equivalents in the languages quoted serve equally as terms for an ideal law, a conclusion which is entirely independent of the question of whether there actually is such ideal law or whether a natural law really exists. This circumstance already shows that the positivist theories cannot be based upon purely analytic definitions of the law since these theories exclude – possibly for good reasons – a certain meaning of the term "law" which is to be found in actual language usage.

---

authors. In addition, cf. ibidem, chart on p. 131). Nevertheless the main focus of sociology of law remains on the facticity of the law.

[11] Cf. e.g. C.E. Alchourrón/E. Bulygin, Normative Systems, Vienna/New York: Springer, 1971.

This impression is reinforced if one examines the individual theories more closely:

Let us start from the example of the highest court of a sovereign country ruling on a legal dispute and rendering a decision that is inconsistent with the law, and let us illuminate these facts from the standpoint of those theories which identify the law – to the exclusion of the normative element – either with the facts of judicial behavior or with a system of norms which correspond to a specific apparatus of sanctions administered by a specific law staff. According to one of these theories, the decision inconsistent with the law is to be qualified as law because it represents a judicial behavior, whereas according to the other, it is qualified as Law because even an unlawful decision usually entails a sanction in case the addressee disobeys. Starting from these theories, it is, however, no longer possible to differentiate between right and wrong decisions. For this would presuppose a *criterion* by which the decision could be assessed and consequently qualified as right, i.e. legally *justified*, or wrong, i.e. legally *unjustified*. Such a standard can only consist in the law in the sense of a system of *norms*, the validity of which is independent of whether it is applied correctly by the administrative organs or not. Therefore, if some judicial practice is praised as being right or blamed for being wrong, this means that the term "law" is being used in sense of a system of *norms* with legal validity (i.e. with ought-validity) in this context. Consequently, the definitions of said sociological theories cannot simply be accounts of a language usage.

The analogue is true for those theories which determine the definition in such a way that international law is denied legal quality.[12] It may be possible to come up with notable arguments in favor of this differentiation. However, there is no denying that the order of the international relationships amongst the states is called "law", viz. international law. A definition of law which wants to be analytic would have to be laid out in such a way that it would include this complex, too.

---

[12] Cf. above, § 2 at n. 35, § 8 at n. 11 and below, § 24 G.

To back up our opinion, reference is made to the comments of Hart.[13] He contrasts the (broader) concept of law of legal positivism with the (narrower) concept of law of Natural Law which incorporates positivity *as well as* certain content-based criteria as characteristics.[14] Hart explains that neither the positivist nor the natural law proponent would be satisfied if he was told that by his concept of law, he had merely correctly reflected a certain language usage, in England or in Germany, for example. It is not a question of the correctness of the reproduction of a language usage, but what really is at stake is the *comparative* merit of a wider or a narrower concept for classifying rules that are effective in social life. A rational *choice* between these two concepts has to be based on the fact that one is superior to the other in the way in which it will assist our theoretical inquiries or advance and clarify our moral deliberations or, indeed, accomplish both.

We therefore hold as an intermediate result: the term "law" is actually used for the denomination of rather different phenomena. It is not assigned a clear-cut meaning which could be reproduced by an analytic definition and proved right or wrong. The positivist definitions exclude the ideational meaning of the word and place their concepts in the normative and/or factual realm although neither one of them is able to claim an all-embracing reflection of actual language usage. Therefore, they are not to be qualified as propositions about an existing language usage.[15]

---

[13] Hart, Concept of Law, p. 209/210. It is Eckman's merit, p. 39 et seqq./129, to have put Hart's somewhat summary comments within a methodological context.

[14] Cf. for example Radbruch, Statutory Lawlessness and Supra-Statutory Law, first published in Süddeutsche Juristenzeitung 1 (1946) p. 105–108, translated by Bonnie Litschewski Paulson and Stanley L. Paulson, Oxford Journal of Legal Studies 26 (2006), p. 1–11, p. 7, quoted below, § 23 A.

[15] The second interpretation possible at this point, viz. that we are here concerned with an incorrect, since incomplete analytic definition, can remain out of consideration because all authors quoted were aware of the existence of the additional meanings of the term "law".

B. Real Definitions

A positivist who, as for example Austin, denies the legal nature of international law but understands it as "international positive morality" might now raise the following objection: "I admit that my concept of law does not reflect language usage since the word 'law' is indisputably used to denote the very object which I also call 'international positive morality'. Nevertheless, I am of the opinion that my concept of law is the solely true one since, in reality, international law *is* not actually 'law'. The habitual language use is simply *mistaken*." Such reasoning shifts the issue onto an entirely different level. It is now no longer a question of whether the positivist definitions correctly reflect language usage but of whether they *correctly describe the object at hand*. This brings a kind of definition known in classical logic as a "real definition" within the scope of our discussion.

I. Basics

"A real definition is a kind of epitome of all that can be said of an object in the light of scientific knowledge at a given time…"[16] Thus, *real definitions are statements about reality*. They contain statements about facts, they *assert* something. Therefore, they must be verifiable and are subject to the criterion of truth. Consequently, they do not differ fundamentally from ordinary empirical statements, which is why some authors conceive of them – in the interest of a clear differentiation of the forms of statements – only as pseudo-definitions.[17]

II. Example: Definition of "Myopia"

Let us have a look at the following definition: "Myopia is a refraction defect of the eye which is either caused by too much refraction power of the optical system (cornea, lens) or by elongation of the eye structure

---

[16] Dubislav, p. 147.
[17] Savigny (quoted in § 19 n. 1), p. 30, speaks therefore of "definitions" only in case of claims about the habitual use (lexical or analytic definition, see above, § 19 A) and stipulations of the meaning of a sign or a word (synthetic definitions, below, § 20 B).

161

itself to the effect that collimated light produces an image in front of the retina." This statement can be tested for its truth by empirical research. However, this presupposes, as remains to be set out in more detail below, that the use of the term "myopia" is already determined either by language usage (above, § 19) or by convention (in the sense to be explained below, § 20 B). That is to say, *it has to be clear which phenomena shall be referred to by the term "myopia"*. Only then will it be possible to make verifiable judgments, in the sense implied by real definitions.

III. Positivist Definitions as Real Definitions?

We will now address the issue of whether the positivist definitions may be apprehended as real definitions. This would mean that they would be verifiable or falsifiable by experience. Since all positivist theories define the concept of law with reference to physical or psychological realities, this should – at first glance – be possible; and moreover, not only with regard to theories which understand the law exclusively as a fact, but also with regard to theories, such as Kelsen's pure theory of law, which include a normative element in their definitions. For, as Kelsen rightly points out, a science is not only empirical if it describes facts taking place in time and space but also if it describes the meaning of certain human acts.[18]

Attempting to derive the concept of law from experience, we will get caught in a vicious circle: the undertaking can only succeed if one already knows which material is deemed to be legal and which facts are deemed to be legal facts. In order to know what law is, one must base one's investigation on experiences which – unlike other experiences – present themselves as legal experiences. *However, strictly logically speaking, this already presupposes the concept of law which is the object of the inquiry.* For how should it be possible to qualify certain phenomena as legal without first knowing what law is? The inquisitive mind, provided that it undergoes critical self-scrutiny, is confronted here with the irritating obstacle that it can only extract from empirical material what it has previously put into it; that the only music it hears is that of

---

[18] Cf. cit. above, § 18 A.

things playing back exactly the notes it first dictated to them! At this point it becomes evident once more that there can be no experience "per se", but that it is always co-authored by the human manner of cognition, which only forms "its own" reality.[19] Depending on the conceptual plan on which – maybe unconsciously – the research is based, the result of such research is influenced one way or the other. We thus conclude that empirical research by itself can never yield a certain concept of law *because it is possible only on condition that there is a concept of law.* One could say: *the concept of law is – from a logical standpoint – not the end, but the beginning of the research: it is not a result, but a postulate* (cf. below, § 20 B.III). It must be emphasized that the order is only logical, not chronological. That is to say, it is not contradictory if a researcher stipulates his concept of law only after detailed analysis of certain experiences. As much as concept formation – from a genetic standpoint – may depend on certain experiences, the concept itself – from a logical standpoint – proves to be independent of such experiences, since it alone enables them to be interpreted as legal experiences! The strict separation of the genetic (psychological) and the logical approach is one of the most important achievements of epistemology.[20] We have encountered this already while discussing the example of Euclidean geometry.[21]

Consequently, a verifiable definition in terms of a real definition is only possible if the material to be explored has already clearly been delimited either by language usage or by a stipulation in the sense to be discussed below, § 20 B, i.e. if the object to be described has been identified by linguistic usage or pragmatic convention. Only if one of these two conditions is met is it possible to make statements which may qualify as "scientific cognitions" in the sense laid out above, § 18. However, in the case of the term "law", a sufficiently accurate language usage does not exist, as has been shown in § 19 A III. A real definition trying to cover an object identified by language usage is therefore impossible. The first of the two conditions therefore falls away. Whereas if a stipulation separates the legal from the extra-legal factors, a real definition is possible

---

[19] Austeda, p. 14.
[20] Fundamental in this point Austeda, p. 9 et seqq and 28 et seqq.
[21] Above, § 16 C.

but, compared to the stipulation made before, relatively inconsequential; for in this case, the decisive problem is of course immediately shifted by one level: then the question is in what terms one has to make the all-decisive stipulation. This variant shall be pursued in the following paragraph, where the upshot will be that the issue cannot be resolved by scientific means.

Hence we arrive at the conclusion that in both cases, the positivist definitions are ultimately not to be qualified as verifiable or falsifiable statements, i.e. as judgments which can be proven or disproven by experience. Once again, it is shown that ultimate justifications are not possible, here with reference to the various positivist definitions of law.

§ 20 Stipulative Definitions

A. Syntactic Definitions

Syntactic definitions are mentioned only for the sake of completeness; they do not have any bearing on the aims pursued by this study so that a more detailed account is unnecessary. According to Klug, a syntactic definition is "a convention (or stipulation) about the admissibility of the replacement of a word – more precisely: of a sign, which may also but need not necessarily be a word – by another, usually shorter one."[1]

B. Synthetic Definitions

I. Basics

Synthetic definitions are the truly "creative" definitions.[2] They stipulate the meaning of a sign or a word. They *postulate* what exactly is to be understood by a sign or a word. Regardless of their character as regulations of language use, in outward appearance they tend to take the form of empirical statements. Thus, for example, the legal definition contained in Art. 10 para. 2 of the Swiss Penal Code reads: "Felonies are offenses punishable by imprisonment of more than three years." However, one always has to bear in mind, that as a matter of logical correctness, this can only mean the following: "By felony *we shall mean* …etc." For it is impossible to prove by any research whatsoever that felony is an offense punishable by imprisonment of more than three years; rather, this had to be *stipulated* by the legislator.

Therefore, as regulations of language use, synthetic definitions do not claim something about reality; they do not express insights but are based on stipulations, on conventions. Consequently, they can neither be true nor false (except for logical errors, of course), *but only useful or not useful.* Because of their ordering character, they are of an *instantly strik-*

---

[1] Klug, Festschrift Emge, p. 39.
[2] Bocheński, p. 82 and 85.

ing resemblance to the axioms[3] but differ from them, nevertheless, in that the axioms call for a certain thinking process, whereas synthetic definitions call for a certain linguistic usage.[4]

At this point, let us address two potential misunderstandings which may arise:

First, it could be argued that the notion of the definition as just sketched out permits a completely arbitrary formation of concepts. In that case, it is impossible to make a choice in favor of either of two contradictory concepts. This is, however, not the case if one opts to work with fruitful concepts, viz. concepts which prove of value. In this case, there is no logical tie, but instead, a teleological one: *it is necessary to take into consideration accepted value judgments and given experiences when forming a concept!* (Cf. the example of the definition of brain death, below.)

Second, there could be a misunderstanding to the point that many scientific and philosophical disputes on conceptual stipulations are demoted to simple questions of terminology by a modern theory of definition, since it is not about truth or untruth. Kantorowicz remarks: "This would be to overlook the fact that behind a dispute on a definition there always lies a problem of classification, and classifications are concerned with the relations not of names but of things. Whether, for instance, a concept ought to be given or refused a name on which important propositions are predicated is a terminological but by no means 'mere' terminological question: the choice does not lie between different terms only, but between the things which they denote."[5] As an example, we return to the above-mentioned legal definition of felony in Art. 10 para. 2 of the Swiss Penal Code. What one wants to understand by felony is not only a terminological question because the term "felony" appears in other contexts and consequently incorporates the meaning assigned to it by the definition in these contexts. According to Art. 24 para. 2, attempted incitement is only liable to prosecution if somebody should have been put up to

---

[3]   See above, § 16 B.II.
[4]   Austeda, p. 63.
[5]   Kantorowicz, p. 9.

committing a felony (as opposed to a misdemeanor or a contravention). Thus it follows from the legal definition of felony in conjunction with Art. 24 para. 2 of the Swiss Penal Code that only the attempted incitement to an offense punishable by imprisonment for more than three years is liable to prosecution. Therefore, the regulation of language use in Art. 10 para. 2 of the Swiss Penal Code possibly results in significant consequences for the accused!

II. Example: Definition of Death in Modern Medicine[6]

The epoch-making achievements of modern medicine have rendered moot the criterion according to which a human being is to be regarded as dead when heartbeat and respiration have stopped (clinical death). If one were to adhere to this definition of death, then this would lead to the following consequences:

1. A patient might possibly be declared dead at a point in time where resuscitation would still be possible (e.g. resuscitation in case of surgical incidents, shock, embolism, cardiac infarction or traffic accidents), thus, where it is possible to restore to life a patient who has passed the point of clinical death.

2. On the other hand, modern heart-lung machines allow for artificially maintaining the respiration and blood flow of a human being whose brain functions (for example due to direct damage through traumatic violence) have *irreversibly* ceased. If one were to adhere to the traditional death criterion, a patient would have to be kept alive as a "heart-lung preparation" by the aid of machines for an indefinite time despite "definitive and irreversible loss of consciousness"[7] (= so-called "brain death").

3. A doctor stopping the machine at this stage would become guilty of voluntary manslaughter. If one wanted to avoid this consequence, one

---

[6] Literature: The Determination of Death in the Context of Organ Transplantation, Medical Ethical Guidelines of the Swiss Academy of Medical Sciences (SAMS), approved by the Senate of the SAMS on 24 May 2005.

[7] This condition must be kept strictly separate from coma (or other states that mimic brain death). By brain death, one understands gross anatomical or fine structural destruction of the brain in its entirety.

would not be able to avoid "assigning the doctor a right to decide on life or death which would exceed the practice properly known as passive euthanasia" since the patient is *per definitionem* still "alive".[8]

4. At this stage, the transplantation of vital organs would plainly be forbidden.

To avoid these consequences, the traditional concept of clinical death has been replaced by the modern concept of *brain death*. Some of the criteria specified by the Swiss Academy of Medical Sciences (SAMS) on 24 May 2005 for determining that the brain has ceased to function in cases of definitive evidence of primary brain injury are the following: coma, bilateral dilation of pupils and absence of papillary light reaction, absence of spontaneous respiration, absence of cough and swallow reflexes, etc.[9]

The brain death thesis as a criterion for human death is, however, not the necessary expression of scientific cognition and therefore not beyond controversy. As a matter of fact, empirical research can only produce evidence of an ongoing process up to the cessation of function of the last cell of the organism several days after clinical death, so that strictly speaking, death cannot be referred to as a "single point in time".

The fact that it is a question of drawing a line somewhere within the process of dying shows quite distinctly that we are ultimately concerned with laying down a postulate, a stipulation, but not with cognition. Thus, the question is not: "When is a person dead?" but rather: "When shall a person be (considered) dead?" Given the impossibility of either empirical or logical verification in this instance, it cannot be a matter of discovering the only true concept of death, but only of developing *rebus sic stantibus* a more or less useful concept of death. To be useful, such a concept must not be chosen arbitrarily, but must be based on given ex-

---

[8] Stratenwerth, Festschrift Engisch (quoted in § 20 n. 6), p. 542. Passive euthanasia is understood to mean the omission of life-prolonging measures. The switching-off of the machine would, on the other hand, be an active acceleration of death, a deliberate act.

[9] Cf. The Determination of Death in the Context of Organ Transplantation, Medical Ethical Guidelines of the SAMS, approved by the Senate of the SAMS on 24 May 2005.

periences and, above all, on value judgments made. A future change in this experience or value basis (if by virtue of medical progress, for example, it became possible to resuscitate a brain-dead person) would of course entail yet another change in the concept of death.

III. The Positivist Definitions of the Law as Stipulations

The previous comments have shown that the positivist definitions of the law cannot be conceived as statements expressing scientific cognition. They are neither assertions about an existing language usage nor real definitions which could be tested for their validity by empirical research. As a result, they can only rank among the kind of definitions explained in the preceding paragraphs (above, § 20 B.I and II): they must be understood as synthetic definitions.[10] The positivist definitions, therefore, do not claim something which could be proven true or false; they are neither true nor false statements but *postulates*. They do not state what the law is but they postulate a certain meaning of the word "law"; they stipulate what *shall* be understood by "law".[11]

For this reason, the question raised at the beginning of this chapter, viz. which of the legal theories is the right one, or more precisely: which one of these theories has found the true "concept" of law, proves to have been formulated inconsistently with logic! The question is not: "What is law?", for, as has been demonstrated, that kind of question cannot be answered in a scientifically objective manner. Instead, the question must

---

[10] The form of definition mentioned above, § 20 A, remains out of consideration since the positivist definitions of law refer to the *meaning* of the term "law" as opposed to only laying down the replacement of one sign (word) by another.

[11] The more recent theory of definition differentiates not only analysis of meaning and stipulation of a meaning but also explication of a term. The latter is taking the centre position between the former two. L. Kuhlen, Typuskonzeption in der Rechtstheorie, Schriften zur Rechtstheorie No. 66, Berlin: Duncker & Humblot, 1977, p. 31:
„... unlike meaning analysis, there remains in the case of an explication a decision leeway which cannot be filled by an ever so comprehensive research into habitual language use. Like synthetic definitions, explications cannot be true or false but only adequate or inadequate."
It is thus reasonable to hold the view that the various definitions of the term "law" are representing explications. Since explications cannot be true or false, either, our argument does not get changed at all.

be: "What shall reasonably be understood by law?" or "On what concept of law do we want to base our assumptions?"

By this approach which, following Kantorowicz, may be called "conceptual pragmatism",[12, 13] the debate on the concept of law is transferred onto a different level: it is no longer a question of truth but a question of delineating a more or less fruitful concept of law. It is not a matter of *discovering* a certain concept but of *forming* a certain concept. The fruitfulness of any definition will have to be judged by asking whether, in view of given experiences and value judgments presupposed as binding, one regards the consequences it entails as acceptable.[14] It will perhaps turn out in the process *that it would be more useful to form not just a single concept, but several concepts: it is not essential for the sociologist of law, the historian of law and the judge to work in their different fields of activity with the same concept.*

This "axiomatic" character of the problem, which consists in the fact that it is ultimately a stipulation that tips the scale with regard to what is deemed to be law and hence what subject-matter a theory has to deal with, has been seen clearly by several positivist authors:

First and foremost, mention must be made of Geiger in this context. As we have seen, he does not assert a claim to absolute truth regarding his concept of law but emphasizes that we are concerned with a question of definition. Definitions are crutches of cognition which should, above all,

---

[12] Kantorowicz, p. 5. This view is shared by: Kramer, ÖZöR NF 23 (1972), p. 116; Bydlinski, Rechtsbegriff, p. 285; Hoerster, NJW 39 (1986), p. 2481, left column; Dreier, NJW 39 (1986), p. 893 et seqq.; Krawietz, Rechtstheorie 18 (1987), p. 216.

[13] B. Horvath, Probleme der Rechtssoziologie, Schriftenreihe zur Rechtssoziologie und Rechtstatsachenforschung No. 20, Berlin: Duncker & Humblot, 1971, p. 28, emphasizes rightly: "And there is absolutely no empirical proof for the proposition that the law can only be given in experience" (our translation). The alignment of positivist theories of law with facticity depends on a *definition* which is itself but the reflection of a certain perception of science.

[14] The view set out here may have to be distinguished from that which says that one is allowed to formulate concepts completely arbitrarily. Apparently like this for example Ross, On Law and Justice, p. 31, who explains that the question of the concept of law is an "arbitrary question of definition". Such a view Hart, Concept of Law, p. 209, is confronting, too. Cf. Eckmann, p. 131. All at the same this remark shows that Ross ranks among the critical positivists (cf. below).

be *serviceable*.[15] In Geiger's case, this concession is especially significant because he is proceeding in a strictly empirical manner in the sense of wanting to understand the law and the social order in general as "facticities, as *relations in reality*". The idea of presenting the definition of law as an "irrefutable" scientific insight would seem to have obvious appeal for this kind of approach in particular.

The "conceptual pragmatism" view is apparent in Weber's work, too: he introduces his concepts of sociology and law with the following phrases: "The word 'sociology' is used in many different senses. In our context it *shall mean* ..."[16] or "An order *will be called law* if it is externally guaranteed ..."[17] The wordings "shall mean" and "will be called" are clearly expressing the postulatory character of the definitions. Weber does not state what sociology or law is "per se". The same is apparent from a remark about the problem of the legal nature of international law, where he explains that such an order would not qualify as "law" according to his terminology, which had been chosen to suit a certain purpose, but that the opposite may very well be true for juristic terminology, nonetheless.

We have already made reference to Hart's explanations: according to Hart, the decision between the (broader) positivist concept of law and the (narrower) one of natural law must be based upon the relative value of the two concept formations for the classification of rules generally effective in social life. It is a question of which of the concepts is superior to the other in the way in which it will assist our theoretical inquiries and/ or further and clarify our moral deliberations. In taking up this position, Hart is emphatically advocating the positivist concept.[18] In this context it is pivotal that Hart does not fall into the trap of assuming he has found the "one true" concept of law in his foundational work.

---

[15] Above, § 9 at the end.
[16] Weber, Law in Economy and Society, p. 1 (our emphasis).
[17] Weber, Law in Economy and Society, p. 5 (our emphasis).
[18] Above, end of § 19 A.III. Hart, Concept of Law, p. 209 et seqq.

Furthermore, the pure theory of law has taken a significant turn in this direction. This is due primarily to *Walter*.[19] Walter emphasizes that the pure theory of law bases the delimitation of the object of cognition on a *choice*.[20] The pure theory of law aspires to be a theory of the positive law and understands law to mean a coercive order set *by men* (and not by a supernatural authority) *for men* which is, by and large, effective.[21] Walter points out expressly that we are concerned here with a "stipulation" in Popper's sense; according to Popper, one can disagree about the usefulness of a stipulation.[22] The second fundamental decision upon which the pure theory of law is based consists in the will to interpret positive, effective coercive systems as *normative systems*, as Ought-systems. As is generally known, this is effectuated by the introduction of a hypothetically presupposed norm, the basic norm. It admits of the interpretation that whatever is ordered by the coercive system effective in social life is also what ought to happen.[23] For a long time, Kelsen has qualified the basic norm as a *hypothesis*.[24] However, since a hypothesis usually denotes a verifiable statement but the basic norm can neither be confirmed nor falsified, objections have been raised against this qualification.[25] Thus, Kelsen later spoke of it as a "fiction".[26] Walter, who rightly disapproves of that qualification just as much,[27] recommends the expression "assumption" in the sense of "stipulation of a proposition as if it were

---

[19] Walter, Rechtstheorie 1 (1970), p. 69 et seqq; idem, ÖZöR 18 (1968), p. 331 et seqq.; regarding the question whether Walter may rest his comments on Kelsen himself: Walter, ÖZöR 18 (1968), p. 343 et seqq.

[20] Walter, Rechtstheorie 1 (1970), p. 75 et seqq./79.

[21] Walter, ÖZöR 18 (1968), p. 336.

[22] Walter, Rechtstheorie 1 (1970), p. 76 n. 35.

[23] Walter, ÖZöR 18 (1968), p. 338.

[24] Cf. for example The Pure Theory of Law, p. 46.

[25] Walter, ÖZöR 18 (1968), p. 339 with further references in n. 32/33.

[26] Kelsen, Die Funktion der Verfassung, Verhandlungen des zweiten Österreichischen Juristentages 1964 II 7. Teil, p. 71: Kelsen expressly bases himself on Vaihinger's "Die Philosophie des Als Ob", Fifth/Sixth Edition, Leipzig: Felix Meiner, 1920. Thus, the pure theory of law does not allege that effective coercive systems *are* valid systems but only describes them *as if* they were. Cf. Kramer, ÖZöR 23 (1972), p. 111.

[27] For by "fiction", one often understands "an assumption, the improvability or impossibility of which is usually understood, a fact which, however, does just not apply to the presumption of the basic norm." See Walter, ÖZöR 18 (1968), p. 339.

valid, for a theoretical purpose".[28] This spells out with the utmost clarity that the pure theory of law, too, must operate axiomatically from certain ultimate postulates which, measured against the positivist concept of cognition, are not verifiable but are nonetheless decisive over the concept of law and the subject-matter of Kelsen's theory.

Depending on whether or not he is aware of the relativity of his concept of law and thus of the relativity of his own theory, one can consequently differentiate the *critical* legal positivist from the *dogmatic* legal positivist. The critical positivist knows that the problem of the concept of law and of the subject of his theory cannot be resolved by scientific means but only by clarifying – stating the relevant reasons – what *he wants* to be understood by the term "law" in order to draw conclusions from his approach. The aforementioned authors would therefore all have to be qualified as critical legal positivists. The dogmatic positivist, on the other hand, believes his distinctions to have made an unchallengeable scientific determination. His theory is, so he believes, the only right one; all the other theories are necessarily wrong. The great risk of dogmatism it is that of hardening the positions, leading to disputes which are fruitless because impossible to settle, and, above all, obstructing the awareness of real problems and how they might be solved. A typical example of dogmatic positivism can be found e.g. in Bergbohm.

C. The Unprovability and Irrefutability of Legal Positivism

We conclude: the positivist definitions of law and the theories derived from them are scientifically unprovable. If one starts from the concept of cognition set out above, there is no possibility to prove that one of these theories is the only right one. For the same reason, however, they are also *irrefutable*. For it is equally impossible to prove by scientific means that either one of these theories is false. *This does not, of course, apply if a theory contains logical contradictions or empirically wrong claims.* In such cases a theory is *not only useless* but simply *false*.

---

[28] Walter, ÖzöR 18 (1968), p. 339.

It would, however, be precipitate to infer from this that the construction of a legal positivist theory might be a misguided enterprise right from the start, simply because one can never determine whether it is true or false. Quite apart from the fact that, subjected to a sufficiently critical analysis, this could equally well be demonstrated for the non-positivist theories, too, the question is whether it is possible to develop an interpretation which makes the endeavors of the legal positivists in particular, and legal philosophers in general, appear to be a meaningful and entirely serious undertaking. We will deal with these issues in the third part of the book.

Third Part

Conclusions

§ 21 Legal Philosophies as Axiomatic Theories of Law

A. The "Axiomatic" Character of Philosophical Thinking

An important aim of this study has been achieved by the results derived from the preceding sections. For now it is clear why the legal positivists take such different views: it is the result of the relative character of the concept of law presupposed in each case. One single concept cannot resolve all the issues that are associated with the understanding of law. "Law is neither a system of norms nor a prediction of the behavior of the authorities, nor a command to the authorities or the citizens, nor a general concept or ideology, nor actual regular behavior, sanctioned behavioral norms, rules of a game or a 'rule of recognition', nor, finally, habits within the frame of a model of legal history or cultural studies. Rather, law is something of all of these at the same time. The various definitions of it are in truth but fragments of a single ontological relation, which are turned into an expression for the law as a whole by an illegitimate generalization."[1] Since the concept of law is based on a *pre-scientific* premise, one may understand very different things by law; however, different definitions of the term necessarily yield different theories. Difficulties arise only for those who are not aware of the postulatory character of definitions properly so-called but believes that philosophical reflection may only build upon assured, if possible "evident" cognitions.[2]

Our research set out from a logical-empirical concept of cognition and yielded the result that by taking such a strict standard as a basis, the legal positivist theories are not verifiable. The question is, what can be derived from this for an understanding of legal positivism. Such an understanding, however, presupposes a certain notion of the tasks of legal philoso-

---

[1] Jørgensen, p. 38 (our translation).
[2] Cf. § 16 B XII and § 17 E in the end.

phy, of its possibilities and limits. It is our intention to develop an interpretation which makes the endeavors of the legal philosopher appear as a fundamentally meaningful philosophical undertaking despite the fact that they are, in principle, unprovable.

This interpretation – to be set out in more detail below – originates from a conception which has been developed for general philosophy by the Austrian epistemologist Austeda in his monograph *Axiomatische Philosophie*, already repeatedly cited. Elementary to this understanding of philosophy is the "insight that philosophy (and with it any philosophical inquiry, actually any philosopheme) proves, on sufficiently profound analysis, to be constructed axiomatically and is therefore only to be understood 'axiomatically', *i.e. it presents a certain (at best: consistently thought-out and therefore error-free and stylistically pristine) development of conclusions based on certain presuppositions.*"[3] A philosophy which is self-critically aware of its axiomatic character must be expected to account for its own premises, openly disclose them, clearly define its own standpoint against others, and advance from its own premises with logical consistency.[4] That is the basic requirement upon it!

By this we do not of course intend to promote the opinion that a philosophy is a concisely constructed axiomatic system offhand comparable to the mathematical and logical systems. Rather, what we mean to express is what Klug calls "*quasi-axiomatic*" (regarding efforts to systemize traditional legal philosophy).[5] In each case this meaning is referred to, it shall be indicated by the use of inverted commas.

In the preceding paragraph we have proved the "axiomatic" character of the legal positivist theories. If in the following, we do not refer to legal positivism alone but to legal philosophy in general, then this is undoubtedly a somewhat premature generalization. This generalization is based upon the assumption that the non-positivist legal theories, e.g. the natural law theories, could also be demonstrated to be "axiomatic" in character, meaning that they, too, have to start from unverifiable premises which,

---

[3] Austeda, p. 171 (our translation).
[4] Austeda, p. 172.
[5] Klug, p. 194.

nevertheless, already embody the "basic presuppositions".[6] The reason why this assumption is plausible is because we were able to *prove the unprovability* of the positivist theories, the fathers of which attach particular importance to a "scientific" approach. The obvious presumption is that the same would be possible for all the other theories. On this presupposition, for which evidence – as stated above – would first have to be produced, a modified view of legal philosophy is thrust upon us.

B. The Theorems of Legal Philosophy as Constructs

According to the view to be developed here, theorems of legal philosophy convey neither cognition nor knowledge but are *constructs.* The task of the legal philosopher is not the reproduction of something existing "per se", but the creation of something new: it does not consist of passively "contemplating" but of actively "creating", "building", "forming". The legal philosopher should attempt to devise constructs which he can account for even in the light of the consequences they entail. Therefore, he would have to test them by *investigating the consequences and making sure that he can accept them.* For the value of his theorems consists in their *fruitfulness* regarding the attainability of theoretical or practical goals but not in their truth. Legal theories should be scrutinized under the aspect of "What do they lead to in practice?"[7] Insofar as the legal philosopher pursues theoretical goals, he is concerned with providing a conceptual instrument which supports and furthers the research of the various jurisprudential branches. On the other hand, if he pursues practical goals by developing a *content-based* legal philosophy, he is concerned with *shaping the real social world in a certain way.* Legal philos-

---

[6] It is impressive to see how the Catholic natural law tradition is criticized nowadays even within the Catholic community itself. Thus Pfürtner, Das Natürlich-Rechte, in: Natur und Naturrecht. Ein interfakultäres Gespräch, Freiburg/Schweiz: Universitätsverlag, 1972, p. 281, concludes: "A truth consciousness formed by positive research, however, must repudiate as unproven or even as demonstrable speculations most of the anthropological premises on which modern scholastic natural law theory bases its propositions." From this unprovability of the natural law theory, one must not at any rate conclude that the formation of natural law theories is a futile philosophical undertaking from the outset. See also below, concluding remarks.

[7] Kriele, ÖZöR 16 (1966), p. 426.

ophy in this sense is "reflected legal politics".[8] *The situation takes on a different complexion, though, if a theory of legal philosophy contains internal contradictions or assumptions which are empirically wrong.* In that case, it has to be classified not just as non-useful but as false![9]

That case apart, jurisprudential constructs have not to be judged according to whether they are true or false, but according to whether, on the one hand, they enable the theoretical understanding of legal phenomena and, on the other hand, they are directed at values which are considered desirable to realize. Legal philosophical ideas do not state anything, and in particular, they are not assertions of facts; but rather, they *invite* us to adopt a specific approach to the law; they contain *proposals* for the theoretical understanding or for the practical shaping of the legal reality.

Based on such an understanding of philosophy of law, it does not make sense to ask, for example, whether there "is" a right to resistance "per se", whether a right to resistance "exists". This type of question results in a controversy which cannot be settled by scientific means. In contrast, it makes sense to ask whether a right to resistance is desirable under certain circumstances, and whether the criteria for its admissibility may be framed with sufficient accuracy. If so, it comes down to "constructing" the corresponding theory of legal philosophy, which justifies a right to resistance and contains justiciable criteria for its admissibility. The accomplishable goal of such an undertaking is not the provability and irrefutability of that approach, but its plausibility on the basis of a reasonable argumentation proceeding from acceptable premises. Thus, it is not the theory that yields an "insight" into a right to resistance, but the desired right to resistance that leads to the corresponding theory! The understanding of philosophy of law sketched here entails the following consequences:

One upshot of the above, first of all, is that any philosophy of law is *temporary*. Since the ideas of legal philosophy are unprovable, one ought to energetically confront any dogmatism purporting to offer definitive answers. Strictly speaking, a theorem of legal philosophy cannot be ver-

---

[8] Such the accurate term by Kriele, ÖZöR 16 (1966), p. 422.
[9] Cf. above, § 21 A.

ified or falsified but must be subject to *criticism* and, should the occasion arise, *revision*.

The second precept that follows from our interpretation is that of pursuing legal-philosophical discourse in the spirit of *tolerance*. A considerate discussion is hardly furthered by everybody trying to disprove everybody else and claiming one's own position to be the only one that is right. A far more conducive procedure is to discern the dependency of both one's own and other people's positions upon approaches that are useful to some extent or other, and to be mindful of the pros and cons of the respective approaches. Exemplary in this respect is Walter's attitude: as a proponent of the pure theory of law who is aware of the "axiomatic" character of a position, he does not object to the theories of recognition as being wrong but concedes that theoretically, there is no objection to such a *construct*. However, he is left with the question of whether it is useful and whether it does not boil down to the same practical result as *Kelsen's*. Walter makes particular reference to the difficult issue of how "recognition" by the members of a legal community is to be ascertained.[10] Such an approach defuses the dispute and redirects it onto a reasonable course.

Third, our approach discloses the legal philosopher's *considerable responsibility* for the theories he develops. Here, a basic difference to positive science becomes apparent: a scientifically provable proposition does not become false simply because it entails undesired consequences. The statement that disease x is incurable according to the latest developments in medical science, for example, is not false merely because it induces despair in the many sufferers from that disease; and the insights of modern nuclear science are not false purely because they made it possible to build the atomic bomb! The situation is entirely different in the case of a theory of legal philosophy: since, as we have seen, such a theory is not subject to the truth criterion as a matter of principle, the matter of the theory's consequences becomes the sole decisive criterion! If, for example, one particular concept of law, such as that advocated by the statutory positivists, could be proven the one true theory, one would

---

[10] Walter, Rechtstheorie 1 (1970), p. 79/80 n. 43.

have to accept it *irrespective of the consequences*. Since this is *demonstrably unfounded*, however, the legal philosopher is at liberty to develop a theory which leads to *justifiable consequences*.

Fourth, under our approach, an ahistorical understanding of legal philosophy proves unsustainable.[11] Ideas of legal philosophy depend on certain historical conditions such as the respective developments in general philosophy or the social, political and legal situation of a certain epoch. Let us pursue this briefly with reference to legal positivism.

C. Historical Relativity of Legal Positivism

The need to apply the reductionist method, which has led the empirical sciences as well as experimental psychology to such evident successes and which consists of orientating oneself only by undeniable logical-empirical facts, becomes apparent in all positivist theories. The positivist is not looking for a profound justification of his theory but a comprehensible one. Experience tells us that it is impossible to achieve both at the same time, since "profoundness" and "comprehensibility" tend to stand in inverse proportion to one another: *the more profound, the less comprehensible* (and presumably more subjective), or *the more comprehensible, the more objective* the line of argument becomes! The positivists' concerns come to the fore in epochs when it becomes necessary to knock back idealistic flights of intellectual fancy, which have resulted in obvious elements of subjectivity, by bringing them down to earth.[12] More recently, as mentioned, this rather negative, criticistic motive has been joined by the positive aspiration to apply to the field of law a method that has proven so successful in the other sciences mentioned above.

Apart from this dependence of legal positivism on certain constellations from the history of philosophy and of science, several authors have pointed out a different kind of historical relativity associated with certain

---

[11] The historical relativity of legal philosophy is referred to by W. Hassemer, article "Rechtsphilosophie", in: A. Görlitz, Handlexikon zur Rechtswissenschaft, Munich 1972, p. 332/333. A self-documenting example for this is, according to Hassemer, the reaction of the post-war German legal philosophy to the Nazi-Regime.

[12] Cf. instructive table regarding eclipses and revivals of natural law in: Brecht, p. 141.

positivist theories of law, namely an ideological-political component that is inherent in them. This relates in particular to the theories of analytical positivism: thus, according to Kriele, the lawgiver's monopoly to legislate (as opposed to simple prerogatives to legislate), which is expressed in the well-known interdiction against interpreting the law, was politically directed against the *claims of jurists to develop the law*.[13] In contrast, the positivist idea of the *sovereignty of states* had been directed, on the one hand, against the *potestas indirecta* of the church, namely the Catholic church, and, on the other hand, against the recognition of a right to resistance on the part of the subjects. In this latter sense, legal positivism is directed against "rebellion, disobedience, anarchy, tyrant killing, civil war, and pleads for order, obedience, domestic peace."[14] The political goal here is to achieve a high degree of *legal certainty* disregarding an individualizing justice.[15] Occasionally, the theories of recognition are justified by the principle of legal certainty as well. Thus, for example, Riezler, according to whom "recognition by the authority who has attained actual, not completely ephemeral, power" constitutes the legal character of a norm.[16] The deeper reason why ideals of natural law should not be mixed with the law in force, understood as explained above, is a need for legal certainty "in the dual sense that it is established and determinable what is legal, but also that everybody may rely upon the courts and other governmental bodies to administer to them the law and only the law."[17]

Therefore, positivist theories may be, but need not necessarily be, politically motivated. A positivist theory, as we have seen, is based upon a concept of law composed of value neutral elements. Hence, there is no basis to presume, *a priori,* that it is ideologically colored. Indeed, the underlying stipulation may equally have been made for non-political

---

[13] Kriele, JuS 9 (1969), p. 150/151.
[14] Kriele, ibidem, p. 152 (our translation).
[15] Radbruch, too, is justifying his positivist theory by the principle of legal certainty: cf. quote above p. 19 et seq.
[16] Riezler, in: Naturrecht oder Rechtspositivismus?, p. 242. Riezler's positivism would have to be attributed to Beling's and Nawiasky's theories of recognition by the "leading class". Above § 6, n. 70.
[17] Riezler, p. 250/251 (our translation).

reasons. This is particularly true for the pure theory of law, in which various authors believed they had discovered ideological traits.[18] We refer to Verdross's comments as a representative example: Verdross argues that if Kelsen's basic norm establishes precisely the effective legal order, and not some other, as the legal authority, the sole reason can be that it is the only kind of order capable of guaranteeing legal certainty for the human society in question. Kelsen's positivism is, therefore, geared to the values of law and order.[19] Verdross has overlooked that Kelsen's choice of the object of cognition (viz. of the effective orders backed by threat) is made for *epistemological* but not for political reasons. Since Kelsen, being a value relativist, negates the possibility of cognition of absolute values, it does not seem to make sense to focus scientific cognition on the object of law in an absolute sense;[20] rather, law has to be something the actual existence of which is revealed by observable events in time and space; these Kelsen sees in the positivity of the law, i.e. in the fact that it is made by men and is by and large effective. It is no less fallacious to infer an ideological tendency (i.e. liberalism) of the pure theory of law, for instance from Kelsen's "negative norm" to the effect that if the legal system does not impose any obligation on an individual regarding a certain behavior then it allows for that behavior.[21] For even taking this norm as a basis, one could construe the most perfect totalitarian police state provided that a sufficient number of ways to behave were expressly forbidden! Kelsen's declared commitments to democracy are not related to his positivism, either, but can be explained from his value relativism.[22]

Whether legal positivism is politically-ideologically bound or not can therefore not be answered generally but only case by case, i.e. *with regard to each individual theory.* Detailed analysis of this would require quite an extensive study and is beyond the objectives we have set ourselves for the purpose of this project, which focuses more on the epistemic aspect of the problem. We are convinced that proof may be fur-

---

[18] Cf. for this purpose e.g. Fechner, ARSP Beiheft No. 6 (1970), p. 199 et seqq.
[19] Verdross, Völkerrecht, 5th Edition, Vienna: Springer, 1964, p. 18.
[20] Walter, Rechtstheorie 1 (1970), p. 77.
[21] Kelsen, Pure Theory of Law, p. 246.
[22] Cf. Kelsen, Was ist Gerechtigkeit? (Vienna, 1953), p. 40 et seqq.

nished regarding some theories, and equally convinced that for certain others, it probably could not.

On the other hand, all legal positivist theories are historically relative insofar as they are – explicitly or implicitly – based upon an understanding of science which has not been applicable everywhere and at all times and which, at the present time, is once again severely contested: it is the ideal of an objective, exact science based on axioms, undefined basic terms and rules of inference.

D. The Question Concerning the Merits and Demerits of the Legal Positivist Theories

On the basis of the interpretation developed in this section, which we refer to as "Axiomatic Theory of Law", we no longer inquire as to the truth or untruth of the legal positivist theories – as explained – but as to their fruitfulness in achieving practical and theoretical objectives. Thus, we inquire as to the practical and theoretical consequences of a construct, i.e. where a certain theory takes us and what purposes it is or is not suitable for. The issue, then, is not to discover to what extent a certain theory is true and to what extent it is false, but to assess its *effectiveness* in dealing with certain theoretical or practical problems. This means abandoning our hitherto value-free attitude, though, because the question as to whether or not certain consequences of a theory are desirable inevitably entails value judgments. Which values are assumed by the present authors can best be seen from the following concrete arguments.

It is the purpose of these explanations to show what difficulties are created by the attempt to lump together all the problems associated with the phenomenon of the law in *one single* theory. The same theory may be suitable for achieving one objective (e.g. the development of a concept of law that is appropriate for inquiries of legal sociology) but quite unsuitable for achieving another (e.g. the development of substantial criteria to guide the judge in filling statutory gaps).

Thus, in the following, we will try to take stock of the *advantages* and *drawbacks* of the legal positivist theories and, on this occasion, seek to identify how, in our opinion, theories of legal philosophy should be assessed. Our aim is, on the basis of an overview of the different varieties of legal positivism, to sketch out the *substantial* arguments and counter-arguments. In order to structure the subject matter, we will start by assessing the arguments and counter-arguments that concern the separation thesis, which it seems propitious to address separately (below, § 22 and § 23). We will then classify the remaining arguments and counter-arguments as applicable either to all varieties of legal positivism (below, § 24 A) or to some varieties of legal positivism only (below, § 24 B to I). So initially we want to dedicate our attention to the field on which the main battle of legal positivism has been fought, which left it largely discredited in our times, i.e. the debate about the positivist separation thesis.

E. The Question as to the Merits and Demerits of the Positivist Separation Thesis in Particular

Two preliminary remarks are necessary in this context:

The arguments for and against the separation thesis may be divided into three categories: the historical (empirical), the normative and the analytical.[23]

An *historical* argument against the separation thesis is that legal positivism in the narrower sense contributed to the horrors of the Nazi regime. This is an historical issue which we will deal with below.[24]

We are confronted with a *normative* argument against the separation thesis if, for example, it is asserted that it complicates the matter of remedying "statutory lawlessness", or in favor of the separation thesis if it is argued that it fosters legal certainty and conceptual clarity.

---

[23] Alexy, ARSP Beiheft 37 (1990), p. 10 et seqq.; see also idem, The Argument from Injustice – A reply to Legal Positivism, p. 20 et seqq., where Alexy explains, however, that on closer inspection, "a third group of arguments, namely, empirical arguments …. become components of analytical or normative arguments." (Ibidem, n. 39).

[24] § 23 , especially § 23 D.

The most substantial *analytical* argument against the separation thesis is that there is a *conceptually* necessary connection between law and morality; that one can not *define* law, including positive law, as anything other than *"a system and an institution whose very meaning is to serve justice."*[25] Alexy has tried to provide evidence that there is such a conceptually necessary connection between law and some kind of morality, indeed even "right" morality.[26] Höffe's criticism, too, is of the same tenor.[27] Likewise, Coleman II most recently defends this view.[28]

From the interim result arrived at so far, however, it follows that only historical and normative arguments may be considered, but not analytical arguments.[29] For the question of whether there is an analytical connection between law and morality depends upon which definition of law is presupposed; and any such definition is based, as we have seen, upon a pre-scientific premise.[30] If one defines "law", for example, as "the epitome of all norms which are set by the body authorized to do so in accordance with a certain procedure and which do not conflict with morality",[31] it follows analytically that there cannot be such a thing as immoral law; hence, there is *a conceptually necessary* connection between law and morality. On the other hand, if one defines "law" in accordance with the understanding of the positivists by using exclusively social facts, then it

---

[25] Radbruch, Statutory Lawlessness and Supra-Statutory Law, first published in Süddeutsche Juristenzeitung 1 (1946) p. 105–108, translated by Bonnie Litschewski Paulson and Stanley L. Paulson, Oxford Journal of Legal Studies 26 (2006), p. 7.

[26] Alexy, ARSP Beiheft 37 (1990), p. 23 et seq.; idem, The Argument from Injustice – A reply to Legal Positivism, p. 22 et seqq.

[27] According to Höffe, it is a specific characteristic of the law that the group of people to which the coercion applies is congruent with the group of people advantaged by such coercion (inwardly-directed coercion) whilst in case of a syndicate of criminals, these two groups diverge (Höffe, p. 161, 168 et seq.). Such cases – and this is the argument against a justice-free definition – are not yet referred to as a legal order (loc. cit., p. 170). It is, however, evident that the Nazi system is referred to as a legal order although the coercion applied by the system did not yield any advantages, but only disadvantages to the Jews. That means that in case of the term "law" there is no established language usage which could be reproduced by an analytic definition (cf. above, § 19 A.III at the end).

[28] Cf. § 15 D above.

[29] In this spirit also Dreier, Recht – Moral – Ideologie, p. 182 et seq.

[30] Above, § 20 B.III, C, § 21 A.

[31] Geddert, p. 193; cf. also loc. cit., p. 207.

follows from this definition that there cannot be any analytical connection between law and morality. Whether one should proceed one way or the other, is, however, precisely the question; and this question can only be answered by means of historical and normative arguments, not analytical ones.

The issues we will address in the following may be divided into those which have a *direct practical* significance and those which do not. By issues with a *direct practical* bearing, we shall mean issues which are directed at how a judge or a legal subject of a certain legal order ought to act in a certain situation. All the other issues, particularly issues which are of interest to the comparative lawyer, the legal historian or the legal sociologist, shall here be called *theoretical* issues.[32] They have no immediate practical, but at most, an indirect practical bearing. Thus the findings obtained by a comparative lawyer may have an indirect bearing on a trial that takes place under a foreign legal system; similarly, facts which the legal sociologist has come across within the scope of legal fact research may have an indirect bearing on the decision of the judge. The distinction suggested here between issues with a direct practical bearing and theoretical issues, i.e. issues that have an indirect practical bearing, is similar to, but not fully congruent with the distinction between the perspective of an observer and the perspective of a participant.[33]

In the following section (§ 22), the arguments militating in favor of the separation thesis shall be set forth for discussion; in the subsequent sec-

---

[32] For the differentiation between theoretical and direct practical meaning see Geddert, p. 31 et seqq. and p. 311.

[33] Alexy, ARSP Beiheft 37 (1990), p. 13 and idem, The Argument from Injustice – A reply to Legal Positivism, p. 25 et seqq., is circumscribing the perspectives of a participant and an observer as follows: "At the centre of the *participant's perspective* stands the judge. When other participants – say, legal scholars, attorneys, or interested citizens – adduce arguments for or against certain contents of the legal system, they refer in the end to how a judge would have to decide if he wanted to decide correctly. The *observer's perspective* is adopted by one who asks not what the correct decision is in a certain legal system, but, rather, how decisions are actually made in a certain legal system." – As one can see, the scope of the questions with immediate practical bearing is basically congruent with the participant's perspective. On the other hand, there are issues amongst the theoretical questions which are not directed at what is actually decided in a particular legal system, for example the problem of the justification of the so-called argument of principle. Cf. below, § 22 D.

tion (§ 23) we move on to the argument which, in its normative version (but not its historical version!), militates preponderantly against it, in our opinion; we call this the "Hitler argument".

§ 22 The Merits of the Positivist Separation Thesis

As we have seen, all positivist theories define their concept of law by means of social facts.[1] From this it follows that all positivist concepts of law are value-free; the positivist abstracts from all legal contents; he deals with the law as it is, but not with the law as it ought to be: in other words, as this is routinely expressed, he conceptually separates law from morality.[2] Two versions of the separation thesis must be kept apart:

1. A distinction has to be made between the law as it is and the law as it ought to be according to a *positive* morality, i.e. the prevailing moral views of a society.

2. A distinction has to be made between the law as it is and the law as it ought to be according to a so-called *critical* morality, i.e. an enlightened morality or natural law.

A. The Usefulness of the Separation Thesis for Sociology of Law, History of Law and Ethnology of Law[3]

A first advantage of this conception is the following: if one were to include certain content-based criteria of justice in the concept of law to the effect that a positive statute not complying with these criteria would not only be "unjust" law but not law at all, then substantial parts of National Socialist law or of the slave law of antiquity would fall outside the scope of investigation of the legal sociologist or the legal historian, although these are the very phenomena that may be of greatest concern

---

[1] Above, § 15 B. The various versions of inclusive positivism always use the empirical or formal criteria of developed legal systems, too. Moral criteria are only brought up if the legal system being described contains such criteria in its rule of recognition (e.g. the amendments of the US constitution or the Canadian Charter of Rights and Freedoms).

[2] Regarding the dual sense of the term "morality", see above, § 2 n. 22 and § 15 B.II.

[3] The list of disciplines may be completed by psychology of law, ethology of law (behavior research) and comparative law. Regarding psychology of law, see R. Jakob/M. Rehbinder (Editors), Beiträge zur Rechtspsychologie, Schriftenreihe zur Rechtssoziologie und Rechtstatsachenforschung, No. 64, Berlin: Duncker & Humblot, 1987, with extensive bibliography on p. 217 et seqq.

to a jurist.[4] The analogue is true for the "laws" of tribal societies which go against our humanitarian ideals, such as the legally authorized killing of children, invalids or old people amongst the Eskimos.[5] Ethnology of law could not address such phenomena since they would not be embraced by the concept of law, and this would undoubtedly amount to an inexpedient constriction of the field of research. For these reasons, the historian of law, the sociologist of law and the ethnologist of law are recommended to base their studies on a positivist concept of law so as not to force the respective object of research by adopting too narrow a notion of what the law is. Which concept of law is the most adequate in individual cases can only be decided on the basis of detailed knowledge of the legal-sociological, -historical and -ethnological material. This does not mean that these disciplines have to work with the same concept. The legal historian and the legal ethnologist are interested in the notions of law of such an early stage that it would not make sense for them to "link the existence and function of the law to institutions such as police, courts, administration etc.; in contrast, anyone who wants to concern himself with the current law will naturally attach importance to these institutions, e.g. in order to distinguish between law and morality."[6]

---

[4] Thus, for example the *actio redhibitoria* (action which the buyer of goods can bring to set aside a contract of sale and claim the return of the entire purchase price against the return of the article) and the *actio quanti minoris* (action which the buyer can bring to obtain an abatement in the purchase price) arose out of the edicts of the *aediles curules* for the sale of slaves and draft animals: Kaser Max/Knütel Rolf, Römisches Privatrecht, 18th Edition, Munich: Beck 2005, § 41 margin no. 38–39 (p. 214 et seq.).

[5] E.A. Hoebel, The Law of Primitive Man, A Study in Comparative Legal Dynamics, First Harvard University Press Publication Edition, Cambridge: Harvard University Press, 2006. In the Eskimos' opinion, society could not compensate for non-productive members. This may be accounted for by the extremely hard conditions of existence to which the Eskimos were subject.

[6] Jørgensen, p. 11 (our translation).

B. The Separation Thesis from the Aspect of Legal Certainty

From the aspect of legal certainty, the separation thesis offers the advantage that the validity of the law cannot be challenged by reference to political, moral, philosophical and theological opinions. Since controversies are likely to arise in these areas, a useful approach is to have questions of social relevance decided authoritatively for the time being and otherwise to refer them "to the arena of the intellectually conducted political debate."[7] Even if one admits that the different political positions are not all equal in merit, that some are better or worse than others, some wiser, some more foolish, it is precisely the question of which one is most meritorious which gives rise to disputes – and which therefore requires a verdict.[8] Thus, the separation thesis is conducive to legal certainty, because everybody is certain what law is and may rely on being granted the benefit of the law, and only the law, by the state authorities.[9]

C. The Separation Thesis and the Problem of Legal Policy

Furthermore, the abstraction from all content-based criteria has the following consequence: any legislator having to create new law or any judge having to decide a case that is not, as yet, provided for by legislation nor by precedent, will not find that positivist theory sheds light on how he should proceed. All positivist theories are sterile precisely with regard to those questions which are to be considered the most important.[10] In response to this, the positivist will argue that legal positivism does not intend to supply a reply to such questions. This objection will have to be accepted; the fact remains, however, that a positivist

---

[7] Kriele, JuS 9 (1969), p. 154; idem, ÖZöR 16 (1966), p. 423 et seqq. (our translation).

[8] Kriele, JuS 9 (1969), p. 154.

[9] Cf. passage by Riezler quoted above, § 21 C at n. 17.

[10] Regarding inclusive positivism, the aforesaid does not apply to the extent that content-based criteria have become part of the rule of recognition. Furthermore, the institutional theory of law (ITL) recognizes rational *de lege ferenda* reasoning to a limited degree. See above, § 13 , and below, § 24 I.

theory only ever states what the law is, but not what new law should look like.

From this, Kriele further concludes that – as a consequence – the separation thesis is vulnerable to the objection that only questions that have been settled and finally decided, but not those that remain unresolved, may be qualified as legal questions;[11] thus, he argues, all juristic issues under discussion at any given time would be excluded from the discourse.[12] Addressing this point, the following remark can be made: the positivist separation thesis does indeed result in the non-qualification of as yet unresolved issues (on both the legislative level and the level of application of the law) as questions of law in the narrower sense, since the positivist contends that in such cases, no law yet exists which one could refer to.[13] To the positivist, such issues are issues of legal policy, i.e. questions about a law that remains to be created in the future. What could be so dangerous about this usage of language defies comprehension, as long as one acknowledges the importance and necessity of legal policy and also grants the judge a degree of competence to act politically, within defined parameters.[14] What would be gained by calling such issues legal issues? The legislators would be forced to look for a law that intrinsically already exists, and would thereby saddle themselves with a host of philosophical problems; and the judges would render even more pseudo-justifications than they already do, just to cover up the fact that they have, in reality, made new law. Refraining from dealing with unresolved issues at a given time in accordance with some law yet to be created, as the positivist imposes upon himself *within the scope of his theory*, by no means bars him from commenting *outside his theory* on

---

[11] Kriele, ÖZöR 16 (1966), p. 419.

[12] Kriele, ÖZöR 16 (1966), p. 420.

[13] To the proponent of a theory of general recognition, there seems to be an exception if certain norms have already been accepted by a majority of a people before they have been stipulated legislatively or judicially, and for the proponent of a theory of sociological positivism if a court practice has already developed independently of the law. In this case it would not be a question of creating new law but of committing to statute *law that, in terms of these theories, already exists.*

[14] Amongst the positivists, only the German statutory positivists deny the judge such competence. Above § 3 text at n. 17–28.

current issues of law creation. Thus, for example, Austin,[15] Weber,[16] Kelsen[17] and Hart[18] have not hesitated to make recommendations with regard to the future creation of law. Austin[19] and Kelsen[20] have actually excelled as successful legislators.

Nevertheless, Kriele's objection is partially justified: the positivist is always in danger of squandering his reasoning power on purely theoretical problems which are often, although interesting and challenging, of next to no practical relevance. The philosophy of law of the future will, in fact, have to address itself to far more concrete issues once again, should it wish to regain its former luster.

D. The Separation Thesis and the Argument from Principles[21]

It is often argued against the separation thesis that legal data is in need of interpretation to a great extent. Such interpretation is, according to

---

[15] For evidence see Löwenhaupt, p. 49 et seqq.

[16] Cf. Rehbinder, Max Weber zum 100. Geburtstag, JZ 19 (1964), p. 332 et seqq.

[17] Métall, p. 110 et seq.

[18] Eckmann, p. 11 and above, § 11 n. 5.

[19] During his two-year political-administrative mission as a commissioner on Malta; cf. Löwenhaupt, p. 39 et seqq.

[20] Kelsen was the intellectual father of the Austrian Constitution of 1920. Cf. Métall, p. 112 et seqq.

[21] Literature: R. Alexy, Zum Begriff des Rechtsprinzips, in: W. Krawietz/K. Opalek/A. Peczenik/A. Schramm (Editors), Argumentation und Hermeneutik in der Jurisprudenz, Rechtstheorie, Beiheft 1 (1979), p. 58 et seqq.; idem, The Argument of Injustice – A Reply to Legal Positivism; idem, ARSP Beiheft 37 (1990), p. 9 et seqq.; C. Bittner, Recht als interpretative Praxis. Zu Ronald Dworkins allgemeiner Theorie des Rechts, Schriften zur Rechtstheorie No. 121, Berlin/Munich: Duncker & Humblot, 1988; J. Burley, Dworkin and His Critics,, Oxford: Blackwell, 2004; F. Bydlinski, Rechsbegriff, p. 221 et seqq., 236 et seqq., 248 und 289; R. Dreier, NJW 39 (1986), p. 890 et seqq.; idem, Rechtstheorie 18 (1987), p. 368 et seqq., 378 et seq.; R. Dworkin, Taking Rights Seriously; idem, No Right Answer?, in: P.M.S. Hacker/J. Raz (Editors), Law, Society and Morality, Essays in Honour of H.L.A. Hart, Oxford: Clarendon Press, 1977, p. 58 et seqq.; idem, A Matter of Principle, Oxford: Clarendon Press, 1985; idem, Law's Empire, Cambridge: Harvard University Press, 1986; H. Geddert, p. 227 et seq.; S. Guest, Ronald Dworkin, 2nd Edition, Edinburgh: Edinburgh University Press, 1997; H.L.A. Hart, The Concept of Law, p. 238 et seqq. (Postscript); idem,

this argument, not possible without recourse to "moral" standards, so-called principles. A clear separation is, therefore, impossible for this reason alone. Currently, the version of this argument most often discussed is the one set forth by Ronald Dworkin, who was H.L.A. Hart's successor as Professor of Jurisprudence at Oxford. In his 1977 book *Taking Rights Seriously*,[22] Dworkin summarizes several treatises – including some published previously – and launches a "general attack on positivism",[23] taking the theory of his predecessor as his target.[24]

I. The Three Main Theses of Positivism from Dworkin's point of View

According to Dworkin, the conceptual foundation of legal positivism consists in the following three theses:

1. The law of a community consists only of rules which are identified not by content but by pedigree[25] (for example on the basis of Hart's rule of recognition). By means of this pedigree test, rules of law may

---

Legal Duty and Obligation, in: idem, Essays on Bentham, Oxford: Clarendon Press, 1982, p. 147 et seqq.; N. Hoerster, NJW 39 (1986), p. 2480 et seqq.; idem, ARSP Beiheft 37 (1990), p. 24 et seqq.; O. Höffe, p. 126 et seqq.; H. Koch, ARSP Beiheft 37 (1990), p. 152 et seqq.; W. Krawietz, Rechtstheorie 18 (1987), p. 209 et seqq., 222 et seqq.; N. MacCormick, Wie ernst soll man Rechte nehmen? Rechtstheorie 11 (1980), p. 1 et seqq.; idem, Legal Reasoning and Legal Theory, Oxford: Clarendon Press, 1994, chapter 9, quoted as Legal Reasoning; F. Michaut, Droits, Revue Française de Théorie juridique (1989), p. 69 et seqq.; idem, Archives de Philosophie du Droit 33 (1988), p. 113 et seqq.; idem, Droits, Revue Française de Théorie juridique (1990), p. 107 et seqq.; A. Ripstein (Editor), Ronald Dworkin, Cambridge: Cambridge University Press, 2007; R. Watkins-Bienz, Die Hart-Dworkin Debatte, Berlin: Duncker & Humblot, 2004, p. 77 et seqq.

22 In Germany, Dworkin's theory has been taken up and partially modified by Alexy, Rechtstheorie Beiheft 1 (1979), p. 59 et seqq., as well as The Argument from Injustice – A reply to Legal Positivism, and Dreier, NWJ 39 (1986), p. 892 et seq. See there for further details.

23 Dworkin, Taking Rights Seriously, p. 22.

24 Dworkin, loc. cit.

25 This is consistent with the characterization made above, § 15 B, i.e. that the legal positivists are defining the law by way of formal criteria. Moral criteria are only brought up by inclusive positivists if the legal system being described contains such criteria in its rule of recognition (e.g. the amendments of the US constitution or the Canadian Charter of Rights and Freedoms).

be distinguished from other sorts of social rules, particularly from those of morality.[26]

2. If a case is not fully covered by such a rule, for example because the rule is vague, it follows that the case may not be decided by applying the law. In such a case, the judge is not legally bound. He must exercise discretion which means he reaches beyond the law and resorts to extra-legal standards.[27]

3. A legal obligation exists when (and only when) "an established rule of law imposes such an obligation. It follows from this that in a hard case – when no such established rule can be found – there is no legal obligation until the judge creates a new rule for the future. The judge may apply this rule to the parties involved in the case at hand, but this is *ex post facto* legislation, not the enforcement of an existing obligation."[28]

II. Dworkin's Criticism of the Three Main Theses of Positivism

Dworkin considers all three theses false:

1. In hard cases, the judge must resort to so-called principles. Principles cannot be identified by a positivist test of pedigree. Rather, the lawyer would have to engage in moral reasoning for this purpose.[29]

2. Even in hard cases, there is only one right answer.[30] Such a decision may not be covered by rules but, to be sure, by principles. The judge does not have discretion but is bound by the principles.

---

[26] Cf. Dworkin, Taking Rights Seriously, p. 17.
[27] Cf. Dworkin, Taking Rights Seriously, p. 17.
[28] Dworkin, Taking Rights Seriously, p. 44, cf. also loc. cit., p. 17.
[29] Cf. Dworkin, Taking Rights Seriously, p. 68. In the chapter "The Model of Rules I" (particularly p. 22–45), Dworkin regards principles as an integral part of the law, whilst in the Chapter "Appendix: A Reply to Critics", he does not want to commit himself as to whether principles are part of law or morality (in whichever sense) or both. Therefore, we will in the following use the term "principles", not "legal principles".
[30] Below, § 22 D.III.3.

3. Thus, even in hard cases the judge does not invent his answer, but *discovers* by means of principles what rights the parties already have.[31]

III. Justification of this Criticism by Dworkin

1. Differentiation of Legal Rules and Principles

Dworkin differentiates between legal rules and principles as two kinds of sources of law.[32] For example, the requirement that a will has to be signed by three witnesses would be a rule.[33] A judge having to decide over the validity of a will could under no circumstances consider a will signed only by two witnesses to be a valid will. "Rules are applicable in an all-or-nothing fashion. If the facts a rule stipulates are given, then either the rule is valid, in which case the answer it supplies must be accepted, or it is not, in which case it contributes nothing to the decision."[34] Distinctive of rules is their way of functioning in case of a conflict: "If two rules conflict, one of them cannot be a valid rule. The decision as to which is valid, and which must be abandoned or recast, must be made by appealing to considerations beyond the rules themselves."[35] This may happen by reference to another rule, one stating, for example, that the rule enacted later is to be preferred.

The mode of operation of principles is entirely different: a principle such as "No man may profit from his own wrong"[36] does not at all costs

---

[31] Below, § 22 D.III.3.
[32] Dworkin, Taking Rights Seriously, p. 22 et seqq. and 71 et seqq.
[33] Dworkin, Taking Rights Seriously, p. 25.
[34] Dworkin, Taking Rights Seriously, p. 24. Koch, ARSP Beiheft 37 (1990), p. 153, rightly makes the following restrictive remark: "As is generally known, not even the 'strict' legal norms with an 'if-then-structure' are of such confined and static character. Rather, given new cases, it is often necessary and possible to interpret the prerequisites stipulated by the law extensively or restrictively in the light of the end of a norm."
[35] Dworkin, Taking Rights Seriously, p. 27. In accordance with Koch, ARSP Beiheft 37 (1990), p. 153, however, this must be qualified by stating that a contradiction between two norms can often be resolved by understanding one norm as an exception to the other.
[36] Dworkin, Taking Rights Seriously, p. 25.

preclude that somebody profits from a wrong he committed. Dworkin quotes the following example: if a man leaves one job, breaking a contract, to take a much higher paying job, he may have to pay damages to his first employer, but he is usually entitled to keep his new salary."[37] Generally speaking, a principle "states a reason that argues in one direction, but does *not* necessitate a particular decision."[38] Principles also differ from rules in the way they operate when they collide: when two principles conflict, one is not – as in the case of rules – valid at the expense of the other; instead, the conflict must be resolved by taking into account the "relative weight" of each.[39]

In further developing Dworkin's thoughts, Alexy has shown that principles give directives which can be satisfied to a greater or lesser degree i.e. they allow for different shades of compliance;[40] in his words, principles contain optimization commands. A rule, on the other hand, can only be complied with or not.[41, 42]

2. The Discovery of the Relevant Principles

Furthermore, the question arises as to how to discover the principles deemed relevant by Dworkin. First of all, Dworkin does not deny that principles can be codified.[43] But how about the other principles which are not codified? According to Dworkin, "a principle is a principle of law if it figures in the soundest theory of law that can be provided as a justification for the explicit substantive and institutional rules of the

---

[37] Dworkin, Taking Rights Seriously, p. 25.
[38] Dworkin, Taking Rights Seriously, p. 26 (emphasis by authors).
[39] Dworkin, Taking Rights Seriously, p. 26.
[40] Alexy, Rechtstheorie Beiheft 1 (1979), p. 79/80; idem, The Argument from Injustice – A reply to Legal Positivism, p. 70.
[41] Alexy, Rechtstheorie Beiheft 1 (1979), p. 79/80.
[42] A distinction different from the one by R. Dworkin and R. Alexy is drawn by Humberto Ávila, Theory of Legal Principles, Law and Philosophy Library 81, Dordrecht: Springer, 2007: According to this author, one and the same legal norm may serve as rule as well as principle; moreover, not only principles but also rules can be weighed, i.e. there is a weight-dimension inherent in them, too.
[43] This follows from Dworkin's explanations, Taking Rights Seriously, p. 27. Art 1 para. I, first sentence, of the German Basic Law, may serve as an example: "Human dignity is inviolable."

jurisdiction in question."[44] The principles of such a theory of law must "try to *justify* the settled rules by identifying the political or moral concerns and traditions of the community which, in the opinion of the lawyer whose theory it is, do in fact support the rules. This process of justification must carry the lawyer very deep into political and moral theory, and well pass the point where it would be accurate to say that any 'test' of 'pedigree' exists for deciding which of two different justifications of our political institutions is superior."[45]

At this point, Dworkin makes a differentiation because "one justification may be better than another ... in two different dimensions: it may prove a better fit, in the sense that it requires less of the material to be taken to be 'mistakes', or it may prove a morally more compelling justification, because it comes closer to capturing sound political morality."[46] In such a case of competing theories of justification, the "theory among these that is morally the strongest provides the best justification, even though it exposes more decisions as mistakes than another."[47]

It is here that Dworkin's attempt to disprove positivism is vulnerable. For either a theory justifies the institutions of the jurisdiction in question without criticizing them, i.e. is in line with the empirically given legal material. This would, however, only (but at least) demonstrate *a relation between the positive law as it is and the deep structure of this positive law as it is*. Thus it can be said with a claim to objectivity and without any moral judgment of one's own that the rules of the Swiss private law on freedom of contract[48] and ownership[49] are based on the principle of private autonomy. Or: modern criminal law systems are based on the guilt principle;[50] the belief in the superiority of the Nordic race (*Rassenprinzip*) and the *Führer*-principle as principles of the positive law

---

[44] Dworkin, Taking Rights Seriously, p. 66.
[45] Dworkin, Taking Rights Seriously, p. 67.
[46] Dworkin, Taking Rights Seriously, p. 340.
[47] Dworkin, Taking Rights Seriously, p. 340.
[48] Art. 19 para. 1 of the Swiss Code of Obligation.
[49] Art. 26 of the Swiss Federal Constitution and Art. 641–729 of the Swiss Civil Code.
[50] Cf. Koch, ARSP Beiheft 37 (1990), p. 157, regarding the Criminal law of the Federal Republic of Germany.

formed part of the legal order of National Socialism.[51] These examples show that the positivist may, in such cases, absolutely bring up a test of pedigree: principles cannot only be verified directly in rules adopted by the positive law or in the form of *rationes decidendi* in precedents, but often also *indirectly* by abstraction from positive rules and precedents.[52] Only if this is not possible, then an explicit moral judgment must be brought to bear in the form of a discretionary decision by the judge, according to the positivist view.

The other possibility is that a theory critically reflects the existing institutions, i.e. partially challenges them. Consequently, in some respects it is out of line with the empirically given legal material. In just such a case, however, the positivist separation thesis, i.e. conceptual differentiation between the law as it is and the law as it ought to be on the basis of such a justifying theory, makes sense once again.

3. The Right-Answer Thesis

The statutory positivists, particularly Bergbohm, supported the dogma of the gaplessness of the law expressed in statutes, as has been laid out above.[53] This opinion can be considered to have been overturned some time ago.[54] Dworkin also develops some kind of gaplessness dogma, admittedly at the level of principles. For he is of the opinion that the legal orders of modern industrial countries always contain *one right* answer, even in hard cases.[55] "For all practical purposes, there will always be a right answer in the seamless web of our law."[56] "It remains

---

[51] Alexy, ARSP Beiheft 37 (1990), p. 22 and idem, The Argument from Injustice – A reply to Legal Positivism, p. 78. The example of National Socialist principles shows that principles, too, might be regarded as highly immoral from a higher standpoint of view which is an argument for, not against the separation thesis.

[52] According to MacCormick, Legal Reasoning, p. 233, principles form part of the law on condition that they can be quoted as reasons for the rules identified by Hart's rule of recognition. As an example, he cites the Apartheid-principle of the law of South Africa (loc. cit., p. 238 et seq.).

[53] § 3 in the end.

[54] Below, § 24 C.

[55] Dworkin, Taking Rights Seriously, p. 280 et seqq.

[56] Dworkin, No Right Answer?, p. 84.

the judge's duty, even in hard cases, to discover what the rights of the parties *are, not* to *invent* new rights *retrospectively*."[57]

This conception cannot be shared. If two principles are in conflict, the judge must deliberate. To come up with a decision, he determines a preference relation, i.e. he must determine under what circumstances one principle is to be preferred to another. *And such determination cannot be derived from the principles themselves.*[58] We are dealing here with an autonomous decision which is independent of the question of identifying the relevant principles. Alexy rightly criticizes: "A perfect theory of the relations of principles would be a theory including all imaginable relations of principles. This theory would provide a solution to all cases. It is, however, not only impossible to factually construct such a theory, but it would also represent a system of rules, i.e. a proposal of the perfect *codification*, and thus no longer qualify as a theory of principles."[59] That there cannot be one right answer on the level of principles is rooted in the very character of the principles sketched out by Dworkin himself.[60]

Dworkin acknowledges, however, that lawyers can be of different opinion on questions of principles;[61] he also acknowledges that even if there is one right answer to a hard case it is pointless to demand that a judge seek to find it because *"there is no way to prove that his is the right answer even if it is."*[62] Nevertheless, he insists on the right-answer thesis because a proposition can be true even if there is no agreed test by which its truth might be demonstrated.[63] We may have to accept this but the question arises whether it makes sense to base a theory on such uncertain grounds.

Suppose for example the Swiss Federal Court had to decide whether a fundamental right not as yet included in the written Swiss Federal Con-

---

[57] Dworkin, Taking Rights Seriously, p. 81 (our emphasis).
[58] Cf. Koch, ARSP Beiheft 37 (1990), p. 159.
[59] Alexy, Rechtstheorie Beiheft 1 (1979), p. 84 (emphasis by authors).
[60] Koch, ARSP Beiheft 37 (1990), p. 159. MacCormick, Legal Reasoning, p. 251, also comes to the conclusion that there cannot be one right solution in hard cases.
[61] Dworkin, Taking Rights Seriously, p. 81 and 279 et seqq.
[62] Dworkin, Taking Rights Seriously, p. 280 (emphasis by authors).
[63] Dworkin, Taking Rights Seriously, gist of p. 81 and p. 282.

stitution is to be incorporated in the catalogue of unwritten fundamental rights. Presumably, some constitutional theorists would develop a theory which includes this controversial fundamental right; other constitutional theorists would develop an opposing theory, according to which this fundamental right does not exist in Switzerland. Following Dworkin's theory, one would have to assume that one group of constitutional theorists was wrong whilst the other was right, but it would not be possible to identify which party was right. Suppose, furthermore, the Federal Court acknowledged this new fundamental right on the occasion of a controversial session. Would this result in the conclusion that the judges representing the minority opinion had been wrong? No, for even now there is a possibility that the majority has erroneously "believed" in the existence of such a fundamental right whilst the minority has rightly realized that this right does not "exist" in Switzerland.

The question is whether such a view of things is realistic. Does it not misconceive the political function of constitutional adjudication? Would it not be more reasonable to adopt the positivist view, according to which the recognition of a new unwritten fundamental right is an act similar to legislation and that there is, as a result, no such right in Switzerland prior to its recognition by the Federal Court? Is it not the lawyer's day-to-day experience that one may in good faith differ over legal questions without imputing an actual "error" to the other party? Does this experience not naturally account for differing opinions of constitutional theorists and judges? Do the precedents in such cases not have the function of an independent source of law?

IV. No Disproof of the Positivist Separation Thesis by the Argument from Principles

Finally, let us touch on the question of whether Dworkin succeeded in disproving the positivist separation thesis. As illustrative material, we refer to the Swiss Matrimonial Law:

The Matrimonial Law of 1907 contained a legal role allocation which assigned "the husband the primacy and main responsibility for the marital community and the wife a position of relative subordination".[64] It is a relict of a patriarchal family law we are dealing with here. In society, however, a gradual shift towards equality of men and women took place. On 22 September 1985, the voters adopted a new Matrimonial Law, with a majority of 921'743 yes-votes prevailing over 762'619 no-votes,[65] which realized gender equality to a great extent and was brought into force on 1 January 1988. This example illustrates that the version of the separation thesis which distinguishes between the positive law as it is and the law as it should be according to positive morality, i.e. according to the moral views prevailing in a society, may be maintained. Despite Dworkin's criticism, it still allows for differentiation between the positive marital law (which included the patriarchal principle as a background structure) as it was until 31 December 1987 and the matrimonial law (embracing the principle of equality as a background structure) as it should be according to the prevailing moral views of the population by no later than 22 September 1985, the date of the vote. This version of the separation thesis is consequently not disproved.

But how about the separation thesis in the version which says that a distinction must be made between the law as it is and a natural law? This version, too, still allows for a differentiation between the positive matrimonial law (including the principle of equality as a background structure), in force since 1 January 1988, and the law as it should be – for example, according to the Aristotelian natural law theory. According to Aristotle, relationships of domination can be found everywhere in nature. In the human being, for example, the mind rules over the body, and amongst the living creatures, the human is the ruler of the animals: "Again, the same holds good of male in relation to female. The male is by nature superior and the female inferior, and the one rules, the other is ruled."[66] Considering that example, it seems to us that this version of the separation thesis is not disproved, either.

---

[64] C. Hegnauer, Grundriss des Eherechts, 1st Edition, Bern: Stämpfli, 1979, p. 93.
[65] C. Hegnauer/P. Breitschmid, Grundriss des Eherechts, 2nd Edition, Bern: Stämpfli 1987, p. 30.
[66] Aristotle, Politics 1254 b.

According to Dworkin, what the argument from principles is about is the proof of a relation between the positive law and its background structure, the latter not being identical with a natural law[67] nor with the prevailing moral views of a population.[68] How the reply to that may be framed from a positivist standpoint has been indicated above.[69] At any rate, the two conventional versions of the separation thesis make no reference to this, and are therefore not refuted by the argument from principles.[70]

---

[67] MacCormick, Rechtstheorie 11 (1980), p. 2 with further references.

[68] Dworkin, Taking Rights Seriously, p. 128 et seq.: "The community's morality [...] is not some sum or combination or function of the competing claims of its members." He paraphrases this "community morality" as "the morality presupposed by the laws and institutions of a community" (loc. cit., p. 126).

[69] Above, § 22 D.III.2.

[70] Geddert, p. 227 et seqq., and Höffe, p. 126 et seq. also come to the conclusion that the argument from pinciples is to be dismissed.

§ 23 The Separation Thesis and the "Hitler Argument"[1]

We will now turn our attention to the one objection to the separation thesis which is considered to be the cardinal proof against legal positivism, and which has manifestly discredited the theoretical positions associated with it, to the point that many jurists today view the legal positivist as an "inferior member of the guild".[2] The objection – we call it the "Hitler Argument" – appears in two versions. According to the version advocated by Radbruch, there are *single* norms "which are unjust to such a degree that they have to be denied validity and/or the very nature of law."[3] According to the other version which is advocated by Höffe[4] and Alexy,[5] *systems* of norms which do not meet certain fundamental criteria of justice do not qualify as legal systems. A tenable reply to the latter version has been sketched out briefly above.[6] Radbruch's version was ignited by the experience with National Socialism which is why we label it *pars pro toto* as the "Hitler argument" against legal positivism, being well aware that other examples apart from the Third Reich could equally be quoted to corroborate it. Its historical version says that positivism rendered the German juristic fraternity defenseless in the face of laws of

---

[1] Literature (selection): Alexy, ARSP Beiheft 37 (1990), p. 14–18; idem, The Argument from Injustice – A Reply to Legal Positivism; Bydlinski, Rechtsbegriff, p. 211 et seq., 277 et seqq.; Dreier, NJW 39 (1986), p. 891 et seq.; Fuller, Harvard Law Review 71 (1958), p. 630 et seqq.; Geddert, p. 217 et seqq.; Hart, Positivism and the Separation of Law and Morals, p. 72 et seqq.; Höffe; Hoerster, Einleitung, p. 9 et seqq.; idem, NJW 39 (1986), p. 2480 et seqq.; idem, Neue Hefte für Philosophie 17 (1979), p. 78 et seqq.; idem, Jahrbuch für Rechtssoziologie und Rechtstheorie 2 (1971), p. 115 et seqq.; idem, ARSP Beiheft 37 (1990), p. 27 et seqq.; Kriele, Recht und praktische Vernunft, chapter 5; idem, ÖZöR 16 (1966), p. 413 et seqq.; Kuhlen; Radbruch, Statutory Lawlessness and Supra-Statutory Law, first published in Süddeutsche Juristenzeitung 1 (1946), p. 105–108, translated by Bonnie Litschewski Paulson and Stanley L. Paulson, Oxford Journal of Legal Studies 26 (2006), p. 1–11.
[2] Riezler, in: Naturrecht und Rechtspositivismus?, p. 239.
[3] Dreier, NJW 39 (1986), p. 891. Regarding Radbruch's argument, cf. below, A.
[4] Höffe, p. 158 et seq.; p. 170 et seq.
[5] Alexy, ARSP Beiheft 37 (1990), p. 16 et seqq., particularly p. 17; idem, The Argument from Injustice – A reply to Legal Positivism, p. 127.
[6] Above, § 21 E after n. 26.

arbitrary and criminal content issued during the Third Reich.[7] Its normative version says that positivism makes it difficult to remedy "statutory lawlessness".[8]

A. The Formulation of the Hitler Argument by Gustav Radbruch

In his famous essay "Statutory Lawlessness and Supra-Statutory Law", the key passages of which we will repeat verbatim, Radbruch wrote the following: "By means of two maxims, 'An order is an order' and 'a law is a law', National Socialism contrived to bind its followers to itself, soldiers and jurists respectively. The former tenet was always restricted in its applicability; soldiers had no obligation to obey orders serving criminal purposes [Military Criminal Code of 1940, § 47]. 'A law is a law', on the other hand, knew no restriction whatever. It expressed the positivistic legal thinking that, almost unchallenged, held sway over German jurists for many decades. 'Statutory lawlessness' was, accordingly, a contradiction in terms, just as 'supra-statutory law' was."[9] "Positivism, with its principle that 'a law is a law', has in fact rendered the German legal profession defenseless against statutes that are arbitrary and criminal. Positivism is, moreover, in and of itself wholly incapable of establishing the validity of statutes. It claims to have proved the validity of a statute simply by showing that the statute had sufficient power behind it to prevail. But while power may indeed serve as a basis for the 'must' of compulsion, it never serves as a basis for the 'ought' of obligation and for legal validity. Obligation and legal validity must be based, rather, on a value inherent in the statute."[10] Radbruch goes on to develop his well-known formula of "statutory lawlessness": "Where

---

[7] Cf. below, § 23 D. W. Ott / F. Buob, Social and Legal Studies, Volume 2, London, Sage Publications, 1993, p. 91 et seqq.

[8] Cf. below, § 23 C.

[9] Radbruch, Statutory Lawlessness and Supra-Statutory Law, first published in Süddeutsche Juristenzeitung 1 (1946) p. 105–108, translated by Bonnie Litschewski Paulson and Stanley L. Paulson, Oxford Journal of Legal Studies 26 (2006), p. 1–11, p. 1.

[10] Radbruch, loc. cit., p. 6.

there is not even an attempt at justice, where equality, the core of justice, is deliberately betrayed in the issuance of positive law, then the statute is not merely 'flawed law', it lacks completely the very nature of law. For law, including positive law, cannot be otherwise defined than as a system and an institution whose very meaning is to serve justice. Measured by this standard, whole portions of National Socialist law never attained the dignity of valid law."[11] Radbruch urged that "we must arm ourselves against the recurrence of an outlaw state like Hitler's by fundamentally overcoming positivism, which rendered impotent every possible defense against the abuses of National Socialist legislation."[12]

Ever since, the Hitler argument has been brought forward in similar form by many great authors such as E. von Hippel,[13] H. Weinkauff,[14] L.L. Fuller,[15] M. Kriele,[16] R. Dreier[17] and R. Alexy,[18] to name just a few.

As one can see, Radbruch's formula is not one hundred percent precise; according to the first formulation, the so-called National Socialist law would not, conceptually, be law at all, whilst according to the second formulation it would be "law" but *not valid* law, which would conform to the notion of a derogative power of natural law. The differentiation is, however, of no importance – as will be explained below – which is why we will not elaborate on it any further.

Radbruch's formula had a lasting influence on the practice of the highest Courts of the Federal Republic of Germany;[19] it also met with an enor-

---

[11] Radbruch, loc. cit., p. 7.
[12] Radbruch, loc. cit., p. 8.
[13] E. v. Hippel, Die positivistische Staatslehre im Nürnberger Prozess und nach dem Grundgesetz, in: Aktuelle Fragen aus modernem Recht und Rechtsgeschichte, Gedächtnisschrift für Rudolf Schmidt, Berlin: Duncker & Humblot, 1966, p. 35 et seqq.
[14] H. Weinkauff, Was heisst das: "Positivismus als juristische Strategie?", JZ 25 (1970), p. 55; idem, in: "Die deutsche Justiz und der Nationalsozialismus", Stuttgart: Deutsche Verlagsanstalt, 1968, p. 18 et seqq.
[15] Fuller, Harvard Law Review 71 (1958), p. 657 et seqq.
[16] Kriele, p. 124.
[17] Dreier, NJW 39 (1986), p. 891, right column.
[18] The Argument from Injustice.
[19] See for example the following decisions: Entscheidungen des Bundesverfassungsgerichts 3 (1954) 58, at 119; 3 (1954) 225, at 232 et seq.; 6 (1957) 132, at 198; 23 (1968) 98, at 106; Entscheidungen des Bundesgerichtshofes in Zivilsachen 3 (1951) 94, at

mous response from the international discourse on legal philosophy by inducing a rebirth of Natural Law during the 1950s and 1960s on the one hand[20] and being questioned by critics of stature, including H.L.A. Hart[21] and Norbert Hoerster,[22] on the other.

The question is whether a narrower concept of law, such as that advocated by Radbruch, is to be preferred to a broader concept, such as that advocated by Hart. Since the time of Hart and to this day, this issue has been understood with ever growing distinctness as a *practical, pragmatic or political one*.[23] "Although the terminology is not uniform, the same is meant. The crux of the discussion is an aspect of the relation between the concepts of 'law' and 'morality', namely the question of which linguistic usage should reasonably be chosen."[24] What is considered decisive is "how different linguistic usages prove themselves in practice in different contexts. This practical test consists first of all of assessing the *consequences* of taking one or the other usage of language as a basis in the given context, then *rating* these as more or less desirable, and finally

---

107; Entscheidungen des Bundesgerichtshofs in Strafsachen 2 (1952) 234, at 237 et seqq.; 2 (1952) 333, at 334; 3 (1953) 357, at 362 et seq. See also Björn Schumacher, Rezeption und Kritik der Radbruchschen Formel, Thesis Göttingen 1985, Part 3. Regarding the problem of the punishability of the East German Border Guards where the German Courts again applied Radbruch's formula, see Knut Seidel, Rechtsphilosophische Aspekte der Mauerschützenprozesse, Berlin: Duncker & Humblot, 1999; Walter Ott, Did East German Border Guards along The Berlin Wall Act Illegally? Comments on the Decision of the German Federal Constitutional Court of 24 October 1996, Israel Law Review 34 (2000), pp. 352–372.

[20] See for example the anthology edited by W. Maihofer (Editor), Naturrecht oder Rechtspositivismus? Second Edition, Bad Homburg v.d.H.: Hermann Genter Verlag, 1966; regarding reception and criticism of Radbruch's formula in legal doctrine, see Schumacher, loc. cit., Part 2.

[21] Hart, Positivism and the Separation of Law and Morals, p. 72 et seqq.

[22] Hoerster, Einleitung; idem, NJW 39 (1986), p. 2480 et seqq. (this essay represents a response to R. Dreier, NJW 39 [1986], p. 890 et seqq.); idem, Neue Hefte für Philosophie 17 (1979), p. 77 et seqq.; idem, Jahrbuch für Rechtssoziologie und Rechtstheorie 2 (1971), p. 115 et seqq.

[23] See above, § 21 A; Hart, Concept of Law, p. 207–212; Kuhlen, p. 77; Kriele, ÖZöR 16 (1966), p. 413 et seqq., in particular p. 422 and 426; Bydlinski, Rechtsbegriff, p. 285; Geddert, p. 41 n. 43, p. 225 et seqq.; Hoerster, Neue Hefte für Philosophie 17 (1979), p. 78, 83 et seq.; idem, NJW 39 (1986), p. 2481.

[24] Kuhlen, p. 77.

choosing the usage category which has *preferable* consequences to those of the alternative."[25]

B. Inhumane Law in the Light of the Different Positivist Theories

As one can see, Radbruch's comments are expressly directed only *against German statutory positivism*. Nevertheless the question arises whether their scope could be extended by analogy to other positivist theories. Thus to begin with, we will look into which variants of the positivist theories are exposed to this allegation. As an example, we choose the Decree concerning the Administration of Penal Justice against Poles and Jews in the Incorporated Eastern Territories of 4 December 1941.[26] Among other things, in Art. I para. 3, the decree provides that a Pole or Jew shall be sentenced to death "if he manifests anti-German sentiments by malicious activities or incitement" (particularly "by making anti-German utterances, or by removing or defacing official notices of German authorities or offices", or generally "if he, by his conduct, lowers or prejudices the prestige or the well being of the German Reich or the German people"). It shall now be analyzed according to which positivist theories such an inhumane legislative act as this decree may be called "law". Said decree is:

1. "Law" in terms of Austin's analytical jurisprudence. For according to Austin, here we would be concerned with a sovereign's command vis-à-vis his subjects, and thus Austin's concept of law would be met. This clearly emanates from the example quoted above, too, according to which we can talk about law even if the sovereign prohibits an innocuous or indeed benign act under penalty of death.[27]

2. "Law" in terms of German statutory positivism.

---

[25] Kuhlen, p. 77/78 (our translation).
[26] Reichsgesetzblatt I, p. 759, quoted from The Mazal Library, A Holocaust Resource, Nuernberg Military Tribunal Vol. III, p. 995 et seq. (www.mazal.org/archive/nmt/03/NMT03-T0995.htm and following page).
[27] Above, § 2 at n. 10.

3. "Law" in terms of Kelsen's pure theory of law. For here we are concerned with a by and large effective, coercive norm posited by the social authority. Since the National Socialist tyranny proved effective within the German Reich, Kelsen's basic norm is to be presupposed[28] as a result of which the subjective sense intended by the National Socialists may be interpreted as objective, i.e. as an objective Ought.[29]

4. *Not law* in terms of the theories of individual recognition. For it is not likely that the victims of such a decree would have given it their consent.[30]

5. Presumably *not law* in terms of that variant of a theory of general recognition which demands the consent of a majority of the population to each individual norm.[31] Explicit recognition is out of question because the option of holding a plebiscite, which existed according to § 1 of the German Plebiscite Act of 14 July 1933, was exercised only three times during the Third Reich,[32] not, however, in this particular case. Whether the Act enjoyed tacit consent could theoretically have been evaluated by way of a representative survey (if this was possible under a totalitarian regime!); today it is no longer possible to say for certain, but the question must probably be answered in the negative. All at the same it remains to be stressed that an inhumane law will qualify as law according to the theory of general recognition if the legal consciousness has been perverted to a degree that results in general approval for such a law.

---

[28] Cf. Kelsen, Pure Theory of Law, p. 48, with regard to the problem of a robber band.

[29] It is not needless to be evocative of Kelsen's interpretation not being imperative; according to the pure theory of law, everybody is free to see but brute force where the Nazis refer to something as "law" (at n. 14).

[30] Of course, this only holds good if one takes the theories of recognition in their strictest form, i.e. accepts them at face value. Because of its obvious untenability, nobody represented such a pure form. Bierling takes refuge to his theory of "indirect recognition", whilst Laun switches over to a theory of general recognition with regard to the validity problem.

[31] Like this Laun, cf. above.

[32] Brodersen, U. (ed.), Gesetze des NS-Staates, Bad Homburg v.d.H./Berlin/Zürich: Gehlen, 1968, p. 14.

208

6. Not (sociological) law in terms of Ehrlich's theory of feeling. For it is not likely that such harmless "misdemeanors" as the ones prohibited by the decree under penalty of death were sufficient to trigger the feeling of revulsion and that this order was supported by an "*opinio necessitatis*". Thus, the decree is not covered by Ehrlich's sociological concept of law. In contrast, if one started from Ehrlich's concept of "living law", its legal character would have to be affirmed: for, as we have seen, the complex of norms of the state law forms part of the living law, too. The effectiveness of the former depends upon the law-enforcement power of the state (which was certainly existent in the case at hand) and may absolutely appear to be in defiance of a large part of society.[33]

7. "Law" in terms of Bierling's, Merkel's, Beling's and Nawiasky's theories of recognition. For if only the legal system as a whole has to be recognized (Bierling, Merkel) or if recognition must be awarded only by the leading class who sets the tone within a society (thus in the example by the National Socialists; cf. Beling, Nawiasky), then the National Socialist coercive order was a legal system and the said norm of the decree was a legal norm.

8. "Law" in terms of Scandinavian legal realism, because for the Scandinavian Realists, the law is the complex of ideas that is expressed in the material of the legislature and the judiciary or, according to Alf Ross, the normative ideology as manifested in decisions of the judges. As a result, the National Socialist norm concepts which have been disclosed in said decree and/or in the behavior of the law staff administering this decree are to be qualified as "legal".

9. "Law" in terms of American legal realism and in terms of the modern sociological theory of coercion which both pivotally rely on the behavior of the law staff. For said norm was a "real rule" since it found expression in the behavior of the law staff: the law staff was prepared to apply and enforce it.

10. "Law" in terms of Hart's theory: for according to Hart, recognition is limited to the fundamental secondary rule which contains the sys-

---

[33] Rehbinder, Eugen Ehrlich, p. 57 et seq.

tem's validity criteria; furthermore, only the *officials* need recognize and apply this secondary rule, whilst for the ordinary citizens it is sufficient to by and large comply with the primary rules. All of these prerequisites were certainly met in Hitler's Reich. That Hart would not deny these rules legal character clearly emanates from the slave-owning society he cites as an example: according to Hart, if a coercive system provides advantages even to just a small group of slave-holders, it qualifies as legal order.[34]

11. Law in terms of exclusive positivism, for the formal criteria contained in the rule of recognition were met.

12. Law in terms of inclusive positivism since the Decree complied with formal as well as the moral criteria of the Nazi ideology (the racial theory, the *Führer*-principle, the sound popular feeling ["*gesundes Volksempfinden*"] and the party program of the NSDAP) contained in the rule of recognition.

13. Law in terms of Weinberger's and MacCormick's institutional positivism. For according to ITL, a legal system comprises not only legal principles, the teleological background of the legal system (e.g. principles of justice) as well as the legal doctrine, but primarily of course, explicitly enacted primary and secondary rules as understood by Hart (norms of conduct and power-conferring norms). In the case under consideration, we are dealing with an explicitly given primary rule, i.e. with a norm of conduct which is thus to be qualified as a legal norm.

It follows from the above that not all positivist theories are exposed to the accusation of the "Hitler argument". Viewed under *this* aspect, the theories that do best are the theory of individual recognition, Ehrlich's theory of feeling as well as the above-mentioned variant of the theory of general recognition; for precautionary reasons, however, we would like to point out right away that just the opposite is true if these theories are applied to other issues (below, § 24 E; § 24 F). The following comments are only concerned with those variants of legal positivism according to which even an inhumane statute is to be regarded as "law".

---

[34] Above, § 11 at n. 34.

C. The Dispute about the Separation Thesis with Regard to Inhumane Law

Suppose lawyer A is a natural lawyer following Radbruch's theory. As a judge, he finds himself confronted with the dilemma, under statutory lawlessness (in an *Unrechtsstaat* or after the collapse of such a state), of having to apply an inhumane law such as the aforementioned decree. Since he takes Radbruch's concept of law as a basis, he will come to the conclusion that this is a case of "statutory lawlessness" and that consequently, having correctly assessed the matter, he has no *legal obligation* to apply the norm in question. Hence, he will refuse to apply the law (although, in an *Unrechtsstaat*, only if he is not afraid of potential martyrdom), and he will do so on the basis of *legal* considerations.

Lawyer B is a positivist of Hart's persuasion. He, too, is confronted with the above situation. On the basis of Hart's conception, he will come to the conclusion that the decree qualifies as law and that, on juridical assessment of his position, he is therefore obliged to apply it. On the other hand, he is nevertheless aware that "there are laws which may have any degree of iniquity or stupidity",[35] and that by concluding that there is a legal duty, the *moral* question of whether one ought to really obey the law or not is not yet decided. Therefore, he, too, will refuse to apply the law (although only if he, too, is not afraid of the potential consequences in an *Unrechtsstaat*), and he will do so by referring to *moral* arguments.

As one can see, both positions – the one acting on the assumption of a content-based concept of law as well as the positivist position – offer a solution to the problem of inhumane law.[36] For the positivist, the judge is bound by the positive law and in an extreme case is, therefore, – legally speaking – obliged to apply even absolutely immoral law; but morally speaking, he is not.[37] From a moral point of view, he may very well refuse to apply an inhumane law. For the supporters of a content-based concept of law, a legal obligation never even comes into existence. The

---

[35] Hart, Positivism and the Separation of Law and Morals, p. 84.
[36] In agreement Geddert, p. 222.
[37] Hoerster, Jahrbuch für Rechtssoziologie und Rechtstheorie 2 (1971), p. 128.

question now arises as to which of these "conceptions" is more useful for the deliberation of these directly practical questions.

The one thing clear for the time being is that the issue of an application of Radbruch's formula – as is evident from Radbruch's own explanations – only arises if one is confronted with a *lex iniustissima:* "The conflict between justice and legal certainty may well be resolved in this way: the positive law, secured by legislation and power, *takes precedence even when its content is unjust and fails to benefit the people*, unless the conflict between statute and justice reaches such an intolerable degree that the statute, as 'flawed law', must yield to justice."[38] Thus normally, there is a legal and moral duty to obey even unjust laws. It is, therefore, impossible to use Radbruch's formula to contest, say, an unjust tax statute, unless that statute touches on the core area aimed at by Radbruch's formula.[39]

Which arguments are produced against Radbruch's formula and to what extent are they conclusive?[40]

I. The Naivety Argument

A first objection, raised by Hart who acknowledges the moral earnestness of Radbruch's passionate appeal, is that Radbruch's view is naïve.[41] According to Hoerster, who formulates Hart's thought with more precision, Radbruch apparently assumes that definitions of legal theory have the potential to improve the morality of the legislator and the citizens.[42] However, according to Hart, there is more behind Radbruch's view than sheer naivety: everything he says is really due to the misunderstanding

---

[38] Radbruch, Statutory Lawlessness and Supra-Statutory Law, first published in Süddeutsche Juristenzeitung 1 (1946) p. 105–108, translated by Bonnie Litschewski Paulson and Stanley L. Paulson, Oxford Journal of Legal Studies 26 (2006), p. 1–11, p. 7 (our emphasis).

[39] According to Bydlinski, Rechtsbegriff, p. 212, this would be the case if income tax and contribution rates added up to more than 100% of the actual income.

[40] Arguments against Radbruch's formula are at the same time arguments in favor of the separation thesis and vice-versa.

[41] Hart, Positivism and the Separation of Law and Morals, p. 74.

[42] Hoerster, Einleitung, p. 9.

that the recognition of a rule as a valid rule of law is equally conclusive of the question: "Ought one obey this rule?"[43]

Hoerster's argument can certainly be endorsed in relation to the citizens. For the citizens do not usually know definitions of legal theory; thus they cannot be influenced by them. In the normal way of things, Hoerster's argument applies to the legislator as well; for politicians are not usually up to date with contemporary philosophy of law.[44]

But how about the courts? At this point, it is necessary to differentiate between the judge *in* a state that misuses the rule of law and the judge *after* the collapse of a state that misuses the rule of law:

1. The Judge in an *Unrechtsstaat*

For a judge in an *Unrechtsstaat*, there is no fundamental difference between Hart's and Radbruch's position. Though both could refuse to apply a law of terror – one by invoking moral reasons, the other by invoking legal reasons – both strategies seem unrealistic under the conditions of government perversion of the rule of law. For "judicial resistance in existing ('established') totalitarian systems – considered in isolation – has no chance of bringing about a change of system. Even collective refusal by the judges to carry out their duties would probably only lead to their removal from office."[45] In a totalitarian state that abuses the rule of law, there are only two possibilities left to the judge who revolts against the regime: either to camouflage his opposition by avidly quoting the ideological phrases of the system while "reserving within the framework of the formally adapted judicature some disguised leeway for contrary judicial judgment"[46] or to resign from office and leave the position to somebody else who would certainly be less scrupulous. Neither alternative, however, really threatens the continuance of the system. Nor

---

[43] Hart, Positivism and the Separation of Law and Morals, p. 75.

[44] The influence of Locke on the framers of the American Declaration of Independence represents an exception. Cf. H. Welzel, Naturrecht und materiale Gerechtigkeit, 2nd, unchanged Reprint of Fourth Edition, Göttingen: Vandenhoeck & Ruprecht, 1990), p. 142 et seqq.

[45] This is, according to Rüthers, Entartetes Recht, p. 216, one of the lessons that National Socialism teaches us.

[46] Rüthers, loc. cit., p. 216 (our translation).

do judges, unlike for example *generals, chiefs of police, industrialists* or *union chiefs, possess a real power base*[47] from which the campaign against the totalitarian government could successfully be advanced. Furthermore, it has to be taken into account that in a state that misuses the rule of law, insubordination requires not only the courage to stand up for one's beliefs, but also *readiness for martyrdom*,[48] and the latter cannot generally be demanded of people, whether they be judges or not. Supposing that Radbruch had meant that a conception such as his would have made the German juristic fraternity more capable of defending itself "against statutes that are arbitrary and criminal",[49] then this view would indeed have to be qualified as naïve. For once such statutes are enacted, the judiciary stands no chance of opposing them in any effective way. To have a realistic chance of success, the battle by juristic means must be fought before the "takeover".[50]

2. The Judge after the Collapse of an *Unrechtsstaat*

The difference between the two positions is, however, apparent when the judge, who is not himself an agent of the government that misused the rule of law but who is – as in the Federal Republic of Germany after the war and again after the collapse of the German Democratic Republic (East Germany) – confronted *ex post facto* with the dilemma of having to apply an inhumane law enacted by such a government.

Hoerster tries to illustrate the complete harmlessness and linguistic adequacy of the positivist phraseology by means of the following example: "*From the point of view of sport* (i.e. according to the rules presently in force), a boxer should try to knock his opponent out. From a moral point of view, however, he should refrain from doing so if he knows that a knock-out will mean physical or psychological ruin for his opponent. In that situation, why should we cease to say … that it is his duty as a sportsman to knock his opponent out if possible? Where is the danger in

---

[47] Rüthers, Entartetes Recht, p. 215.
[48] Kriele, p. 123.
[49] See above, § 23 A at n. 10 (our translation).
[50] Rüthers, Entartetes Recht, p. 215.

such a use of language, considering that we clearly say at the same time that he has the overriding *moral* duty not to do it?"[51]

The answer to this question is obvious, because there will hardly ever be a boxer who will care about his *moral duty* not to harm his opponent as long as he knows it is his *duty as a sportsman* to knock his opponent out. This is proved by the countless cases in which boxers have suffered permanent physical damage or died as a result of the injuries received in the ring. This deplorable state of affairs could only by changed by obliging the sportsman not only morally, but also by the rules of sport, not to ruin his opponent. Theoretically, this could be achieved in two different ways: either by changing the boxing rules presently in force, or by starting from a different linguistic stipulation; for example by including the reservation "*neminem laedere*" in the concept of the sportsman's duty. Only the first variant is practically realizable since the second would hardly be understood amongst sportsmen.

The analogue is true for the problem of inhumane law: *if a judge knows that he is not even legally obliged to apply a particular law, he will be more likely to refuse to apply it than if he is legally bound to by the law and can "only" state moral reasons for his refusal.* Hoerster concedes this.[52] Judges of civilized states should be allowed to refuse the application of inhumane orders by reference to the *legal literature* and *not only for reasons of moral philosophy* and *moral theology*. Though definitions of legal theory are normally not capable of improving the morals of the legislator or the citizens, *they can certainly influence the adjudicative practice of the courts as long as they are acknowledged as prevailing doctrine by the legal literature.* The fact that inhumane orders may be qualified as "law" from a sociological, historical or ethnological point of view (since the sociologist, the historian and the ethnologist of law must each work with different concepts of law if their research is to be fruitful[53]) does not prevent such orders from being denied legal character when it comes to the question of the law to be applied by a judge of a modern, civilized state. For this reason alone it is justifiable to start from

---

[51] Hoerster, Jahrbuch für Rechtssoziologie und Rechtstheorie 2 (1971), p. 128.
[52] Hoerster, NJW 39 (1986), p. 2482, left column, and idem, JZ 34 (1979), p. 824.
[53] Above, § 22 A.

a narrower concept of law based on a minimal content in this context. Such a stipulation would have the advantage that at least the most fundamental principles of a critical morality would fall within the *scope of responsibility* of the courts, since such principles would be legal principles at the same time. Good illustrative material may be drawn from the application of Radbruch's formula in post-war judicial practice. Let us look at one of these cases, which was based on the following facts:[54]

The Claimant, a Jewess, had emigrated to Switzerland in 1939. Pursuant to § 2 of the 11th Ordinance of 25 November 1941 (Reichsgesetzblatt I, p. 722 et seqq.), issued by virtue of the Reich's Citizenship Law, she lost her German nationality. Pursuant to § 3 of said Ordinance, this denaturalization entailed that the ownership of the assets of the person in question was acquired by the German Reich. She left a securities deposit with the Defendant, a bank. This deposit remained listed unchanged under the name of the Claimant in the Defendant's books during the Nazi regime and for some time afterwards. After the end of the war, the Claimant relocated her domicile to the Federal Republic of Germany and claimed release of the securities in the aforementioned deposit.

The Great Civil Senate of the Federal Court *(Grosser Senat für Zivilsachen des Bundesgerichtshofes)* denied the legal character of the confiscation "though formally dressed up as a law."[55] Amongst other reasons, they referred to the "supra-legal principle of equality" which is even beyond the constitution-making power's reach. That it was violated followed clearly from the fact that "the confiscation of assets" was only imposed on a "group of persons distinguished solely by racial aspects."[56] Thus, the Claimant had been the owner and holder of the securities all along, and did not therefore need to rely on the now stale claim pursuant to the German restitution laws.

According to Hart's theory, the claim would have had to be dismissed. The Claimant would have lost ownership and possession of the securities due to the legally valid, but morally condemnable confiscation. And the

---

[54] BGHZ 16 (1955), p. 350 et seqq. (354).
[55] Loc. cit., p. 353.
[56] Loc. cit., p. 353.

judge of the German Federal Republic would have had to tell her:
"Though you may have a moral right to the securities, I have to dismiss
your claim on legal grounds."[57] However, such a result would have been
an *affront*. The appropriate result, viz. a decision in favor of the Claimant, can only be arrived at by declaring §§ 2 and 3 of the 11th Ordinance
issued by virtue of the Reich's Citizenship Law null and void and by
integrating the criteria Hart wants to have discussed in categories of
moral philosophy within the realm of the legal by way of Radbruch's
formula.[58] In this way one enables the court to base its decision on such
criteria. A court must be able to decide a *legal* dispute by means of *legal*
reasons, not by means of moral-philosophical ones. A decision based on
moral principles is to be considered, at most, if the positive law incorporates them by including a specific reference to them[59] or else if issues of
interpretation or gap-filling are at stake.

---

[57] The question arises here whether the judge, based on Hart's theory, may have re-
plied: "On legal grounds I would have to dismiss your claim, but nevertheless, I will
decide in your favor on moral grounds since the 11th Ordinance is too unjust to be
applied." In other words: Would a judge, according to Hart, be allowed to opt for the
legally wrong solution for *moral* reasons? As Hart's comments on the denunciation
case reveal (see below, § 23 C.IV, text at n. 75 et seqq.), this is not the case. For Hart
does not explain there that the judge may simply ignore on moral grounds the woman's positive-legal right to denunciate and thus convict her but he says that one would
either have to let the woman go unpunished or punish her pursuant to the introduction of a frankly retrospective law. I.e. Hart does not grant the judge the liberty to
ignore a positive legal right or norm on moral grounds when writing an opinion. At
most, the judge could refuse to apply the law for moral reasons and resign from his
office. Therefore, it only applies to an ideal type of legal positivism when Geddert,
p. 223, writes that one would always arrive at the conclusion that "natural lawyers
and legal positivists would agree on the behavior indicated if only they agreed on
what morality demands in the case at hand."

[58] At this point, one could raise the objection that it would have been the duty of the
legislator to retroactively repeal the 11th Ordinance after the end of the war and that
the affronting result was due to a deficiency of the law and not to Hart's theory. A
rejoinder to this is, however, the argument that courts were at all times again and
again confronted with constellations where the legislator had remained inactive. It is
precisely this kind of a situation which necessitates that the courts get support from
legal doctrine so that it is, in our opinion, nevertheless a deficiency of Hart's theory
that it does not provide such support. The situation is, however, different in criminal
cases. See below, § 23 C.IV.

[59] Cf. Hoerster, NJW 39 (1986), p. 2481.

Hoerster has raised the question: "Why should we refuse to refer to governmental orders, which – for example because of their blatant injustice – in our opinion should not be followed, as *valid law*?"[60] The answer which shall be given here in the sense of an interim conclusion is: because we are then able to solve some civil law cases in a more satisfactory manner.

II. The Confusion Argument

Another argument against Radbruch's formula is that it causes confusion. Hart writes: "For if we adopt Radbruch's view, and with him and the German courts make our protest against evil law in the form of an assertion that certain rules of law cannot be law because of their moral iniquity, we confuse one of the most powerful, because it is the simplest, forms of moral criticism. If with the Utilitarians we speak plainly, we say that although positive laws may be law, they may be too evil to be obeyed. This is a moral condemnation which everyone can understand and it makes an immediate and obvious claim to moral attention. If, on the other hand, we formulate our objection as an assertion that these evil things are not law, here is an assertion which many people do not believe, and if they are disposed to consider it at all, it would seem to raise a whole host of philosophical issues before it can be accepted ... when we have the ample resources of plain speech we must not present the moral criticism of institutions as propositions of a disputable philosophy."[61] Hoerster assents to this statement[62] and quotes the following example:

"A white American, for example, who wants to tour South Africa in his dark skinned wife's company and is concerned about the details of the tour, will hardly be reassured by the 'natural law' information that the norms of Apartheid in force in that country are not valid law because of the blatant human rights abuse."[63]

---

[60] Neue Hefte für Philosophie 17 (1979), p. 82.
[61] Hart, Positivism and the Separation of Law and Morals, p. 77 et seq.
[62] NJW 39 (1986), p. 2482, left column.
[63] NJW 39 (1986), p. 2481, left column (our translation).

Serious terminological difficulties need not be feared at this point, however. The necessary differentiations can be expressed by very simple attributes of "law".[64] For instance, one can say with Hart that the Apartheid norms are law backed with coercive measures by the state but too evil to be obeyed. One may, however, just as well say that Apartheid norms are mere commands of the South African rulers which give raise to the expectation of certain coercive measures in case of disobedience; they are, however, not real law. Both ways of saying this, the positivist and the non-positivist, allow for adequate expression of what was in our mind, and the fears of Hoerster's white American are justified in any case.

A rejoinder to Hart's argument that Radbruch's formula causes confusion is therefore that for the lawyer, this is not the case. The latter is used to having to work with much more difficult dogmatic constructions, in matters of civil law, for instance. Radbruch's somewhat more complex construction, consisting of a combination of factual validity and ideal validity, is therefore hardly likely to ask too much of the average lawyer.

III. The Risk of Anarchy

Hart and Hoerster see a further difficulty of Radbruch's formula in acknowledging that it could promote anarchy:

Hart writes: "Older writers who, like Bentham and Austin, insisted on the distinction between what law is and what it ought to be, did so partly because they thought that unless men kept these separate they tended to hastily and without counting the cost to society make judgments that laws were invalid and ought not to be obeyed."[65] And Hoerster explicates in this context:

"There is no kind of guarantee or even likelihood that the morality included by the respective judge or citizen in his concept of law is, in fact, an 'enlightened' morality! ... Normally, the person concerned will base her moral concept of law on her own moral ideas. Nevertheless, there are

---

[64] Bydlinski, Rechtsbegriff, p. 286.
[65] Hart, Concept of Law, p. 211.

generally no grounds for supposing that the *moral ideas* of any individual or any particular society are more enlightened in any sense whatsoever (e.g. 'more human' or 'more just') than the *norms of the positive law* of the respective state. Let us for example compare the attitude of our population to the regulation of the Basic Law *(Grundgesetz)* regarding the legitimacy of capital punishment. The fact is, there are not only judges and citizens – as the opponents of legal positivism suggest time and again – who, confronted with the 'Nazi laws', would prefer to follow a more human morality; there are equally judges or citizens who, confronted with 'democratic' laws (e.g. those of the Weimar Republic or the Federal Republic of Germany), would prefer to follow a Nazi morality!"[66]

We cannot, however, see a risk of anarchy in the application of Radbruch's formula.[67] For it follows from Radbruch's above-quoted explanations that the positive law assured by statute and power takes precedence even if its content is unjust and fails to benefit the people. That the judge or the citizen may each start from his own concept of law based on his subjective moral ideas is out of the question. It is true that opinions on what the law requires vary a great deal. Thus we have an *unreliable sense of justice*. There is, on the other hand, a world-wide consensus on what is considered as despicable and thus objectionable at least according to the moral awareness of the vast majority of the population. We therefore have a *more reliable sense of injustice*. Only if this area, which is no longer seriously challenged in developed countries, is affected, does an application of Radbruch's formula come into question. Despite the vagueness of Radbruch's formula which is something that it has in common with any blanket clause this area may be at least roughly delimited: it includes phenomena such as the Gulag archipelago, concentration camps, slavery and the slave trade, genocide, mass deportations as well as discrimination based on color, race, sex, and background. The core area being thus objectivized, there is no room for augmenting the concept of law with subjective ideas of a Nazi morality.

---

[66] NJW 39 (1986), p. 2482, left column (our emphasis).
[67] In agreement Bydlinsky, Rechtsbegriff, p. 288.

As far as capital punishment is concerned, one may not go so far as to assert that it infringes this core area, as long as it is imposed in a criminal proceeding in accordance with due process. As is generally known, not even the European Convention of Human Rights prohibits the death penalty.[68] Only Protocols No. 6 and No. 13 to the Convention provide for the respective prohibition.[69] It remains to be hoped, however, that our legal culture will keep progressing towards the day when capital punishment, just like torture, will be self-evidently ranked amongst the absolutely inadmissible and despicable institutions of any rule-of-law criminal justice system.

IV. The Charge of a Hidden Strategy in Criminal Cases

A further argument against Radbruch's formula is that it might result in a covert strategy in criminal cases by neglecting to disclose that, in reality, the formula helps to evade the principle of non-retroactivity in criminal law *("nullum crimen sine praevia lege poenali")*.

The following case decided by the Federal Supreme Criminal Court *(Bundesgerichtshof in Strafsachen)* may serve as an example to illustrate the problem:[70] The persons accused had, as members of the Gestapo, assisted in displacing Jews to Eastern Europe. The Stuttgart jury court found them not guilty of accessoryship to deprivation of liberty, committed in office, resulting in death (§ 239 of the German Criminal Law Code of 1871) since they had not been aware of violating the law in force; this was based on the Order of the Reich President for the Protection of Peo-

---

[68] Article 2 (1), second sentence. Cf. Frowein/Peukert, Europäische Menschenrechtskonvention, EMRK-Kommentar, Second Edition, Kehl am Rhein/Strassburg/Arlington: Engel 1996, p. 33/34.

[69] Protocol No. 6 to the Convention for the Protection of Human Rights and Fundamental Freedoms concerning the abolition of the death penalty dated 28 April 1983 and Protocol No. 13 to the Convention for the Protection of Human Rights and Fundamental Freedoms, concerning the abolition of the death penalty in all circumstances. The Swiss Federal Assembly has ratified Protocol No. 6 (SR 0.101.06) on 20 March 1987 (BBl 1987 I 1018) and Protocol No. 13 (SR 0.101.093) on 3 May 2002 (BBl 2003, 4209).

[70] BGHSt 2 (1952), p. 234, (237 et seq.).

ple and State of 28 February 1933 which had provided the legal foundation of the Gestapo's activities.

The Federal Supreme Criminal Court overruled this interpretation of the law. Said order could not, according to the view of the Federal Supreme Criminal Court, give the Gestapo carte blanche to violate that core area of the law "which, according to the legal consciousness of all civilized peoples, may not be infringed by a statute or other governmental measure."[71] The Federal Supreme Court circumscribes this core area as follows: "It comprises certain principles of human behavior considered as inviolable which have developed over time amongst all civilized people on the basis of concurrent moral concepts and which are considered legally binding, whether or not certain legal orders seemingly allowed for their violation."[72] Therefore, the acquittal of the defendants on the grounds that they were not aware of the illegality of deprivation of liberty represented by the displacement of the Jews was not deemed to be justified.[73]

The decision is, above all, notable because it expressly addresses the issue of the right to protection from retroactive criminal laws in the following words:

"This does not mean that the behavior of the persons accused is measured against norms which entered into effect only later, and nor are the defendants expected to have answered the question of whether it was right or wrong based on principles not valid at the time or no longer valid. That they were not familiar with the few indispensable principles for human coexistence which form part of the fundament and core area of the law that lives in the knowledge of right and wrong of all civilized peoples, or that they could have misjudged the binding nature of such principles irrespective of their recognition by the state, is all the less reasonable a presumption, since they had been exposed to the impressions whereby such convictions are formed at a time before National Socialism had been able to unfold its disorientating and tainting propaganda. ... Only

---

[71] loc. cit., p. 238.
[72] loc. cit., p. 237 (our translation).
[73] loc. cit., p. 242.

in this way can the phrasing of the judgment be understood that the defendants had had 'an obscure feeling that the Jews suffered injustice' but nevertheless believed that carrying out their official duties did not 'violate the law in force'."[74]

Hart addresses this issue on the basis of a shocking denunciation case.[75] In 1944, a woman, desiring to get rid of her husband, reported to the authorities derogatory remarks he had made about Hitler while home on leave from the German army. "The husband was arrested and sentenced to death, ... though he was not executed but sent to the front .... In 1949, the wife was prosecuted in a West German court for an offence which we would describe as illegally depriving a person of his freedom *(rechtswidrige Freiheitsberaubung)*. ... The wife pleaded that her husband's imprisonment was pursuant to the Nazi statutes and hence that she had committed no crime. ... The court of appeal to which the case ultimately came held that the wife was guilty"[76] on the basis of a natural law justification. Hart disapproves of this approach and writes:

"There were, of course, two other choices. One was to let the woman go unpunished; one can sympathize with and endorse the view that this might have been a bad thing to do. The other was to face the fact that if the woman were to be punished it must be pursuant to the introduction of a *frankly retrospective* law and with a full consciousness of what was sacrificed in securing her punishment in this way. Odious as retrospective criminal legislation and punishment may be, to have pursued it openly in this case would at least have had the *merits of candor*. It would have made plain that in punishing the woman a choice had to be made between two evils, that of leaving her unpunished and that of sacrificing a very precious principle of morality endorsed by most legal systems.

---

[74] loc. cit., p. 239 et seq. (our translation).

[75] Judgment of 27 July 1949, Oberlandesgericht, Bamberg, Süddeutsche Juristen-Zeitung 5 (1950), p. 207 et seq., Harvard Law Review 64 (1951), p. 1005.

[76] Hart, Positivism and the Separation of Law and Morals, p. 76. Strictly speaking, the case as it is discussed by Hart should only be discussed as a hypothetical case since it has not been reported correctly. Cf. corrigendum in: Hart, Concept of Law, p. 303 et seq.

Surely if we have learned anything from the history of morals it is that the thing to do with a moral quandary is not to hide it."[77]

If one applies these considerations to the other case,[78] then either those defendants would also have had to be acquitted, since the Gestapo order would have had for a result the legality of the morally condemnable displacement of the Jews; or punishment would have been possible if the Federal Republic of Germany had enacted a frankly retrospective criminal law for such acts, although this would only have been possible by way of an amendment to Art. 103 para. 2 of the Basic Law ("An act may be punished only if it was defined by a law as a criminal offense before the act was committed").

The question that now arises is whether the aforementioned justification of the Federal Supreme Criminal Court regarding the principle of non-retroactivity in criminal law is well founded.

It is, first of all, undoubtedly correct that the defendants were not convicted due to principles entering into effect only later. For these principles were creations of western culture (and doubtless other cultures); they had obtained cultural validity long before National Socialism came to power, and Germany was part of this culture. But were they part of the law with unrestricted validity during the Third Reich, too? Could a National Socialist judge have convicted a member of the Gestapo and the woman desiring to be rid of her husband, back then, of accessoryship to deprivation of liberty and of deprivation of liberty committed through another person respectively? Could he have argued that, even back then, the law in force had to be interpreted to the effect that the deportation or denunciation was illegal? Undoubtedly not. "A judge regarding the conduct of the woman [or of the Gestapo officers; authors' note] as illegal back then would not have been interpreting the applicable law but rather – maybe in the name of some higher law – taking a firm stand against the applicable 'law' and he would doubtlessly have been aware of this fact."[79] This leads us to conclude that the Gestapo officers as well as the

---

[77] Hart, Positivism and the Separation of Law and Morals, p. 76 et seq. (our emphasis). In the same spirit Hoerster, NJW 39 (1986), p. 2481, right column.

[78] Above, § 23 C.IV, text following n. 70.

[79] Geddert, p. 228.

woman were convicted of acts that had not been defined as punishable in a law before they were committed. And that is what matters for the purposes of the *nulla poena sine lege* principle. The term "lex" in this principle refers to the *positive* law, not to a higher law,[80] for the principle would not make any sense otherwise.[81] From this it follows that even the strategy supported by Radbruch's formula – just like the positivist one – requires a restriction of *nulla poena sine lege* in such cases. It is just that in this case the restriction is made by the *judge*, whereas according to Hart's proposal it is made by the *legislator*. The reasons given for the judgment are thus not convincing inasmuch as they represent an attempt to substantiate that this approach does not violate the principle. At any rate the principle was only restricted and not completely repealed. For only the order then suspending the illegality of the acts of the accused persons (Order of the Reich President for the Protection of People and State of 28 February 1933) was not recognized as valid; the conviction, however, was based on the Criminal Law Code of 1871 which had continued in force for the duration of the Third Reich. Hart's denunciation case is similar. The accused had exercised her positive legal right to report an offense. The Appellate Court *(Oberlandesgericht)* Bamberg had explained that a behavior was illegal in terms of § 239 of the German Criminal Law Code of 1871 (wrongful deprivation of liberty) even if "the right exercised is admittedly in accordance with formal positive law but such exercise nevertheless grossly infringes upon the sense of equity and justice of all decently thinking men."[82] Thus, the judgment regarding illegality had taken place on the basis of a supra-positive norm; the conviction, however, was based on the German Criminal Law Code of 1871.

Both perceptions, Hart's as well as Radbruch's, do not bypass the dilemma of either having to leave a blatant wrong unatoned or having to restrict a fundamental principle in accordance with the rule of law. After all, the restriction seems tolerable if a justifying norm is overruled only on condition that it violates the most fundamental principles of human

---

[80] Geddert, p. 229.

[81] The principle "nulla poena sine lege" only endures if it is strictly obeyed. Cf. Grünwald, Zeitschrift für die gesamte Strafrechtswissenschaft 76 (1964), p. 15.

[82] Süddeutsche Juristenzeitung 5 (1950), p. 207 et seq.

coexistence, which were recognized in the moral consciousness of all civilized nations at the time when the crime was committed.[83]

In our opinion, the charge that the application of Radbruch's formula leads to a hidden strategy is, therefore, true. It would have been more honest if one had opted for the positivist strategy in Germany after the war, i.e. if one had made provision to amend Art 103 para. 2 of the Basic Law, for example with an exception clause annulling the most evil justificatory Nazi laws with *ex tunc* effect.

So much for the normative arguments for and against the separation thesis. In the next section, we will turn to the historical version of the Hitler argument.

D. German Statutory Positivism and National Socialism[84]

It is necessary to draw a distinction between the problem discussed in the preceding paragraph and the historical question of whether legal positiv-

---

[83] Cf. in this context Art. 7 para. 2 of the European Convention of Human Rights. According to this rule, "the conviction or punishment of a person guilty of an act or omission which was punishable according to the principles generally recognized by civilized people" may not be excluded by Art. 7 para. 1 (where the principle "nulla poena sine lege" is stated). This was meant to ensure that the prohibition of retroactive criminal laws would not extend to laws which were enforced at the end of World War II in order to sanction war crimes, treachery and cooperation with the enemy. Cf. J.A. Frowein/W. Peukert, Europäische Menschenrechtskonvention, EMRK-Kommentar, 2nd Edition, Kehl am Rhein/Strassburg/Arlington 1996, p. 327.

[84] Literature (selection): Alexy, The Argument from Injustice – A Reply to Legal Positivism; W. Ott/F. Buob, Did Legal Positivism Render German Jurists Defenceless during the Third Reich?, Social and Legal Studies 2 (1993), p. 91 et seqq.; Baratta, ARSP 54 (1968), p. 325 et seqq.; U. Brodersen, Gesetze des NS-Staates, Bad Homburg v.d.H./Berlin/Zurich: Gehlen, 1968; G. Dilcher, Der rechtswissenschaftliche Positivismus, ARSP 61 (1975), p. 497 et seqq.; H. Dreier, Die Radbruch'sche Formel – Erkenntnis oder Bekenntnis? in: H. Mayer (Editor), Staatsrecht in Theorie und Praxis, Festschrift für Robert Walter zum 60. Geburtstag, Vienna: Manz, 1991, p. 120 et seqq.; E. Franssen, Positivismus als juristische Strategie, JZ 24 (1969), p. 766 et seqq.; H. Hannover/E. Hannover-Drück, Politische Justiz 1918–1933, Bornheim-Merten: Lamuv-Verlag, 1987; M. Hirsch/D. Majer/J. Meinck (Editors), Recht, Verwaltung und Justiz im Nationalsozialismus. Ausgewählte Schriften, Gesetze und Gerichtsentscheidungen von 1933 bis 1945, 2nd, unchanged edition, Baden-Baden: Nomos, 1997; H. Kramer, Entstehung, Funktion und Folgen des nationalsozialistischen

ism did in fact open the door to the possibility of fascist legal doctrine and its manifestations in National Socialist judicial practice. This should be prefaced with the remark that, at best, only German statutory positivism comes into consideration as the potential cause; for the realist theories (sociological and psychological positivism) and the pure theory of law were clearly not the prevailing doctrine during the Weimar Republic. Hart's positivism, the institutional theory of law as well as exclusive and inclusive positivism are ruled out of consideration for chronological reasons.

I. The Juristic Fraternity [85]

Any attempt at sketching a picture of legal thought and the application of the law during the National Socialist era necessitates an examination of those who applied it and their position within the political system. For every type of state it is indispensable to ensure the "conformity of the juristic fraternity"[86] in order to secure the state's very existence, since in modern states "real power, which is manifested in the management of the administration ... is necessarily and unavoidably in the hands of officials."[87] Viewed from this angle, Rottleuthner argues that when exam-

---

Rechtssystems. Ein Literaturbericht, Kritische Justiz 20 (1987), p. 218 et seqq.; F. Kübler, Der deutsche Richter und das demokratische Gesetz, AcP 162 (1963), p. 104 et seqq.; D. Majer, Grundlagen des nationalsozialistischen Rechtssystems, Stuttgart: Kohlhammer, 1987, p. 60; I. Maus, Bürgerliche Rechtstheorie und Faschismus, 2nd Edition, Munich: Wilhelm Fink, 1980; idem, Juristische Methodik und Justizfunktionen im Nationalsozialismus, ARSP Beiheft 18 (1983), p. 176 et seqq.; I. Müller, Furchtbare Juristen. Die unbewältigte Vergangenheit unserer Justiz, Munich: Kindler, 1987; H. Rottleuthner (Editor), Recht, Rechtsphilosophie und Nationalsozialismus, ARSP Beiheft 18 (1983); idem, Substantieller Dezisionismus. Zur Funktion der Rechtsphilosophie im Nationalsozialismus, ARSP Beiheft 18 (1983), p. 20 et seqq.; B. Rüthers, Unbegrenzte Auslegung; idem, Entartetes Recht; M. Walther, Hat der juristische Positivismus die deutschen Juristen wehrlos gemacht? Kritische Justiz 21 (1988), p. 263 et seqq.; H. Wrobel, Der Deutsche Richterbund im Jahre 1933. Skizze eines Ablaufs, Kritische Justiz 15 (1982), p. 323 et seqq.

[85] Hannover/Hannover Drück (quoted in § 23 n. 84); Müller (quoted in § 23 n. 84); Rottleuthner, ARSP Beiheft 18 (1983), p. 22 et seqq.; Kübler, AcP 162 (1963), p. 104 et seqq.; Wrobel, Kritische Justiz 15 (1982), p. 323 et seqq.

[86] Rottleuthner, ARSP Beiheft 18 (1983), p. 22.

[87] M. Weber, Parlament und Regierung im neugeordneten Deutschland, in: Gesammelte politische Schriften, Second Edition, Tübingen 1958, p. 308.

ining the history of the judiciary since the empire, the question which requires an explanation is not why the judiciary conformed to the National Socialist system after 1933 but rather *why the judiciary functioned during the Weimar Republic.*[88]

In the first half of the nineteenth century the jurists were among the most important proponents of liberal ideology. The parliamentarians which met at the Paulskirchen Assembly in May 1848 included 94 professors of law and over 110 judges.[89]

After the founding of the empire and Bismarck's appointment as chancellor in 1878, he introduced a radical reform of the judiciary with the aim of purging it of its liberal elements and thus instrumentalizing the practice of the courts.[90] By drastically reducing the number of courts Bismarck achieved the dismissal of judges belonging to the ten oldest age-groups, i.e. those whose political consciousness stemmed from the revolution era (1848). In addition, free posts for judges were blocked for the next ten years, which permitted in turn a massive lengthening of the legal training period: three to four years of study leading up to the first state exam, followed by a clerkship (*Referendarzeit*) of three, or mostly four years prior to the second state exam, followed by a term as an assessor averaging between five and ten years. All this without pay and, what is more, in Prussia only persons able to deposit a considerable amount of money and command the annual income of 1500 Marks considered as befitting their rank and station could be admitted to a clerkship. The education and training costs of a Prussian judge thus amounted to a sum which could only be afforded by the upper middle class, i.e. sons of judges and other officials. In addition, the fact that a candidate for a post as judge could be dismissed forthwith during the entire training period without any legal procedure to be followed ensured a *rigorous attitude of submission to authority*, particularly as jurists of liberal mind increasingly began to turn to the newly created free bar. From the point

---

[88] Rottleuthner, ARSP Beiheft 18 (1983), p. 23.

[89] Th. Rasehorn, Justizkritik in der Weimarer Republik. Das Beispiel der Zeitschrift "Die Justiz", Frankfurt a.M./New York: Campus Verlag, 1985, p. 110.

[90] Cf. Hannover/Hannover-Drück (quoted in § 23 n. 84), p. 21 et seqq; Müller (quoted in § 23 n. 84), p. 14 et seqq.

of view of social prestige, however, judges, and even more so lawyers, ranked considerably lower than public prosecutors and administration jurists who were subject to official instructions and therefore closer to the authorities. Accordingly, senior judicial posts were filled by public prosecutors of long standing, who along with the administration jurists, were for the most part recruited from the aristocracy. It was this lower status, which was reflected by the comparatively low rates of pay for judges, which meant that they felt particularly threatened by the social and political changes beginning to take place.[91]

After the founding of the Weimar Republic the provisional government decided to incorporate the imperial judges into the republican state structure rather than implement the old social-democratic principle of election.[92] Ernst Fraenkel summed up the situation of these judges in a democratic state as follows: "He used to pass judgment 'in the name of the King' … Now he is supposed to judge 'in the name of the people', the people for whom in the course of becoming what he is today he has nothing but contempt … The whole officialdom of the old regime was royalist by education, conviction and tradition. A judge was a royalist for the sake of his inner well-being, as well. No branch of officialdom therefore had more difficulty in adapting to the new circumstances than the judiciary."[93] Moreover, due to the inflation, the economic situation of the judiciary became increasingly similar to that of the workers, a development which furthered the forming of a front against the workers and their organizations during the whole period of the Weimar Republic.[94]

Nonetheless, the judges and public prosecutors who belonged to the Association of German Judges pressed in no uncertain terms for an independent, objective, formal-juristic and apolitical judiciary which would decide the parties' disputes with complete detachment: "German judges consider it as a matter of course their duty to judge according to the law and the precepts of justice alone and to be just to every person, regardless of his status. For them neither the political opinions of the

---

[91] Kübler, AcP 162 (1963), p. 109 et seq.
[92] Hannover/Hannover-Drück (quoted in § 23 n. 84), p. 21.
[93] E. Fraenkel, Zur Soziologie der Klassenjustiz, Berlin 1927, p. 12.
[94] Kübler, AcP 162 (1963), p. 113.

persons appearing before the court are of relevance, nor is the form in which the state is governed."[95] This formula was, however, inspired by Richard Thoma's so-called 'two soul theory' which allowed the judiciary to differentiate between the purely coincidental republican form of state and its "real", inherent nature, the latter alone determining the judges' duty of obedience.[96] This standpoint allowed the judiciary to exclude from their considerations all those consequences of the new regime which contradicted their political and social attitudes by labeling them as "political".

Hannover and Hannover-Drück (1987) have documented most impressively the effect of this anti-democratic attitude on the practice of the courts, above all in criminal cases with political aspects.[97] Perhaps the most meaningful data, for their brevity, are those collected in 1922 by Emil Julius Gumbel, professor of mathematics, relating to the political murders of the preceding years.[98] The figures for 1918–1922, adjusted in 1991 by Füsser, are:[99] 308 murders committed by right-wingers as against 21 by left-wingers. For every left-wing murder there were on average 2.57 (in total 54) suspects who were the subject of investigations by the examining magistrates, while for every right-wing murder there were on average only 0.39 (in total 121). Of the 54 left-wing suspects 37 were convicted, while of 121 right wing suspects only 11 were convicted. The murders committed by left-wingers incurred 13 death penalties and those committed by right-wingers one death penalty.

---

[95] Deutsche Richterzeitung 1923, column 1, quoted by Kübler, AcP 162 (1963), p. 116.

[96] Kübler, AcP 162 (1963), p. 115 et seq.

[97] Hannover/Hannover-Drück (quoted in § 23 n. 84).

[98] E.J. Gumbel, Vier Jahre politischer Mord, Berlin-Fichtenau: Verlag der neuen Gesellschaft, 1922, Reprint: Heidelberg: Das Wunderhorn, 1980. Gumbel's statistics suffers from some methodological deficiencies which is why we rely on Füsser's (see n. 100) reassessed numbers. The fact that Gumbel's assertions were essentially correct remains, however, unchanged.

[99] Klaus Füsser, Republikfeindliche Tendenzrechtsprechung in Weimar? Zur Aussagekraft der Gumbel-Mordstatistik, Zeitschrift für Rechtssoziologie 12 (1991), p. 89 et seq. We have calculated the number of death sentences on the basis of the data provided by Füsser, loc. cit., p. 90.

	Right-wingers	Left-wingers
Total of murders committed	308	21
Average of suspects per murder subject to investigation	0.39 (in total: 121)	2.57 (in total: 54)
Total of subjects convicted	11 (1 death penalty)	37 (13 death penalties)

The crisis of confidence in the judiciary provoked by this practice[100] – insofar as it was admitted to at all – was put down to criticism of the judiciary by the Republican Association of Judges and left-wing parties which, it was alleged, had artificially created a crisis by generalizing a small number of wrong judgments. The German Association of Judges responded to the demand made by the Republican Association of Judges for a more democratic-republican spirit among the judiciary by insisting upon apolitical judges, and accused the republicans of trying to politicize the judiciary.[101]

Within a year of Hitler's seizure of power in 1933 all German judges were amalgamated into the Association of German National Socialist Jurists; the German Association of Judges disbanded itself. The German judiciary's credo of political neutrality was unable to assert itself under the new system.[102] Rottleuthner holds the general insecurity among the judiciary responsible for this, rather than ideological affinities:[103] politi-

---

[100] B. Schulz, Der Republikanische Richterbund (1921–1933), Frankfurt a.M./Bern: P. Lang, 1982, p. 95 et seqq.

[101] Schulz (quoted in § 23 n. 101), p. 134 et seqq.

[102] Regarding the whole process of "Gleichschaltung", i.e. alignment of the complete life of Germany to the Nazi model, see Wrobel, Kritische Justiz 15 (1982), p. 323 et seqq. In 1938, 54.28% of all the judges were organized in the National Socialist German Workers Party (NSDAP) or its sub-organizations; the majority of them also took actively part in the political work. In this regard, see D. Majer, Die ideologischen Grundlagen des nationalsozialistischen Rechtsdenkens, dargestellt am Beispiel der NSDAP (Justiz und NSDAP), in: Niedersächsische Landeszentrale für politische Bildung (Editor), Justiz und Nationalsozialismus, 1985, p. 119 et seqq., particularly p. 125 et seq.

[103] Rottleuthner, ARSP Beiheft 18 (1983), p. 24 et seqq.

cally motivated postings, changes in court organization, a new training system, the assumption of control over specialist literature and corrections made to judgments by various bodies (police, Gestapo, SS, Hitler) assured that the law was applied in conformity with the new ideology. The new legal terms, such as *völkisches Gedankengut* (voelkish ideology)*, Gemeinschaft* (community allegiance)*, Rasse* (race)*,* and *Blut und Boden* (blood and soil), were of no practical use in the judgment-making process. In combination with the *Führer*-principle, i.e. the permanent possibility of interference by other bodies in the original judicial domain, they allowed the political leadership to instrumentalize the judiciary at will, using the label *Volksnähe* (populism).[104]

II. The Binding Nature of the Law on the Judge[105]

Central questions in the discussion concerning the role of the judiciary in the National Socialist era are the method of decision-making, and in particular the binding nature of law on the judge. Ever since Radbruch's essay "Statutory Lawlessness and Supra-Statutory Law"[106] to the present day, it has been held that it was legal positivism which paved the way for fascist legal doctrines and which was responsible for the unresisted incorporation of the judiciary into the Third Reich.[107] However, an increasing number of authors have begun to disagree with this view[108] – as indeed a veritable flood of literature concerning the National Socialist period has appeared.

---

[104] Rottleuthner, ARSP Beiheft 18 (1983), p. 29.

[105] Franssen, JZ 24 (1969), p. 766 et seqq.; Wieacker, p. 430 et seqq.; Dilcher, ARSP 61 (1975), p. 497 et seqq.; Maus (quoted in § 23 n. 84); idem, ARSP Beiheft 18 (1983), p. 176 et seqq.; Rüthers, Unbegrenzte Auslegung; idem, Entartetes Recht; Rottleuthner (quoted in § 23 n. 84); idem, ARSP Beiheft 18 (1983), p. 20 et seqq.; Kübler, AcP 162 (1963), p. 104 et seqq.; Brodersen (quoted in § 23 n. 84; Hirsch/Majer, Meinck (quoted in § 23 n. 84), Walther, Kritische Justiz 21 (1988), p. 263 et seqq. (our translation).

[106] Above, § 23 A.

[107] See compilation of literature by Maus (quoted in § 23 n. 84), n. 74 and n. 79; see also Rottleuthner, ARSP Beiheft 18 (1983), p. 20 et seqq.

[108] Cf. e.g. Baratta, ARSP 54 (1968), p. 325 et seqq., particularly p. 327 et seq. and 339 et seqq.; Franssen, JZ 24 (1969), p. 766 et seqq.; Maus (quoted in § 23 n. 84), p. 39 with references to further literature; Walther, Kritische Justiz 21 (1988), p. 263 et seqq.

The criticism of legal positivism presupposes however that this doctrine was predominant[109] during the Weimar period and during the National Socialist era. As we shall show, this of all things was not the case.

The framework for German conceptual jurisprudence (*Begriffsjurisprudenz*) was provided by the Historical School of Law which founded a new, systematic science of private law with an awareness of methodical considerations.[110] While Dilcher attested that Savigny's conception of law was essentially open to the humanities and social sciences,[111] the further development of Savigny's conception through the constructive method of the Pandectists and through *Begriffsjurisprudenz* precluded a methodological reception of any non-juristic discipline. This conception of law deduced its normative rules and their application purely from the "system, concept and doctrine"[112] of legal science; extra-juristic values and aims such as social, economic, moral, political or religious considerations were not considered to be of legal relevance. Through this scientific method, with its historical focus on the abstract Roman law of trade, the science of Pandectism had the effect of placing the domain of private law in the hands of scientifically trained jurists, i.e. representatives of the bourgeoisie, thus removing it from the clutches of the state.[113] At a point in history in which state and society were growing apart, the importance attached to the will of the private individual amounted to a decision in favor of the *autonomy of private law* – a decision ideally suited to the then prevailing political situation in Germany. By renouncing material, social-politically motivated restrictions of their private law conception, Savigny and *Begriffsjurisprudenz* had opted for a liberated bourgeois society with an authoritarian state.[114]

---

[109] In the same vein, Walther, Kritische Justiz 21 (1988), p. 263
[110] Wieacker, p. 367 et seqq.
[111] Dilcher, ARSP 61 (1975), p. 497 et seqq.: Dilcher recognizes a relation to societal reality in the dualism of historical and philosophical elements in legal science adopted from the 18th century by Savigny by interpreting "historical" as meaning "empirical" (p. 505) as well and by assuming that Savigny still conceived of the historical and the political as parallels (p. 506 and 515 et seqq.).
[112] Wieacker, p. 431.
[113] Dilcher, ARSP 61 (1975), p. 518.
[114] Dilcher, ARSP 61 (1975), p. 519; regarding the alternative methodological-political positions (Jhering, Gierke, Marx) see Dilcher, p. 520 et seqq.

With the conclusion of the delayed German *codification process* towards the end of the nineteenth century, *state legislation* took the place of legal development at the hands of learned jurists. The codification was, however, less the product of the people's will than "the work of a ministerial bureaucracy rigorously committed to scientific precepts" very much in the Pandectist tradition.[115] Hence legal conceptualism *(Begriffsjurisprudenz)* began to be replaced by *German statutory positivism* which held law as a whole to be identical with statutory law enacted in the form prescribed by the constitution and postulated that the legal order, or even statutory law, contained no regulatory lacunae (the gaplessness postulate).[116]

During the second half of the nineteenth century the constructive method was also applied to constitutional law by Jhering, Gerber and Laband. Von Oertzen summarized the general opinion of the social and political tendencies which manifested themselves in the new constitutional doctrines as follows: "The independence from ideological and political value judgements as alleged by the rigorously scientific school of constitutional thought is mere pretence. In reality 'legal method' serves to uphold the existing social order by confining itself to a formal preoccupation with public law as it stands and precluding any form of substantial criticism … After the founding of the empire, the German bourgeoisie waived the implementation of its constitutional ideals regarding freedom; it reached a saturation point and concluded a compromise with the aristocratic-conservative forces dominating the state, assuring it economic and social freedom of movement by retaining a state formally governed by the rule of law, while the real state power is left in the hands of the monarchy and its officialdom."[117] Von Oertzen does add, however, that while the positivist constitutional doctrine did indeed conserve the formal structures, substantively it was not conservative but brought about the consolidation not of conservative but of liberal ideas, which had sprung primarily from the concepts of the formal state governed by

---

[115] Wieacker, p. 459. F. Kübler, Kodifikation und Demokratie, JZ 20 (1969), p. 645 et seqq.

[116] Wieacker, p. 459; cf. above.

[117] P. von Oertzen, Die soziale Funktion des staatsrechtlichen Positivismus, Frankfurt am Main: Suhrkamp, 1974, p. 321 et seq. (our translation).

rule of law *(formaler Rechtsstaat)* and of state sovereignty *(Staatssouveränität)*.[118]

The *statutory positivist approach* to law relies in particular on confidence in the stability of the political situation within the state and on the guarantee that the "right" solution will be found by the legislator. This confidence already began to appear problematic to the German judiciary with the strengthening of parliament towards the end of the Wilhelmine era; it was shattered by the First World War and its aftermath.[119] This led during the first years of the Weimar Republic to the judiciary taking a critical stance towards law enacted by the state, reflected for example by appeals in the German Judges' Gazette to the judiciary to break with statutory law and decide freely according to judge-made law.[120] Senate president Reichert exemplified this attitude in 1926 as follows: "Law is not what the legislator arbitrarily orders according to his own subjective opinion, even if he means well thereby. People in general only feel, esteem and cherish as law that which can be said to be law according to the *objective* standards: that which an upright consciousness of what is right and wrong dictates to the legislator, who must not consider himself as unfettered lord and master, but as the vessel in which law is born, in the sense that there can only be *one law, the common law of all the people.*"[121]

Rüthers has shown inter alia with the example of free revaluation what effect this attitude had on the practice of private law in the Weimar Republic.[122] Due to inflation, the principle "A Mark is a Mark", which permitted gold Mark debts to be fulfilled through paper Mark payments, led de facto to a currency-related expropriation of creditors. The *Reichsgericht* abandoned this principle in a decision of 28 November 1923,[123] applying § 242 of the German Civil Code (good faith clause), a decision

---

[118] von Oertzen (quoted in § 23 n. 118), p. 322.
[119] Rüthers, Unbegrenzte Auslegung, p. 95. Kübler, AcP 162 (1963), p. 110 et seqq.
[120] Kübler, AcP 162 (1963), p. 113 et seqq.
[121] M. Reichert, Rechtswende?, JW 55 (1926), p. 2791 et seqq. (emphasis in original; our translation).
[122] Rüthers, Unbegrenzte Auslegung, p. 64–90.
[123] Entscheidungen des Reichsgerichts in Zivilsachen, vol. 107, p. 78; Entscheidungen des Reichsgerichts in Zivilsachen, vol. 101, p. 145, had ruled the opposite.

which was justified in view of the general state of emergency.[124] The *Reichsgericht* went further and granted the judges the power to revalue mortgage debts in accordance with good faith, i.e. to determine a new rate of exchange and thus make a fundamental economic and political decision. When the government subsequently planned to solve the revaluation problem differently from the Reichsgericht, the Association of Judges made a formal protest to the government and hinted that the Reichsgericht might declare the statutory solution invalid should it in any way detract "the well foundedness of revaluation *in the law*".[125] The first statutory regulation, enacted in February 1924,[126] prescribed an obligatory rate of 15 percent for an exhaustive list of the economically most important types of claim, leaving all other types of investment free, as a compromise. Even if it permitted the Reichsgericht to find its way back to its positivistic notion of law[127] and adhere to it during the following years, this decision, the statement by the Association of Judges, and the judicial correction of contracts as a result of a change of the economic situation,[128] made one thing very clear: the background to these decisions and statements was formed by economic, political and social considerations and relationships which were in every way capable of suppressing traditional legal method and robbing the law of its binding nature should social reality render this necessary. "As the state was denied any real authority, the laws enacted by it could only be of limited validity."[129]

---

[124] Cf. Rüthers, Unbegrenzte Auslegung, p. 69 et seqq., particularly p. 76.

[125] 53 Juristische Wochenschrift (1924), p. 90, emphasis supplied.

[126] Dritte Steuernotverordnung of 14 February 1924, RGBl I 1179.

[127] See for example the judgment of 4 November 1927: "The legislator is all-powerful and bound by no other limits than those which he has imposed on himself in the Constitution or in other enactments" (Entscheidungen des Reichsgerichts in Zivilsachen, volume 118, p. 327).

[128] Rüthers, Unbegrenzte Auslegung, p. 13–63: These corrections of contracts were achieved by judicial broadening of the terms of unacceptability and economic impossibility. Cf. also F. Dessauer, Recht, Richtertum und Ministerialbürokratie, Mannheim/Berlin/Leipzig 1928, p. 1–92.

[129] O. Kirchheimer, Politische Justiz, Verwendung juristischer Verfahrensmöglichkeiten zu politischen Zwecken, Reprint, Hamburg: EVA Europäische Verlagsanstalt, 1993, p. 315 (English edition: Kirchheimer, Political Justice: The Use of Legal Procedure for Political Ends, Princeton, N.J.: Princeton University Press, 1961).

This conflict between fidelity to the law and free judge-made law is also reflected by the contemporaneous discussion of methodological questions, which focussed in particular on the application of the law by the judge. It was above all the reform movement of interest-orientated jurisprudence *(Interessenjurisprudenz)* which managed to establish itself as an alternative to German statutory positivism, rather than the secondary free law school *(Freirechtsschule),* which advocated that the judge should depart from the law if he considered that its application would be unjust in the case in point.[130] *Interessenjurisprudenz,* while also assuming that the legal order had gaps[131] *(lacunae)* and postulating more freedom for the judge, insisted in principle that he is bound by the law.[132] Heck's own so-called divergent theory postulated, albeit with reticence, that the judge should be entitled to correct the law in the event of a change in circumstances unforeseen by the legislator. In so doing the judge should be bound by the legislator's evaluation of interests and may only in exceptional cases, where the law yields no clues at all, rely on the legal consciousness of contemporary society (subjective-teleological interpretation).[133] This basic fidelity to the law in Heck's teaching was also apparent in his criticism of the *Reichsgericht's* revaluation judgment discussed above.[134] His reverence of the legislator was one of the reasons why *Interessenjurisprudenz,* which dominated the Weimar period, was again highly controversial at the time of Hitler's seizure of power in 1933.[135]

During the Weimar era several changes also took place in the field of constitutional law. Central in the new controversy regarding method was the question of judicial review of legislative acts against the background of the principle of equality as laid down in Art. 109 Para. 1 of the Weimar Constitution *(Reichsverfassung).* Judicial review of legislative enact-

---

[130] Wieacker, p. 579 et seqq.

[131] P. Heck, Gesetzesauslegung und Interessenjurisprudenz, AcP 112 (1914), p. 1 et seqq., 21; Wieacker, p. 574,; Rüthers, Entartetes Recht, p. 34.

[132] Heck, AcP 112 (1914), p 2.

[133] Rüthers, Unbegrenzte Auslegung, p. 140; Heck, AcP 112 (1914), p. 176 et seqq., 189 et seqq., 196 et seqq., 218 et seqq.

[134] Heck, AcP 122 (1924), p. 221.

[135] Rüthers, Unbegrenzte Auslegung, p. 270 et seqq.; idem, Entartetes Recht, p. 36 et seqq.

ments was recognized for the first time by the *Reichsgericht* in a judgment given on 4 November 1924.[136] During the conference of Professors of Constitutional Law in 1926 in Münster, Erich Kaufmann, a former rigorous constitutional positivist – advocated a new approach influenced by Natural Law: "...the State does not create the law, the State creates laws; *and the State and its laws are both subject to the law.*"[137] He was vehemently criticized by proponents of the positivist doctrine including Anschütz, Thoma, Kelsen and Naviasky, who felt that holding a court judgment superior to an act of parliament conflicted with the democratic character of the Constitution.[138] Kelsen inquired after the political background to the call for metaphysics and natural law: "I do not wish to examine here whether and to what extent the departure of certain circles within the judiciary from the legal positivism which has hitherto been accepted without question is sociologically connected with changes in the political structure of the legislature. At any rate there is no mistaking that there are jurists who formerly considered the judge to be strictly bound by the law and who are now invoking Natural Law in order to grant the judiciary considerable freedom with regard to the law; and that the judiciary has remained more or less untouched by those changes in the political structure which manifest themselves in the way Parliament is constituted, so that between the present judiciary and jurists in general there is not the political contrast which exists between the jurists as a whole, or at least parts thereof, and parliament."[139] The whole controversy illustrates an aspect which went completely unnoticed in the discussion regarding the judiciary after the Second World War: the statutory positivism of the Weimar Republic was still informed by the doctrine of

---

[136] RGZ 111, p. 320 et seqq.; however, Rottleuthner, ARSP Beiheft 18 (1983), p. 21, points out that though the Reichsgericht has approved judicial review in this as well as in practically all other *Reichsgericht* decisions referred to time and again, it has, apart from two exceptions, never declared invalid a legislative enactment.

[137] Quoted from Rüthers, Entartetes Recht, p. 33.

[138] Cf. Rüthers, Entartetes Recht, p. 33 et seq.; Franssen, JZ 24 (1969), p. 772 et seq.

[139] Kelsen's contribution to the discussion, published in *Veröffentlichung der Vereinigung der Deutschen Staatsrechtslehrer* no. 3, Berlin/Leipzig: Walter de Gruyter,1927, p. 54.

a "democratic source of law",[140] pursuant to which the content of a law was deemed to be "right" not because it was materially bound to hierarchically superior law, "but by the democratic nature of the legislative process itself",[141] an aspect of which the pioneers of a popular renewal of the law were well aware. Thus Carl Schmitt wrote in 1935: " 'A law' means something completely different, theoretically and practically, depending on whether one is talking of a law of a constitutional monarchy, of a state with a parliamentary legislature or a modern *Führer*-state."[142] In a state governed by the rule of law, which he equated with a liberal constitutional state, it was only by virtue of law-making by the freely elected representatives of the people in accordance with the prescribed procedure that laws became legal norms applying to all. In the *"deutsche Rechtsstaat Adolf Hitlers"* (Adolf Hitler's German state under the rule of law), in effect the law meant *the plans and the will of the Führer"*, so that – in Schmitt's words – the "hollow" statutory state (*Gesetzesstaat*) had been superseded.[143]

Thus, he hints at the main *targets of hostility* for Nazi legal thought (and they are easier to localize than their substantial cores): inter alia, it was *anti-democratic*, *anti-liberal* and *anti-positivistic*.[144] Karl Larenz wrote in 1934: "A renewal of German legal thought is unthinkable *without a radical departure from positivism and individualism*."[145] For with the dissolution of the dualistic structure of the state and a non-state-controlled society, "the respective jurisprudential type of thinking must also

---

[140] R. Wiethölter, Rechtswissenschaft, Frankfurt am Main: Fischer, 1968; reprint: Basel/Frankfurt am Main, 1986, p. 295; cf. Maus (quoted in § 23 n. 84), p. 27 et seqq., particularly p. 40 et seq.; E. Topitsch, Einleitung zu H. Kelsen, Staat und Naturrecht: Aufsätze zur Ideologiekritik, 2nd Edition, Munich: Fink, 1989, p. 22 et seqq.; Franssen, JZ 24 (1969), p. 768.

[141] Maus (quoted in § 23 n. 84), p. 42.

[142] C. Schmitt, Der Rechtsstaat, in: H. Frank (Editor), Nationalsozialistisches Handbuch für Recht und Gesetzgebung, Munich: Zentralverlag der NSDAP, 1935, p. 24 et seqq., p. 29.

[143] Schmitt (quoted in § 23 n. 143), p. 30 et seqq.

[144] Rottleuthner, ARSP Beiheft 18 (1983), p. 27; cf. A. Kaufmann, Rechtsphilosophie und Nationalsozialismus, ARSP Beiheft 18 (1983), p. 1 et seqq. with corresponding quotations.

[145] K. Larenz, Deutsche Rechtserneuerung und Rechtsphilosophie, Tübingen: Mohr 1934, p. 15 (emphasis by authors).

be discarded."[146] Thus, Heinrich Lange celebrated the *release* from *"the chains of statutory positivism"*,[147] which meant "renouncing the creative element in the law" and which "with its too rigid conception of the binding nature of the law lamed the judge's sense of responsibility."[148] Erik Wolf contrasted the liberal ideal of the happiness of the individual with the "exclusive obligation of each individual for the national community",[149] and described the National Socialist state as a "state of material justice for the national community" in which the freedom of the judge was "fettered neither by arbitrariness nor by a formal and abstract principle of security under the law." Instead, the state received its contours – and, if necessary, its limits – from "the popular notion of justice as manifested in the laws and personified by the *Führer*."[150] Law and custom, law and morals should in future be one[151] and the unrealistic methodological dualism of "is" and "ought" should be discarded.

Even though there was no official, consistent National Socialist legal philosophy, it is possible to identify central issues which, as Rottleuthner has noted, are characterized by the *völkische Rechtsidee* (the voelkish or popular notion of law), a closely related racial theory and the *Führer*-principle.[152] Elements of this new legal thought found their way into the legal order through the legislator; a number of measures and special laws were enacted which directly furthered National Socialist aims, above all in the fields of criminal law, racial policy, economic and fiscal law. The laws were often *conspicuously short, full of indeterminate legal concepts* and prefaced by *ideological preambles*[153] containing the political program for the law in question. In many central areas of the legal

---

[146] C. Schmitt, Über die drei Arten des rechtswissenschaftlichen Denkens, Berlin: Duncker & Humblot, 2006, originally published 1934, p. 66 (our translation).
[147] H. Lange, Die Entwicklung der Wissenschaft vom bürgerlichen Recht seit 1933, Tübingen: Mohr, 1941, p. 39.
[148] Larenz (quoted in § 23 n. 146), p. 13.
[149] E. Wolf, Das Rechtsideal des nationalsozialistischen Staates, ARSP 28 (1934/35), p. 348 et seqq., p. 349.
[150] Wolf, ARSP 28 (1934/35), p. 352.
[151] Cf. Rüthers, Entartetes Recht, p. 26.
[152] Rottleuthner, ARSP Beiheft 18 (1983), p. 27; Majer (quoted in § 23 n. 103), p. 123 et seqq.
[153] Cf. Maus, ARSP Beiheft 18 (1983), p. 180; I. v. Münch, Einleitung zu Brodersen (quoted in § 23 n. 84), p. 17.

order, however, and in particular in private law (with the exception of a few new individual enactments, such as the Marriage Act and the Testament Act), the provisions which had already applied during the Weimar period remained in force.[154] Rüthers has established the following instruments of revaluation for the traditional legal order:[155] The proclamation of the *völkische Rechtsidee*, which was, so to speak, supra-positive and pre-existent, created with its dualism between supra-positive and positive law the possibility of declaring unpopular old laws to be inapplicable since they ran contrary to the new legal conception. *The creation of new sources* of law such as the *will of the Führer, the national community* and *the party program* led, by force of their number, the vagueness of their contents and the open question of the hierarchical relationship between them, to general legal uncertainty in practice and thus also to great uncertainty among those applying the law, but was nevertheless celebrated as a *victory over normativism*.[156] The proper interpretation of the old law was achieved by the extensive use of existing and the addition of new general clauses and indeterminate legal concepts, all of which were to be interpreted *"in the spirit of National Socialism"*,[157] and by the identification and filling of gaps. This also explains why Philipp Heck's doctrine could not remain the dominant method under National Socialism, although Heck himself considered it perfectly suitable:[158] On the one hand his notion of "interests" was accused of being individualistic, since he placed the particular interests of the individual on the same footing as the national and ethical interests of the community. His "ideological neutrality" lacked an immanent methodological acknowledgement of the peo-

---

[154] Rüthers, Entartetes Recht, p. 19; with regard to the whole topic, cf. Rüthers, Unbegrenzte Auslegung.

[155] Cf. Rüthers, Entartetes Recht, p. 22 et seqq. with further references.

[156] K. Michaelis, Wandlungen des deutschen Rechtsdenkens, in: K. Larenz (Editor), Grundfragen der neuen Rechtswissenschaft, Berlin: Junker und Dünnhaupt Verlag, 1935, p. 59: "The attempt to factually determine the hierarchical relationship of the sources of law and their relevance for the judge would of course amount to a relapse into the thinking to be overcome."

[157] C. Schmitt, Nationalsozialismus und Rechtsstaat, JW 63 (1934), p. 713 et seqq., p. 717: "All indeterminate concepts, all the so-called general clauses are to be applied absolutely and unconditionally in the spirit of national socialism."

[158] Rüthers, Entartetes Recht, p. 37.

ple's legal ideas.[159] On the other hand, the leading role of the legislator in *Interessenjurisprudenz* in filling secondary gaps in the law was in contradiction to the revocation of legislative programming in National Socialist law.[160]

The only difference between the application of the "old" and the "new" law lay in the question of *judicial review*, which was confined to the laws passed before National Socialism.[161] Legal method, on the other hand, was the same for both types of law,[162] although a lack of specifically National Socialist methodological doctrines can be ascertained.[163] A controversy did, however, arise regarding the correct method for the popular renewal of the law, which spread to all legal disciplines and in which *all non-positivistic* schools of thought participated, each claiming to be suitable for solving the problem.[164] However, the professors involved in the dispute were left to themselves by the courts.[165] The theoretical discussion focused on two related notions, the first being the *Theorie der konkret-allgemeinen Begriffe* (theory of concrete-general concepts), as propounded trenchantly by Larenz, which with its preoccupation with individual cases led to a situative dynamization of legal concepts and thus achieved the desired changes in law by deliberately altering concepts. Thus, for example, the notion of the capacity to have rights and duties (*Rechtsfähigkeit*) was no longer tied to the individual person and was thus radically changed. Instead of being an abstract no-

---

[159] Rüthers, Unbegrenzte Auslegung, p. 271 et seq.

[160] Maus, ARSP Beiheft 18 (1983), p. 180.

[161] Maus, ARSP Beiheft 18 (1983), p. 179 et seq.; Larenz (quoted above § 23 n. 146).

[162] Larenz wrote that judges were not absolutely bound by National Socialist laws: "It would be a misapprehension of the *Führer's* will to hold him to an expression which does not have a significance compatible with the spirit of the national legal order. A judge who interprets and supplements the law pursuant to the living legal will of the community acts in conformity with the *Führer's* will ... The judge is obliged to recognize and apply every law which is enacted with the *Führer's* will as law; but he must apply it in the *Führer's* spirit, according to current legal will, the community's concrete idea of law." Larenz (quoted above § 23 n. 146), p. 35 et seq.

[163] Maus, ARSP Beiheft 18 (1983), p. 182; H.-J. Koch, Die juristische Methode im Staatsrecht, Frankfurt: Suhrkamp, 1977, p. 103 et seqq.

[164] Rüthers, Unbegrenzte Auslegung, p. 276; idem, Entartetes Recht, p. 32 et seqq., p. 52 et seqq.; Maus, ARSP Beiheft 18 (1983), p. 182 et seqq.

[165] Rüthers, Entartetes Recht, p. 53.

tion ("any person") the person was viewed as being a member of a concrete community: "What is decisive for the legal status of the individual is no longer the fact that he is a person, but his concrete role: he might be a farmer, soldier, intellectual, spouse, member of a family, official."[166] Through this manipulation of concepts the Nazi racialist and community ideology was smuggled into the legal system and the fundamental values of the equality and dignity of each individual abolished.[167] The second concept, Carl Schmitt's *konkretes Ordnungsdenken* (concrete concept of order) aimed (with its subordination of enacted law to the people's concrete way of life) at raising the social adequacy of legal concepts and thus generally subordinating the laws and the practice of the courts to existing power structures and social conditions.[168]

Nevertheless, the practice of the courts remained more or less unaffected by these methodological controversies and attained practically any desired result by means of general clauses and the formula alluding to the public good, and by resorting to other instruments or revaluation such as the *völkische Rechtsidee* (popular notion of law) and the new doctrine of the sources of law.[169] In criminal law, too, where prosecution was characterized by a dualism between the police and the judiciary since the seizure of power,[170] the courts greatly assisted the legal renewal. Without the law having been changed, penal practice was tightened up by means of extensive interpretation of what constituted a punishable offense and by tougher sentences. The relevant standards were obtained for the most part through directives, recommendations and suggestions from the judicial administration.[171] The intention was to create a new National Socialist penal law which, "unlike the formal liberal notion of right and

---

[166] Larenz (quoted above § 23 n. 146), p. 40.
[167] Rüthers, Unbegrenzte Auslegung, p. 302 et seqq.; idem, Entartetes Recht, p. 76 et seqq.; Maus, ARSP Beiheft 18 (1983), p. 183 et seq.
[168] Maus, ARSP Beiheft 18 (1983), p. 184 et seqq.; Rüthers, Entartetes Recht, p. 63 et seqq.
[169] Rüthers, Entartetes Recht, p. 52.
[170] L. Gruchmann, Rechtssystem und nationalsozialistische Justizpolitik, in: M. Broszat/ H. Möller (Editors), Das Dritte Reich. Herrschaftsstruktur und Geschichte, Munich: Beck, 1983, p. 83 et seqq., p. 85 et seq.
[171] D. Majer, "Fremdvölkische" im Dritten Reich, Boppard: Boldt Verlag, 1981 (nearly unchanged reprint: 1993), p. 593 et seqq.

wrong" would be based on the idea of material justice: "Laws and the law are not identical, for laws are merely indispensable but necessarily incomplete sources of information about the law."[172] This new penal law system, which also contained offenses with retroactive effect, no longer needed the principle of *nulla poena sine lege*: "Any person who commits an act which the law declares to be punishable or which is deserving of penalty according to *the fundamental conceptions of penal law and sound popular feeling*, shall be punished. If there is no penal law directly covering an act, it shall be punished *under the law of which the fundamental conception applies most nearly to said act*."[173] Characteristic of this approach, which is *diametrically opposed to German statutory positivism*, is the fact that both euthanasia operations[174] and the massacres in the concentration camps were *carried out without any clear statutory basis*.[175]

Thus an expanding radius of action for judgments unrelated to the law can be observed in all fields of law and court practice. As the National Socialist state was, however, characterized by the dualist structure which Ernst Fraenkel was the first to analyze[176] – the state governed by norms

---

[172] H. Frank, Nationalsozialistische Leitsätze für ein neues deutsches Strafrecht, 1. Teil, Third Edition, Berlin: Deutsche Rechts- & Wirtschaftswissenschaftliche Verlags-Gesellschaft, 1935, p. 5 et seqq., cited by Hirsch/Majer/Meinck (quoted in § 23 n. 84), p. 434 et seqq. (our translation).

[173] § 2 of the Gesetz zur Änderung des Strafgesetzbuches of 28 June 1935 [Decree amending certain provisions to the penal code], published in Reichsgesetzblatt 1935, vol. 1, p. 839; translation by Permanent Court of International Justice, Consistency of certain Danzig legislative decrees with the constitution of the free city, Advisory Opinion No. 27, PCIJ, Ser. A./B., 1935, p. 4 [http://www.worldcourts.com/pcij/eng/decisions/1935.12.04_danzig/option_ii/1935.12.04_danzig.pdf].

[174] Cf. Ott, Festschrift für Robert Walter zum 60. Geburtstag, Vienna: Manz, 1991, p. 519 et seqq.

[175] For the Final Solution of the Jewish Problem see below, § 24 , text at n. 191 et seqq. Regarding euthanasia, cf. E. Klee, Euthanasie im NS-Staat. Die Vernichtung lebensunwerten Lebens, 3rd Edition, Frankfurt a.M.: Fischer, 1983; H.-W. Schmuhl, Rassenhygiene, Nationalsozialismus, Euthanasie, Göttingen: Vandenhoeck & Ruprecht, 1987; on the killings in the concentration camps: I. Arndt, Antisemitismus und Judenverfolgung, in: Broszat/Möller (quoted in § 23 n. 171), p. 209 et seqq.

[176] E. Fraenkel, The Dual State: A Contribution to the Theory of Dictatorship. Translated From the German by E.A. Shils, in Collaboration with Edith Lowenstein and Klaus Knorr. Reprint of Oxford University Press 1941 Edition, Clark, N.J.: The Lawbook Exchange, Ltd., 2006.

can at any time be suspended in favor of a state governed by interventionist measures – the increased freedom of decision for the judges did not lead to a widening of the judiciary's powers as a whole. On the contrary, the creation of special jurisdictions and the widening of police power led to large areas of social life being removed from the jurisdiction of ordinary courts. The independence of the judiciary was also affected.[177] Above all, there was only *one* standard for the exercise of this newly created leeway in decision-making: that set by National Socialist values – values which, in many cases, judges could have rejected by declaring themselves to be bound by the law.

Summing up, we may draw the following conclusions:

The allegation that legal positivism, and in particular German statutory positivism, was responsible for the legal desolation under National Socialism is demonstrably false. Statutory positivism had already lost its leading role during the Weimar Republic, and National Socialist legal thought was diametrically opposed to positivist thinking. The technique favored by the Nazis of inserting masses of general clauses into their laws (for example "sound popular feeling" in § 2 of the Penal Code in the version of 28 June 1935), the open abolition of the *nulla poena sine lege* principle in the same part of the Code, the numerous interventions in penal proceedings against SS and SA members,[178] the mass killings of patients in mental hospitals and care homes (*Heil- und Pflegeanstalten*) as a result of the *Führer*'s secret euthanasia order of 1 September 1939[179]

---

[177] Maus, ARSP Beiheft 18 (1983), p. 181; Gruchmann (quoted in § 23 n. 171), p. 94.

[178] Weinkauff, p. 113/128.

[179] The Authorization is worded as follows:
"Adolf Hitler Berlin, 1 September 1939
Reichsleiter Bouhler and Dr. med. Brandt are instructed, under responsibility, to broaden the powers of physicians to be designated by name in such a way that persons terminally ill as far as anyone can judge may be granted mercy killing after the most careful evaluation of their condition.
signed Adolf Hitler."
Quoted from Ernst Klee, "Euthanasie" im NS-Staat. Die "Vernichtung lebensunwerten Lebens", 3rd Edition, Frankfurt a.M.: Fischer, 1983, p. 100 (authors' translation). Cf. Ott, Festschrift für Robert Walter, Vienna: Manz, 1991, p. 519 et seqq.
The *Oberlandesgericht Frankfurt* correctly denied this order the character of a law even in the formal sense in 2 Süddeutsche Juristenzeitung (1947), p. 623 et seq. It is

and the genocide of Jews,[180] *could all have been resisted in no uncertain terms from the statutory positivist viewpoint.*

The fact that the majority of German jurists served the National Socialist "renewal" is to be explained rather by their authoritarian way of thinking since Bismarck's reforms of the judiciary and by their anti-democratic and anti-liberal views, coupled with massive interventions by the political leadership in the judicial domain.

E. Result

Our assessment of the merits and demerits of the positivist separation thesis shows that it is quite adequate for some of the single legal disciplines such as history of law, psychology of law, sociology of law, ethology of law, ethnology of law and comparative law.[181] The argument from principles does not represent an imperative argument against it, either.[182] Thus the separation thesis is suitable for theoretical issues (i.e. issues with no direct practical bearing).[183] From a directly practical point of view, it offers the advantages of furthering legal certainty[184] and forcing a forthright strategy in dealing with the legacy of the Nazi state's perversion of the rule of law in criminal cases.[185]

Otherwise, as far as issues with a direct practical bearing are concerned, the disadvantages prevail. Legal positivist theories do not provide the judge or the legislator with guidance as to how he is to create new law.[186] Furthermore, an ethically enriched concept of law[187] facilitates the pro-

---

significant that the *Reichsjustizminister* Dr. Gürtner himself considered the killings as bereft of a valid legal basis. For further references, cf. Evers 4 n. 1.

[180] The Holocaust, too, went without any legal basis – even from a positivist standpoint (except for ITL). Cf. below, § 24 , text at n. 191 et seqq.

[181] Above, § 22 A.

[182] § 22 D, in particular § 22 D.IV.

[183] For the differentiation between issues with a direct practical bearing and theoretical issues see above, § 21 E.

[184] Above, § 22 B.

[185] Above, § 23 C.IV.

[186] Above, § 22 C.

[187] For an ethically enriched concept of law, see the proposals worthy of consideration at Dreier, NJW 39 (1986), p. 896, and Bydlinsky, Rechtsbegriff, p. 317 et seq.

cess of remedying statutory lawlessness after the collapse of such a government (except in relation to criminal cases); the separation thesis produces repugnant results in such cases, as has been exemplified above.[188] If one wants to avoid this, the solution suggesting itself first of all is to stipulate the concept of law in such way that it does not cover blatantly inhumane orders anymore. The judges of civilized countries should be able to refuse the application of such orders for legal, and not just for moral reasons. The judge, as opposed to the legal theorist, is not interested in the law as a social phenomenon but *in the law which he has to apply*. Therefore, the most obvious thing for the judge to do is to only refer to the binding law as "law".[189]

Finally, it must be kept in mind that the term *"Recht"* is part of legal, but also of everyday language. If a concept needs to be comprehensible to non-experts as well, the entrenched associations must not be neglected.[190] The thesis that there is no relation between *"Recht"* and *"Gerechtigkeit"* is probably very hard to understand for a layperson in German-speaking parts of the world; possibly the one way of making it comprehensible is to undergo the discipline of legal positivist thinking. Things are different in English, where it is obvious that "law" and "justice" do not necessarily form a pair. Probably this was one of the reasons why English theorists (Hobbes, Austin, Bentham, Hart) were the first to formulate the separation thesis.

Dissenters to the solution presented here may argue that the diversity of the opinions on issues of justice bars us from including content-based criteria in the concept of law. In our opinion, this objection is no longer compelling in today's circumstances. For, as Bockelmann points out, we do not know and will never know "how we have to legally organize this world in order to turn it into a heaven on earth. However, we do know quite a bit about what not to allow if it is not to be turned into hell."[191]

---

[188] Above, § 23 C.I.2.
[189] Eckmann, p. 44.
[190] This is emphasized by Jørgensen, p. 27.
[191] P. Bockelmann, Ist die Rechtswissenschaft wirklich eine Wissenschaft?, in: Das Rechtswesen, Lenker oder Spiegel der Gesellschaft? 12 Beiträge nach einer Sendereihe des "Studio Heidelberg", Süddeutscher Rundfunk (Heidelberger Studio, 49), Munich: Piper, 1971, p. 29 (our translation).

According to Fechner, too, there is – notwithstanding all uncertainties about what it is that law and morality require – a worldwide consensus nowadays on what is to be regarded, according to the moral awareness of the majority of all people, as abhorrent and thus utterly reprehensible.[192] For example, nobody seriously disputes the idea that *war crimes, slavery and slave trade, mass deportations or depriving women of their rights are in violation of universal human rights*; in our times, he contends, a universal cultural awareness has become established.[193]

Where there is evidence, however modest, for a "basis of intersubjectivity" at least regarding what may never be tolerated in any circumstances, then it is hard to see why one should not make recourse to it. For there is nothing, particularly no epistemic reason, that bars us from tackling this particular issue not starting from a positivist construct, but from a material construct whereby regulations that violate the minimal principles of human dignity are on no account to be regarded as law. In doing so, it will probably be most advisable not to content ourselves with blanket clauses (e.g. "human dignity is inviolable") but, beyond these, to proceed casuistically, i.e. to build groups of typical cases which must be assumed to involve such a violation no matter what.

---

[192] E. Fechner, article "Rechtsphilosophie", in: Handwörterbuch der Sozialwissenschaften VIII, Stuttgart/Tübingen/Göttingen: Mohr, 1964, p. 754, right column.
[193] G. Dahm, Völkerrecht I, 2nd edn., Berlin: De Gruyter 1989, p. 132 et seq.

§ 24 The Remaining Merits and Demerits of the Positivist Theories

A. General Aspects

A major asset of all positivist theories is that their object of investigation is determinable and delimitable against other objects of investigation by means of *verifiable* criteria. The concept of law of each theory is, as we have seen, based upon a pre-scientific premise and therefore, strictly speaking, not verifiable. However, once one has accepted the concept of a theory, it is normally clearly determinable whether something is "law" in terms of this theory or not. Thus the positivist knows what he is talking about. In this regard, he has a clear advantage over the natural lawyer; for the latter, even after having affirmed the existence of eternally valid legal principles, finds himself confronted with problems teeming with philosophical intricacies: for example, the question as to where these eternally valid principles are rooted (e.g. in reason, in an objective system of values or in God's will and wisdom), how mankind can access such eternal guidelines (for example through divine revelation or through the voice of the human conscience) and what content they would have in concrete terms.[1] The positivist, on the other hand, refers to the power of a sovereign, to the laws of a state, to the coercive order regularly prevailing, to the behavior of the citizens or the courts and to the actions of an apparatus of sanctions respectively – all of these being social facts which may be established beyond doubt –, and he knows what the law is *hic et nunc*, what he has to deal with. This only seems to pose a difficulty for the psychological varieties of legal positivism, since although psychological processes are undoubtedly equally real, they are not given in time *and* space but only in time, and are therefore not directly observable. On closer inspection, however, this difficulty proves irrelevant for those varieties of psychological positivism which content themselves with some sort of *carte-blanche* acceptance. If all that one needs to recognize are the constitutional norms concerning the enactment and the validity of laws (Bierling), or the supreme imperative "Obey my directions"

---

[1]   Fechner, p. 183/184.

(Merkel) or just the system as a whole (Nawiasky, Beling), every effective coercive order is of course "recognized" in this sense as long as the citizens do not successfully revolt against it. Likewise, this difficulty has no significance for the Scandinavian legal realism since this school wants to develop the "ideas of behavior" relevant to the law from legislative and judicial material, i.e. from something that exists in time and space. A difficulty arises, however, if one frames psychological positivism in such a way that recognition by the majority must refer to every single norm individually. In this case, the question is how the fact of such recognition can be established. Contrary to the misgivings expressed in many quarters, nowadays this is possible in principle since modern sociology disposes of methods for determining average valuations. A particularly useful option are public opinion polls "where the questioning of a representative sample of the populace allows for an inference as to the opinion held by the total".[2] The opinion poll conveys a more exact picture of public opinion than a plebiscite since representative polls allow for more differentiated questions.[3] Statistical research and probability calculus provide information about how large a sample has to be for the margin of error not to exceed the necessary degree of accuracy.[4] Thus, Kelsen's objection that it is impossible to establish the recognition of legal norms is, in principle, no longer true.[5]

A further example is the principle of effectiveness emphasized in particular by the pure theory of law. Despite considerable fluctuations, on the whole effectiveness is the yardstick which influences international practice regarding the recognition of a new state and its government.[6]

---

[2] W. Birke, Richterliche Rechtsanwendung und gesellschaftliche Auffassungen, Cologne: Verlag Dr. Otto Schmidt KG, 1968, p. 52.

[3] Birke, p. 53.

[4] Birke, p. 54.

[5] Kelsen, Hauptprobleme, p. 357 et seqq.

[6] Regarding these issues, cf. I. Seidl-Hohenveldern/T. Stein, Völkerrecht, 10th edition, Cologne/Berlin/ Bonn/Munich: Heymanns, 2000, p. 326: Trying to put the coexistence of the subjects of international law on a realistic basis, public international law attributes more importance to "the normative power of the factual" than domestic law. There have always been endeavors at enforcing the proposition "*ex iniuria ius non oritur*". However, sooner or later the practical need to establish relations with the actual rulers of a territory – even if they had come into power through an injustice according to international law – has always prevailed. See also H. Krieger, Das

The principle of effectiveness says "that according to general international law, a government which, independent of other governments, exerts effective control over the population of a certain territory, is the legitimate government; and that the population that lives under such a government in this territory constitutes a 'state' in terms of international law, regardless of whether this government exerts this effective control on the basis of a previously existing constitution or of one established by revolution."[7] It is instructive of this that the courts of the United States of America at first refused to recognize acts of the revolutionary Russian government as legal acts, on the grounds that they were not acts of a state but of a robber band.[8] However, after the coercive order established by the revolution had proved effective over a long period of time, it was recognized as a legal order and the respective government as a government of the state. As long as international practice follows the principle of effectiveness (which need not remain the case for all time) one cannot deny that the positivism of the pure theory of law hits the mark in this point (viz. regarding the legitimation of states under international law); in fact he who "lifts the veil and does not close his eyes" is faced by *nothing but the "Gorgon's head of power"!*[9]

Apart from these obvious advantages, however, all positivist theories exhibit – one way or another – the deficiency of being too one-sided and rendering certain aspects in terms of absolutes.[10] Naturally, this objection is raised mainly by those theorists who start out from a different epistemological position and who believe that an "essence", a certain "quality of nature and value" forms part of the law, too.[11] From such a standpoint,

---

Effektivitätsprinzip im Völkerrecht, Schriften zum Völkerrecht, Berlin: Duncker & Humblot, 2000; G. Dahm, quoted above Völkerrecht I, 2nd edition, Berlin: de Gruyter, 1989, p. 132 et seq.

[7] Kelsen, Pure Theory of Law, p. 215.

[8] Kelsen, Pure Theory of Law, p. 50.

[9] Thus Kelsen, in his contribution to the discussion on the occasion of the conference of the German constitutional lawyers in 1926, Veröffentlichung der Vereinigung der Deutschen Staatsrechtslehrer No. 3, Berlin/Leipzig, 1927, p. 55.

[10] Cf. for example Henkel, p. 500 et seq., and Fechner, p. 64. Kelsen, Hauptprobleme, p. 42, emphasizes that it is "self-evident that the formal, strictly normative point of view of the lawyer is one-sided and in no way capable of covering the entire phenomenon of the law."

[11] Thus Henkel, p. 501.

all varieties of legal positivism are of course deficient from the outset, since they only address the "real" but not the "ideal" side of the law. But even if one shifts one's standpoint onto the same epistemological ground as the legal positivists, one cannot help but find the view constricting (except in the cases of Hart's, McCormick's and Weinberger's theories as well as exclusive and inclusive positivism). For even what may still be regarded as "real" on the basis of strict epistemological positivism is further constricted by the legal positivists in a certain respect, in that – depending on their orientation – they predominantly investigate either normative, sociological, psychological or formal matters to the exclusion of the others. The deficiencies resulting from this can better be pointed out, however, by examining each theory individually, which is what we will turn to now.

B. The Merits and Demerits of Austin's Analytical Jurisprudence

According to Austin, the concept of command is "the key to the sciences of jurisprudence and morals."[12] How modern such a basic conception is to the date, is proved by the attempts of contemporary proponents of analytical value theory to qualify moral judgments or rather value judgments as "imperative" or "prescriptive" utterances (as opposed to "descriptive" empirical sentences).[13] However, this approach is contested nowadays even within analytical value theory.[14] A discussion of the very complex value judgment problem would go beyond the scope of this work. Apart from its topicality, being discussed in the works of numerous jurisprudents,[15] the command theory is to be praised for its simplicity and the aptness with which it captures the phenomenon of criminal law. Analytical jurisprudence also gives an accurate account of the law from the standpoint of a *politician* who "understands the law as an instrument of

---

[12]   Austin, Province, p. 21.

[13]   This is pointed out by Hart, Positivism and the Separation of Law and Morals, p. 58.

[14]   E.v. Savigny, Die Philosophie der normalen Sprache. Eine kritische Einführung in die "ordinary language philosophy", Frankfurt a.M.: Suhrkamp, 1993, p. 216 et seqq.

[15]   Cf. authors quoted by Larenz, Methodenlehre, 6th edition, 1991, p. 253 n. 5.

governance and will therefore regard legal norms as commands endowed with a sanction or imperatives."[16]

The most important objection against the command theory is that there are legal rules which cannot be interpreted as commands since – as we have already pointed out – they do not lay down a sanction.[17] Amongst these are rules on legal competency, on the acquisition, transfer or loss of rights, on the legal status of persons or associations of individuals as well as on the acquisition and loss of "legal power" (e.g. power of authority).[18] As pointed out by Larenz, it is admittedly possible to rescue the command theory of law logically by saying that such rules fulfill only an *auxiliary function*.[19] Thus, for example, the rule on the formation of a power of authority becomes significant in practice only in combination with a legal act – entered into by the agent in the name of the principal with a third party – from which duties of the principal and the third party may then arise. The legal rule on the formation of a conferred power of authority would, therefore, not yet be a complete legal rule but only a sentence serving to circumscribe one of the requirements of another legal rule, and duties reinforced by a sanction would only arise in conjunction with the latter. *At this point it becomes clear that it is almost always possible to rescue a theory by way of auxiliary constructions and that, therefore, one may rarely disprove ideas of legal philosophy in a stringent manner*, which tends to support the adequacy of our interpretation of philosophical thinking. Thus the command theory of law cannot be proved false; one can only object that it appears forced since it has been bought at the price that "almost all sentences which the jurist is used to regarding as 'legal rules' (*Rechtssätze*) take on the character of mere auxiliary explanatory sentences."[20]

Further deficiencies of Austin's conception have been pointed out in particular by Hart. Hart argues that habitual obedience of the subjects

---

[16] Jørgensen, p. 11.
[17] § 2 at n. 33 et seqq.
[18] Larenz, Methodenlehre, 6th edition, 1991, p. 254 et seq.; Henkel, p. 42.
[19] Larenz, p. 185 (to be found only in: Methodenlehre der Rechtswissenschaft, Second Edition, Berlin/Heidelberg/New York: Springer, 1969).
[20] Larenz, p. 185 (to be found only in: Methodenlehre der Rechtswissenschaft, Second Edition, Berlin/Heidelberg/New York: Springer, 1969).

vis-à-vis a sovereign is possible only with "a monarch sufficiently long-lived for a 'habit' to grow up." This scheme does not apply to legislature with a changing membership and "a fortiori not to an electorate".[21] The command theory is confronted with a particular difficulty if one considers the case of a democracy. Since here it is ultimately the bulk of the voters which must be regarded as sovereign, "in this case the bulk obeys the bulk, that is, it obeys itself."[22] Thus the image of a superior commander and a subjected person who follows the commands as devised by the command theory proves insufficient for a democracy. The only resort is to distinguish between the legislator in his capacity as an official person and in his capacity as a private person. Although according to Hart, there is nothing objectionable in this form of expression, this distinction presupposes power-conferring rules (so that one knows when an active citizen exercising his political rights is acting as legislator and when as a private person) which, as we have seen, cannot be interpreted as coercive commands.[23]

Further deficiencies of Austin's theory are that it is unable to account for the phenomena of international and of customary law. The rules of the first he includes with positive morality whilst he must interpret the latter as a tacit command of the sovereign provided that it has been recognized by a court. Hart argues here that customs can be law before they have been applied by a court[24] and that the legislature and *a fortiori* the electorate know only rarely about a court decision in which a rule of customary law was applied; which is why the legal status of customs cannot be explained by the idea of tacit order.[25]

---

[21] Hart, Positivism and the Separation of Law and Morals, p. 59.
[22] Hart, Positivism and the Separation of Law and Morals, p. 60.
[23] Hart, Concept of Law, p. 42; Eckmann, p. 60.
[24] Hart, Concept of Law, p. 46/47; Eckmann, p. 60.
[25] Hart, Concept of Law, p. 48.

C. The Merits and Demerits of German Statutory Positivism[26]

The advantages of the model of statutory positivism are obvious: apart from its simplicity, it especially has the advantage which we have determined, in § 24 A above, for the positivist theories in general and which consists in a clear and verifiable criterion for the legal status of a rule. Whilst proponents of psychological and sociological positivism will possibly have to engage in protracted inquiries to determine whether something is or is not law in terms of their theory, the statutory positivist may, in answering the question of what law is, simply refer to the official compilation of the rules and regulations of a state and spare any further research. In addition, it has to be conceded to the statutory positivist that in the modern constitutional state, the state law in its various forms of appearance (constitution, statute, regulation) has become a dominant source of law.

Furthermore, the statutory positivist doctrine of the judge as mere "subsumption machine" has experienced an unexpected revival in the recent past by the possibility to employ computers in the law application process.[27] As far as one can tell today, the application of automated law finding processes is "obviously only up for discussion where legal consequences tie in unambiguously and exclusively with external facts which are quantifiable and finite in number to the effect that the ever-infinite variability of the concrete situation ('individual case justice') simply does not flow into the decision-making process."[28] This is particularly true for simple applications of subsumption such as the determination of tax, salary and pension sums, insurance benefits as well as traffic fines.[29] At least within these limits, the statutory positivist model applies.

---

[26] For a detailed account of the history of criticism of the statutory positivist law application model in the 19th century, see Ogorek, p. 76 et seqq.
[27] Cf. Klug, p. 174 et seqq.
[28] F. Wieacker, Recht und Automation, Festschrift für Eduard Bötticher, Berlin: Duncker & Humblot, 1969, p. 399.
[29] Wieacker (quoted in § 24 n. 28), p. 399.

255

Disapproving of statutory positivism, Ophüls has tried to furnish proof that this theory is logically unworkable.[30] The proposition that all valid norms (norms in force) including those containing the validity criteria are man-made or are derivable from positive law[31] leads to a logical contradiction. Ophüls' key argument is based on the "recursivity" of the norms of the positive law. According to Ophüls, this means "that none of them is valid *per se* by virtue of its content but that its validity is constituted by a positive legislative act justifying it."[32] On the basis of this definition, Ophüls correctly proves that at least the highest norm, which contains the validity criteria from which the positive legal system derives its validity, may not itself be derivable from a positive legislative act. Thus, Ophüls reproduces the argument which has previously been formulated by Kant in his "Metaphysics of Morals":[33] even if one was to imagine an external legislation containing nothing but positive laws, "a natural law constituting the authority of the legislator (i.e. the power of binding others at his will) would nevertheless have to precede it." This basically shows nothing but the "axiomatic" character on which we place so much emphasis and which is typical of each legal positivist theory and thus of statutory positivism as well, *since the underlying chain of deductions must necessarily be broken off at one point and instead be replaced by at least one nonproven premise.* Such a premise by no means has to be a natural law proposition, as Ophüls and Kant believed, but may be a simple definition of law. To the question as to why, of all things, the orders of the legislator are to be regarded as the law in force, the statutory positivist might simply reply: because they are the law in force *by virtue of the definition accepted by me!* One may consider this explanation to

---

[30] Ophüls' explanations, NJW 21 (1968) II p. 1746, are, according to his own words, directed against the German statutory positivism of the 19th century.

[31] Ophüls, NJW 21 (1968), II, p. 1750.

[32] Ophüls, NJW 21 (1968), II, p. 1750. The argument of the non-contingency of the validity norms is untenable, as has been revealed by Hoerster's subtle considerations (ARSP 56 [1970], p. 47 et seqq.), since validity norms – just like the rules of substantive law – may vary from legal system to legal system and are therefore contingent.

[33] I. Kant, *The Metaphysics of Morals*. Trans. Mary Gregor. New York: Cambridge University Press, 1996.

be poor; it is not, however, logically contradictory.[34] Therefore, the objection of logical untenability does not hold.

Things are of course different if one assesses the effectiveness of the statutory positivist construct in terms of comprehension of the phenomenon of judge-made law. According to the fundamental analyses of Esser,[35] Wieacker,[36] Larenz,[37] Meier-Hayoz,[38] Canaris[39] and Bydlinski[40] to mention only a few of the more modern publications, there can be no doubt today that – apart from deciding on completely trivial legal cases and excluding from the application of law those areas in which the use of a computer is possible – judicial activity is not limited to a stringently logical decision-making process. The statutory positivist model would only apply if one succeeded in *strictly* axiomatizing the positive legal system and putting it into the form of a *calculus*. The limits of the axiomatizability of the law are equally the limits of German statutory positivism. Since this criticism of German statutory positivism has already been brought forward countless times, dwelling on this point would be preaching to the choir.

---

[34] Hoerster, ARSP 56 (1970), p. 51, refers additionally to the possibility to see the supreme constitutional norm itself as the supreme legal validity criterion.

[35] Vorverständnis und Methodenwahl in der Rechtsfindung: Rationalitätsgrundlagen richterlicher Entscheidungspraxis, Frankfurt a.M.: Athenaeum, 2nd Edition, 1972.

[36] Gesetz und Richterkunst. Zum Problem der aussergesetzlichen Rechtsordnung, Schriftenreihe der juristischen Studiengesellschaft Karlsruhe No. 34, Karlsruhe: Müller, 1958.

[37] Methodenlehre der Rechtswissenschaft, 6th Edition, Berlin/Heidelberg/New York/Tokyo: Springer, 1991.

[38] Der Richter als Gesetzgeber, Zurich: Juris, 1951.

[39] Systemdenken und Systembegriff in der Jurisprudenz, entwickelt am Beispiel des deutschen Privatrechts, Schriften zur Rechtstheorie No. 14, 2nd Edition, Berlin: Duncker & Humblot, 1983.

[40] Juristische Methodenlehre und Rechtsbegriff. Second Edition, Vienna/New York: Springer 1991.

D. The Merits and Demerits of Kelsen's Pure Theory of Law

We have already touched on the pure theory of law on several occasions above. First of all, in the chapter on the unprovability of the legal positivist theories, we have seen that Kelsen ranks amongst the critical positivists, i.e. amongst those positivists who are aware of the "axiomatic" character of their theory.[41] One may even say: in no other positivist theory is the axiomatic character as pronounced and unmistakable as in the pure theory of law; it is a textbook example of a theory which self-critically reflects on itself and, in that respect, is a laudable model for all those, whether or not they agree with it.

Moreover, we have defended the pure theory of law against the charge of being ideologically biased.[42] The limitation of scope in Kelsen's theory is not the result of political but of epistemic considerations. Typical of this is the fact – for which Métall has furnished impressive literal proof[43] – that there is hardly any political ideology of which the pure theory of law has not been suspected. This factor, however, militates for rather than against the purity of Kelsen's theory.

The pure theory of law aspires to interpret the positive, effective coercive orders as *normative* systems, as *Ought*-systems.[44] This approach is fruitful for the judge and the dogmatist, for both are looking for justifications of solutions to legal cases; and such justifications may only follow from

---

[41] See above, § 20 B.III.

[42] Above, § 21 C.

[43] R. A. Métall, (quoted in § 21 n. 18), Internationale Zeitschrift für Theorie des Rechts 10 (1936), p. 163 et seqq., with numerous references to further readings. Cf. also Kelsen, Introduction to the Problems of Legal Theory, Translation of the First Edition of the Reine Rechtslehre or Pure Theory of Law, translated by Bonnie Litschewski Paulson and Stanley L. Paulson, Oxford: Clarendon Press, 1992, p. 3: "Fascists declare that the Pure Theory is on the one side of democratic liberalism, while liberal or social democrats regard it as a trail-blazer for Fascism. Communists write off the Pure Theory as the ideology of capitalistic statism, while nationalists and capitalists write it off sometimes as Bolshevism, sometimes as covert anarchism. There are those who assure us that the Pure Theory is intellectually related to Catholic scholasticism, and others who believe that it has the characteristic of Protestant political and legal theory."

[44] Walter, ÖZöR NF 18 (1968), p. 336.

norms but never from social or psychological facts. To replace legal dogmatics by sociology of law or by psychology of law is consequently impossible.

Another advantage to be pointed out is that Kelsen's theory of interpretation has been largely corroborated by the more recent developments in legal methodology.[45] If nowadays the method of interpretation is widely characterized as a topical approach[46] which, as such, is based on the weighing of arguments and counterarguments, then this supports Kelsen's view whereby methods of interpretation only ever lead to one possible result, but never to one which is solely and exclusively correct.[47] The topical method is creative;[48] if interpretation is to be a topical procedure, it must consequently also be creative; and this is exactly what is claimed by Kelsen's theory of interpretation as an act of will, as a *law-creating* act and not a cognitive act.[49]

Furthermore, the theory of the hierarchical structure of the law is conceived in such a manner that it can account for the phenomenon of the unlawful judicial decision. Recall the example of the practice of the Swiss Federal Court regarding the question of whether cartels may or may not opt for the legal form of a non-profit association (Art. 60 et seqq. Swiss Civil Code).[50] Kelsen argues that the fact that "the legal order confers the force of a final judgment to a decision of a court of last instance means that not only is a general norm valid which predetermines the content of the judicial decision, *but also a general norm according to which the court may itself determine the content of the individual norm* [judgment; authors' note] *to be created by the court."*[51] Thus, the court of last instance is – according to this conception – authorized even to rule *in contradiction to* the legal norm, which in turn allows for understand-

---

[45] Rightly emphasized by Walter, ÖZöR NF 18 (1968), p. 350/351 n. 84.
[46] An example for such a catalogue of topoi are the elements of interpretation: Grammatical, systematical, historical and teleological element.
[47] Kelsen, Pure Theory of Law, p. 352.
[48] W. Ott, Jurisprudenz und plausibles Argumentieren, in: Aspekte der Rechtsentwicklung, Festschrift Meier-Hayoz, Zurich: Schulthess, 1972, p. 32 et seqq.
[49] Kelsen, Pure Theory of Law, p. 353.
[50] See below, § 24 F.
[51] Kelsen, Pure Theory of Law, p. 269 (emphasis by authors).

ing an unlawful practice – such as that of the Swiss Federal Court, quoted above – as valid positive law.

One of the most fundamental objections raised against the pure theory of law is that Kelsen cannot follow through the disparity of Is and Ought.[52] Larenz claims that the positing of the basic norm ultimately derives its justification from the fact that a certain coercive order functions as such – thus, the Ought actually results, by way of a detour via the epistemic postulate of the "basic norm", from the Is (which Kelsen considers, as such, to be devoid of value), i.e. from sheer facticity![53] However, in this form the objection does not succeed, for Kelsen does not say: the coercive order X is an effective order, therefore it is an order which ought to be (which would in fact represent an inadmissible deduction of an Ought from an Is); he only says: if one wants to *interpret* an effective coercive order X as a *normative* order, one must *presuppose* a basic norm which states that one ought to behave as the historically first constitution X and the norms set according to it prescribe. However, according to Kelsen, *nobody is forced to follow this interpretation and to accept the basic norm.*[54] From this one can see that the basic norm *does not result from the facticity of X* but is deliberately *"stipulated"* in order to conceive the factual – admittedly only *hypothetically* – as that which ought to be. Therefore, from the standpoint of logic, Kelsen's separation of Is and Ought is not put in jeopardy.[55] However, one must concede the following to the critics: as regards content, the basic norm is formulated in such a manner that it refers in each case to an *effective* coercive order and declares such an order to be hypothetically normative so that the positive law, understood as an effective coercive order, may *never* be contradic-

---

[52] Larenz, p. 73; E. Kaufmann, Kritik der neukantischen Rechtsphilosophie, Reprint of 1921 Edition, Aalen: Scientia, 1964, p. 30 et seqq.; Fechner, ARSP Beiheft NF 6 (1970), p. 209/210; K. Engisch, Besprechung der zweiten Auflage von Kelsen, Reine Rechtslehre, ZStrW 75 (1963), p. 602.

[53] Larenz, p. 74.

[54] Cf. above, § 4 at n. 11 et seqq.

[55] This has been emphasized by Walter, ÖZJ 16 (1961), p. 478. The invulnerability of this basic thesis has been established by Klug; cf. U. Klug, Die Reine Rechtslehre von Hans Kelsen und die formallogische Rechtfertigung der Kritik an dem Pseudoschluss vom Sein auf das Sollen, in: U. Klug, Skeptische Rechtsphilosophie und humanes Strafrecht I, Berlin/Heidelberg/New York: Springer, 1981, p. 99 et seqq.

tory to the corresponding basic norm.[56] On the other hand, the only co-ercive orders for which the basic norm is not presupposed are those which are not sufficiently effective, as for example in the case of a robber band whose power is inferior to that of the state.[57] Thus the decisive criterion of whether or not a basic norm is stipulated is whether or not the coercive order in question is sufficiently effective, i.e. something *factual* which seems to justify the criticism. But this criterion does not provide Kelsen with the premise for a logical deduction of the basic norm (in which case the latter would not have to be stipulated but could be proved![58]); rather, the orientation towards the factual is only the (epistemic) *motive* for the stipulation of the basic norm.

Raz levels the further criticism that the theory of the basic norm is based on circular logic: "He (Kelsen) can only identify the legal system with the help of the basic norm whereas the basic norm can be identified only after the identity of the legal system has been established."[59] In order to examine the truth of this charge, we will pursue this question with reference to Swiss law:

The first step is the following: the starting point is the hypothetical basic norm, which reads, "Coercive acts ought to be performed under the conditions and in the manner which the historically first state constitution, and the norms created according to it, prescribe." The historically first constitution in which Switzerland established itself autonomously, i.e. not under the dictates of foreign powers, as a confederate state, was that of 1848 (cf. Bereinigte Sammlung der Bundesgesetze und Verordnungen von 1848–1874, BS, vol. I, [Bern]). Around a quarter of a century later, in accordance with the rules of the old constitution, the people and cantons consented to a new one, namely that of 1874. In 1999 once again, the Swiss constitution underwent a total revision, and the new constitution entered into force on 1 January, 2000.

---

[56] See above, § 4, text following n. 14.
[57] See above, § 4 at n. 17.
[58] Walter, ÖJZ 16 (1961), p. 478, rightly observes: "... that which is inferable does not have to be presupposed hypothetically."
[59] Raz, Kelsen's Theory of the Basic Norm, in: idem, The Authority of Law, Reprint of 1979 edition, Oxford: Oxford University Press 2002, p. 122.

The second step consists of examining whether these constitutions and the norms prescribed by them have been effective by and large. This is obviously the case. Hence the Swiss legal order in its currently valid form is identified.

In a third step, the hypothetical basic norm for the Swiss legal system can now be stated more precisely: "Coercive acts ought to be performed under the conditions and in the manner which the *Federal Constitution of 1848*, and the norms created according to it, prescribe [meaning, in particular, the Federal Constitutions of 1874 and 1999]." How this procedure is based on circular logic is impossible to discern.

A further objection targets Kelsen's concept of the legal norm. A complete legal norm is, for Kelsen, only one which authorizes a certain individual (viz. an organ of the legal order) to direct a coercive act as a sanction against another individual.[60] Thus, the "Ought" refers first and foremost to the sanction, but not directly to the behavior of a subject of the legal order which is the condition of the imposing of the sanction.[61] Therefore, in the example of a murder statute, the Ought only applies to the sanction to be imposed in case of murder, but not the behavior of not killing. From this one might be inclined to conclude that Kelsen's legal norm is addressed primarily to the organs of the legal order but not to its subjects.[62] Hart opposes such a view with the argument that it conceals the specific character of the law as a *means of social control*. "A punishment for a crime, such as a fine, is not the same as a tax on a course of conduct, though both involve directions to officials to inflict the same money loss. What differentiates these ideas is that the first involves, as the second does not, an *offence or breach of duty* in the form of a violation of a *rule set up to guide the conduct of ordinary citizens*."[63] Against this, the following objection might be raised: Kelsen does not misconceive the function of the law as a means of social control: for even if – according to him – the norm directly stipulates the sanction as a legal obligation and is therefore addressed to the officials, this does not rule

---

[60] Kelsen, Pure Theory of Law, p. 34.
[61] Kelsen, Pure Theory of Law, p. 118 et seq.
[62] Like this Eckmann, p. 67, and Hart, The Concept of Law, p. 35 et seq.
[63] Hart, The Concept of Law, p. 39 (our emphasis).

out the *indirect* consequence that the behavior associated with the sanction appears to be *prohibited*, or that the opposite behavior appears to be legally *commanded*. Kelsen explicitly states that if a certain sanction *ought* to be executed in the event of a certain behavior, this already implies that the behavior conditioning the sanction is prohibited, and that the opposite behavior is commanded.[64] Hart's tax example can be accounted for by Kelsen's theory as well: if a tax law stipulates a certain income tax for a certain income, one cannot really say that the legal order forbids the realization of that income and imposes income tax as a sanction in case of non-compliance! Meanwhile, according to Kelsen, the legal norm would have to be worded as follows: if A realizes a certain income and does not pay the tax owed on it, then A is to be exposed to enforcement of payment of the amount of the tax owed plus interest on account of the delay. In this case, it is not the realization of a certain income that is forbidden by the positive law, but the non-payment of the legal tax, and it is the latter which conditions the coercive act. Thus, even the case of a statutory tax may be explained by Kelsen's theory, provided one rephrases the legal norm in the above-mentioned manner.

Kelsen does, however, encounter difficulties with his concepts of legal obligation and subjective rights. An individual has an obligation to behave in a certain way if, and only if, a legal norm attaches a coercive act to the opposite behavior as a sanction.[65] Ross and Welzel argue, against this, that defining the concept of legal obligation in this way leads to an infinite regress. For in this case, even an official can only be obligated inasmuch as he is subject to the coercive act of a higher official, etc.[66] Kelsen tries to escape this dilemma by assuming that the highest officials of the state do not have a duty, but only an authorization to impose a sanction.[67] However, this construction is not compatible with habitual language use, according to which the highest officials of the state, too, are *obligated* rather than merely authorized to act in a certain manner, by constitutional norms not backed by a threat.[68] Kelsen's concept of 'right'

---

[64] Kelsen, Pure Theory of Law, p. 25.
[65] Kelsen, Pure Theory of Law, p. 115.
[66] Ross, Realistic Jurisprudence, p. 75; Welzel, p. 14.
[67] Kelsen, Reine Rechtslehre, p. 124, n. ** (quoted from German edition).
[68] This is rightly pointed out by Welzel, p. 14/15.

equally leads to an incompatibility with habitual language use. According to Kelsen, a right is a private right in the technical sense if the legal order accords an individual the legal power to bring about *by lawsuit* the enforcement of the fulfillment of an obligation existing toward him.[69] If one accepts this concept, then the individual incapable of acting cannot have a right, for the legal order does not endow him with the legal power to take action! Only his statutory representative has this capacity.[70] Consequently, Kelsen must understand the rights and obligations concerned as the legal representative's rights and obligations.[71] If one wants to avoid this interpretation because the representative is obligated to exert this power *in the interest of the represented individual incapable of acting*, then one is left with the conclusion that such rights and obligations are *without a subject*![72] With his characteristic implacability, Kelsen is honest enough to pick up on the unfavorable implications resulting from his approach. For let us try to understand what this boils down to: a right without an entitled party, a right without a subject? Both consequences, the assumption of a right or obligation of the representative as well the assumption of a right without a subject are arguably untenable, and only avoidable if one starts out from different definitions which are better adapted to habitual language use. In this point, it seems to us that Hart's conception is superior to Kelsen's; we will address Hart's specific method of concept analysis separately.[73]

If one wants to use the pure theory of law for *practical* purposes, i.e. not just as a theory describing the positive law as such,[74] one can enrich its basic norm with moral content, which would be something like the following:

"One ought to behave as prescribed by the historically first constitution and by the norms stipulated in accordance with it, provided that these *do not contradict the United Nations Universal Declaration of Human*

---

[69] Kelsen, Pure Theory of Law, p. 145.
[70] Kelsen, Pure Theory of Law, p. 160.
[71] Kelsen, Pure Theory of Law, p. 161.
[72] Kelsen, Pure Theory of Law, p. 161.
[73] See below, § 24 G, text at n. 123 et seqq.
[74] Cf. § 4, first sentence, above.

Rights of 1948." This declaration is not yet positive law, and therefore belongs to morality. In spite of that, its content would be easy to ascertain because the declaration is written down in a United Nations document. And Kelsen, whose position is that of an observer of everything on a meta-level, could maintain his value-relativism. This would turn the pure theory of law into practical philosophy. Thus, it is shown that enrichment of the basic norm with moral content is not bound to Hart's theory, as has always been assumed in the literature, but could also be extended to other forms of positivism.

E. The Merits and Demerits of Psychological Positivism[75]

A strength of the legal theories referred to as "theories of recognition" is first of all that the law must normally meet with a positive attitude from society in order to be effective.[76] Experience shows that, usually, rules which have lost their resonance with the members of a legal society will no longer be enforced by the coercive apparatus.[77] A self-documenting present-day example is the influence of changed sexual morals on criminal court decisions.[78]

The individual theories of recognition have to be credited for providing the most plausible bindingness of a legal obligation on an empirical basis: if one is to perform the transfer from the Is to the Ought, from the sheer fact to the legal obligation – and herein lies a central question of philosophy of law – then the approach that can probably best be sus-

---

[75] Kelsen, Hauptprobleme, p. 346 et seqq. and 355 et seqq.; Yoon (quoted below § 5 A n. 3)
[76] Henkel, p. 548.
[77] Raiser, Einführung, p. 72/73.
[78] Cf. for example BGE 96 IV 64 where the Swiss Federal Court had to rule on the Swedish movie "I am curious", containing several realistic cohabitation scenes, in the light of the former, repealed Art. 204 Ziff. 1 of the Swiss Criminal Code (repealed effective 1 October 1992). The court explained that legal practice could not refrain from being open to a general change in attitude towards sexuality and the reduction of sensitivity related thereto. A criminal judge must apply Art. 204 Ziff. 1 of the former Swiss Criminal Code with reserve and only if the portrayal of the sexual acts clearly runs counter to "the moral views of the prevailing majority of the population."

tained is to rely on the approval of the individual affected. The binding-ness of the authoritative power of the law then lies in the self-obligation entered into by the individual on the basis of recognition. Interpreted in the strict sense, this theory is obviously untenable, however: if one asked for a deliberate, voluntary act of approval by all legal subjects regarding all the contents of legal norms, a breach of law could very rarely be sanctioned, for hardly any lawbreaker would voluntarily recognize a norm that was not in his favor. Therefore, Laun switches to a theory of general recognition when it comes to the problem of the authority of law[79] whilst Bierling finds a remedy in his theory of "indirect recogni-tion".[80] We will proceed to deal with the advantages and difficulties of such "*carte-blanche* recognition".

If one takes a granular look at those theories of recognition which have reinterpreted the concept of recognition in such a way that it is sufficient to recognize the legal order as a whole (like this Bierling, Merkel), or which accept as persons responsible for recognition only the leading class which sets the tone (Beling, Nawiasky), the following advantages surface: such conceptions allow for Art. 102 of the Basic Law of the Federal Republic of Germany *(Grundgesetz)*, the provision abolishing capital punishment in Germany, to be understood as valid law even though a majority of the population – admittedly a steadily decreasing majority – has approved of the death penalty ever since the said provision of the Basic Law was enacted.[81] Furthermore, these versions of the the-ory of recognition avoid the difficulty resulting from the fact that only a small proportion of the population actually reads the laws. Thus, the results of a survey held in the 1950s in Norway showed that only a small number of home-helps knew the basic essentials of their legal status and, of these, only few based their information on the law.[82] Of course, such

---

[79] § 5 A. II at n. 40.

[80] We showed in above § 5 A I in the end how the problem of Is and Ought could be solved by means of a basic norm that fits with Bierling's system.

[81] W. Maihofer, Gesetzgebung und Rechtsprechung im Spannungsfeld von Staat und Gesellschaft, in: Bockelmann Paul et al. (Contributors), Das Rechtswesen – Lenker oder Spiegel der Gesellschaft?, Munich: Piper, 1971, p. 54.

[82] Jørgensen, p. 50 n. 1.

cases cannot be discussed in terms of norm recognition or anything of the sort.

Let us finally look back upon the former interpretation of the illegal matchmaking rule of the German Criminal Code by the German Federal Court in Criminal Matters: according to BGHSt 6 (1954) 46 et seqq. and 17 (1962) 230 et seqq., non-prevention of sexual intercourse between fiancés of full age[83] (at that time 21 years), and even more so between fiancés who have not yet attained legal age, was looked upon as indictable abetting of fornication. Since it was the court's opinion that sexual intercourse was, in principle, only to take place in marriage, sexual intercourse between unmarried people also had the characteristics of fornication – even if they were genuinely engaged.

Empirical research revealed, however, that the majority of the German population had diametrically opposed ideas.[84] Therefore, the relevant norms of the German Criminal Code as interpreted by the German Federal Court in Criminal Matters could have been understood as valid law by the theory of recognition only if one was content with recognition by the "leading class which sets the tone" (thus in this case by the highest judges), or recognition by the population of the legal order as a whole.

On the other hand, in waiving real recognition of single norms, the said versions of psychological positivism entail the disadvantage that one is giving away a weapon to establish the wrongful character of a statutory or judicial rule on an empirical basis. If one understood the theory of recognition as declaring that only norms enjoying the real recognition of the members of a legal society are part of the law, this would possibly allow for furnishing empirical proof (i.e. without recourse to natural law propositions) that a statutory or judicial rule is "statutory or judicial lawlessness" and thus lacks, in reality, the character of law. In particular,

---

[83] BGHSt 17 (1962) p. 235.

[84] Maihofer, p. 50. By the 4th Statute Regarding the Reform of the German Criminal Law dated 23-11-1973, the rules regarding illegal match-making (§§ 180, 181 old version of the German Criminal Code) were transformed into a protection provision for minors so that the practice of the Federal Court in Criminal Matters lost its basis. The example shows that it is not the custom, in the long run, to enforce a judicial practice in opposition to social morality.

when one considers the case of a totalitarian and authoritarian regime, the potential political relevance of this version of psychological positivism, which has been pointed out in a different context[85] is quite apparent. But then one encounters difficulties with these theories in the examples discussed above, because in every case the legal character of those rules would have to be denied due to the lack of real recognition by the population. Furthermore, a theory of recognition in this latter version does not allow for distinguishing the law from other social orders. This set of problems has been investigated by Rehbinder on the basis of Ehrlich's theory of recognition:

As we have seen, Ehrlich does make the legal norm independent from its valid enactment in the state, and transfers it by means of his concept of the living law as a concrete behavioral norm into the relevant society.[86] As is generally known, his answer to the problem of distinguishing a legal order from other social orders consists of his "feeling theory": the decisive criterion for the distinction is the feeling triggered by breaches of norm. According to Ehrlich, a legal norm is a norm whose breach entails the strongest emotion release, viz. revulsion. In reality, this criterion is not viable, for how should one ever be able in practice to distinguish between "those shades of feeling named by Ehrlich, i.e. revulsion (breach of a legal norm), indignation (violation of a norm of morality), disgust (indecency), disapproval (tactlessness), ridiculousness (offense against etiquette) and critical disapproval (non-observance of fashion)."[87] For this reason, modern sociological legal theory is – following Weber and Geiger – based upon the existence of a specific law staff. Only this control entity turns a norm into a legal norm. We will concern ourselves with the merits and demerits of such a conception in subsection F, below.

---

[85] § 23 B at n. 31.
[86] Rehbinder, Eugen Ehrlich, p. 124.
[87] Rehbinder, Eugen Ehrlich, p. 123 (our translation). However, Rebhinder shows that the conception of Ehrlich, who shifts the law directly into the life of the group, is nevertheless still of significance for a modern theory of sociology of law (p. 141).

F. The Merits and Demerits of Sociological Positivism

A first advantage of those sociological theories which relate the binding character of law to the actual behavior of a law staff is that they allow for a clear distinction between the law in action and rules which have never been enforced in practice or are no longer enforced.[88] The fruitfulness of such a conception is apparent, for example, if one looks at the decisions of the Swiss Federal Court regarding the question of whether a cartel may opt for the legal form of a non-profit association.

In the 1930s, the Swiss Federal Court had decided that cartels might opt for the legal form of a non-profit association as provided for in Art. 60 et seqq. of Swiss Civil Code on condition that they did not operate a business carried out in a commercial manner.[89] This practice was, as is now admitted by the Swiss Federal Court, *illegal* under Art. 59 para. 2 and 60 para. 1 of the Swiss Civil Code which provide for associations to be non-commercial in purpose. Therefore, the Swiss Federal Court changed its judicial practice in BGE 88 II 209 et seqq. and decided that an organized body of people could only be subject to the law of associations if it was pursuing a non-commercial purpose. In BGE 90 II 333 et seqq., however, it returned to its former practice: It explained that a strict interpretation of the above-mentioned legal provisions could at best be justified if the question had never previously been ruled upon by the courts. Then one would require organizations to heed the wording of the statutory provisions to the letter. According to the court, however, the circumstances made this quite a different matter. Professional organizations had in fact taken root in the legal form of associations. Many of them played an important part in the economic and social life of Switzerland. The courts had accepted this practice for almost 30 years. A legal situation having become established with the courts' approval could not be overturned in the absence of any means of providing for a transitional regulation. The consequences of such a turnaround would be highly disagree-

---

[88] Jørgensen, p. 29/30.
[89] Decision of 5 December 1934, Journal des Tribunaux 1935 I 66 et seqq., confirmed in BGE 62 II 32 et seqq.

able for the professional organizations and their members as well as for third parties.[90]

Taking a sociological validity concept as a basis, the phenomenon of an illegal judicial practice, as in the case discussed above, may be accounted for as follows: for the sociological positivist, the (illegal) rule "A trade association [in the sense of cartels and professional associations; authors' note] can opt for the legal form of an association as provided for in the Swiss Civil Code, Art. 60 et seqq., if it does not run a business carried out in a commercial manner" is law because that and only that (rather than the much stricter regulation pursuant to the Swiss Civil Code) is actually applied by the law staff. It alone is a "real rule", i.e. living law; the solution required by the Swiss Civil Code, i.e. that associations must always pursue a non-commercial purpose, is nowadays just a "paper rule" – as regards trade associations not running a commercial business – since the law staff lacks the willingness to apply it.

Furthermore, sociological positivism adequately reflects the attorney at law's perspective of the law: for the attorney "does not want to know how the officials *ought to behave* but how they actually *do behave*. Only then will he be able to predict to his client whether he will be granted his right or not."[91]

Finally, the sociological conception correctly illustrates that in the majority of cases, the application of the law is based on an alogical decision and that consequently, judicial precedents must be recognized as a source of law. Today, the norm-generating function of judicial decisions is emphasized particularly by the proponents of modern "value-oriented jurisprudence" ("jurisprudence of values"). The question that surfaces is whether the development from the formal rationality of Pandectism through statutory positivism towards the end of the 19th century and at the beginning of the 20th century up to modern "judicial law-making" might not be best understood as an evolution towards "judicial positivism".[92]

---

[90] BGE 90 II 343.
[91] Rehbinder, Einführung, p. 55 (our emphasis). Along the same lines Jørgensen, p. 11.
[92] Rüthers, Unbegrenzte Auslegung, p. 476.

With regard to the experience of validity *(Geltungserlebnis)* of legal rules, the sociological explanation may at least in parts be accurate: sometimes, the members of a legal society consider a rule to be law because a sanction is to be expected in case of disobedience. In such cases, the experience of validity is a consequence of the sanction that is to be expected.[93]

A first drawback of a purely sociological approach to the law consists in its being useless to the judge. It is of no use to the judge to know that law is what he will do or that it is the order which is backed by the probability of the occurrence of physical or psychological coercion. For the question which the judge is confronted with is just how he *should* act or which rule he *should* leverage. Thus, the judge is looking for a *justification* of his decision and such justification may only be supplied by the law in terms of a normative system, but not by the law in terms of a complex of social facts. Otherwise, an illegal decision would be impossible and, as Kantorowicz notes, one might just as well staff the supreme court with nine generals since there is no doubt that they would know how to enforce their decisions.[94]

In addition, the adoption of a sociological concept of law excludes the law of tribal societies (without court organization);[95] even if administrative "organs" such as chieftains, magicians, shamans, tribal elders, tribal courts or the Germanic "*Thing*" (assembly of all men able to bear arms) have formed, they fulfill functions that are also political, ritual and military in character, and thus cannot be regarded as a judicial specialist force, as "law staff" in the sociological sense.[96] There is equal difficulty in understanding the rules of public international law as law, for lack of a mandatory international jurisdiction.[97] Moreover, certain constitutional

---

[93] Jørgensen, p. 31.

[94] Kantorowicz, Rechtswissenschaft und Soziologie: ausgewählte Schriften zur Wissenschaftslehre, Karlsruhe: C.F. Müller, 1962, p. 114.

[95] Jørgensen, p. 30.

[96] Kantorowicz, p. 68 et seq. The "law" investigated by the ethnologists is thus in the majority of cases not law in the sociological sense. Before a law staff has formed, law and morality are not to be separated. A preliminary stage of law governs, the so-called "*Sittenrecht*": Rehbinder, Eugen Ehrlich, p. 129.

[97] Jørgensen, p. 30; Kantorowicz, p. 14.

provisions which cannot be submitted to a court or any other administrative body would not rank as law;[98] Jørgensen refers us to the example of the constitutional provisions on the date of the initial meeting of the Danish parliament.[99]

A further objection against the depicted sociological conception is that many norms are addressed to the members of a legal society but not to the officials, and consequently they are conducive primarily to the prevention rather than the solution of conflicts. Therefore, according to this opinion, it is forced and exaggerated to tie the law primarily to the behavior of the law staff.[100] However, this problem may easily be tackled by introducing into a sociological concept of law not the actual reaction of the law staff as a criterion but the reliance on the *willingness* of the staff members to react.[101] Likewise, a rule that everybody complies with voluntarily and thus needs no enforcement is then law in the sociological sense, since it, too, has a chance of being enforced by the law staff against an eventual law-breaker.

Against both the command theory of law and the sociological theory of coercion, one may argue that there are legal norms which do not order people to do something or prohibit them from doing something, and which thus cannot be obeyed or enforced by a law staff. "Let us take a rule specifying the ways in which a valid will or contract is made. If the conditions provided for by the laws are not met, the contract will be null and void, but there is neither breach or violation of an obligation nor a sanction, neither a wrong nor a reaction to a wrong."[102] These pitfalls may, however, be avoided if one makes use of the conception – primarily developed by Bulygin – which differentiates between *obedience* to and *use* of rules.[103] A secondary rule cannot be obeyed,[104] but it can be *used* in order to justify a decision. Thus, the law in the sociological sense

---

[98] Bulygin, ARSP Beiheft 41 (1965), p. 57.
[99] Jørgensen, p. 30
[100] Like this for example Kantorowicz, Rechtswissenschaft und Soziologie, ausgewählte Schriften zur Wissenschaftslehre (§ 24 n. 94), p. 109, and Jørgensen, p. 50.
[101] Rehbinder, Eugen Ehrlich, p. 130.
[102] Bulygin, ARSP Beiheft 41 (1965), p. 41.
[103] Bulygin, ARSP Beiheft 41 (1965), p. 45 et seqq.
[104] Cf. Rehbinder, Eugen Ehrlich, p. 130 n. 12.

is constituted not only by norms for which there exists a chance of enforcement by the law staff in case of disobedience, but also by norms *which may be used by the law staff to justify a decision.*

Finally, it might be argued against the "prognostic" theories that the foreseeability of a decision rests, of all things, upon the knowledge of the legal rules.[105] Consequently, one cannot just simply tie the law to the behavior of the law staff. Ross tries to avoid this dilemma by not proceeding behavioristically but by integrating a psychological element into his theory.[106] According to Ross, the law is a normative ideology expressing itself in the decision behavior of the judges from where it can be accessed. However, as we have seen above, this source of cognition is not open to the judge since he cannot develop the law from his own decision behavior but must know what the law is *before* he comes to a decision. Consequently, there must be a different access to the ideology for him, viz. the study of the laws, judicial precedents as well as legal doctrine. If one admits this, then the question arises as to why one should rely exclusively on the decision behavior of the judges to find the law and whether the law could not be revealed more directly through said sources (without the unnecessary detour via verification against future judicial behavior).

If, finally, as Ross assumes, opinions of a court largely represent nothing but a "façade of justification"[107] which does not reflect the true reasons for the decision which have motivated the judge, then one would – as is emphasized by Jørgensen – risk being thoroughly misinformed by studying court decisions alone;[108] and the forecasts of the legal dogmatists on future decisions made on this basis would probably miss their target most of the time.

---

[105] Jørgensen, p. 32.
[106] See above, § 23 B at n. 31.
[107] Ross, On Law and Justice, p. 152.
[108] Jørgensen, p. 101.

G. The Merits and Demerits of Hart's Legal Theory[109]

Hart's conception has the advantage of being based on the *social reality of the respective legal order*. He does not need to understand his "rule of recognition" which contains the *identification and validity* criteria of the system as a "transcendental-logical prerequisite" of any legal order, but simply construes it as a rule varying in content from system to system but nevertheless determinable for each individual legal system, a rule which manifests itself in a complex, but normally concordant practice engaged in by the courts, the "officials and private persons when identifying the law by reference to certain criteria."[110] In other words, the existence of the rule of recognition is a social fact which – laying claim to objectivity – may be determined by any neutral observer of the system; thus it comes within the facts which may be regarded as "real" even from the standpoint of a strictly epistemic positivism. – Hart systematically abstains from assuming an – even merely hypothetical – Ought-validity of a legal *system as a whole*. A legal order exists or does not exist; the question of whether it can, from a higher-order point of view, be regarded as legitimate or not presupposes the application of measures of value and is independent of the question of the existence of the legal order.[111]

It must be stressed, however, that the said social facts first have to be interpreted in the light of the constitution so that one is able to identify them as validity criteria (cf. A. Ross's chess example in § 6 B above, text at n. 22 et seqq.). For the said facts are not brute facts (like rocks or planets, for example) but so-called *institutional* facts (such as boundary stones, or legal persons).[112] Their *real* side consists in the social practice

---

[109] For critical reviews see: Above, § 22 D; Fuller, Harvard Law Review 71 (1958), p. 630 et seqq.; Alexy, ARSP Beiheft No. 37 (1990), p. 9 et seqq.; idem, The Argument from Injustice – A reply to Legal Positivism, p. 18 et seq.; Raz, Norms, p. 149 et seqq.; idem, Concept, ch. VI-IX; idem, AL, p. 90 et seqq.; Finnis, p. 11 et seqq., p. 163, 312 et seqq., 357 et seqq.; re: Dworkin, see above, § 22 D. V.A. Menchaca, Hart und der Rechtsbegriff, in: W. Krawietz/Walter Ott, Formalismus und Phänomenologie im Rechtsdenken der Gegenwart, Festgabe für Alois Troller zum 80. Geburtstag, Berlin: Duncker & Humblot, 1987, p. 73 et seqq.

[110] Hart, Concept of Law, p. 110.

[111] Hart, Concept of Law, p. 107 et seq.

[112] See § 13 above, text at n. 15 et seqq.

described, whereas their *ideal* side consists in the *meaning* of this social practice. And this ideal side is *normative*; hence the term 'rule'. Unless this distinction is noted, anyone might easily make the mistake of thinking that Hart is drawing an illogical inference from Is to Ought, from the social practice to the normative.

Thus, the rule of recognition clearly differs from Kelsen's "hypothetical basic norm". Hart argues against Kelsen that it is a needless reduplication to assume the same content of the basic norm for all legal systems, viz. that the constitution ought to be obeyed.[113] A constitution is accepted and exists if the courts and officials of the system actually identify the law in accordance with the criteria it provides.[114] According to Hoerster, who agrees with Hart on this point, there is no objection to regarding the highest constitutional norm of the respective legal system *itself* as the highest legal validity norm.[115] Meanwhile Hart's polemic against Kelsen is defective, which has been pointed out by Eckmann and Dreier.[116] For Kelsen, unlike Hart, is not content with understanding the legal system as (an institutional) social fact, but wants to understand the effective coercive orders – even if only hypothetically – as orders of normative character. The problem of how an actual coercive order becomes a coercive order of normative character can, from Kelsen's point of view, only be solved by presupposing a norm which interprets the given effective coercive order as one which ought to be. In Kelsen's system, the basic norm is by no means a futile reduplication, although one can also agree with Hart and Hoerster that the cognitive value of the basic norm can be assessed as marginal. Nor is it true, furthermore, that the basic norm always has the same content. For the basic norm makes reference to the historically first constitution and the norms of a state which have been set in accordance with it. But the historically first constitution differs

---

[113] Hart, Concept of Law, p. 293. Here Hart uses Kelsen's unduly shortened version of the basic norm. See the correct version in § 4 n. 11, text after § 4 n. 15 and here, text after n. 116.

[114] Hart, Concept of Law, p. 293.

[115] Hoerster, ARSP 56 (1970), p. 51.

[116] Eckmann, p. 124; Dreier, Sein und Sollen, Bemerkungen zur Reinen Rechtslehre Kelsens, JZ 27 (1972), p. 332.

from one legal system to another.[117] For Switzerland the basic norm would read: "People shall behave as prescribed by the Federal Constitution of 1848 and the norms set in accordance with it (meaning, in particular, the Federal Constitutions of 1874 and 1999)."

According to Hart's theory, the fundamental secondary rule and thus the legal system as a whole must only be accepted by the officials. The ordinary citizens may do this as well but it is not a necessity; for a legal system to exist, the only requirement on the part of the ordinary citizens is that they *by and large obey the primary rules* of the system;[118] their actual acceptance is unnecessary. This conception, of course, features the same merits as those observed with Beling's and Nawiasky's (recognition of the law by the "leading class which sets the tone") theories of recognition. It also allows for comprehending as "law" rules which do not partake of recognition by the citizens, be it because the latter have different views from the legislating or law administering bodies or because they have no knowledge at all of the content of law.[119] On the other hand, just as in the case of the theories of recognition, this entails the drawback that the legal character of a norm imposed by an irresponsible ruler or judge cannot be denied on the basis of empirical proof that such a norm engenders indignation among the majority of citizens.

As we have seen, Hart's rule of recognition of a developed system provides for several validity criteria. In particular, it contains the criterion that the rules expressed in a judicial decision are to be recognized as valid law.[120] It is, however, questionable whether the rules expressed in judicial decisions must, as Hart seems to assume,[121] always be primary rules. In reality, courts *apply and make secondary rules, too.* Let us cite the special formal regulations of holographic wills in the Swiss Civil Code of 1907 as an example: according to Art. 505 of the Swiss Civil Code of 1907 the holographic will has to be wholly written by the divisor's own hand, inclusive of the indication of year, month, day and place

---

[117] Cf. the examples in § 24 D at n. 66–67 and § 24 D, text at n. 63 above.
[118] Hart, Concept of Law, p. 112/116.
[119] See above, § 24 E at n. 81.
[120] Above, § 11 at n. 51
[121] Above, § 11 n. 51, Hart, Concept of Law, p. 73

of making, and it must be signed by the divisor. Up to the year 1990, the Swiss Federal court applied this rule rigorously. Then it began to gradually ease the formal requirements. In BGE 116 II 129 it held that an evidentially wrong date shall not lead to the nullity of the testament provided that the fault is not based on the divisor's intention and that the correctness of the date is of no significance whatsoever. Eventually, the Swiss Federal Court applied these newer principles not just to the date but also to the place where the last will was made (BGE 117 II 145). Following the revision of the marriage law and the law of succession, the legislator implemented these judicial modifications in the Swiss Civil Code. Art. 505 of the revised Swiss Civil Code abandons the statement of the place as a formal requirement and the newly inserted Art. 520a specifies the circumstances under which an incorrect or incomplete statement of year, month or day does not lead to the nullity of the testament. Both articles have been in force since January 1, 1996.

Hart's rule of recognition is, however, as he admits himself, unable to account for international law. Since there is neither an international legislature nor courts to which the states are obligatorily subject, nor centrally organized sanctions, international law bears more resemblance to a simple system of primary rules than a developed legal system. According to Hart, it is arguable that international law not only lacks secondary rules of change and adjudication but also a unifying rule of recognition containing the sources of the law as well as criteria for identifying the rules that belong to the system.[122]

Hart's method of concept analysis is based partly on Wittgenstein's language philosophy, to wit less on Wittgenstein's debut publication, the *Tractatus logico-philosophicus*, than on his *Philosophical Investigations* published posthumously.[123] According to Wittgenstein's later conception, words of a language do not serve only to mirror reality; that use of words does not exhaust the functions of language; words can, for example, be

---

[122] Hart, Concept of Law, p. 214.
[123] L. Wittgenstein, Philosophical Investigations: The German Text, with a Revised English Translation, 50th Anniversary Commemorative Edition (Hardcover), translated by G.E.M. Anscombe, Oxford: Wiley-Blackwell, 2008. See Eckmann, p. 101 et seqq.

employed to express a command, a request or a question. Then language has a different function because no reference to any particular object is made. According to Wittgenstein, the *meaning* of a word is in large part identical to its *use in ordinary language*. The method for language analysis and for investigating philosophical problems that results from this is based on investigating how particular verbal expressions are used in everyday language. Hart takes up this theory and explains that expressions such as "right", "duty", and "corporation" do not have the primary function of standing for or describing anything,[124] which is why we cannot find facts which correspond to these words. These words have an entirely different meaning: in Hart's opinion, they derive their meaning *"from the manner in which they function in conjunction with legal rules."*[125] In our judgment, the fruitfulness of such a method of inquiry is immediately clear if one calls to mind that it renders impossible a definition of the term "right", as undertaken for example by Kelsen. As we have seen, based on his concept of right, Kelsen is forced to accept that an individual incapable of acting cannot have rights. The rights concerned are either the rights of the legal representative of the individual incapable of acting, or they are rights "without a subject".[126] However, it is indisputable that jurists constantly refer to the rights of persons who are incapable of acting. A proponent of Hart's method would explain a legal term by taking a sentence in which the term plays its characteristic role (thus, in the above example, "child A has a right against X"). In doing so, he would automatically define the right in such a way that it would include these cases, rather than on the contrary having to explain that the jurists were erroneously speaking of rights in these cases![127] In an analogous way, Hart arrives at the differentiation between primary and secondary rules which is of fundamental importance to him. The difference between them is revealed to him first of all in *how one speaks*

---

[124] Hart, Definition and Theory in Jurisprudence, reprinted in: Essays in Jurisprudence and Philosophy, p. 31.

[125] Eckmann, p. 105.

[126] See above, § 24 D at the end.

[127] Hart's approach in analyzing the concept of right and his conclusions are explained in more detail by Eckmann, p. 106 et seqq.

about them.[128] If, in making our last will and testament, we will ensure that the document complies with certain validity provisions which are, according to Hart, secondary rules, the issue will not – as in the case of a primary rule – be addressed as *violation of a duty* but it will only be said that *the will is null and void* or has no legal effect.[129]

Here and elsewhere, it is imperative to point out that there is only little evidence of Wittgenstein's philosophy in Hart's *Concept of Law*. Hart's preface to the *Concept of Law* confirms this finding when he explains that his "book may also be regarded as an essay in descriptive sociology."[130] Here, Hart's clearly positivist attitude shows. Above all, however, we would like to draw attention to Hart's comments on the wider positivist concept of law versus the narrower Natural Law concept of law.[131] Hart explains that neither the positivist nor the natural lawyer would be satisfied if he was told that his concept of law was merely correctly reflecting the linguistic usage in, for example, England or Germany.[132] According to Hart, not only the correct reproduction of the linguistic usage is at stake (which would be in accord with Wittgenstein's method) but also "the comparative merit of a wider or narrower concept of classifying [...] rules generally effective in social life", i.e. a rational *choice* between these two concepts.[133] Here, Wittgenstein's method does not apply since linguistic usage employs the term "law" to denote entirely different phenomena.[134] Therefore it is just not Hart's concern here to explain the word "law" in terms of English or German habitual language use and to thus apply Wittgenstein's method. Hart's own concept of the positive law[135] does not conform to an inquiry into the use of the word "law" in English language, either (apart from the differentiation between primary and

---

[128] Eckmann, p. 61/62; Hart, Concept of Law, p. 28: "The radical difference in function between laws that confer such powers and the criminal statute is reflected in much of our normal ways of speaking about this class of laws."

[129] Hart, Concept of Law, p. 28.

[130] Hart, The Concept of Law, p. vi.

[131] Cf. above, § 19 A.III in the end and § 20 B.III at n. 18.

[132] Hart, The Concept of Law, p. 209.

[133] Hart, The Concept of Law, p. 209.

[134] See above, § 19 A.III.

[135] Above, § 11 in the end.

secondary rules), but to philosophical considerations of a different nature.

Moreover, the success of Hart's method of investigation depends on whether linguistic usage is sufficiently consistent, as regards the terms of law to be investigated. This difficulty surfaces with Hart's analysis of the validity concept. As we have seen, Hart's use of the term "validity" always just refers to an internal validity, i.e. validity within a given system. According to Hart, one usually only speaks of the validity of a rule if the speaker has established its existence by deduction from a presupposed higher rule. From this, two things follow: only the subordinate rules of a system can be legally valid, but not the rule of recognition. And: by validity of a norm, Hart does not understand a factual, but a normative validity, an Ought-validity.[136] Eckmann is of the opinion that this analysis of the validity concept is inconsistent with habitual language use, according to which the validity criteria of a constitution, which make up the rule of recognition, are referred to as valid law.[137] For even the rule of Art. 140 para. 1 lit. a. and Art. 142 para. 2 of the Constitution of the Swiss Confederation, according to which revisions of the Federal Constitution must be submitted to the vote of the People and the Cantons, is looked upon as valid law; i.e. in habitual language use, there is a *validity of the validity criterion* itself.

We do not agree with the critique mounted by Eckmann. For the highest constitutional norm derives its validity from the rule of recognition. The fact that the supreme criteria of the validity of the constitution can also be found in the rule of recognition does not mean a needless reduplication. For when it comes to the rule of recognition, it is necessary that the supreme criteria of the constitution are *rooted in social practice* by the officials accepting and applying such criteria.

That the criteria contained in the constitution and in the rule of recognition do not necessarily coincide may be shown by the example of the non-existence of a statute prohibiting intercantonal double taxation un-

---

[136] Hart's and Kelsen's theories concur in the normativity of the respective validity concept.
[137] Eckmann, p. 122/123.

der the Constitution of the Swiss Confederation of 1874. According to Art. 46 para. 2 of the Constitution of 1874, the Parliament was empowered to enact a statute against the double taxation of persons with links to two or more Cantons. In reality, such a statute was never drafted. Instead, the Federal Supreme Court developed a differentiated practice regarding this issue. Based on the social fact thesis, it is clear that the practice of the Federal Supreme Court represents the law in force on this issue and that the delegation of the power to Parliament is a mere paper rule.

H. The Merits and Demerits of Inclusive and Exclusive Positivism

When assessing the merits and demerits of these two new forms of legal positivism, one must differentiate between two main problems:

First: the question of whether the judges, when interpreting fundamental rights of moral content included in the constitution, are creating new law (as according to exclusive positivism) or not (inclusive positivism).

Second: the question of whether moral criteria are to be incorporated in the rule of recognition (as according to inclusive positivism) or whether the content of the rule of recognition is to be limited to formal sources such as legislative acts, case law and customs (exclusive positivism).

It is important to understand that these two questions are logically *independent of each other*. This means that one may be a proponent of soft positivism[138] – which was Hart's original position – and nevertheless emphasize the creative role of the courts,[139] or one may be an adherent

---

[138] Hart, Concept of Law, p. 250.

[139] Hart, Problems of the Philosophy of Law, in: P. Edwards (ed.), The Encyclopedia of Philosophy, Vol. 6, New York: Macmillan, 1967, p. 271: "It is of crucial importance that cases for decision do not arise in a vacuum but in the course of the operation of a working body of rules, an operation in which a multiplicity of diverse considerations are continuously recognized as good reasons for a decision. These include a wide variety of individual and social interests, social and political aims, and standards of morality and justice; and they may be formulated in general terms as principles, policies, and standards. In some cases only one such consideration may be relevant,

of a kind of sources thesis and nevertheless argue that the judge – when interpreting the constitution – is only declaring the rights the parties already have. However, under the latter conditions, judge-made law could no longer qualify as a legal source, as has become apparent with German statutory positivism.[140]

A case discussed by Waluchow[141] on the basis of the considerations of the Canadian Court of Appeal, viz. Andrews v. Law Society of BC, is particularly suitable for answering the first of the above questions.[142]

The Law Society of BC had denied Andrews the licence to practice law since Andrews did not have Canadian citizenship. The question raised before the court was whether the requirement of Canadian citizenship as a prerequisite to practice law was violating sec. 15 of the Canadian Charter of Rights and Freedoms. Sec. 15 of the Canadian Charter of Rights and Freedoms falls under the title "Equality Rights" and reads:

> **15.** (1) Every individual is equal before and under the law and has the right to the equal protection and equal benefit of the law without discrimination and, in particular, without discrimination based on race, national or ethnic origin, colour, religion, sex, age or mental or physical disability.

According to sec. 15, any law or other legal instrument is unconstitutional if it discriminates against individuals unless such discrimination can be justified under sec. 1 of the Charter.[143] Sec. 1 states:

> **1.** The Canadian Charter of Rights and Freedoms guarantees the rights and freedoms set out in it subject only to such reasonable limits prescribed by law as can be demonstrably justified in a free and democratic society.

The main issue with which the court was confronted was whether the citizenship requirement enjoined by the Law Society represented a dis-

---

and it may determine the decision as unambiguously as a determinate legal rule"; Waluchow, p. 233 et seq.

[140] Cf. above, § 3, text at n. 17 et seqq.

[141] Waluchow, p. 149 et seqq.

[142] 4 WWR 242 (BCCA). The Court of Appeal's decision was later upheld (3 to 2) by the Supreme Court of Canada. See Waluchow, p. 149, with reference to *Law Society of BC v. Andrews*, [1989] 56 DLR (4th) 1.

[143] Waluchow, p. 149.

crimination. According to Waluchow, this brought forth the moral and philosophical question of how discrimination was to be defined in order to interpret sec. 15.[144]

The Court of Appeal discarded a first definition submitted by the Law Society and accepted by the Trial Court.

A second definition, this time proposed by Andrews, was dismissed by the Court of Appeal as well.

The appellate court judges finally accepted a third definition:

"D3: L is discriminatory if it draws any unreasonable or unfair distinctions, distinctions which are unduly prejudicial."[145]

The judges then applied this definition to the Andrews case. They ruled that the citizenship prerequisite imposed by the Law Society was in fact discriminatory and thus in violation of sec. 15. It was "neither fair nor reasonable for someone in Andrews's position to be denied the licence to practise law."[146] What remained to be examined was whether the violation was admissible as an exception under sec. 1. In this point, the Court could rest on principles with regard to the application of sec. 1 laid down by the Canadian Supreme Court in Regina v. Oaks.[147] In application of these principles, the Court came to the conclusion that the discriminating requirement of citizenship could not be justified based on sec. 1. It could not be said of the apparent goals that they were related in a clear and reasonable way to societal concerns which were urgent and essential.[148] The effects of the chosen means were not proportional to the importance of the pursued goals; and they were not related to them in a rational manner either: *"Citizenship is in no way a necessary condition of being a good lawyer."* In the Court's opinion, this was furthermore corroborated by the absence of such a requirement in other common-law jurisdictions.[149]

---

[144] Waluchow, p. 150.
[145] Waluchow, p. 151, with reference to Andrews, at p. 250–252.
[146] Waluchow, p. 152.
[147] Waluchow, p. 153, with reference to R. v. Oaks [1986] 1 SCR 103, 50, CR (3d) 1.
[148] Waluchow, p. 154.
[149] Waluchow, p. 154 (our emphasis), with reference to Andrews, at p. 257.

Andrews's appeal was therefore granted. The citizenship requirement was invalid due to its being unconstitutional.[150]

After having come to the conclusion that moral arguments play in fact an important part in Charter cases, Waluchow addresses the question of whether they do this at least in part in the capacity of a test for the existence or the content of valid laws.[151]

Again with reference to Andrews, Waluchow answers this question in the affirmative as well, because:

Following exclusive positivism, the Court did not enforce a pre-existing right (to equality) against a measure that was void from the beginning (citizenship requirement) when it based its decision on the unfairness of the citizenship requirement. Rather, it made use of its authorization stated in sections 15 (equality) and 52 (supremacy of the constitution) to make unconstitutional what would otherwise have been perfectly valid law. The Court did not discover a *collision of law* but a *collision of law and morality*. With its decision, the Court enforced *a non-legal, moral right* and thus at the same time made a *new right*. With the decision, the *lawyers* were assigned *a new right* in the sense of *no longer being subject to the citizenship requirement.* As an authoritative act, *the decision of the court had the power to create such new right, just as acts of a Parliament*, which are themselves often *based on political morality*, obviously have the ability to create new legal rights.[152]

According to Waluchow, the exclusive account is contrary to the Canadians' intuition.[153] Generally, they understand the Charter as certifying fundamental legal rights which they have in relation to the government and the administration. The contrary view, viz. that the Charter makes reference to non-legal, moral rights, on the basis of which the courts are empowered to create new legal rights and to override what would otherwise be valid law, flouts this understanding.[154]

---

[150] Waluchow, p. 154.
[151] Waluchow, p. 155.
[152] Waluchow, p. 158.
[153] Waluchow, p. 158.
[154] Waluchow, p. 158 et seq.

This criticism of Waluchow's overemphasizes the indeterminacy of Charter Rights from an exclusive positivist's standpoint. The Canadian Charter as a modern constitutional document, in force since 17 April 1982, describes with great precision which criteria may lead, for example, to discrimination. It lists no less than nine of them: race, national or ethnic origin, color, religion, sex, age or mental or physical disability.[155] *Even the citizenship which played a major part in Andrews's case is explicitly mentioned.* An adherent of exclusive positivism would surely not allege that sec. 15 only contained a reference to non-legal, moral rights, on the basis of which the judges were empowered to create new legal rights. Sec. 15 is not a judicial creation; it in fact guarantees the respective equality rights to the Canadians even *before a court has ruled.* However, in certain cases, the framing of such a fundamental right in concrete terms is incumbent on the courts, and it is *only within these limits* that the judge acts as a *law creator.* If the viewpoint of inclusive positivism was right, Andrews could have been sure of being awarded the licence to practice law even *before* the trial had started. But could he really be sure of this? Is such a view realistic? Of course not. It neglects the *aleatory* nature of legal practice. A strong indication for the exclusive account is the fact that Andrews *lost* before the *Trial Court, won* before the *Court of Appeal* and also *won – though only with the closest possible result (3 to 2)* – before the *Supreme Court.* Thus two judges of the Canadian Supreme Court voted in favor of the Law Society. It is confirmed knowledge of modern legal methodology that, when interpreting the law or even filling gaps, judges are developing the law.[156] However, that judges have a creative role and sometimes make new law has been widely accepted in common law jurisdictions as well.[157]

Prior to the decision of the Canadian Supreme Court, it was unclear whether foreign nationals could practice as lawyers in Canada. *It would only have taken one* of the three Supreme Court judges who voted in

---

[155] Cf. above, § 24 H, citation preceding n. 143.

[156] See above, § 24 n. 37–40.

[157] See for example Kenneth Einar Himma, Final Authority to Bind with Moral Mistakes: On the Explanatory Potential of Inclusive Legal Positivism, Law and Philosophy 24 (2005), p. 3 et seq.

favor of Andrews *to have voted differently*, and the legal situation in Canada would be *precisely the opposite*.

Waluchow himself acknowledges that standards of political morality like those found in the Canadian Charter can of course sometimes be subject to various kinds of indeterminacy: "In cases where indeterminacy figures, judges are thought to play a leading role in shaping the contours of the political morality legally recognized in the Charter. They do so, as they do in any other area of law where indeterminacy is encountered, by exercising their discretion and creating new legal rights. The exercise of this discretion should be, and normally is, sensitive to the linguistic, philosophic, and historical contexts within which rights of political morality are rooted. But this still leaves room for a measure of authoritative judicial creativity, for Thomistic 'determination'. In cases where such creativity is present, judges will do as the exclusive account claims they always do when Charter rights, whose interpretation requires appeal to political morality, are in play. They will create new legal rights and use these to invalidate existing legal rights. The Charter's regions of indeterminacy are perhaps greater than in many other areas of law where more closely textured terms are used, terms like 'vehicle', 'radio telegraph', and 'assault'. But terms like 'equality', 'discrimination', and 'liberty' are not so open-textured as to admit of no determinate meaning whatsoever."[158]

This is the perfect description of the judge's creative role with the sole exception that the exclusive account does not claim that terms like "equality", "discrimination", "liberty" have no significance. This has been shown above on the basis of sec. 15 of the Charter.[159]

A further objection raised against the exclusive account is that "… the existence and the content of a law, and the legal right or obligation it purports to establish, can never, under any circumstances and to any degree, be a function of moral considerations …"[160] This claim is unfounded. We have seen above[161] that judges both apply and develop the

---

[158] Waluchow, p. 159.
[159] Cf. above, § 24 H at n. 155.
[160] Waluchow, p. 156.
[161] § 12 A.I.

law; in doing the first, they apply their *legal* skills whereas in doing the second they use *moral* arguments. If a legal question is not covered by norms derivable from the legal sources, the law is indeterminate in this point. If judges decide such cases, they will inevitably break new *legal* ground, and their *decision develops new law*. Naturally, such decisions are at least in part based on *moral* and other non-legal considerations.[162]

The exclusive account, according to Waluchow, also stands in contradiction to sec. 52 (1) of the Constitution Act which states that the Constitution is the supreme law of Canada and that any law violating the constitution is not effective to the extent of the violation.[163] As a matter of course, violations would not only come into existence upon the judge's declaration of their existence.[164]

This objection may also be refuted by the adherent of exclusive positivism: of course, judicial decisions do have *retroactive* effect according to exclusive positivism. The law or the measure which is inconsistent with the Constitution is invalidated with *retroactive* effect, which means that it is deemed null and void from the outset.

Furthermore, Waluchow argues that exclusive positivism could not account for why a legal remedy "should be forthcoming following a successful Charter challenge."[165] The basis for such a remedy is provided by sec. 24 (1) of the Charter:

> **24.** (1) Anyone whose rights or freedoms, as guaranteed by this Charter, have been infringed or denied may apply to a court of competent jurisdiction to obtain such remedy as the court considers appropriate and just in the circumstances.

The reason for the failure of exclusive positivism is, in Waluchow's view, simple: according to this approach, no legal rights would have been infringed *before* the court decision was passed. All legal rights which might exist would only come into being *with* the Court's decision.[166] "But if so, then why should a remedy be forthcoming? The offending party

---

[162] Raz, AL, p. 48 et seqq.
[163] Waluchow, p. 159 et seq.
[164] Waluchow, p. 160.
[165] Waluchow, p. 162.
[166] Waluchow, p. 162.

violated no one's legal rights! He may have violated a moral right, but surely it is not the task of the judiciary to enforce non-legal, moral rights against perfectly valid legal rights."[167]

The rejoinder to this argument is obvious, too: if, according to exclusive positivism, the Court's decision renders the law in question invalid with retroactive effect, then the law is considered *invalid from the outset*. Hence, for instance, a criminal prosecution based on this invalid law is null and void from the outset as well, and is a viable ground for a legal remedy.

In reply to the question initially asked, we may thus conclude that the judges are, when interpreting constitutional rights of moral content, creating new law, as exclusive positivism claims. The difference from inclusive positivism is, however, minor, since Waluchow also concedes that Charter rights might be so inconclusive as to call for judicial creativity, and that in such cases, the judges are creating new legal rights. The difference between the two positions, therefore, is solely the following: according to exclusive positivism, the judges *always* create new law when the interpretation of Charter rights requires appeal to moral or other non-legal standards. According to the inclusive account, this is only necessary *in some cases*.

Let us now turn to the second issue raised in the beginning of this paragraph, viz. whether the content of the rule of recognition must be limited to *formal sources* such as legislation, case law and custom (in accordance with the sources thesis of exclusive positivism) or whether *moral contents* of constitutional rights may be included in the rule of recognition as well. Let us take the following example: the legislature of state X enacts a law by the formally correct procedure, prohibiting Muslim teachers at public schools from wearing an Islamic headscarf in class. This law is challenged as unconstitutional by the women teachers.

The Supreme Court of state X must first of all check the law for its formally correct enactment. This requirement we have already held as given. At this point, there is no difference between inclusive and exclu-

---

[167] Waluchow, p. 162.

sive positivism. It is equally easy to *identify* the relevant moral criterion. To do so, the Supreme Court must only look into whether the constitution of state X guarantees freedom of religion. It is much more difficult to assess whether the law violates the freedom of religion guaranteed by the constitution. According to the exclusive account, the judges are creating new law when a constitutional right requires appeal to moral considerations: if they come to the conclusion that the freedom of religion of the Muslim teachers is infringed, they will create *a new right for the latter which entitles them to wear a headscarf in class.* This new right was not fully evident from the guarantee of freedom of religion itself prior to the decision. The challenged law is, in the case at hand, *annulled with retroactive effect* and *deemed null and void from the beginning.* According to the inclusive account, freedom of religion is incorporated in the rule of recognition as an identification and validity criterion. Following this approach, the judges *discover* – also based on moral evaluation – *a right the Muslim teachers are already entitled to*. If, in the opinion of the court, a right of the Muslim teachers is infringed which is valid according to that moral criterion, they will state that the challenged law is invalid *ab initio.*

Given these circumstances, one must ask with regard to the two approaches: what is the difference which makes the difference?

An adherent of exclusive positivism would not deny either that it is not sufficient just to check for the formal requirements of a law, and that the judges must subsequently raise the question of the constitutionality of a law. And, with regard to the subject matter, an adherent of inclusive positivism would engage in the *same moral considerations* as the adherent of exclusive positivism. The inclusive positivist would, however, claim that he is discovering a right the Muslim teachers already have whereas the exclusive positivist would assert that he is *only granting* Muslim teachers their rights *by his decision.*

By way of the authority argument, however, Raz claims that it must be possible to identify orders emanating from an authority without recourse to the dependent reasons [e.g. moral considerations; authors' note] which the order purportedly decides. If this conception is applied to the law, it follows that the core of Charter Rights is authoritative in Raz's terms but not the penumbra. For prior to the judgment, the Muslim teachers would not know with certainty whether the prohibition on wearing a headscarf violates their right to freedom of religion. In order to do so, they would have to engage in moral considerations, and these are uncertain.

But does this confute the authoritative nature of the law? Scarcely. For the Supreme Court's decision is rendered in the form of an *official act* and can easily – without recourse to moral or other reasons – be *identified* by reference to *social facts alone*. It hereby meets the criteria of an authoritative act in terms of Raz, irrespective of its content. It emanates from a formal source in terms of the sources thesis, viz. from the case law.

More or less the same applies to Raz's functional argument. "It is an *essential* part of the function of law in society to mark the point at which a *private view* of members of the society, or influential sections or powerful groups in it, *ceases to be their private view and becomes* (i.e. lays a claim to be) a view binding on all members *notwithstanding their disagreement with it*. It does so and can only do so by providing *publicly ascertainable* ways of guiding behaviour and regulating aspects of social life."[168] It is correct that the behavior of the ordinary citizen can only be guided if it is possible to clearly, i.e. without the necessity of interpretation, determine the content of the rules applicable to them. However, if two parties are in conflict with one another, e.g. about contractual rights and duties, a court will have to decide authoritatively, even if this necessitates the interpretation of contractual or statutory regulations. And such a court decision will then replace the dependent reasons applicable to the parties before. Or: if the direction of somebody's conduct fails and this person commits a crime, a court will decide authoritatively on the gravity of guilt and the extent of the penalty. The reasons presented by the public prosecution and defense no longer count.

In other words: the fact that the civil, criminal and constitutional courts must interpret legal rules time and again does not change the authoritative character of their decisions. And in cases that are never taken to

---

[168] Raz, AL, p. 51 (our emphasis); a critical exploration of Raz's theory can be found in Martin, M., Judging Positivism, Oxford: Hart Publishing, 2014.

court, the authoritative character of the law is self-proving. Therefore, inclusive positivism cannot be refuted by means of the functional argument.

The same holds true for the sufficiency component endorsed by Dworkin and Coleman I,[169] i.e. the claim that there are legal standards which owe their status as law to their being true moral principles although their truth cannot be demonstrated (e.g. "no man should profit from his own wrong"). At the moment a court draws on such a principle in order to justify its opinion, it is authoritatively deciding on the validity of this principle in a legal system and, as a result, it renders the question of the truth of the principle obsolete.

From this it can be concluded that although the controversy between exclusive and inclusive positivism is theoretically important, it is of hardly any significance for the solution of practical cases subject to constitutional jurisdiction. The examples of the Muslim headscarf case and Andrews have made this quite clear. Following exclusive positivism, one may say that the sources of law are of purely formal nature and that constitutional constraints of moral content are not to be included in the rule of recognition. One may, however, also argue that these constitutional constraints of moral content are to be ranked as part of the rule of recognition since they represent identification and validity criteria just like the formal sources. The fact that they are usually vaguer than formal criteria does not necessarily militate against this conception held by inclusive positivism. For the decision of the constitutional court interpreting a fundamental right is, again, of authoritative nature, even in terms of exclusive positivism. Both positions are conceivable although in our judgment, exclusive positivism gives a more realistic account of constitutional jurisdiction. The ambivalence of both positions is evident also from the fact that Hart, as we have seen, originally supported soft positivism, which he later, in the Postscript to the Second Edition of the Concept of Law, called into question. For, he argues, it is an open question whether moral values have an objective standing and therefore, it

---

[169] Cf. above, § 12 B.IV at n. 44.

must remain an open question whether or not to include moral criteria in the rule of recognition.[170]

The reasons why we ultimately lean towards exclusive positivism, apart from the more realistic account of constitutional jurisdiction already mentioned, are the following:

As we have seen above, all variants of legal positivism which are based on Hart subscribe to the social fact thesis[171] which is supplemented by the conventionality thesis.[172] According to this thesis, the validity criteria of the rule of recognition rest upon a *social convention* amongst the persons which hold *official* functions. The existence of such convention is dependent upon whether the officials apply (external aspect) as well as accept (internal aspect) the validity criteria. From the standpoint of inclusive positivism, such a convention would also have to cover – apart from the formal validity criteria – the *contents of fundamental rights*. This is hardly feasible, however, since the officials cannot at any point in time foresee which problems will be submitted to the constitutional court in the future. Therefore, the social convention could only embrace the *legal frame* of the fundamental rights. This frame may be kept general, if, for example, the constitution states: "Every individual is equal before and under the law without discrimination." Such a provision would leave the interpretation almost entirely to the courts. The legal frame may, however, be considerably more precise as we have seen with Sect. 15 of the Canadian Charter of Rights and Freedoms.[173] Here, the leeway of the courts would be narrower. According to exclusive positivism, the social convention could, in contrast, only cover the *legal frame* of the fundamental rights, *but not their moral content*, to begin with. For this reason, it seems advisable not to incorporate moral contents as identification and validity criteria into the rule of recognition but to limit the latter to formal sources as demanded by exclusive positivism.[174] This result is independent of whether moral values have an objective standing

---

[170] Hart, Concept of Law, p. 254 and above, § 11 at n. 56.
[171] § 12 B.I.
[172] § 12 B.II.
[173] Cf. above, § 24 , text below n. 142.
[174] Cf. above.

or not. For even if one could justify moral judgments just as well as all other judgments, it would be impossible for officials to foresee which questions will be submitted to the constitutional court in the *future*. One cannot know about the future, one can only speculate.

If the fundamental rights with moral content are listed as in the USA or in Canada in the Amendments to the US Constitution or in the Canadian Charter of Rights and Freedoms, the judge can simply look through these lists and know which rights are guaranteed in his country. The philosophical problem of justifying such rights does not arise for him thus far. For although these rights have moral content, their *legal framework* can still be incorporated into the rule of recognition; for this is *source-based*. However, the problem of interpretation arises subsequently in any case, and here the judge must engage in moral considerations. But there is no theory which circumvents this problem. – It is a different matter, then, when a principle is exclusively *content-based*. In this case the concerns according to Hart's later view are justified, and it is wiser not to take such a criterion into the rule of recognition before it has been positivized through legislation or legal adjudication.

Moreover it is a fact that some substantive issues about the content of the law are controversial. For the United States of America, Himma mentions the questions regarding the permissibility of abortion and capital punishment. In such cases, somebody must be authorized to have the final word. It is uncontested that legal systems such as those of Great Britain, Canada as well as the United States grant such authority to a court.[175] If, however, the rule of recognition grants a court general legal authority to bind officials with either one of two conflicting decisions on whether something is in compliance with the moral principle P, then P can no longer function as a sufficient or as a necessary validity criterion. For then the officials practice a rule according to which they are bound to recognize as law *whatever the courts have declared to be in compliance with P*. If the respective criterion was written out in the rule of recognition, it would *no longer be content-based but source-based*.[176]

---

[175] Himma, Final Authority, p. 3.
[176] Himma, Final Authority, p. 30 et seq.

I. The Merits and Demerits of MacCormick's and Weinberger's Institutional Theory of Law[177]

A first plus to be highlighted is that Weinberger and MacCormick are among the critical positivists who are aware of the "axiomatic" character of their theory. Thus, according to Weinberger, the institutional view is based on *stipulations*; the ontological and conceptual framework of ITL has in principle a stipulative character.[178] For MacCormick, too, conclusions are substantiable only within theoretical frameworks which are essentially constructs and therefore, for their part, not justifiable in the same way.[179] The question is consequently not whether the institutional or the traditional ontology is true but which ontology fits certain realities better. The two authors also openly disclose the underlying *Weltanschauung* on which ITL is based: it is that of a skeptical and relativistic *Weltanschauung*, viz. ethical non-cognitivism.[180] Therefore they do not – as institutional theories often tend to do[181] – gloss over the "mists of the institutional" with a seemingly scientific vocabulary. Furthermore, the separation of law and morals as well as the non-derivability postulates guarantee that the factual is not per se legitimized as that which ought to be: MacCormick and Weinberger do not allege that what is in reality is also reasonable. In contrast to the continental European positivist theories, ITL acknowledges to a certain degree the possibility of rational *de lege ferenda* argumentation: viz. (a) by analysis of the contextual relations between the relevant facts and by analysis of the consequences of our actions and (b) by assessment of the inner consistency of our value judgments.[182] To this extent, the adherent of ITL can, therefore, contribute to the question of how future law is to be shaped even though according to this theory, the decisive points are switched by statements which are cognitively not provable. Furthermore, ITL must be singled out for

---

[177] Literature: MacCormick/Weinberger, ITL; idem, IRP; Rüthers, Entartetes Recht; idem, Neues zum institutionellen Rechtsdenken? – Einige Literaturhinweise, Zeitschrift für Rechtssoziologie 8 (1987), p. 139 et seqq., especially 141 et seqq.

[178] Weinberger, IRP 18.

[179] MacCormick, IRP 58.

[180] See above, § 13.

[181] Cf. Rüthers, Zeitschrift für Rechtssoziologie 8 (1987), p. 147.

[182] See above, § 13.

special praise for taking a balanced position beyond normativism and realism.[183]

The main advantage of this theory is that it is not exposed to the argument from principle from the start.[184] If positive law comprises not only explicitly enacted primary and secondary rules, in Hart's sense, but also legal principles, rules of interpretation, even the entire teleological underpinning of the legal system as long as they are effective in the argumentation of legal practice, these elements must neither be interpreted as a natural law nor as parts of positive morality. This means that problems of interpretation and gap-filling become resolvable on the level of the positive law. To some extent, ITL can provide criteria for the identification of legal principles: sometimes, legal principles may be established directly on the basis of positivized legal rules or on the basis of precedents in the form of *rationes decidendi*, and sometimes also indirectly by way of abstraction from positive legal norms and precedents.[185] If, however, one does not succeed in delivering such proof, there is no clear criterion of pedigree by means of which one could identify legal principles. In such cases, what remains is a pointer that the judge is allowed to make a discretionary decision on the basis of his own moral judgments. As any positivist theory, ITL fails the judge as well as the legislator if the issue at stake is to develop the law with regard to so far unknown problems.

Furthermore, the partial breakaway from purely formal validity criteria, at least by Weinberger,[186] results in a broadening of the *observation perspective*. This has the advantage that the reality of a legal system is seen in a more comprehensive sense and can be better described thus than on the basis of the constricting conventional view. Take, for example, the reality of the legal system of National Socialism: if both its teleological background and legal doctrine, to the extent that these elements have a positive-social existence, also rank as positive law, then the *Führer*'s will, the people's community identified and defined by race *("artbe-*

---

[183] See above, § 13.
[184] See above, § 22 D.
[185] Cf. Weinberger, Gedächtnisschrift für René Marcic, p. 500 et seq.
[186] MacCormick's position in this point remains unclear.

stimmte Volksgemeinschaft"), the party program of the NSDAP, the National Socialist worldview and sound popular feeling *("gesundes Volksempfinden")* may all be understood as sources of law, as per the National Socialist legal doctrine.[187] Thus, ITL is suited to capturing and describing indisputable realities in relation to the law.

As much as this approach is advantageous from the perspective of the observer, its impact is fatal if one switches to the *perspective of the participant*. The partial breakaway from clear positivist pedigree criteria for the identification of valid law by Weinberger entails that, for example, Hitler's secret letter of authorization dated 1 September 1939, which was the basis for the euthanasia operations on mentally handicapped and mentally ill persons as well as invalid patients in sanatoriums and care homes, must be understood as valid law.[188] For in this case, we are undoubtedly dealing with "practical information which has obtained positive-social existence" in the sanatoriums and care homes. That in the institutional sense, it is a legal norm rather than any other form of social norm, is evident from the fact that legal doctrine – as has been mentioned above – declared the *Führer*'s will a source of law.[189] No doctor could have been held to have acted illegally on the basis that Hitler's letter of authorization was not valid law, not having been published in the *Reichsgesetzblatt* (and lacking recognition by the population).[190]

The analogue is true for the "Final Solution of the Jewish Problem" *(Endlösung der Judenfrage)*. The question of when the Holocaust decision was made is controversial among historians. Some indicate March 1941, others September/October 1941, but the majority view tends to-

---

[187] Rüthers, Entartetes Recht, p. 27 et seq., with numerous references.

[188] For wording of the authorization see above, n. 180.

[189] Rüthers, Entartetes Recht, p. 28 et seq. with further references.

[190] The legal character of said letter has rightly been denied from a formal point of view already by the OLG Frankfurt, Süddeutsche Juristenzeitung 2 (1947), p. 623/624. Furthermore, the OLG argues that a secret order could never partake of recognition by the citizens. Such recognition is, however, constitutive for the order's legal character. Cf. Süddeutsche Juristenzeitung 2 (1947), p. 625/626.

wards 31 July 1941, based on a letter from Göring to SS General Heydrich bearing that date.[191]

The German historian Christian Gerlach, on the other hand, refers to a confidential speech given by Hitler on 12 December 1941.[192] According to this account, Hitler is said to have delivered a speech to the approximately 50 *Gauleiter* and *Reichsleiter* (political heads of districts), the highest council of the NSDAP in his private rooms in the *Reichskanzlei* (Chancellery of the Reich). The content of this speech is known to us inter alia through a diary entry by the Reich Minister of Propaganda, Joseph Goebbels, dated 13 December 1941, as well as through a *Regierungstagebuch* (protocol of the Reich government) entry dated 16 December 1941 by the Governor-General of occupied Poland, Hans Frank: *Hitler did not order but had authorized what had already been practiced in many places.* By 12 December 1941, a million Jews had already been killed.

This example shows that the extinction of the Jews had also begun *without any positively ascertainable basis* and was later based upon a *confidential* speech by Hitler or on the *circular letter* of the Reich Security Main Office mentioned above. In contrast to other positivist theories, ITL arrives here at a different conclusion. From an institutional point of view, the confidential speech and the circular decree were valid law. As a result, nobody involved in the "Final Solution" could have been accused of violating the law in force back then by participating in the ex-

---

[191] The letter which sounds harmless to the uninitiated is worded as follows:
"Supplementing the task assigned to you by the decree of January 24, 1939 [reference is made to a written communication by Göring to Reichsinnenminister Frick, which was thus not understood as 'simple letter'; authors' note], to solve the Jewish problem by means of emigration and evacuation in the best possible way according to present conditions, I hereby charge you to carry out preparations as regards organizational, financial, and material matters for a total solution (Gesamtlösung) of the Jewish question in all the territories of Europe under German occupation.
Where the competency of other central organizations touches on this matter, these organizations are to collaborate..."
Quoted from H.G. Adler, Der verwaltete Mensch, Studien zur Deportation der Juden aus Deutschland, Tübingen: Mohr, 1974, p. 84 et seq. (Translation cf. http://www.historyplace.com/worldwar2/timeline/order1.htm).
[192] http://www.holocaust-history.org/december-12-1941/

termination of the Jews. Any person involved could have appealed to these sources by way of justification.[193]

Here once again, it is evident that the value of different positions of legal theory must be rated differently depending on the goals they are used to pursue. The more suitable a legal theory is for treating a theoretical issue (for example sociology of law, history of law, and ethnology of law), the less suitable it is for the solution of directly practical issues, and vice-versa. Thus, ITL will be ascribed a high degree of suitability for the depiction of realities close to the law, and at the same time its suitability for the direct solution of practical problems will be poorly rated.

The authors did not succeed, either, in developing a position beyond natural law and legal positivism. Although ITL stands beyond natural law theories, it falls within the realm of positivism – as the English subtitle "New Approaches to Legal Positivism" as well as the German term *"Institutionalistischer Rechtspositivismus"* reveal. ITL represents a strong version of legal positivism in the sense explained above (i.e. it combines an ethically neutral concept of law with ethical relativism in the supra-positive sphere).[194] Such a conception is neither compatible with a strong version of natural law theory (i.e. natural law derogates from contradictory rules of the positive law) nor with a weak version of natural law theory (i.e. natural law is a standard against which positive law is rated). A reconciliation of natural law and positivism is only possible if one combines a weak version of natural law theory with a weak version of legal positivism, just as British legal positivism (Hobbes, Bentham, Austin, Hart) has always done; i.e. by using an ethically neutral concept of law and at the same approving of the possibility of practical cognition in the sense of natural law or a rational foundation of morals.

---

[193] Cf. above, text following n. 180. Note that institutional positivism did not have to be considered in the above deliberations since this conception was developed decades after World War II.

[194] Above, § 15 B.II at the end, and § 13 n. 8 regarding Weinberger's position.

Concluding Remarks:
Natural Law as a Cultural Creation

In this book, we have attempted to show that the endeavors of legal philosophers in general and of legal positivists in particular may be understood as a fundamentally meaningful undertaking *even if one acts on the assumption of an epistemic positivism* (this would be true *a fortiori* if one were to choose a less strictly epistemic position as a starting basis). Nobody has pointed out the one true path so far, and presumably nobody will be able to show a universally acceptable route in the foreseeable future. However, on the basis of the interpretation developed here, one may extract a meaning from legal philosophy in any case even if one takes the strictest demands on human cognition as a basis, viz. those of philosophical positivism.

If one proceeds on this assumption, then legal philosophy – unlike the single sciences – is not concerned with finding truths. Legal philosophies convey neither cognition nor knowledge. Rather, they are theoretical constructs which have been developed for achieving certain goals. They are to be judged by whether – in the light of these presupposed goals – they lead to acceptable or unacceptable consequences, but not by whether they are true or false. Our analysis of the legal positivist theories has shown that the results of such an assessment can differ greatly depending on the issue to which an individual theory is applied. The choice of particular approaches yields varying results which are suitable for some sets of problems but not for others.

Therefore, future efforts should be targeted less on devising the one and only theory which solves all problems of the law. Rather, one should try to work with a plurality of theoretical approaches, and not in an arbitrary manner but in the knowledge of *why this particular* approach was chosen over another approach to solve *a particular* problem.

On the basis of the suggested interpretation of legal philosophy, the idealist legal philosophies (not embraced by this book), particularly the natural law theories, appear in another light. They are *creations* of occidental culture, if not of other cultures also.[1] If one proceeds on the assumption of a positivist concept of cognition *(which – as we have seen – is not imperative)*,[2] human rights in the sense of legal entitlements vis à vis the state are not something innate to every person, irrespective of their culture, from the outset. Thus, the natural lawyers who have postulated the human rights have not *discovered* something which has always been there, but rather *created* what had not been there before. *Human rights are thus based on a cultural innovation, not on a scientific discovery. So-called natural law does not emanate from nature, but from culture. It is not a natural law, but a cultural law!* It does not make sense, therefore, to allege that freedom of religion is innate to a member of a pre-state tribal society. For freedom of religion only becomes important in a certain context: viz. when the unity of religion has broken up, as is the case, for example, in Western European society since the Reformation. In tribal communities, however, unity of faith prevails. Furthermore, freedom of religion is a right which is primarily directed against the state. A pre-state tribal society lacks this quality as well. In the same way, one can only speak of freedom of the press where there is a press. Before the invention of the press, there could not be any press freedom, either.

Therefore, the question to be directed at a natural law theory – just as at any other legal philosophy – is not: is it true or is it false? (unless there is a *contradiction in terms* or the theory contains *propositions disproved by experience. Then such a theory is not only non-useful but false*[3]) but: what would adherence to such philosophy mean for our lives and for

---

[1] Apparently, there are no more than two standards which are valid in almost all cultures: viz. the prohibition on killing members of *one's own* group (with exceptions such as, for example, capital punishment) and the prohibition on practicing sexual relations between close blood relatives (so-called incest taboos). Cf. F.H. Schmidt, Verhaltensforschung und Recht, Berlin: Duncker & Humblot, 1982, p. 90 et seqq., 169, 172 et seq. Cultures with settled forms of life additionally know "*in rem*" relations to movable things and land. Cf. Simon Roberts, Order and Dispute. An Introduction to Legal Anthropology, Harmondsworth (etc.): Penguin Books, 1979, p. 100 et seq. *To this extent, natural law theories are not cultural creations but expressions of supra-cultural standards.*

[2] Cf. above, and introduction to § 16 .

[3] Cf. above, § 21 , text preceding n. 9.

extra-human nature? A legal philosophy – as consistent and well-founded as it may otherwise be – will never be accepted by jurists in the long run if it does not prove of value in the practical world, in the fray of everyday life and legal practice. This practical test consists, firstly, in asking what the consequences would presumably be if, in a given context, one set out from this theory or another; in then evaluating the relative desirability of these consequences; and, finally, in developing a philosophy whose consequences would be preferable to the consequences of the other theories. *Thus, a legal philosophy and, in particular, a natural law theory is acceptable if it proves its worth through its practical (or theoretical) consequences.*

Over the course of history, unacceptable theories of natural law (e.g. the right of the strongest in Calicles or the justification of slavery in Aristotle) and acceptable theories of natural law (e.g. the theory of innate human rights) have been developed. Thus the most important innovations to our legal and constitutional order that we hold dear go back to the natural law of Enlightenment thinkers of the 17th and 18th centuries. These ideas proved remarkably fruitful. Essentially we are still drawing from this wellspring. Although these natural law theories do not represent collections of truths, particularly eternal truths, nevertheless they are *sense-outlines* for shaping human existence; and as such, they are accorded a function which is indispensable – in defiance of all the "realism" that is so fashionable today.

The concerns of both the idealist and the realist-positivist philosopher would be answered if one could transform

> the *ideality* of the idealist's conceptions into the *positivity* of law, so as to meet the positivist's demand for *objectivity* in the identification of law.

In short, our appeal for the future is this:

> *To pursue objectivity of ideality through positivity!*

Summary and Results

1. According to the conception developed in the First Part of this work, our decisive criterion for the classification of the different variants of legal positivism can be identified with what we call the "positivity of law in the broader sense".[1] The characteristics of positivity are at the same time the distinguishing features of each respective theory's concept of law.

On the basis of this criterion, three main types of legal positivism may be distinguished, viz. analytical, psychological and sociological positivism. An exceptional position is held by Hart's theory, inclusive and exclusive positivism on the one hand, and by Weinberger's and MacCormick's institutional theory of law on the other, all of which combine elements of the three main groups.

2. The analytical positivisms (above, § 2–4) basically identify the positivity of the law with the setting or imposition of rules by a state authority.

For Austin, the law consists of the epitome of all commands set or imposed by the highest political authority, the sovereign of an independent political society, upon its subjects. Unlike an ordinary request, a command is characterized by the fact that it is backed by threats and that the sovereign may enforce it by imposing an evil in case of disobedience. Furthermore, Austin emphatically stresses the conceptual (analytical/logical) separation between the law as it is and the law as it ought to be, i.e. between law and morals, characteristic of any positivist theory: from the fact that a rule violates principles of morality it cannot be concluded that it is not a legal rule; and from the fact that a rule is morally desirable it cannot necessarily be inferred that it is a legal rule. However, critics of legal positivism usually omit the fact that, according to the positivist view, there is an *empirical* relation between law and morals: moral conceptions have an impact on law, and conversely, the law has an impact on moral ideas.[2]

---

[1] § 1 B.II and § 1 B.V, scheme on p. 8.
[2] See above, § 11 text at n. 8 and § 15 text at n. 25.

For German statutory positivism, the law is all and only that which has been promulgated as law by the respective ruler of a state according to the formally correct procedure. Furthermore, a particular law application theory is characteristic of German statutory positivism: the application of law shall amount to nothing more than sheer deduction from the norms of the statutory system, which is interpreted as a self-contained, gapless whole.

For the pure theory of law, the law is a normative and coercion-threatening system set in place by men, which is by and large effective. Since Kelsen always understands validity in the sense of normative validity, the ultimate reason for the validity of such a system cannot consist in a fact but only in a norm. This basic norm which does not actually exist but is only presupposed hypothetically, says that one ought to behave in conformity with what the *historically first* constitution and the norms created in accordance with it prescribe. The "point of imputation" in which the unity of the legal system is expressed is nothing but the state in the juridical sense. Understood like this, the state is identical with the legal system.

3. Psychological positivism (§ 5 and § 6) identifies the positivity of the law in certain contents of feeling and consciousness:

The so-called theories of *individual* recognition (Bierling, Laun) are based on the recognition of each single norm-addressee; the theories of *general* recognition (Merkel, Jellinek) on the recognition of the majority of norm-addressees. A centre position is taken by Beling's and Nawiasky's theories, which deem the ideas of the *leading class* that sets the tone to be authoritative.

Scandinavian legal realism, which is characterized by a particular hostility towards metaphysics, sees positivity in a psychological reality, viz. in imperatively operating notions of behavior which are expressed in the legislative and judicial material. It is the task of legal science to identify these contents of consciousness by means of linguistic analysis. With Ross, who attempts a synthesis between the psychological and the sociological approach, legal norms are characterized by being felt as binding by the judges (psychological aspect) and therefore being applied (sociological aspect). Jurisprudence is a branch of psychology and sociology; the propositions which it brings forth are predictions of some future judicial behavior which may be verified or falsified by experience.

4. Sociological positivism (above, §§ 7–10) identifies the positivity of the law with certain human behavior patterns, viz. the behavior patterns of the so-called group members or of the so-called "law staff".

According to Ehrlich, the main emphasis of law development is neither on legislation nor on jurisprudence nor on judicial decisions but *on society* itself. What Ehrlich calls social law consists of the rules with which the people in fact align their behavior. Such rules are supported by an *"opinio necessitatis"* and trigger a *feeling of revulsion* in case they are violated (theory of feeling). Apart from the norms of the social law, Ehrlich also knows the norm complexes of the juristic law and of the state law; all these classes of norms combined constitute the so-called "living law".

The sociological coercion theory (Weber, Geiger), on the other hand, is based on the existence of a *specific law staff*. The law is the order which is guaranteed by the probability that in case of breach of norm, a staff of people holding themselves ready especially for that purpose will react by applying a characteristic coercion. The validity of the law in terms of the sociological coercion theory is the probability of the occurrence of some specific coercion, exerted by a staff of people who stand by in readiness for that express purpose.

In the case of certain forms of American legal realism, not only the positivity of the law, but the law as such is identified with the behavior of certain people, especially of judicial officials. According to another variant of American legal realism, the law consists of the prophecies of what the courts are likely to do in fact (Holmes). The validity of such "rules of description and prediction" (Llewellyn) may be verified by the observation of judicial behavior.

5. A centre position between the main forms of legal positivism is taken by the theories of Hart (§ 11) as well as inclusive and exclusive positivism (§ 12), on the one hand, and of MacCormick and Weinberger (§ 13) on the other hand. According to Hart, the law consists of the so-called

primary rules which motivate individuals to a certain behavior (e.g. the rules of the criminal law) and the *secondary rules* which confer private or public power (e.g. the rules regarding legislative powers). The most important secondary rule is the "rule of recognition" which contains the ultimate *identification and validity* criteria of a system. The rule of recognition exists in the form of a complex, but normally concordant, practice by courts, officials, and private persons of identifying the law with reference to certain criteria. For Hart, the positivity of the law consists on the one hand in the psychological fact that the officials accept the rule of recognition (the internal aspect) and, on the other hand, in the sociological fact of its application by them (the external aspect). It is sufficient if the ordinary people only by and large comply with the primary rules. Thus Hart's theory contains psychological, sociological and analytical elements. It coincides with German statutory positivism and the pure theory of law in being based on a normative validity concept.

In the aftermath of Dworkin's criticism of Hart's theory, analytical legal philosophy faced up to the question of whether the rule of recognition in Hart's sense can incorporate moral values as ultimate criteria for legal validity (above, § 12). This led to the emergence of two new doctrinal trends: whilst the proponents of *exclusive positivism* dismiss the incorporation of moral values, the adherents of *inclusive positivism* consider their incorporation possible though not necessary. Like any other validity criteria forming part of the rule of recognition, moral values must be expressed in the concordant practice of the legal officials.

Campbell's Legal Theory of Ethical Positivism does not change the concept of law in H.L.A. Hart's sense, either.[3]

According to Weinberger's and MacCormick's institutional theory of law (§ 13), the law comprises not only the explicitly given primary and secondary rules in Hart's sense, but also the so-called principles of law, indeed, the whole teleological background of the law (e.g. postulates of justice), as well as legal doctrine, in so far as these elements have a positive social existence, i.e. have become effective in legal practice.

---

[3] § 14 in the end.

6. At the end of the First Part, an attempt is made to develop a useful concept of legal positivism (above, § 14 and § 15). The following features are mentioned as characteristic of all positivist theories:

First: it is characteristic of all positivist theories that they try to do without metaphysical assumptions. They refrain in particular from presupposing the existence of God, a world of absolute ideas or values, a teleologically determined nature or an invariable nature of mankind and/or from searching for the "nature", the "idea" or the "essence" of the law.

Second: all legal positivists define the law with reference to physical realities, i.e. facts of the spatiotemporal external world (social fact thesis), and/or with reference to psychological realities, i.e. facts of the mental inner world. This entails the following two consequences: law can only ever be something which – in one of the ways explained above – has become positive, i.e. real. All law is positive, and only positive law is law. And: the law as it now exists, i.e. has become positive within the terms of a particular theory, is to be strictly separated conceptually (analytically/logically) from the law as it ought to be (the positivist separation thesis). A norm cannot lose its legal quality simply by force of being deemed immoral from a higher standpoint. Conversely, Coleman II most recently advocated the connection thesis.[4]

Third: all positivist theories exhibit a relativist tendency. They are not based on characteristics which remain unchanged but on variable factors, viz. on what the respective sovereign promulgates, for example, or what the majority of the citizens of a particular society recognize, or the behavior of certain persons in a society. This leads of course to a relativization of the contents of law. The interim result this yields is that the German conceptual jurisprudence of the 19th century may not be rated as positivist in this sense since it did not have a relativist leaning.

7. All legal positivist theories are implicitly or explicitly based on the premises of general philosophical positivism. In the Second Part, we investigated whether one of these theories may be proved true from the standpoint of a modern positivist epistemology. From such a position,

---

[4] Cf. § 15 D above.

only logical-empirical methods are appropriate for the verification or falsification of scientific statements (above, § 16–18). In doing so one must keep in mind that this basic requirement of philosophical positivism is based upon a convention which cannot itself be proved by the logical-empirical method (above, § 18 A). A proposition is deemed logically true only on condition that it can be proved true by means of the presupposed axioms, definitions, non-defined basic terms and rules of inference of a deductive system. On the other hand, a statement is considered empirically true if it can be integrated without contradiction within the lawful context of a multitude of perception statements and certain theoretical premises. Contrary to widespread opinion, the application of logical-empirical methods is not confined to the natural sciences. The validation of the adequacy of such an understanding of science for jurisprudence is, however, beyond the scope of this work; the authors' sole concern is to be on the same level as the legal positivists who, in all events, all built – consciously or unconsciously – on this understanding of science.

In accordance with the conception developed in the First Part, the various legal positivist theories differ most of all in how they define positivity and (closely related to that) the law itself. The respective concepts of positivity in the broader sense[5] and of the law necessarily result in different theories. The question of whether one of the legal positivist theories can be proved true is therefore reduced to the question of whether one of the legal positivist *definitions* of the law can be proved true. For this purpose, we revert to the modern theory of definition (above, § 19 and § 20). According to the concept of cognition developed in the First Part, only logical-empirical methods are considered for verification or falsification. The most important kinds of definition are assertions regarding an existing linguistic usage (analytical definitions), real definitions as well as stipulations of a certain linguistic usage (synthetic definitions). Analytical definitions are determinations (not stipulations) of the meaning which a word has or of the use that it has. The words "bumblebee", "wife" and "stallion" were quoted as examples. The positivist definitions of the law cannot be such analytic definitions, however, be-

---

[5]   § 1 B.II and § 1 B.V., scheme on p. 8.

cause in habitual language use – as is shown – the word "law" is used to denote quite disparate phenomena. All positivist definitions eliminate the ideal meaning of the word and locate their concepts in the normative and/ or factual sphere, without implying that any one of them could claim to give an all-embracing account of the actual use in language. Real definitions, on the other hand, are *not definitions in the strict sense but empirical descriptions* of an object that is already sufficiently identified. An example of this would be the definition of "myopia". The problem of defining the law in the sense of a real definition is that a real definition is only possible if the object to be described has already been sufficiently identified on the basis of language usage or a pragmatic agreement. The first possibility is disqualified from consideration, as we have shown; as regards the second option, the real definition is relatively insignificant compared to whatever prior convention has been reached. For this shifts the decisive question up a level, to the matter of what linguistic convention one should agree upon. The positivist definitions of the law can therefore only be what are known as synthetic definitions, i.e. conventions which stipulate the meaning of the word "law". Thus, they do not assert anything which could be proven true or false, but rather, they are postulates; they do not determine what the law is but they posit a certain meaning of the word law. The example of the updated stipulation of the concept of death in modern medicine demonstrates that characterizing a definition as a regulation of conventional language use does not imply a free ticket for arbitrariness. Therefore, the so-called "*axiomatic" character* of legal positivism is constituted in all theories being ultimately reducible to postulates which, in themselves, – measured against the concept of cognition adopted by philosophical positivism – are not verifiable or falsifiable. *Consequently there are no ultimate justifications, neither in the exact sciences nor, most certainly, in philosophy*.

8. It would nevertheless be premature to conclude from this that the development of a legal positivist theory is a misguided enterprise from the start. For, as we show in the Third Part, it is possible to develop an interpretation which makes the endeavors of the legal positivists appear a fundamentally meaningful undertaking (above, § 21). This corresponds to the interpretation of legal philosophical thinking which we name "*Ax-*

iomatic Theory of Law" in this work. Unless a legal theory contains empirically wrong statements or logical contradictions (§ 20 C), according to our conception, legal philosophical theorems do not convey cognition but are constructs, which – unlike empirical scientific theories – are not subject to the truth criterion but are to be accepted or rebutted *on the basis of their own consequences*. The value of legal philosophical thoughts consists therefore not in their scientific truth but in their *usefulness for attaining theoretical or practical goals*.

Hence, the line of inquiry in the third part of this book does not ask to what extent the legal positivist theories are true and to what extent they are false, but seeks to ascertain their merits and demerits, i.e. what they are suited for and what they are not (above, § 22–24). The most fundamental point of contention within the positivist discussion so far has been the dispute regarding the separation thesis, principally in the light of the experiences during the Third Reich. Positivism is accused of surrendering the law to whatever power holds sway, and thus opening the floodgates to political abuse (we call it the *"Hitler argument"*). The allegation, first raised by Radbruch, that legal positivism, and in particular German statutory positivism, was responsible for the legal desolation under National Socialism,[6] is demonstrably false if one looks at the historical facts. As shown above,[7] statutory positivism had already lost its pre-eminence during the Weimar Republic, and National Socialist legal thought was diametrically opposed to positivist thinking. The technique favored by the Nazis of inserting masses of general clauses into their laws (for example the notorious "sound popular feeling" in § 2 of the Penal Code in the version of 28 June 1935), the open abolition of the principle of *nulla poena sine lege*[8] (in the same part of the Code), the numerous interventions in penal proceedings against SS and SA members, the mass killings of patients in *Heil- und Pflegeanstalten* based on the *Führer*'s secret Euthanasia Order dated 1 September 1939[9] as well as the genocide of the Jews[10] met none of the statutory positivist criteria

---

[6] See above, § 23 A.
[7] § 23 D.
[8] See above, § 23 at n. 174.
[9] See above, § 23 n. 180 and § 24 I , text at n. 188.
[10] See above, § 24 I.

whatsoever. The fact that the majority of German jurists served the National Socialist "renewal" is to be explained rather by *their authoritarian way of thinking, since Bismarck's reform of the judiciary*, and by *their anti-democratic and anti-liberal views*, coupled with *massive interference in the judicial domain* by the *political leadership*.

Those theories which arrive at the conclusion that inhumane law can have legal quality are transferring the problem from the legal into the moral realm. In concrete terms, this means that a judge would be *legally* but not *morally* obliged to apply an inhumane law. However, since a judge – especially after the collapse of a state that misused the rule of law – will be willing to refuse the application of law more easily if he possesses not just moral but also legal criteria to justify his refusal, it seems to the authors that regarding this issue, a non-positivist approach including certain minimal guarantees in the relevant concept of law is a better solution (except for criminal cases, due to the prohibition of retroactive criminal laws).

An ethically enriched concept of law facilitates the process of remedying statutory lawlessness following the collapse of a state that misused the rule of law. In such cases, the separation thesis leads to inequitable results, as was shown and exemplified above (§ 23 C.I.2). Furthermore, as we also set out in detail above (§ 22–24), other merits shared by all positivist legal theories are that they define the object of their investigations by means of verifiable criteria, and have directed our attention to the *real factors of law-making*. On the other hand, they almost all – the exceptions being Hart's theory, inclusive and exclusive positivism as well as Weinberger's and MacCormick's institutional theory of law – share the demerit of being too one-sided in certain respects, and of making either normative or psychological or sociological aspects absolute. However, as regards the efficacy of the various legal positivist theories for the understanding of certain issues, this has to be assessed for each theory individually. The results of such an assessment will vary considerably depending on what kind of theory is applied to which set of problems. A theory may be useful for addressing one issue (e.g. development of a concept of law that is useful to the judge, illumination of the structure of legal norms), but not for handling another issue (e.g. accounting for the legal character of international law, apprehending the process of judicial interpretation or developing a concept of law that is seminal for legal sociological and legal historical research). From this it follows that it may cause big problems to try to lump all kinds of phenomena together in one concept of law.

On the basis of the suggested interpretation of the "axiomatic approach to law", the natural law theories which have not been discussed in this work also appear in a different light. They are *creations* of occidental culture (and perhaps other cultures, too). The natural lawyers who postulated (for example) human rights did not discover something pre-existent but created something hitherto non-existent. Human rights are based on *cultural creation*, not on *scientific discovery*. The question to be addressed to a natural law theory – as for any other legal theory – is not whether it is true or whether it is right. On the contrary, we can only find out if a legal philosophy, especially a natural law theory, is acceptable by asking whether, *by virtue of its practical and/or its theoretical consequences, it proves its worth*.

In the course of human history, unacceptable natural law theories have been developed. Amongst the unacceptable natural law theories were, for example, Callicles's power of the stronger or the justification of slavery by Aristotle; acceptable natural law theories like the theory of innate human rights have also been developed. So the most important innovations of our own legal and state order date back to the natural law theory of the Enlightenment of the 17th and 18th century. These ideas have proved incredibly fruitful. Essentially we are still feeding from this source. Though these natural law theories are not a collection of truths, especially eternal truths, they are still ideal conceptions for the ordering of human existence by means of law; and as such they have a function which is indispensable – in defiance of all modern insistence on realism.

Both the idealist's conceptions and the concerns of the realist-positivist philosopher would be addressed if one could transform the *ideality* of the idealist's conceptions into the *positivity* of law, so as to meet the positivist's demand for *objectivity* in the identification of law. In short, our appeal for the future is this:

To pursue objectivity of ideality through positivity!

311

Select Bibliography

Alchourrón, C.E./*Bulygin,* E.: Normative Systems, Vienna/New York: Springer, 1971.

Alexy, R., The Argument from Injustice – A reply to Legal Positivism, first published as: Begriff und Geltung des Rechts, translated by Bonnie Litschewski Paulson and Stanley L. Paulson, Oxford: Clarendon Press 2002; cit. Alexy, Argument from Injustice.

Alexy, R. Theorie der Grundrechte, 5th Edition, Frankfurt am Main: Suhrkamp 2006.

Alexy, R.: Zum Begriff des Rechtsprinzips, in: W. Krawietz/K. Opalek/A. Peczenik/A. Schramm (Editors), Argumentation und Hermeneutik in der Jurisprudenz, Rechtstheorie Beiheft 1, Berlin: Duncker & Humblot 1979, p. 58 et seqq.

Alexy, R.: Zur Kritik des Rechtspositivismus, ARSP Beiheft 37 (1990), p. 9 et seqq.

Aiwart, H.: Recht und Handlung, Tübingen: Mohr Siebeck 1987.

Austeda, F.: Axiomatische Philosophie. Ein Beitrag zur Selbstkritik der Philosophie, Erfahrung und Denken No. 10, Berlin: Duncker & Humblot 1962.

Austin, J.: The John Austin Collection, vol. I: Lectures on Jurisprudence or the Philosophy of Positive Law 1–2, 4th Edition, Bristol: Thoemmes 1996.

Austin, J.: The Province of Jurisprudence Determined, ed. by Wilfrid E. Rumble, Cambridge: Cambridge University Press 1995.

Ávila, H.: Theory of Legal Principles, Law and Philosophy Library 81, Dordrecht: Springer 2007.

Bärsch, Cl.-E.: Der Gerber-Labandsche Positivismus, in: M.J. Sattler (Editor), Die deutsche Staatslehre im 19. und 20. Jahrhundert, Munich: List 1972, p. 43 et seqq.

Baratta, A.: Rechtspositivismus und Gesetzespositivismus, Gedanken zu einer "naturrechtlichen" Apologie des Rechtspositivismus, ARSP 54 (1968), p. 325 et seqq.

Baurmann, M./*Kliemt,* H. Rechtspositivismus auf die leichte Schulter genommen? Österreichische Zeitschrift für Soziologie 10 (1985), p. 121 et seqq.

Beling, E. Vom Positivismus zum Naturrecht und zurück, Festgabe für Philipp Heck, Max Rümelin und Arthur Benno Schmidt, Tübingen: J.C.B. Mohr, 1931.

Bergbohm, K.: Jurisprudenz und Rechtsphilosophie I, Leipzig: Duncker & Humblot, 1892.

Bierling, E.R.: Juristische Prinzipienlehre I-V, Reprint of the 1894–1917 edition, Aalen: Scientia 1975–1979, 1986; cit. Bierling, Prinzipienlehre I-V.

Bierling, E.R.: Kritik der juristischen Grundbegriffe I-II, Reprint of the Gotha 1877/1883 edition, Aalen: Scientia 1965; cit. Bierling, Kritik I/II.

Bittner, C.: Recht als interpretative Praxis. Zu Ronald Dworkins allgemeiner Theorie des Rechts, Schriften zur Rechtstheorie No 131, Berlin: Duncker & Humblot, 1988.

Bjarup, J.: Skandinavischer Realismus. Hägerström, Lundstedt, Olivecrona, Ross, Kolleg Rechtstheorie III/1, Freiburg/Munich: Alber 1978.

Bobbio, Norberto: Giusnaturalismo e positivismo giuridico, 2nd Edition, Milano 1972.

Bocheński, J.M.: The Methods of Contemporary Thought, New York and Evanston: Harper & Row, Publishers, 1968

Brecht, A.: Political Theory: The Foundations of Twentieth Century Political Thought, Princeton, New Jersey: Princeton University Press, 1970.

Bonifacio, M., Komplementäres Recht, Schriften zur Rechtstheorie 221, Berlin: Duncker & Humblot, 2004.

Bulygin, E.: Der Begriff der Wirksamkeit, ARSP Beiheft 41 (1965), p. 39 et seqq.

Bydlinski, F.: Juristische Methodenlehre und Rechtsbegriff, Second Edition, Vienna/New York: Springer, 1991.

Campbell, T. D.; The Legal Theory of Ethical Positivism, Aldershot et al.: Dartmouth Publishing Company Limited, 1996, quoted hereinabove as Campbell, LEP.

Campbell, T., Prescriptive Legal Positivism: Law, Rights and Democracy, London: UCL Press, 2004.

Cattaneo, M.A.: Il positivismo giuridico inglese, Hobbes, Bentham, Austin, Milano: Dott. A. Giuffrè, 1962.

Coing, H.: Grundzüge der Rechtsphilosophie, 5th Edition, Berlin, New York: Walter de Gruyter, 1993.

Coleman, Jules, Negative and Positive Positivism, Journal of Legal Studies XI (1982), p. 139 et seqq., cit. Coleman I, p. 139 et seqq.

Coleman, Jules, The Architecture of Jurisprudence, The Yale Law Journal 10/4 [2011], p. 2 et seqq., cit. Coleman II, p. 2 et seq.

Di Trocchio, F., Der Grosse Schwindel, Betrug und Fälschung in der Wissenschaft, Frankfurt am Main/New York, 1994

Dreier, R.: Der Begriff des Rechts, NJW 39 (1986), p. 890 et seqq.

Dreier, R.: Neues Naturrecht oder Rechtspositivismus? In Erwiderung auf W. Krawietz, Rechtstheorie 18 (1987), p. 368 et seqq.

Dreier, R.: Recht – Moral – Ideologie, Frankfurt am Main: Suhrkamp, 1981.

Dreier, R.: Sein und Sollen, Bemerkungen zur Reinen Rechtslehre Kelsens, JZ 27 (1972), p. 329 et seqq.

Dubislav, W.: Die Definition, 4th Edition (reprint of Third Edition), Hamburg: Felix Meiner Verlag, 1981.

Dworkin, R.: Taking Rights Seriously, London: Gerald Duckworth & Co. Ltd., 1977.

Dworkin, R.: Law's Empire, Reprint of 1986 Edition, London: Fontana Press, 1990.

Dworkin, R.: No Right Answer?, in: P.M.S. Hacker/J. Raz (Editors), Law, Society, and Morality, Essays in Honour of H.L.A. Hart, Oxford: Clarendon Press, 1977, p. 58 et seqq.

Eckmann, H.: Rechtspositivismus und sprachanalytische Philosophie. Der Begriff des Rechts in der Rechtsphilosophie H.L.A. Harts, Schriften zur Rechtstheorie No. 15, Berlin: Duncker & Humblot 1969.

Ehrlich, E.: Fundamental Principles of the Sociology of Law, Translation of Grundlegung der Soziologie des Rechts by Walter L. Moll, Reprint Edition, New York 1975.

Evers, H.-U.: Der Richter und das unsittliche Gesetz, Berlin: de Gruyter, 1956.

Fechner, E.: Ideologische Elemente in positivistischen Rechtanschauungen, dargestellt an Hans Kelsens "Reiner Rechtslehre", ARSP Beiheft No. 6 (1970), p. 199 et seqq.

Fechner, E.: Rechtsphilosophie. Soziologie und Metaphysik des Rechts, Second Edition, Tübingen: Mohr, 1962.

Fuchs, W.R.: Exakte Geheimnisse. Knaurs Buch der modernen Mathematik, Munich/Zurich: Knaur 1966.

Fuller, L.L.: Positivism and Fidelity to Law – A Reply to Professor Hart, Harvard Law Review 71 (1958), p. 630 et seqq.

Gächter, Th./*Rea-Frauchiger*, M. A.: Willkürfreiheit als Geltungsvoraussetzung des Rechts, Das Willkürverbot gemäss Art. 9 BV im Licht der Debatte um Inclusive und Exclusive Positivism, in: Sandra Hotz/Klaus Mathis (Editors), Recht, Moral und Faktizität. Essays in Honor of Walter Ott, Zurich/St. Gallen: Dike, 2008, p. 79 et seqq.

Geddert, H.: Recht und Moral. Zum Sinn eines alten Problems, Berlin: Duncker & Humblot 1984.

Geiger, Th.: On Social Order and Mass Society, Selected Papers, Chicago: The University of Chicago Press, 1969.

Geiger, Th.: Vorstudien zu einer Soziologie des Rechts, ed. by Manfred Rehbinder, Schriftenreihe zur Rechtssoziologie und Rechtstatsachenforschung, vol. 65, 4th Edition, Berlin: Duncker & Humblot, 1987.

Gonseth, F.: Elementare und nichteuklidische Geometrie in axiomatischer Darstellung und ihr Verhältnis zur Wirklichkeit, Zurich: Orell Fuessli, 1955.

Harris, J.W., Legal Philosophies, 2nd Edition, London/Edingburgh/Dublin: Butterworth, 1997.

Hart, H.L.A.: Definition and Theory in Jurisprudence. An inaugural Lecture delivered before the University of Oxford on 30 May 1953 (Oxford 1953), reprinted in H.L.A. Hart, Essays in Jurisprudence and Philosophy, Oxford: Clarendon Press 1983, p. 21 et seqq., hereinabove referred to as "Hart, Definition".

Hart, H.L.A.: The Concept of Law, Second Edition, Oxford: Oxford University Press 1994, hereinabove referred to as "Hart, The Concept of Law".

Hart, H.L.A.: Positivism and the Separation of Law and Morals, Harvard Law Review 71 (1957/58), p. 593 et seqq., reprinted in: H.L.A. Hart, Essays in Jurisprudence and Philosophy, Oxford: Clarendon Press 1983, p. 49 et seqq., hereinabove referred to as "Hart, Positivism and the Separation of Law and Morals".

Henkel, H. Einführung in die Rechtsphilosophie, Grundlagen des Rechts, Second Edition, Munich: C.H. Beck, 1977.

Hilbert, D.: Die Grundlagen der Geometrie. Mit Supplementen von P. Bernays, 13th Edition, Stuttgart: Teubner Verlag, 1987, hereinabove referred to as "Hilbert, Grundlagen".

Hilbert, D., E. J. Townsend (Translator), Foundations of Geometry, Whitefish: Kessinger Publishing Company, 2006.

Himma, K. E., Inclusive Legal Positivism, in: Jules Coleman and Scott Shapiro (eds.), Kenneth Himma (assoc. ed.), Oxford Handbook of Jurisprudence and Legal Philosophy, Oxford: Oxford University Press, 2002; hereinabove referred to as "Inclusive Legal Positivism".

Himma, K.E., Final Authority to Bind with Moral Mistakes: On the Explanatory Potential of Inclusive Legal Positivism, Law and Philosophy 24 (2005), pp. 1–45, hereinabove referred to as "Final Authority".

Hoeffe, O.: Politische Gerechtigkeit. Grundlegung einer kritischen Philosophie von Recht und Staat, 3rd Edition, Frankfurt am Main: Suhrkamp 2002.

Hoerster, N.: Einleitung zu H.L.A. Hart, Recht und Moral. Drei Aufsätze, Göttingen: Vandenhoeck and Ruprecht, p. 5 et seqq., hereinabove referred to as "Hoerster, Einleitung".

Hoerster, N.: Grundthesen der analytischen Rechtstheorie, Jahrbuch für Rechtssoziologie und Rechtstheorie 2 (1971), p. 115 et seqq.

Hoerster, N.: Zum begrifflichen Verhältnis von Recht und Moral, Neue Hefte für Philosophie 17 (1979), p. 77 et seqq.

Hoerster, N.: Verteidigung des Rechtspositivismus. Würzburger Vorträge zur Rechtsphilosophie, Rechtstheorie und Rechtssoziologie, Frankfurt am Main: Alfred Metzner Verlag, 1989.

Hoerster, N.: Zur logischen Möglichkeit des Positivismus, ARSP 56 (1970), p. 43 et seqq.

Hoerster, N.: Zur Verteidigung der positivistischen Trennungsthese, ARSP Beiheft No. 37 (1990), p. 27 et seqq.

Hoerster, N.: Zur Verteidigung des Rechtspositivismus, NJW 39 (1986), p. 2480 et seqq.

Hoerster, N.: Was ist Recht? Grundfragen der Rechtsphilosophie, Munich: Beck 2006.

Hotz, S./*Mathis,* K. (Editors), Recht, Moral und Faktizität. Essays in Honor of Walter Ott, Zurich/St. Gallen: Dike, 2008.

Jellinek, G. Allgemeine Staatslehre, Third Edition, Berlin: Häring, 1914.

Jørgensen, St.: Recht und Gesellschaft, Göttingen: Vandenhoeck, 1971.

Jori, M.: Legal Positivism, Dartmouth: Dartmouth Publishing Company, 1992.

Juhos, B./*Schleichert,* H.: Die erkenntnistheoretischen Grundlagen der klassischen Physik, Erfahrung und Denken No. 12, Berlin: Duncker & Humblot, 1963.

Kantorowicz, H.: The Definition of Law, Cambridge: Cambridge University Press, 1958.

Kantorowicz, H.: Some Rationalism about Realism, Yale Law Journal 43 (1934), p. 1240 et seqq.

Kaufmann, A.: Rechtsphilosophie im Wandel. Stationen eines Weges, Second Edition, Cologne: Heymanns, 1972.

Kelsen, H.: Eine "Realistische" und die Reine Rechtslehre, Bemerkungen zu Alf Ross, On Law and Justice, ÖZöR NF 10 (1959/60), p. 1 et seqq.

Kelsen, H. Hauptprobleme der Staatslehre, entwickelt aus der Lehre vom Rechtssatz, Second Reprint of the 1923 Second Edition, Aalen: Scientia 1984, hereinabove referred to as "Kelsen, Hauptprobleme".

Kelsen, H.: Introduction to the Problems of Legal Theory, translated by Bonnie Litschewski Paulson and Stanley L. Paulson, Oxford: Clarendon Press, 1992, hereinabove referred to as "Kelsen, Introduction to the Problems of Legal Theory".

Kelsen, H.: Pure Theory of Law, Translated from the Second (Revised and Enlarged) Edition by Max Knight, Clark, New Jersey: The Lawbook Exchange, Ltd., 2005, hereinabove referred to as "Kelsen, Pure Theory".

Kelsen, H.: Was ist juristischer Positivismus?, JZ 20 (1965), p. 465.

Klee, E.: Euthanasie im NS-Staat. Die Vernichtung lebensunwerten Lebens, 3rd Edition, Frankfurt am Main: Fischer, 1983.

Klug, U.: Der Handlungsbegriff des Finalismus als methodologisches Problem, in: Philosophie und Recht, Festschrift für C.A. Emge, Wiesbaden: Steiner, 1960, p. 33 et seqq.

Klug, U.: Juristische Logik, 4th Edition, Berlin/Heidelberg/New York: Springer, 1982.

Koch, H.J.: Zur Methodenlehre des Rechtspositivismus. Das Prinzipienargument – eine methodische Widerlegung des Rechtspositivismus?, ARSP Beiheft 37 (1990), p. 152 et seqq.

Kolakowski, L., Positivist Philosophy, London: Penguin Books, 1972.

Koller, P. Meilensteine des Rechtspositivismus im 20. Jahrhundert, in: O. Weinberger/W. Krawietz (Editors), Reine Rechtslehre im Spiegel ihrer Fortsetzer und Kritiker, Forschung aus Staat und Recht No. 81, Vienna/New York: Springer, 1988.

Kraft, V.: Erkenntnislehre, Vienna: Springer, 1960.

Kramer, E.A.: Kelsens "Reine Rechtslehre" und die "Anerkennungstheorie", Festschrift für Adolf J. Merkl, Munich/Salzburg: Wilhelm Fink Verlag, 1970, p. 187 et seqq.

Kramer, E.A.: Zum Problem der Definition des Rechts. Vier Antworten auf eine Frage des Augustinus, ÖZöR NF 23 (1972), p. 105 et seqq.

Kramer, Matthew H., Where Law and Morality Meet, Oxford: Oxford University Press, 2004.

Krawietz, W. Neues Naturrecht oder Rechtspositivismus? Eine kritische Auseinandersetzung mit dem Begriff des Rechts bei Ralf Dreier und Norbert Hoerster, Rechtstheorie 18 (1987), p. 209 et seqq.

Kriele, M.: Grundprobleme der Rechtsphilosophie, 2nd Edition, Münster: LIT Verlag, 2004.

Kriele, M.: Recht und praktische Vernunft, Göttingen: Vandenhoeck & Ruprecht, 1979.

Kriele, M.: Rechtspositivismus und Naturrecht – politisch beleuchtet, JuS, Zeitschrift für Studium und Ausbildung 9 (1969), p. 149 et seqq.

Kriele, M.: Rechtspflicht und die positivistische Trennung von Recht und Moral, ÖZöR 16 (1966), p. 413 et seqq.

Kuhlen, L.: Normverletzungen im Recht und in der Moral, in: M. Baurmann/H. Kliemt (Editors), Die moderne Gesellschaft im Rechtsstaat, Freiburg/Munich 1990: Alber, 1990, p. 63 et seqq.

Kübler, F.: Der deutsche Richter und das demokratische Gesetz, AcP 162 (1963), p. 104 et seqq.

Lacey, N.: A Life of H. L. A. Hart: The Nightmare and the Noble Dream, Oxford: Oxford University Press 2004.

Lange, H.: Die Entwicklung der Wissenschaft vom bürgerlichen Recht seit 1933, Tübingen: Mohr, 1941.

Larenz, K.: Deutsche Rechtserneuerung und Rechtsphilosophie, Tübingen: Mohr, 1934.

Larenz, K.: Methodenlehre der Rechtswissenschaft, 6th Edition, Berlin et al.: Springer, 1991.

Laun, R.: Recht und Sittlichkeit, Third Edition, Berlin: Springer, 1935.

Löwenhaupt, W.: Politischer Utilitarismus und bürgerliches Rechtsdenken. John Austin (1790–1859) und die "Philosophie des positivien Rechts", Schriften zur Rechtstheorie No. 28, Berlin: Duncker & Humblot 1972.

Lumia, G.: Empirismo logico e positivismo giuridico, Milano: Giuffre', 1963.

MacCormick, D.N.: Legal Reasoning and Legal Theory, Oxford: Clarendon Press 1994, hereinabove referred to as "Legal Reasoning".

MacCormick, D.N.: Wie ernst soll man Rechte nehmen?, Rechtstheorie 11 (1980), p. 1 et seqq.

MacCormick, D.N.: H.L.A. Hart, Stanford, California: Stanford University Press 1987 (Reprint).

MacCormick, D.N./*Weinberger,* O.: Grundlagen des institutionalistischen Rechtspositivismus, Schriften zur Rechtstheorie No. 113, Berlin: Duncker & Humblot 1985, referred to hereinabove as "MacCormick, IRP" or "Weinberger, IRP".

MacCormick, D.N./*Weinberger,* O.: An Institutional Theory of Law. New Approaches to Legal Positivism, 2nd Print, Dordrecht: Reidel, 1992, hereinabove referred to as "ITL".

Maihofer, W. (Editor): Naturrecht oder Rechtspositivismus? Reprint of 1962 Edition, Darmstadt: Wissenschaftliche Buchgesellschaft, 1966.

Marmor, A., Exclusive Legal Positivism, in: Jules Coleman and Scott Shapiro (eds.), Kenneth Himma (assoc. ed.), Oxford Handbook of Jurisprudence and Legal Philosophy, Oxford: Oxford University Press, 2002, p. 104 et seqq.

Martin, M., Judging Positivism, Oxford: Hart Publishing, 2014.

Maus, I.: Aspekte des Rechtspositivismus in der entwickelten Industriegesellschaft, in: Arndt, Adolf et al., Konkretionen politischer Theorie und Praxis, Festgabe für Carlo Schmid, Stuttgart: Klett, 1972, p. 124 et seqq.

Merkel, A.: Elemente der allgemeinen Rechtslehre, in: Gesammelte Abhandlungen aus dem Gebiet der allgemeinen Rechtslehre und des Strafrechts, Strassburg: K.J. Trübner, 1899, hereinabove referred to as "Merkel, Elemente".

Merkel, A.: Juristische Enzyklopädie, 5th Edition, Berlin: Guttentag, 1913, hereinabove referred to as "Merkel, Enzyklopädie".

Métall, R.A.: Hans Kelsen. Leben und Werk, Vienna: Verlag Franz Deuticke, 1969.

Miedzianagora, J.: Philosophies positivistes du droit positif. Bibliothèque de philosophie du droit No. 12, Paris: Pichon, 1970.

Nawiasky, H.: Allgemeine Rechtslehre als System der rechtlichen Grundbegriffe, Second Edition, Einsiedeln: Benziger 1948.

Noll, P.: Gesetzgebungslehre, Reinbek bei Hamburg: Rowohlt, 1973.

Ogorek, R.: Richterkönig oder Subsumtionsautomat? Zur Justiztheorie im 19. Jahrhundert, Frankfurt am Main: Klostermann, 1986.

Ophüls, C.F.: Ist der Rechtspositivismus logisch möglich?, NJW 21 (1968) II 1745 et seqq.

Ott, W.: Kann man heute noch Rechtspositivist sein? ZSR NF 96 (1977) I 441 et seqq.

Ott, W.: Das Verhältnis von Sein und Sollen in logischer, genetischer und funktioneller Hinsicht, ZSR NF 103 (1984) I 345 et seqq.

Ott, W. (with W. Krawietz, Editors), Formalismus und Phänomenologie im Rechtsdenken der Gegenwart, Festgabe für Alois Troller zum 80. Geburtstag, Berlin: Duncker & Humblot, 1987.

Ott, W.: Die Trennung von Recht und Moral in der Rechtstheorie H.L.A. Harts, in: H. Holzey/G. Kohler (Editors), Verrechtlichung und Verantwortung, studia philosophica, Supplementum 13 (1987), p. 179 et seqq.

Ott, W.: The Varieties and Limitations of Legal Positivism, Vera Lex 7 (1987), p. 17 et seqq.

Ott, W.: Bericht von einem Besuch bei Prof. H.L.A. Hart in Oxford, Rechtstheorie 18 (1987), p. 539 et seqq.

Ott, W.: Die Radbruch'sche Formel. Pro und Contra, ZSR NF 107 (1988) I 335 et seqq.

Ott, W.: Der Euthanasie-Befehl Hitlers vom 1. September 1939 im Lichte der rechtspositivistischen Theorien, in: H. Mayer (Editor), Staatsrecht in Theorie und Praxis, Festschrift Robert Walter zum 60. Geburtstag, Vienna: Manz, 1991, p. 519 et seqq.

Ott, W.: Der Rechtspositivismus, 2nd Edition, Berlin: Duncker & Humblot, 1992.

Ott, W.: (with Buob, F.) Did Legal Positivism render German Jurists defenceless during the Third Reich?, in: Sol Picciotto, Carol Smart (Editors), Social and Legal Studies, Volume 2, London: Sage Publications, 1993, p. 91 et seqq.

Ott, W.: Did East German Border Guards along The Berlin Wall Act Illegally? Comments on the Decision of the German Federal Constitutional Court of 24 October 1996, Israel Law Review vol. 34, 2000, p. 352 et seqq.

Ott, W.: Die Vielfalt des Rechtspositivismus, Würzburger Vorträge zur Rechtsphilosophie, Rechtstheorie und Rechtssoziologie, vol. 51, Baden-Baden: Nomos 2016.

Palazzolo, V. Del positivismo giuridico, Rivista internationale di filosofia del diritto 44 (1967) 616 et seqq.

Pattaro, E.: Der italienische Rechtspositivismus, Rechtstheorie (1974), p. 67 et seqq.

Paulson, S.L./*Stolleis,* M. (Editors), Hans Kelsen, Tübingen: Mohr Siebeck, 2005

Poincaré, H.: Science and Hypothesis, New Dover Edition, Mineola: Dover Publications Inc, 1952.

Popper, K.: The Logic of Scientific Discovery, London and New York: Routledge Classics, 2002.

Radbruch, G.: Statutory Lawlessness and Supra-Statutory Law, trans. Bonnie Litschewski Paulson and Stanley L. Paulson, Oxford Journal of Legal Studies, p. 1 et seqq.; first published as "Gesetzliches Unrecht und übergesetzliches Recht", in: Süddeutsche Juristenzeitung 1 (1946), p. 105–108.

Radbruch, G. Rechtsphilosophie, 8th Edition, Stuttgart: Köhler 1973.

Radbruch, G. Rechtsphilosophie: Studienausgabe, edited by Ralf Dreier and Stanley L. Paulson, Second Edition, Heidelberg: Müller 2003.

Raiser, Th.: Grundlagen der Rechtssoziologie, 4th revised Edition of "Das lebende Recht", Tübingen: Mohr Siebeck, 2007.

Raiser, Th.: Einführung in die Rechtssoziologie, 4th Edition, Frankfurt am Main: Metzner, 1985.

Raz, J., The Authority of Law, Reprint of 1979 edition, Oxford: Oxford University Press, 2002, hereinabove referred to as "AL".

Raz, J., Authority, Law, and Morality, in: Ethics in the Public Domain: Essays in the Morality of Law and Politics, Oxford: Clarendon Press, 1994, hereinabove referred to as "ALM".

Raz, J., Practical Reason and Norms, New Edition, Oxford: Oxford University Press, 1999, hereinabove referred to as "Norms".

Raz, J., The Concept of a Legal System, Reprint of Second Edition, Oxford: Clarendon Press, 1999, hereabove referred to as "Concept".

Rehbinder, M.: Die Begründung der Rechtssoziologie durch Eugen Ehrlich, Schriftenreihe des Instituts für Rechtssoziologie und Rechtstatsachenforschung der Freien Universität Berlin No. 6, 2nd Edition, Berlin: Duncker & Humblot, 1986, hereinabove referred to as "Rehbinder, Eugen Ehrlich".

Rehbinder, M.: Einführung in die Rechtssoziologie, Frankfurt am Main: Athenaeum Verlag, 1971.

Rehbinder, M.: Rechtssoziologie, 6th Edition, Munich: Beck, 2007.

Reich, N.: Sociological Jurisprudence und Legal Realism im Rechtsdenken Amerikas, Beihefte zum Jahrbuch für Amerikastudien No. 23, Heidelberg: Winter, 1967.

Riebschläger, K.: Die Freirechtsbewegung. Zur Entwicklung einer soziologischen Rechtsschule, Schriftenreihe des Instituts für Rechtssoziologie und Rechtstatsachenforschung der Freien Universität Berlin No. 11, Berlin: Duncker & Humblot, 1968.

Riezler, E. Der totgesagte Positivismus, in: W. Maihofer (Editor), Naturrecht oder Rechtspositivismus? Reprint of 1962 Edition, Darmstadt: Wissenschaftliche Buchgesellschaft, 1966, p. 239 et seqq.

Roma, E.: Positivism and the Connection of Law and Morality, ARSP 58 (1972), p. 397 et seqq.

Ross, A.: On Law and Justice, London: Stevens, 1958; Reprint: Clark, N.J.: Lawbook Exchange, 2007.

Ross, A.: Towards a Realistic Jurisprudence. A Criticism of the Dualism in Law, Copenhagen: Einar Munksgaard, 1946, hereinabove referred to as "Ross, Realistic Jurisprudence".

Rottleuthner, H. (Editor): Recht, Rechtsphilosophie und Nationalsozialismus, ARSP Beiheft 18, Wiesbaden: Franz Steiner Verlag, 1983.

Rottleuthner, H.: Substantieller Dezisionismus. Zur Funktion der Rechtsphilosophie im Nationalsozialismus, ARSP Beiheft 18, Wiesbaden: Franz Steiner Verlag 1983, p. 20 et seqq.

Rüthers, B.: Die unbegrenzte Auslegung. Zum Wandel der Privatrechtsordnung im Nationalsozialismus, 6th Edition, Heidelberg: Mohr Siebeck, 2005, hereinabove referred to as "Rüthers, Unbegrenzte Auslegung".

Rüthers, B.: Entartetes Recht, Second Edition, Munich: C.H. Beck, 1988, hereinabove referred to as "Rüthers, Entartetes Recht".

Scarpelli, U.: Cos è il positivismo giuridico. Diritto e cultura moderna No. 2, Milano: Edizioni di Comunità, 1965.

Schmidt, E.: Gesetz und Richter. Wert und Unwert des Positivismus, Karlsruhe: C.F. Müller, 1952.

Schmitt, C.: Über die drei Arten des rechtswissenschaftlichen Denkens, Third Edition, Berlin: Duncker & Humblot, 2006, originally published 1934.

Schmitt, C.: Der Rechtsstaat, in: H. Frank (Editor), Nationalsozialistisches Handbuch für Recht und Gesetzgebung, Munich: Zentralverlag der NSDAP, 1935, p. 24 et seqq.

Schmitt, C.: Nationalsozialismus und Rechtsstaat, JW 63 (1934), p. 713 et seqq.

Schneider, G.: Der Ursprung des Positivismus in der Gestalt des Historismus, ARSP 58 (1972), p. 267 et seqq.

Schreiber, H.L. Der Begriff der Rechtspflicht: Quellenstudien zu seiner Geschichte, Berlin: Walter de Gruyter, 1966.

Sebok, Anthony James, Legal Positivism in American Jurisprudence, Cambridge: Cambridge University Press, 1998.

Seiffert, H.: Einführung in die Wissenschaftstheorie I, Sprachanalyse, Deduktion, Induktion in Natur- und Sozialwissenschaften, 13th Edition (unchanged), Munich: C.H. Beck, 2003, hereinabove referred to as "Seiffert I".

Shuman, S.I.: Legal Positivism. Its Scope and Limitations, Detroit: Wayne State University Press, 1963.

Stegmüller, W.: Probleme und Resultate der Wissenschaftstheorie und Analytischen Philosophie, Band I, Erklärung, Begründung, Kausalität, 2nd, extended and improved Edition, Berlin/Heidelberg/New York: Springer, 1983.

Summers, R.S.: Pragmatic Instrumentalism and American Legal Theory. A Summary Statement, in: Rechtstheorie 13 (1982), p. 257 et seqq.

Summers, R.S.: Pragmatischer Instrumentalismus und amerikanische Rechtstheorie, Kolleg Rechtstheorie III/2, Freiburg im Breisgau: Alber, 1983.

Székessy, L.: Gerechtigkeit und inklusiver Rechtspositivismus, Münsterische Beiträge zur Rechtswissenschaft, Band 150, Berlin: Duncker & Humblot 2003.

Troper, M.: Les théories volontaristes du droit, in: P. Amselek/Ch. Grzegorczyk (Editors), Controverses autour de l'ontologie du droit, Paris: Presses Universitaires de France, 2000.

Tsatsos, Th.: Zur Problematik des Rechtspositivismus. Für und Wider einer Denkmethode in der Staatsrechtslehre, Res publica No. 13, Stuttgart, Kohlhammer, 1964.

Twining, William, Karl Llewellyn and the Realist Movement, London: Weidenfeld and Nicolson, 1973.

Uren, W.J.: Criteria of Legal Positivism. Some Implications of the Legal Positivists View of the Relation of Law to Morality, ARSP 55 (1969), p. 183 et seqq.

Vicen, F.G.: El positivismo en la Filosofía del Derecho contemporánea. Madrid: Instituto de Estudios Políticos, 1950.

Vogel, H.-H.: Der skandinavische Rechtsrealismus. Arbeiten zur Rechtsvergleichung No. 56 (Frankfurt am Main: Metzner, 1972).

Walter, R.: Der gegenwärtige Stand der Reinen Rechtslehre, Rechtstheorie 1 (1970), p. 69 et seqq.

Walter, R.: Die Reine Rechtslehre in der Kritik der Methodenlehre von Larenz, ÖJZ 16 (1961), p. 477 et seqq.

Walter, R.: Die Trennung von Recht und Moral im System der Reinen Rechtslehre. Bemerkungen zu Kriele, Rechtspflicht und die positivistische Trennung von Recht und Moral, ÖZöR NF 17 (1967), p. 123 et seqq.

Walter, R.: Kelsens Rechtslehre im Spiegel rechtsphilosophischer Diskussion in Österreich, ÖZöR NF 18 (1968), p. 331 et seqq.

Waluchow, W.J., Inclusive Legal Positivism, Oxford: Clarendon Press, 1994

Watkins-Bienz, R.: Die Hart-Dworkin Debatte, Schriften zur Rechtstheorie 220, Berlin: Duncker & Humblot, 2004.

Weber, M.: Max Weber on Law in Economy and Society, ed. with introduction and annotations by Max Rheinstein, translated from: Max Weber, Wirtschaft und Gesellschaft, 2nd Edition (1925), by Edward Shils and Max Rheinstein, Cambridge, MA: Harvard University Press, 1954.

Weinberger, O.:Logische Analyse als Basis der juristischen Argumentation, in: W. Krawietz/R. Alexy (eds.), Metatheorie juristischer Argumentation, Berlin: Duncker & Humblot, 1983, p. 159 et seqq.

Weinberger, O.: Norm und Institution. Eine Einführung in die Theorie des Rechts, Vienna: Manz, Vienna, 1988.

Weinberger, O.: Recht, Institution und Rechtspolitik. Grundprobleme der Rechtstheorie und Sozialphilosophie, Stuttgart: Franz Steiner, 1987.

Weinberger, O.: Rechtslogik, 2nd Edition, Berlin: Duncker & Humblot, 1989.

Weinberger, O.: Zur Idee eines Institutionalistischen Rechtspositivismus. Gleichzeitg eine Auseinandersetzung mit Hans Kelsens Setzungspositivismus, Revue Internationale de Philosophie 35 (1981), p. 487 et seqq.

Weinberger, O.: See also MacCormick/Weinberger.

Weinkauff, H.: Die deutsche Justiz und der Nationalsozialismus, Ein Überblick, in: "Die deutsche Justiz und der Nationalsozialismus", Quellen und Darstellungen zur Zeitgeschichte XVI/1, Stuttgart: Deutsche Verlagsanstalt, 1968, p. 18 et seqq.

Weinreb, E.: Law as a Kantian Idea of Reason, Columbia Law Review 87 (1987), p. 472 et seqq.

Weinreb, E.: Legal Formalism: On the Immanent Rationability of Law, Yale Law Journal 97 (1988), p. 949 et seqq.

Welzel, H.: An den Grenzen des Rechts. Die Frage nach der Rechtsgeltung, Cologne: Westdeutscher Verlag, 1966.

Wieacker, F.: Privatrechtsgeschichte der Neuzeit unter besonderer Berücksichtigung der deutschen Entwicklung, 2nd Reprint of 1967 Edition, Göttingen: Vandenhoeck & Ruprecht, 1996.

Wolf, E.: Das Rechtsideal des nationalsozialistischen Staates, ARSP 28 (1934/35), p. 348 et seqq.

Wolf, J.-C.: Bemerkungen zu Walter Otts Beitrag, Studia Philosophica Supplementum 13 (1987), p. 203 et seqq.

Wolf, J.-C.: Zur Trennung von Recht und Moral in der analytischen Rechtsphilosophie, Studia Philosophica 44 (1985), p. 34 et seqq.

Yoon, Z-W.: Rechtsgeltung und Anerkennung am Beispiel von Ernst Rudolf Bierling; Nomos, Baden-Baden 2009

Glossary

Aarnio, A. 109

Adler, H. G. 297

Alchourrón, C. E. 158

Alexy, R. 69, 94, 184–186, 192–199, 203, 205, 226, 274

Alwart, H. 99, 114

Anschütz, G. 17, 18, 21, 238

Aristotle 132, 201, 301, 311

Augustinus 28

Austeda, F. 128, 134–138, 141, 147, 155, 163, 166, 176

Austin, J. 7– 16, 70–72, 89, 91, 106, 110–118, 161, 192, 207, 219, 247, 252–254, 298, 302

Baratta, A. 17, 21, 103, 226, 232

Baurmann, M. 56

Behrend, J. 23

Beling, E. 34, 43, 44, 181, 209, 250, 266, 276, 303

Bentham, J. 9–12, 69–71, 91, 106, 118, 193, 219, 247, 298

Bergbohm, K. 17–22, 113, 115, 173, 198

Bierling, E. R. 34–39, 106, 208, 209, 249, 266, 303

Bismarck, O. 228, 246, 310

Bittner, C. 192

Bjarup, J. 45

Bobbio, N. 103

Bocheński, J. M. 128–131, 134, 138–145, 148, 155

Bolyai, J. 133

Bonifacio, M. 138, 142

Brandeis, L. D. 65

Brecht, A. 9, 12, 104, 118, 138, 180

Brodersen, U. 208, 226, 232, 240

Brouwer, L. 134

Bulygin, E. 45, 49, 50, 158, 272

Bydlinski, F. 170, 192, 203, 206, 212, 219, 257

Campbell, T. D. 7, 107, 108, 305

Canaris, Cl.-W. 257

Cardozo, B. N. 65

Casper, G. 65

Cattaneo, M. A. 9, 105

Cohen, F. S. 65, 69

Coing, H. 45, 65, 103, 115, 154

Coleman, J. 7, 69, 71, 83, 84, 92, 105, 112, 120–124, 185, 291, 306

Comte, A. 114

Dahm, G. 248, 251

Dilcher, G. 226, 232, 233

Di Trocchio, F. 144, 145

Dreier, H. 19, 226

Dreier, R. 170, 185, 192, 193, 203, 205, 206, 246, 275

Dubislav, W. 155, 156, 161

Dworkin, R. 69, 83, 84, 92, 107, 192–202, 274, 291, 305

Eckmann, H. 9, 10, 14, 33–35, 45, 47, 69, 70, 72, 74–82, 103, 170, 192, 247, 254, 262, 275, 277–280

Ehrlich, E. 52–55, 58, 106, 114, 157, 209, 210, 268, 271, 272, 304

Index